CITIES, DESIGN &
EVOLUTION

CITIES, DESIGN & EVOLUTION

STEPHEN MARSHALL

Routledge
Taylor & Francis Group

LONDON AND NEW YORK

First published 2009
by Routledge
2 Park Square, Milton Park, Abingdon, Oxon OX14 4RN

Simultaneously published in the USA and Canada
by Routledge
270 Madison Ave, New York, NY 10016

Routledge is an imprint of the Taylor & Francis Group, an informa business

Typeset in Univers Light and Interstate by RefineCatch Limited, Bungay, Suffolk
Printed and bound in Great Britain
by The Cromwell Press, Trowbridge, Wiltshire

British Library Cataloguing in Publication Data
A catalogue record for this book is available from the British Library

Library of Congress Cataloging-in-Publication Data
Marshall, Stephen, 1967–
    Cities design and evolution / Stephen Marshall
        p. cm.
    1. City planning.   2. Cities and towns.   I. Title.
    HT166.M2593 2007
    711′.4—dc22   2007021591

ISBN10: 0–415–42329–5 (pbk)

ISBN13: 978–0–415–42329–8 (pbk)

CONTENTS

0.0 • Kunsthaus, Graz.

ILLUSTRATION CREDITS

PREFACE

For the first time in history, more than half of the world's population will now be living in urban areas. As humanity is increasingly becoming an urban species – as cities and suburbs and squatter settlements sprout and sprawl across the Earth's surface – the concern for how to plan and design urban areas has arguably never been greater. And yet, we are not necessarily so sure any more how best to plan cities. Indeed, it has seemed sometimes as if planning has been part of the problem.

This book originated in an attempt to find a way of better devising the physical layout of urban areas, partly in reaction to the chequered performance of city planning in the postwar decades. The original focus of scrutiny was to do with urban structure – how things like buildings and streets and neighbourhoods and town centres are put together. It soon became clear that this topic was inextricable with the processes of formation over time. And so, the scope of inquiry duly expanded to cover topics like urban morphology, historical development, planning intentions and design theory. The study of relationships between processes and patterns in turn seemed to benefit from an infusion of ideas from contemporary science, on issues such as complexity, emergence and, ultimately, evolution.

In covering this ground, I have been conscious of what evolutionary biologist Geerat Vermeij refers to as the hazardous journeys between disciplines, journeys which nonetheless can be fruitful, at least to those doing the travelling. I am aware that this work can only give partial glimpses of some territories that, while unfamiliar and perhaps exotic to some readers, are already settled by 'natives' to those disciplines. At times we press on past some territories without alighting, or only take in selective highlights, for the sake of the overall journey. This indeed goes for the treatment of urban planning and design, as much as for other disciplines.

I hope that the reader will forgive this licence, and understand why this has been necessary. In order to understand cities, we do need to venture out beyond the nominal limits of urban studies, to visit architecture, geography, history, social sciences, physical sciences and even occasionally the life sciences. The urban scholar is sometimes indeed an inter-disciplinary tourist: foraging for nuggets of wisdom from other fields, especially those that are easily accessible and available in the English language. It is hoped that readers from other fields will not mind the selective incursions into their own territories. If it is of any comfort, the territory of urban planning itself has been visited or settled by many people originating from other fields – including architects, engineers, geographers and social scientists, not to mention the occasional stenographer, biologist, engraver, journalist and mathematician.

In writing this book, then, I have been conscious of having to simul-taneously address different audiences, steering a course between simplicity and oversimplification, and between generalisation and case-specific detail. Clearly, one could increase the number of scholars, cities or species referred to; but it is hoped that the coverage here is sufficient to get the main argu-ments across. In many cases, the end-notes represent the truncated stumps of tangential arguments that if fully elaborated in the text would have resulted in a book at least twice the size; and perhaps we can be content to leave those arguments for another day.

In the end, it is hoped that this book will help built-environment pro-fessionals, scholars from other disciplines, and the wider public understand how cities are, have been and could be put together. It does not suggest directly what anyone in particular should do. But it can perhaps – it is hoped – assist understanding of cities, their design and their evolution, from which understanding readers may make their own choices.

This book is drawn from an evolving lineage of research that has a shared ancestry with my earlier book *Streets and Patterns*. Rather than a descendant of that work, this book is perhaps better regarded as a younger sibling. The two are complementary in scope and compatible in argument, but in the end each does its own thing in its own way.

The ideas in this book obviously build from many precedent ideas; this is seen not least in the bibliography and reference to individuals named in the text. In the most general sense, I have benefited from discussions with colleagues in the Bartlett School of Planning, and the 'extended family' of the Bartlett faculty at University College London. In particular, I have been stimulated by the work of Bill Hillier, Alan Penn, Michael Batty and Philip

Steadman who have shown that it is possible and fruitful to apply diverse insights from science to urbanism. Looking back, before coming to University College London, I had some kind of interest in most of the topics covered in this book; but perhaps it was only since coming to UCL that it seemed possible and natural to attempt to connect these, and combine them in a single work. I have also been stimulated and supported by David Banister and Peter Hall who have encouraged me in pursuit of my research, and led by example in terms of getting research done and turning the results into books.

With regard to the direct creation of this book, I am indebted to Nick Green and Philip Steadman who provided incisive comments on early versions of the manuscript. These helped me sort out some of the main messages from red herrings, leading me to sharpen some arguments and soften others. I am also grateful to Torbjörn Einarsson, Ming Cheng, Ferdinando Giammichele and Nick Woolley for providing constructive comments and feedback on draft chapters of the manuscript. And I would also like to thank Treasa Creavin for providing feedback and encouragement throughout the writing of the book. The final product has undoubtedly benefited from all of these contributions.

I am grateful to all those individuals and organisations who have permitted use of their graphic material in the book (see Illustration Credits). I would also like to thank the staff at Taylor and Francis, in particular Katy Low and Jeff Mallinder for assistance with image permissions; Sue Dickinson for copy editing; Donna White and the team at RefineCatch Limited for getting the book through production; and Caroline Mallinder for her faith in the project from the outset. I would like to record, finally, thanks to my family for support and encouragement throughout the research and writing of the book.

Stephen Marshall
London, 18th May 2008

1 INTRODUCTION

Cities are the ultimate human-made habitats, and yet – among all species – it is perhaps only humans who create habitats that are not fit to live in. Urban environments can be sufficiently alienating that – for hundreds or even thousands of years – we have sometimes regarded them as unwelcome encroachments on the countryside. This is as if the wilderness were still the most fitting home of *Homo sapiens*, and cities were alien 'carbuncles' on the face of the Earth, rather than seeing urbanisation as a process of adapting the planet to be a *more* human-friendly habitat (Figure 1.0, opposite).

What is more, it seems that *modern planned* urban environments are often perceived to be worse than traditional 'unplanned' ones. That is, our modern cities – especially some deliberately planned parts of them – are often perceived as inhuman, alienating environments: with ugly and brutal 'concrete jungles', landscapes of barren tarmac, looming slab blocks and gloomy undercrofts (Figure 1.1).[1]

Any town or city – traditional or modern – may suffer from a poor-quality environment. But it is in modern planned towns that the failure of town planning is most abject – where so much effort has been made, for so dubious a benefit. When we learn of new towns whose best appreciated parts are those predating their modern planned parts; when urban writers refer to the 'horrors of town planning' knowing that the reader will recognise the association; when modern environments are described as 'most hated', that their inhabitants would be happy to see torn down again, we should really sit up, stop in our tracks – temporarily halting the bulldozers and 'pause printing' our urban blueprints – and question the purposes and methods of planning.[2]

1.0 • Terraforming the Earth for humanity (Brasilia under construction).

1.1 • Modern urban environments, planned by humans for other humans: (a) Red Road flats, Glasgow; (b) Building complex, Finchley,, London; (c) Pedestrian landscape, Glasgow.

(a)   (c)

In what other fields of human endeavour would the deliberate, professionally designed product be routinely assumed to be *worse* than products arising in the absence of the efforts of that profession? In other fields we are used to modern, purpose-built artefacts performing better than old, makeshift ones, or adaptations from nature. A cup is better for drinking out of than a hewn-out piece of rock, or a cupped hand. A computer – or abacus – is better for calculation than a handful of stones, or a handful of fingers. In these contexts, we take it for granted that modern goes along with 'new, improved', and that purpose-built means functional.

But this is not necessarily the case when it comes to cities and urbanism. A new, modern, planned and purpose-built city is not necessarily more attractive, functional or successful than an old, 'unplanned' one.[3]

How could this urban conundrum come about? How is it that we of all species – with intelligence, forethought and creativity, and with technology, learned culture and collective political will at our disposal – have managed to create deliberately planned urban habitats that are often less attractive and more dysfunctional than the unplanned rambling urbanism of historic old cities?

If we can find answers to this specific conundrum, perhaps we shall be able to address the more general concern of this and any other book on urban planning and design: that of how to create better urban areas.

PLANNING AT THE CROSSROADS

The last few decades have seen what must be one of the most dramatic reversals in urban design history. Figure 1.2 shows Le Corbusier's sketch of the urban revolution in which the traditional urban fabric was replaced by a modern urban order in many cities in the decades following the Second World War. But today we often see the reverse: where we once had planned superhighways, we now favour traditional-style streets; where once we built tower blocks, we now have terraces, and where once we had open-plan landscapes we now have enclosed squares and courtyards. A Modernist revolution has been resisted and to some extent supplanted by what amounts to a neo-traditional counter-revolution.

Neo-traditional urbanism

The counter-revolution – neo-traditional urbanism – may be described as the philosophy and practice of recreating the best of traditional urbanism for today. This means, for example, forming buildings into terraces and court-yard blocks, having mixed-use streets fronted by houses, shops and public buildings, and so on. The US-originating New Urbanism movement – perhaps the most significant movement in urban planning and design in recent decades – contains a significant strand of neo-traditionalism in this regard. Associated groups and individuals in many other parts of the world also

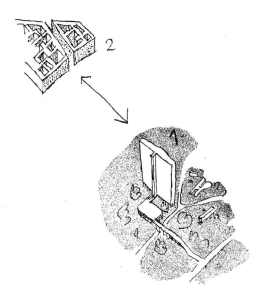

1.2 • Le Corbusier's revolution, the great twentieth-century transformation from a traditional urban fabric to a modern landscape (2 → 1). In some countries, there is now a reversal (1 → 2). In others (2 → 1) is the direction of progress.

favour the creation of buildings and streets in the traditional style. Since the late 1980s, neo-traditional urbanism has become increasingly influential, with the successful completion of smaller- and larger-scale urban developments (Figure 1.3).[4]

In many respects, the products of neo-traditional urbanism seem to offer advantages over the alienating landscapes of old Modernism. But, if neo-traditionalism is to be a clear and robust alternative to Modernism, it seems that some questions need to be answered, that follow from the inherent nature of neo-traditionalism.

First, *what* should neo-traditional urbanism be emulating, and *why*? Are the good things claimed for traditional urban forms because of their forms or because of their traditionalism? Are they good because of or despite being planned or unplanned? Should neo-traditionalism be emulating the *planned* forms of the past, that were Modernist set-pieces of their day: the formal streets and squares of Edinburgh New Town, or London's Bloomsbury estate? Or should the exemplars be the *unplanned* forms of the past: the labyrinthine wynds and closes of Edinburgh Old Town, or the historic alleys and courts of the City of London?

This question is particularly apposite in the twenty-first century, as the nature of the object to be emulated – the city itself – is changing. Whereas

(b)

1.3 • Neo-traditional urbanism: (a) Courtyard, Richmond-upon-Thames; (b) Urban space, Poundbury, Dorchester; (c) Street with colonnade, Richmond-upon-Thames. Compare with Figure 1.1.   **(a)**   **(c)**

before cities were quite distinct physical and political entities, with a definite centre ringed by suburbs, we now have a scatter of urban forms and functions all over the place: a hundred-mile sprawl of edge cities and out-of-town 'centres', industrial and office 'parks' and 'campuses'. In this context, urban agglomerations are becoming so large, sprawling and interwoven with their surroundings that it is hard sometimes to grasp what a city is any more. We today have cities without downtowns, suburbs without cities, 'neighbourhoods' without neighbours, 'communities' without civics, and many other combinations that do not seem to fit our understanding of what a city ever was. As a result, it is not any more clear what a city is, to emulate in the first place.[5]

Over and above this, there is the question of *how* to emulate traditional urbanism. Neo-traditional urbanism implies, after all, some kind of planning intention. How do we recreate the kind of 'good old urbanism' that was *not* master-planned in the first place – the kind that perhaps evolved incrementally over a long time, as in traditional settlements?[6]

Although neo-traditionalism is a reaction to Modernism, in form, style and emphasis, the methods of design and planning are not so different from those of Modernism. Neo-traditionalism still has professional planners and architects dreaming up urban creations, embracing the idea of whole settlements as designable, planned units, set forth on master plans. But these are the very kinds of thought and practice that were subject to the classic critiques of Modernism.

The seeds of dissent against Modernist planning were sown as far back as the 1960s, by radical writers such as Jane Jacobs and Christopher Alexander. Jane Jacobs shook up the world of planning in her classic work *The Death and Life of Great American Cities*. She argued against the 'sacking of cities' in the hubristic pursuit of planning principles of dubious theoretical validity and unproven practical value. She castigated the *failure* of town planning. Meanwhile, Christopher Alexander, in his influential essay 'A City Is Not a Tree', was similarly questioning the top-down approach to planning settlements.[7] In other words, Jacobs and Alexander were not simply criticising the Modernist style of buildings, or modern highways, but the processes of planning and design, even questioning the legitimacy of professional planning and city design themselves.

Crucially, these concerns are still relevant today. This is seen in the grand designs of contemporary master-planning, neo-traditional or otherwise. And in many rapidly developing cities, planning and modernity seem to be alive and well, as modernistic towers of concrete, steel and glass thrust upwards, serviced by a new generation of modern highways and public transport systems, while the older streets and courtyards are torn down and swept away. This gives the issue of urban planning and design a particular urgency.

City planning seems to be at a crossroads. Should we be more modern or more traditional; should we have more or less planning? Are we going back or forward; should we go left or right?[8]

The key debates

In effect, the problem of modern urban planning can be unpacked into two separate strands of debate concerning Modernism and planning.

The first debate pits Modernism against traditionalism. This can be related to corresponding debates between modern music versus traditional music, modern art versus traditional art, or modern architecture versus traditional architecture. The preference for modern versus traditional urbanism is not just the prerogative of professionals, politicians or princes, but concerns all of us, in our preferences for the kind of village, town or city we choose to live in, do business in, or visit as a tourist.

The second debate is to do with planning versus absence of planning: to what extent should cities, towns, neighbourhoods and regions be planned? On what basis should someone decide whether any of us should be allowed to build a shed in our own garden? This issue of 'planning' is not just about the built environment, but relates to wider issues of political economy: the preference for more or less state intervention in industry, education, health, and any other sector.

The choices of what kind of building, city or political state to live in go to the heart of the debates concerning urbanism as concern this book. These issues come to a head when we consider the case of traditional 'unplanned' urbanism. If we want planning, or if we want Modernism, we have plenty of theories to guide us. But if we wish to replicate the intricate functionality of traditional 'unplanned urbanism', we perhaps need a better understanding of how this urbanism came about.

UNDERSTANDING URBANISM

Cities are all the same, cities are all different.
Graham Vickers[9]

Cities are all different, yet they have a recognisably urban form, an identifiable kind of urban order, that makes us easily recognise a city when we see one. There is something 'city-shaped' about cities that we recognise despite the

1.4 • The intricate order of a traditional urban form: Arbil, Iraq.

differences between individual cases. What is the nature of cities as urban objects? How can we understand their form and function?

Consider the curious urban specimen of Arbil, Iraq – the ancient Arbela of Mesopotamia (Figure 1.4). In one sense this urban form is chaotic, as compared with a rectangular street-grid; on the other hand, it possesses a subtle intricate order that makes it a certain recognisable kind of settlement: it is coherent, not an arbitrarily 'random' form. An observer from space – and terrestrial readers from the present day – might wonder how this form came to be the way it is, just as we might regard an anthill.

Each individual city is unique, in its whole and its parts. But there is a general pattern to cities, which includes the presence of town centres, neighbourhoods and suburbs, and the shape of their street patterns. While these will be manifested in different ways in each city, there will be basic kinds of order which will be common to all, to a greater or lesser extent. To help understand this, let us take a closer look at traditional urbanism.

Traditional urbanism

The appeal of traditional urban forms is undoubtedly partly to do with reasons of aesthetics, subjective stylistic preferences, or site-specific respect for historical contexts. But a powerful argument that makes traditional urbanism worthy of attention – whatever the style and whatever the context – is that traditional urban forms often actually *function* better than their modern counterparts.[10]

1.5 • Scruton's forks: modern and traditional. Which is more functional?

The philosopher Roger Scruton has made the point about aesthetics versus functionality very simply by illustrating the case of a modern fork and a traditional fork (Figure 1.5). Either fork could be considered aesthetic in its own way. But while the modern fork is functional-*looking*, the traditional fork is actually more functional – more comfortable and finely balanced – for using to eat with.[11]

A similar case can be made in favour of traditional urban forms. People like walking around the pedestrian-friendly streets of historic city centres, sitting in pavement cafes in public plazas or courtyards, among different kinds of shops, residences and civic buildings. In effect, the traditional format of mixed-use streets and squares is more functional than the so-called functionalism of many Modernist designs, with their 'concrete jungles' of buildings on stilts and service roads, and segregated land uses. This means that when we compare an old town next to a new town, the old town is not like a museum-piece – or a magnificent but outmoded dinosaur – but may continue to function, as an urban place, as well as or better than the modern equivalent (Figure 1.6). While some traditional urban environments are deliberately planned, we need to consider what produced the intricate functional order of traditional 'unplanned' urbanism.

The argument from design

The urban writer Lewis Mumford, contemplating a series of medieval town plans, noted that although each was unique, according to its unique situation, the plans seemed together to present a recognisable pattern. Mumford reflects:

> The consensus is so complete as to the purposes of town life that the variations in detail only confirm the pattern. The consensus makes it look, when one views a hundred medieval patterns in succession, as if there were in fact a conscious theory that guided this townplanning. [*sic*][12]

In other words, the form and functioning of traditional towns and cities seem so well fitted to each other that they look as if they must have been deliberately designed this way (Figure 1.7). They appear 'too well planned' to have arisen by chance.

This sentiment has a resonance with the 'argument from design' in biological and theological thought: the view that the intricate harmonious workings of nature must be explained by the existence of a conscious designer.[13] Tom Turner remarks:

1.6 • Traditional urbanism is good because it is functional. (a) Urban space, Stockholm; (b) Street, Taxco, Mexico; (c) Colonnaded walkway, La Rochelle, France. Compare with Figures 1.1 and 1.2.

(a)

(b)

(c)

In the seventeenth century, it was argued that as the world resembles a watch, but with infinite complexity, there must be a grand watchmaker: God. The built environment equivalent of this argument may be described as 'the watchmaker argument for the existence of planners': as towns and landscapes are complicated structures, that must have master plans.[14]

However, in the case of the town plans of Figure 1.7, while parts of them were planned, they were not all planned by the same hand. Yet, they seem to have a typical characteristic form to them. Is it possible that these similarities in form could have arisen by chance, or is there something else at work here?

If all towns were planned, it would suffice to consult a history of town planning to learn how those towns came to be. If all towns were planned,

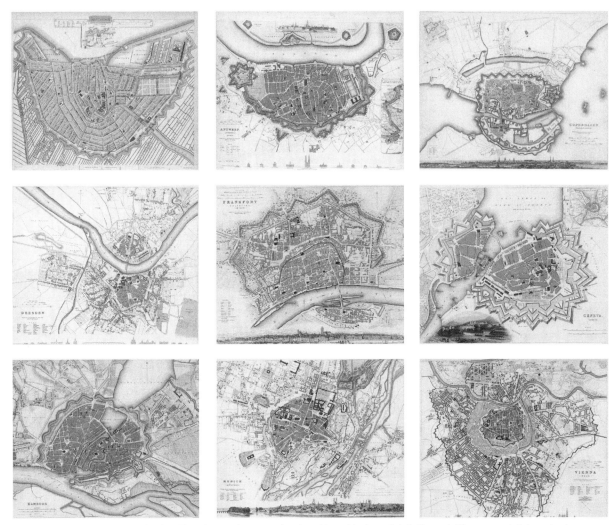

1.7 • European nineteenth-century city plans. These have an almost organic order, with combinations of similarities and differences, and of planned and 'unplanned'.

moreover, we should just replicate or adapt those plans, in order to create another town. However, if we consider the more typical case of the 'unplanned' town, we have to investigate more widely and deeply to find explanation for the pattern of its growth.

LEARNING FROM SCIENCE AND NATURE

The genius of man may make various inventions . . . but it will never discover a more beautiful, a more economical, or a more direct one than nature's.
Leonardo da Vinci[15]

We see ordered patterns everywhere in the natural world (Figure 1.8). It has been the task of science to seek explanations for these patterns, that add up to what we recognise as order.[16]

Conscious acts of human will and creativity have often seemed – historically at any rate – to lie outside the domain of scientific explanation. But not all products of the human world are necessarily determinate artefacts. Towns and cities, for example, seem to contain a degree of indeterminacy that would not be seen in a work of art such as a painting, or the design of a building.

While twentieth-century physics may have dispelled the idea of a 'clockwork universe', it has still taken some time for us to overcome the idea of 'clockwork town planning', in which people are assumed to scuttle about from homes to workplaces and back as if part of some complicated but predictable mechanism.[17]

However, our scientific understanding of the world has moved on since conventional city planning was born. We no longer see the universe as an entirely predictable, deterministic place. We now see it more as a complex, sometimes chaotic place, but one where we can still find patterns in the complexity. Advances made by emerging sciences of complexity and chaos theory have helped to unlock the underlying order in a variety of phenomena previously considered so trivial as to not require an explanation, or too complex or inscrutable to attempt it.[18]

For example, scientists now examine the structure of social networks, such as 'small world networks' that tend to organise themselves in distinctive patterns which are neither completely regular nor completely random. Or, they can study the structure of the internet, which no single person or agency controls, but which nevertheless has a characteristic pattern to it.[19]

In these cases, the broad aggregate patterns we observe are based on complex local interactions between individual elements. While these interactions of individual elements may themselves be un-coordinated or chaotic, the overall patterns might be recurring and familiar. This is a kind of order: but order without a plan.

It has taken some time to recognise this notion of order without a plan. Mitchel Resnick refers to the 'centralized mindset', a 'bias' that makes

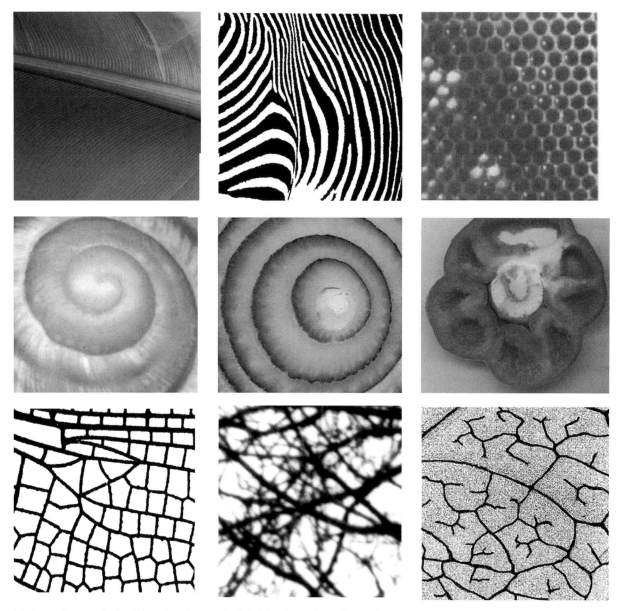

1.8 • Patterns in nature: Feather; Zebra stripes; Honeycomb; Shell; Onion; Pepper; Dragonfly wing; Tree branches; Pea stipule.

people think there must be 'single causes', leaders or seeds behind events or organised things; while decentralised approaches have been 'ignored, undervalued, and overlooked'. However, he notes, in recent years there has been a growing fascination with ideas such as decentralisation and self-organisation. Michael Batty interprets the implication for the urban sphere: the need for 'a dramatic shift in the way we think about cities'.[20]

But, while the ideas of complexity and self-organisation are starting to percolate into urban scholarship, converting these into useful strategies for actually planning or designing cities remains unfinished business. Not least, the urban questions needing to be answered are not just to do with creating order in the absence of planning, but also *functionality* – or fitness of purpose – in the absence of planning. This invites us to consider a further scientific idea: that of evolution.

Evolution

As Theodosius Dobzhansky classically asserted, 'Nothing makes sense in biology except in the light of evolution'. But beyond even its significance to biology, or indeed science, evolution has been described by Jared Diamond as the 'most profound and powerful idea to have been conceived in the last two centuries'. The idea of evolution not only directly transformed biology, but had profound repercussions for philosophy, metaphysics and theology, and has also been applied in areas as diverse as politics, sociology, psychology and literature, by the likes of Marx, Spencer, Freud, and H.G. Wells.[21] Evolutionary thinking has also been applied to the technical and design fields, including the evolution of tools, artefacts, and architecture – notably in the work of Philip Steadman, John Ziman and others. But evolutionary thinking has not been applied to cities and urbanism in such a significant systematic sense.[22]

Patrick Geddes' classic book *Cities in Evolution*, while peppered with biological and evolutionary references, was really more about 'civics' and 'city design' than a systematic application of evolutionary theory to understanding urban change. In any case, Geddes' interpretation of biological evolution was unconventional, and requires caution when applying to cities or anything else. Finally, *Cities in Evolution* was written almost a century ago – an age before motorways, malls, television, computers, antibiotics, and indeed the 'modern synthesis' of genetics and evolutionary theory. So the time seems ripe to apply some renewed evolutionary thinking to cities.[23]

The argument from evolution

Evolution implies that we can have functional order in nature, but without any designer or master planner. The 'argument from evolution' suggests that adaptive incremental change can lead to great transformations and a diversity of forms in the long term. This means a combination of continuity and change – neither a series of capricious metamorphoses, nor a steady unfolding towards an foreseeable goal. The kinds of change are in response to the environment, in such a way that the things we see are apparently functional or fit for purpose – they 'work' in the context of the environment that they are adapted to.

Evolution helps explain why things differ and are yet related to each other through space and time. Richard Dawkins' idea of a 'Museum of All Possible Animals' elucidates the idea of a 'solution space' of possible forms, in which all actual animal forms, however diverse, are physically related to each other, and to all *possible* forms (Figure 1.9). In effect, science sets out the field of possibility, through which natural history forges an actual trajectory. This trajectory is identifiable with evolution.[24]

Evolutionary theory can help provide answers to explain the forms of living things, and how these are well matched to their 'functions', even in the absence of 'design'. Can this be applied to cities?

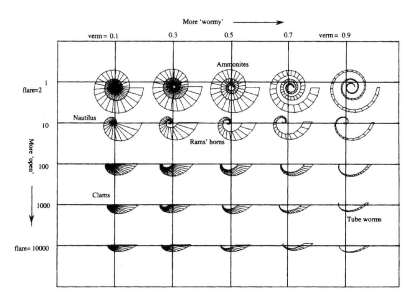

1.9 • The Museum of All Shells. This shows a rank and file of shells, according to two variables relating to 'worminess' and 'openness'. This is a subset of the Museum of All Possible Animals.

The evolutionary challenge

Applied to biology, evolutionary theory had to do several things. For a start, it had to recognise that the complex functionality of living things demanded a special kind of explanation in the first place. Second, it had to demonstrate that evolution actually took place – that species did indeed change and diverge over time. This included being clear about what was actually evolving. Finally, it had to propose the mechanisms by which evolution came about. It was the achievement of Charles Darwin and Alfred Russel Wallace in connecting these that led to the crystallisation of evolution as the 'most important concept in biology'.[25]

When interpreting urban evolution, the stakes are somewhat more modest and the task more straightforward. This is not to say the story is not complex and contested in its own way; but it is in a different league, and a challenge in order of magnitude less than what was faced by the biological evolutionists. For a start, we *know* what mechanisms create buildings and cities – this is the stuff of human imagination, design and construction. Also, we have good evidence of the fact of urban change. As well as seeing things being built and torn down in front of us, we have a good urban equivalent of the 'fossil record': we have both good archaeological evidence of ancient cities, as well as historical documentary evidence of designs and plans, and records of the planning intentions of city founders and city rulers. Putting these together is the least we can do.

If anything, the challenge is to recognise the urban change as a kind of evolutionary effect in the first place, whatever the differences from biological evolution. That is to say, urban change is neither a succession of independent acts of creation, punctuating an otherwise static world; nor is it a steady unfolding towards a mature form, like an unfurling flower.

The challenge of this book is, in a sense, to see how learning from science and nature – in particular from evolution – can help us to understand urbanism, and hence inform the choice of paths to take from the crossroads of city planning and design.

THIS BOOK

The aim of the book, then, is to arrive at a better understanding of cities, their design and their evolution, and the relationships between purposive intervention and historical processes of evolution and the resulting urban patterns and products. This understanding can help crystallise possible alternatives for designing or planning cities in the future. Is there some way that avoids the Modernist misadventures of the 1960s and 1970s, without simply replicating the forms of the past; some way of achieving functional urbanism between the extremes of rigidly planned order or a laissez-faire free-for-all?

To address this agenda, the book draws from a combination of existing and new research into urban history, planning and design theory, and scientific insights into relationships between processes and patterns, forms and functions. This does not presume to be a comprehensive explanatory theory of urbanism, nor an empirical account of how any particular cities came to be the way they are. Rather, it suggests a general framework, or a series of linked perspectives, within which different aspects of urbanism may be arranged and hence – it is hoped – better understood.

In the end, the book does not recommend any particular course of planning or design action. The decision as to what is 'good' city form will depend on the context of time and place, and individual purposes. That context and those purposes are assumed to be supplied by the reader. That said, some indications of how the understanding of the book could be applied to practice are suggested.

A few words on scope and focus

At its broadest level, this book is concerned with urban planning and design: the physical nature and structure of cities, how cities have been shaped, the elements of the city that are used as the basis for design, and how different elements may be used towards future design. A few words on what is meant by 'cities', 'design' and 'evolution' will help set the scene for the rest of the book.

Cities

The book tends to refer primarily to cities, rather than other kinds of settlement, not because the city is grander than the town, but because the term city captures all of the urban components and complexities that the book is concerned with, whether this applies to a small historic city of a few thousand people or a modern megacity of ten millions. That said, the scope of the book properly applies to settlements of any kind, including towns and villages.

More specifically, the book focuses on the physical fabric and structure of cities. While cities are ultimately also constituted by a wide array of non-physical considerations – social relations, economic forces and energy flows, and so on – the book's primary attention is given to the basic physical stuff of cities: things like streets, buildings and plots of land – tangible things that can be pointed to, located, walked around – things that can be physically designed. In other words, the book is mainly about the planning and design of the 'hardware' of the cities, rather than its 'software'. The two are closely interlinked in practice, but they are conceptually quite distinct, forming a natural division of labour when it comes to their design or management.

Design

The book interprets design as referring to the devising or creating of some finite object at a given point in time for a definite purpose. In this sense we talk of a machine or building being designed. A planned city could, in an extreme case, be described as designed if its whole form were preconceived in advance of being built as a finite set-piece. More usually, however, we use the word planning in contradistinction to design, to indicate the generation of something that is not a finite object, but something that is developed incrementally over time and not ever 'finished'. The relationship between design and planning will be explored in the course of the book.

Evolution

This book treats evolution as a general concept that can be applied to cities, and other human artefacts and systems, as well as in biological contexts. In doing so, evolution is taken to refer to the effect of adaptive transformation over time; and this can be interpreted with respect to cities and species, even though the precise nature of the contributory processes will vary from case to case. This is like the way we can apply the term 'adaptation' as a general concept across different contexts, albeit that it has a specialist meaning within biology.

On the one hand, this means that using the term evolution is not just a figure of speech – like saying metaphorically that 'a city is a living organism'. On the other hand, as we shall see, using the term evolution does not imply that urban evolution is equivalent in detail to biological phenomena. The argument of this book does *not* require the reader to believe that cities are somehow literally alive, or to seek urban analogues for sex, cells, genes, and so on.

Rather, evolution is treated as a concept that is general enough that it can be interpreted in both biological and non-biological contexts; but specific enough that it is clearly distinct from other kinds of change – growth, development, metamorphosis, adaptation and emergence – that may also be interpreted in both the natural and built environment. In other words, this book argues that what happens to cities when they evolve is a real effect, whatever word is used to describe that effect; we would still need a word to describe this effect, even if we did not recognise evolution in other contexts.

1.10 • Venus Fly Trap, the intricate functionality of nature.

Therefore, addressing evolution is not some romantic fancy, which somehow brings human artifice closer to nature. It would only be a fanciful contrivance by either imposing human motives and tendencies on nature (as if Venus Fly-Traps really 'planned' to trap flies, or were really 'designed' to do so), or by the converse, claiming to be sprinkling the magic of a pure, sagacious nature on the mundane, muddled world of urban planning.

Certainly, we can admire nature for its beauty, as we admire the beauty of a historic town or urban quarter. But just as we do not emulate traditional urbanism because it is traditional, we do not look to nature because it is natural; but we can learn from nature where it can provide us with useful insights into how things work (Figure 1.10).

Outline of the structure and main arguments

The belief that a city is – or should be – an 'organic whole' pervades much of planning theory and practice. This affects not only our understanding of how cities 'are', but how they could or should be planned. As we shall see, much of this book is concerned with understanding the relationships between the parts and the whole, the changes in the parts and the whole over time, and the planning and design of those parts and wholes.

After this Introduction, Chapter 2 sets out the context of the 'problem' of city planning as tackled in this book, by examining Cities, Planning and Modernism. We shall see how city planning is concerned with the creation of urban order, and the particular activity of 'city design' which is directed at designing the city as a whole.

To understand how a city is 'put together,' we need to understand the urban 'building blocks' involved; and Chapter 3, Articulating Urban Order, investigates what these units are and how these may be put together, generating the different kinds of order we see in planned and 'unplanned' cities. Chapter 4 then explores the Social Logic of Urban Order, suggesting the social reasons behind why we have urban units such as buildings, streets and cities in the first place.

In order to plan or design a city as a whole, we need to understand the nature of that whole, or the Kind of Thing a City Is. Chapter 5 explores different conceptualisations of the city, and argues that, while a city may be 'organic', this does not mean it is an organism, a corporate whole. Rather, a city is more like an ecosystem, whose components are partly in cooperation, but partly in competition. In effect, the order of the whole arises from the interactions between the parts.

Chapter 6 therefore considers how functional order might be created in the absence of design or planning of the whole, through the concepts of

Emergence and Evolution, with reference to examples from nature and other phenomena. Here, the case is made for recognising evolution as a generic concept that can be applied outside biology.

The next two chapters then apply the concepts of emergence and evolution to understanding cities and urbanism. Chapter 7, Emergent Urban Order, and Chapter 8, Cities in Evolution help explain how, even in the absence of overall 'city design', we have seen the emergence and evolution of traditional urban forms – and Modernist and contemporary ones.

In effect, we can recognise an evolutionary perspective or paradigm that is different from either a 'creationist' (city-as-designed-object) or 'developmental' (city-as-growing-organism) one. Chapter 9, Planning, Design and Evolution, explores the implications of this evolutionary understanding, for application to the urban context. Finally, Chapter 10 draws general Conclusions on the book, while looking out to new horizons beyond.

Notes

1 By 'unplanned' it is meant 'not wholly planned', rather than 'wholly not planned'. On the idea of no settlement being wholly unplanned, see Kostof (1991: 52), Sitte ([1889] 1945: 52). On the alienating nature of modern urban environments: Martin (1999: 167) describes the new architecture and planning of the 1960s and 1970s as 'grim and alienating'; Alexander (1979: 237) refers to people complaining about the 'merciless inhuman quality of their environment'; Alexander gives many examples of 'bad' Modernism in *The Nature of Order*, see, for example, Alexander (2002a: 14; 2002b, xiv–xv; 2005: 32–33).

2 New towns: Marshall (2006a); 'horrors': Turner (1996: 22); 'most hated': Hebbert (1993: 434).

3 Millions of people live in cave-dwellings, but these have been deliberately designed and adapted to human use, as opposed to unadapted natural caves occupied by animals (Rudofsky, 1965; Golany and Ojima, 1996).

4 See, for example, Katz (1994); Hebbert (2003); Southworth (2003); Hebbert (2005a).

5 Sudjic (1992); Garreau (1992); Ellin (1996); Batty (2005: 18); Koolhaas (2005); Davis (2006); Batty (2008a).

6 As Moudon (1987) has pointed out, the design of successful places takes time: 'it took at least 400 years of repeated design activity, which followed a few hundred more years of just "using the space" to make Piazza San Marco in Venice'. Johnson-Marshall (1966: 12–13) suggests 1,000 years of the evolution of Piazza San Marco.

7 Jacobs (1962); see also commentary by Batty (1999); Kolson (2001: 166). 'The Failure of Town Planning' appeared as the subtitle to the Penguin edition of Jacobs' book (1962). Alexander (1966). Before them, Camillo Sitte ([1889] 1945) and Patrick Geddes (1915) had argued against mechanistic town planning.

8   Perhaps planning is always at, or approaching, a crossroads of one sort or another. For one treatment of the topic, see Simmie (1993).

9   Vickers (1998: 11).

10   This also accords with Alexander who argues against replicating the past for its own sake (1966: 47). More recently, Bressi asserts: 'New Urbanism is not a romantic movement' (1994: xxv).

11   Scruton (1979: 241) points out that the traditional fork is 'adapted to the needs of daily life'. The modern fork is also functional to the extent its function is to look functional. See also Lang (1994), Hillier (1996) and de Botton (2006) for discussion on Modernism and functionality.

12   Mumford (1961: 302–303). See also Rudofsky's (1965) exposition of *Architecture without Architects*; Dickinson (1961: 364) on recurring common features of towns of Flanders.

13   See, for example, Sagan (1974); Steadman (1979); Dawkins (1991: 4); F. Dyson (1998: 186); Jones (1999: 91), Ayala (2007: 8568).

14   Turner (1996: 56).

15   Richter (1952: 103).

16   See, for example, Sagan (1977), Grande and Rieppel (1994), Bowes (1996), Bak (1996), Camazine (2003); Blunt (2004), on Linnaeus; Carroll (2006).

17   The 'clockwork universe' is associated with Newton and Laplace. See, for example, Jencks (1997a: 7); Saunders (1997: 52); Gribbin (2005: 18).

18   See, for example, Holland (1995), Coveney and Highfield (1995); Gribbin (2005); Batty (2005); Batty (2008a); Chapter 5.

19   Watts and Strogatz (1998); Watts (1999); Dodge and Kitchin (2001); Barabási (2002); Batty (2007, 2008b).

20   Resnick (1997: 5); Resnick (1997: 4); Batty (2005: xix; 2007, 2008b).

21   Dobzhansky (1973); Diamond (2001: vii), Strickberger (2000: 53), Jones (1999: xxv).

22   Steadman (1979, 2008), Ziman (2000), Wheeler *et al.*, (2002). See Chapter 6. In effect, these address artefacts and systems that may be component parts of cities.

23   The scope of *Cities in Evolution* is best summed up by its subtitle: *An Introduction to the Town Planning Movement and to the Study of Civics*. Parts of it were written as far back as 1910 (Tyrwhitt, 1949: ix). Geddes' interpretation of evolution – which differs from both the Darwinian evolution of his day and neo-Darwinian thinking of today – is first set out in Geddes and Thomson (1889) and reaffirmed in Geddes and Thomson (1911) and Thomson and Geddes (1931). Batty (1995a) suggested the time is ripe for uniting neo-Darwinian thinking and urbanism . . .

24   Dawkins (1997: 182). Dawkins' Museum of All Possible Animals is derived from another metaphorical allusion, the philosopher Daniel Dennett's Library of Mendel – a vast library of all possible genomic descriptions or DNA sequences based on permutations of the four letters of the 'genetic alphabet' (Dennett, 1996: 111). Dennett's Library is itself an allusion to José Luis Borges' *Library of Babel* con-

taining a vast but finite range of books of all possible permutations of letters. *The Library of Babel* has its own history and pre-history . . . (Borges, [1962] 1998: 13). Incidentally, Patrick Geddes conceived of an 'Index Museum' – a visual classification of all knowledge, or *Encyclopedia Graphica*. A monograph on this unpublished typescript is entitled 'Museums: Actual and Possible' (Meller, 1980: 210).

25   'Evolution is the most important concept in biology': Mayr (2001); Dawkins on living things requiring a special kind of explanation (1991: 1, 6); the challenge faced by Darwin: Ayala (2007: 8567).

2 CITIES, PLANNING AND MODERNISM

Hippodamus, son of Euryphon, a native of Miletus, the same who invented the art of planning cities.

Aristotle, *The Politics*[1]

Le Corbusier was one of the most inventive and influential architects of the twentieth century, or any century. His work inspired a generation of architects and planners – and provoked another. Le Corbusier is famous for some of the most iconic urban images of the twentieth century – that still look dramatic and futuristic today. With its looming skyscrapers of reinforced concrete, steel and glass, set in open space and connected by high-speed roads and interchanges, Le Corbusier's urbanism could be regarded as forming the quintessential Modernist landscape (image opposite).

As we saw in Chapter 1, Modernist landscapes, as actually built, were not always loved by the public. Modernist planning was implicated in this, as the very way in which cities were being structured was hindering the creation of the intricate functionality of traditional towns. If Modernist planning is part of the urban problem, then we need to understand better both planning and Modernism.

The problem of Modernist planning cannot simply be one of planning, since we see many examples of traditional urban planning – not least the planned cities of ancient Greece – that are admired and applauded by contemporary neo-traditionalists. The roll-call of cities that started life as newly planned or founded settlements after all includes historic London and old New York, ancient Rome and the once 'new Rome' of Istanbul, as much as Brasilia, Canberra or Welwyn Garden City.

Then again, the problem of Modernist city planning cannot simply be the presence of modern features – individual modern buildings, with interior bathrooms and lifts; or modern metro systems with electric lighting and tele-communications. These modern features can each be regarded as being successful in their own right, and definite improvements on their historic predecessors, and adopted without demur as 'good' Modernism. If the essence of Modernist city planning is not in the individual parts, then the 'planning' must be in the packaging.

To get to grips with the 'problem of Modernist planning' we need to unpick the package that is city planning, and the connotations of Modernism. What is the relationship between planning and Modernism? Can we discard Modernism, but keep town planning?

This chapter shall investigate cites, planning and Modernism, and how these are related. We shall do this with reference to historical and con-temporary examples of urban planning and planned cities. First, let us unpack the concept of city planning. We shall do this by first identifying four classic elements of city planning that will be important for the understanding of planning through the rest of the book: planning intention, city design, urban ordering, and the use of plans as planning instruments. Then, we shall turn to explore the rise and fall of Modernist city planning, in doing so addressing the meaning of Modernism, and interpreting Modernist city planning in terms of the classic elements of planning identified herein. Finally, we turn to post-modern urbanism, and consider to what extent this is a continuation or refutation of Modernist planning. This chapter therefore serves to articulate the 'problem' of Modernist city planning that the rest of the book will be seeking to resolve.

CITY PLANNING

Hippodamus of Miletus, the ancient Greek, has sometimes been heralded as the 'father of town planning'. Allowing for the vagaries of translation and historical interpretation, Hippodamus is variously credited with having invented 'the art of planning cities', the 'divisioning of cities', the division of cities into 'blocks' or 'precincts', and the tripartite disposition of public, private and sacred spaces. He is also often associated with gridiron planning, and is credited with laying out the street-plan of Piraeus. Then again, in Aristotle's *Politics*, it is primarily as a 'utopian' thinker that Hippodamus is being examined.[2]

Clearly these are not the same things. The different ways in which we interpret what Hippodamus of Miletus actually invented or practised reflects different aspects that could variously represent – or add up to – what we mean by town or city planning. It will be useful to unpack the different elements of planning in order to get to grips with this issue.

Plans and planning

At the outset of *Urban and Regional Planning*, Peter Hall goes back to first principles and interprets the meaning of the term planning:

> planning as a general activity is the making of an orderly sequence of action that will lead to the achievement of a stated goal or goals. . . .
> It may, but need not necessarily, include exact physical blueprints of objects.[3]

At a fundamental level, Hall is noting that a plan can mean an *intention* (as in a plan to go to London or New York) or a physical representation (a street-plan of London or New York). The latter may be regarded as an *instrument* of planning.

These two distinct meanings could apply to intentions or instruments that had nothing to do with cities or urbanism: a planning intention could be a budget for an event; a blueprint could be a specification for a machine. Therefore, when unpacking the meaning of 'city planning' for the purposes of this book, it will be useful to recognise two further interpretations of planning that are associated with the physical planning of cities. These shall be referred to as *city design* and *urban ordering*, and these go to the heart of the sense of planning as treated in this book.[4]

We can first introduce city design and urban ordering by placing them in the middle of a 'cosmic pyramid'[5] with planning intention at the top, and planning instruments at the bottom (Figure 2.1).

Before interpreting these four elements with respect to planning settlements, we can quickly see the distinctions of meaning by considering the case of a building – say, a family house. The *intention* is to create a family home to live in. The *design* is the architectural design of the house – the specific arrangement of walls and floors to create rooms, and so on. The *ordering* is the general consistency of relationships between individual components – for example, the way bricks are ordered in a regular pattern or 'bond', irrespective of the final shape the brickwork makes. Finally, the *instruments* of architecture include plans, elevations and cross-sections.

Let us return to the urban scale, and look at these four elements in turn: planning intention, city design, urban ordering and planning instruments.

2.1 • Four classic elements of city planning.

I. Planning Intention

II. City Design

III. Urban Ordering

IV. Planning Instruments

Planning intention

Planning intention is concerned with envisioning and precipitating a desired future state. City planning is typically associated with objectives that are ultimately social and political. We can identify at least three degrees to which a future desired state might be planned for.[6]

The first degree of planning is simply that of maintaining an existing desired state into the future (or, selectively retaining desired parts of an existing state). This could be a purely routine concern, like planning maintenance of the streets to prevent or remedy potholes. Or, it could imply more proactive intervention to maintain a given satisfactory condition within an anticipated changed future context. For example, if the birth rate or water level is rising, then it is prudent to provide for new or larger schools, or flood defences, to maintain adequate provision into the future. This first degree of planning, however modest, can be recognised indeed as an act of planning, not least since failure to do it would be regarded as a 'failure of planning'.

A second degree of planning would be to create and provide for a desired future state that is in some way better than the present, for example, by providing *more* schools per child, or *better* paved roads. This second degree in effect creates an improved state tomorrow, for today's society.

A third degree of planning would attempt to create a future desired state for an 'improved' society. This could be equated with 'Utopian' planning and social engineering. Here, the attempt is to change society for the better, *through* planning. This could mean providing – or withholding provision of – things compatible with a supposed better society. For example, a plan that provided a public library in every neighbourhood, rather than a public house, could help promote a society with more education and less alcohol. In this relatively mild form, this could be interpreted as aiming to realise the latent good intentions of people as they currently are, without necessarily trying to change attitudes or behaviour. A stronger form would actively stimulate changed attitudes or otherwise attempt to 'engineer' improved behaviour.[7]

Note that although the third case is closest to being 'utopian', the second case is still making an assumption about what an improved state of affairs would be, and even the first case is making selective judgement about which parts of the present state warrant propagation into the future (the smooth road surfaces, rather than the potholes). All, therefore, rely on assumptions about a future desired state, not just the more overtly 'utopian'. All, therefore, have a political element to them; none is a purely technical exercise.[8]

City design

City design refers to the design or planning of a city in a definite form at a given point in time, as a finite, whole unit. This sense of design is equivalent to the design of a building, or machine, any other artefact, as a whole unit, for a particular purpose. Although the term city design is the main focus here, corresponding terms may be used for other kinds of urban unit: town design, neighbourhood design, village design, and so on. In each case, 'design' implies creation of a single finite product, that once designed is then constructed, and hence 'finished'.

A second aspect of city design is that the 'whole' is composed of sub-components that support the functioning of the whole. While any city may come to have different specialised areas – for example, marketplace, residential quarters, industrial areas – in a planned city these are decreed in advance, in such a way that they support the city's functioning as a whole.

As a third connotation of city design, the recognition of a whole at any scale also allows reconstituting, reinventing or repackaging of elements. For example, recognition of a town as an urban unit allows recognition of a cluster of individual shops and public buildings as a 'town centre'; and a planned town allows 'town centre design' as a specific exercise over and above the placement or design of individual shops or public buildings.

The idea of the city as unit of design is deeply connected with several other city planning concepts: newly founded settlements; functional special-isation and subdivision of parts; neighbourhood 'cells'; and optimisation for the good of the whole. These may all be considered contingent on and subsidiary to the idea of the city as unit of design.[9] Lewis Mumford, one of the most influential urban writers of the twentieth century, expressly saw the whole city as the unit of design. City design could be applied to the restructuring of an existing urban accretion, or it could be applied to the founding of a new city.[10]

The case of city design is most clearly seen in the case of designs for ideal cities that are often clearly finite, bounded, and composed of supporting sub-components, and devised as a whole for a particular planning intention. Vitruvius included in his *Ten Books of Architecture* a description of an ideal city, with the symmetrical order of the octagon, devised in such a way as to optimise control of the 'eight winds' (Figure 2.2) – a specific city design to meet an explicit planning intention.[11]

Edinburgh's Georgian 'New Town' was laid out as a residential suburb to the north of the original settlement. This was a finite composition in the form of a hierarchical orthogonal grid, with squares, main streets, minor streets and alleys (Figure 2.3). As such, this was a case of 'suburb design', or 'town

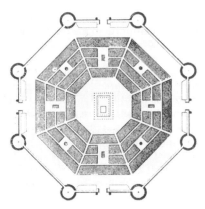

2.2 • Vitruvius' ideal city.

2.3 • Craig Plan, Edinburgh.

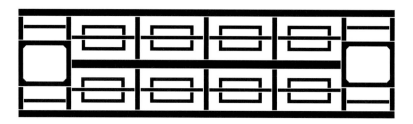

design', although later it became integrated within the city as a whole, forming the central business district.

With city design, as interpreted here, the whole city may be composed of identifiable sub-components – such as neighbourhoods or blocks – that are themselves objects of design. Similarly, neighbourhoods or blocks may be composed of streets that are definite objects of design; and streets may be composed of buildings that are definite objects of design. By this level, we are back down to building design: the scale of architecture.

Urban ordering

Urban ordering refers to the creation of order through consistency of urban 'building-blocks' and their relationships. This is referred to as urban (rather than town or city) ordering, since it is independent of settlement type: this kind of order would apply whether relating to a development of a few buildings or a large city or urban region.

While a city design may incorporate urban ordering, urban ordering does not necessarily presume any overall 'whole' that is being designed. In other words, the ordering is independent of being part of any particular finite product that it may ultimately form part of. In the case of a brick building, the way that bricks are laid in a particular 'bond' is a kind of order, and different kinds of bond are possible that can be put together to create many different overall designs – whether a garden wall, the walls of a house, an aqueduct, and so on. Or, a classical building has a vocabulary of columns, pediments, and so on, that can form a kind of 'kit of parts' (Figure 2.4).[12] Similarly, at the urban scale, it is possible to have streets joined together in some kind of order, but without any neighbourhood design. Or, one might have internally ordered towns and cities that are seen to form conurbations, but with no 'conurbation design'.

An example of internal ordering would be the ordering of the ground plane – the order one sees on a city plan. We could refer to this as *ground-plane ordering* – or, more simply, *ground-planning*. Perhaps the most commonly recognised form of ground-planning is the ordering of the street layout

2.4 • A 'kit of parts'. This can form the basis of order, whatever the ultimate finite design that might be assembled. The illustration shows an interpretation of typical elements by Alexander 'Greek' Thomson.

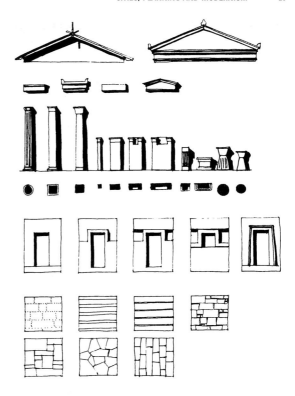

on a grid pattern; although other kinds of regular order are possible – for example, branching cul-de-sacs, or even hexagonal plans. If Hippodamean town planning refers to the presence of a rectangular grid, this is only a small subset of many kinds of planning.[13]

Among the oldest known examples of planned cities, urban order can perhaps be seen most clearly in street patterns. In the Indus Valley civilisation of around 2150 BC, the city of Mohenjo-Daro, for example, had a regular street-grid and a division into public and private spaces. Meanwhile, Kahun in Egypt has been suggested as the earliest known example of the use of the gridiron. Hippodamus of Miletus (as mentioned above) is associated with the idea of laying out cities on a regular gridiron pattern; this came to be known as a 'Hippodamean' grid. Hippodamus' own home town, Miletus, was replanned on a regular grid formation (Figure 2.5 a). These cases of regular street-grids – as instances of urban ordering – neither presuppose nor preclude the possibility that city design was also involved.[14]

In contrast to Edinburgh's New Town, Glasgow's Blythswood New Town grid is not so much a finite design, but has been described as 'the open-

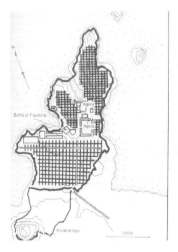

(a)

(b)

2.5 • Urban order through orthogonal geometry, that is capable of indefinite extension: (a) Ancient Miletus; (b) Glasgow's Blythswood 'New Town'.

ended Hippodamian grid par excellence' (Figure 2.5 b). Indeed, a time-travelling Hippodamus would feel quite at home in the urban order of 'Hippodamian' Glasgow – a city complete with Alexander 'Greek' Thomson's classical architecture (Figure 2.4).[15]

The open-ended grid became the norm for many cases of newly settled or newly colonised land, such as in the New World of the Americas. Part of the reason for the practicality of the grid is that it is easy to conceive and set out on the ground. This is partly due to its regular, *ordered*, nature.[16]

While urban ordering is in principle independent of city design, it can be used to support the creation of an ordered city design. For example, a gridiron layout could help provide the internal structure of a city design that relates the different parts to the whole.

As well as ground-planning, another kind of ordering could simply be the very relationships between houses in streets or blocks, whereby each house faces a street at the front, and has a garden at the back. Here, the street–house–garden combination represents a basic kind of order (building blocks and relationships) whether or not the streets or houses themselves have any regularity of size, shape, alignment, or anything else.

Planning instruments

We can regard a plan – in the sense of a two-dimensional representation of the ground plane – as a planning instrument. Other planning instruments include elevations and cross-sections, geographical information systems (GIS), models, codes, regulations, design briefs and guidelines, and so on. Any of these instruments may be used to support the activities of ground-planning, urban ordering and city design, and hence help fulfil ultimate planning intentions. Then again, in principle such kinds of instrument do not necessarily imply the creation of any of these planning functions. For example, a building plan could be simply a record of some existing spatial arrangement, and nothing to do with future intention.[17]

Just as planning in general does not require ground-planning, ground-planning (and planning in general) does not require the use of plans. Two-dimensional ground-plane order can be created by surveying methods that allow those physically laying out a set of streets to generate straight lines, in parallel and perpendicular formations, without the need for an abstract representation. In antiquity, the *groma* was used to lay out perpendicular intersections and hence orthogonal grids (Figure 2.6). It too could therefore be regarded as a 'planning' instrument, even if it were not used in conjunction with any plan. So the order of ancient Greek cities, for example, that we today

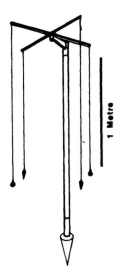

2.6 • Groma, a surveying device used to lay out perpendicular intersections and hence orthogonal grids.

could see so clearly from a plan, or from the air, could be generated without the aid of either paper plans or an aerial perspective.[18]

Urban order can also be created through codes, ordinances and other kinds of regulation. For example, codes have been used historically to legislate for things like building orientation, building type and height, street width, and so on, without the use of a plan, or without the design of any particular building being preconceived in advance. A clear example of an urban code in contradistinction to an urban plan is that of the building code introduced after the Great Fire of London. This created urban order – a consistency to London's streets – without an overall finite design. So, coding can provide a way of 'planning without plans'.[19]

The 'classic' city planning package

City planning, then, can be regarded as a combination – or conflation – of planning intention, city design, urban ordering, and the use of plans as instruments (Figure 2.7). This could involve – but need not involve – any of the following: utopian planning intentions; city founding; land use zoning; ground-planning, gridiron layouts; and the use of plans as two-dimensional representations of proposals. We could identify a classic 'ultimate' planned city featuring all of the foregoing features; but perhaps we can allow the term 'planned city' to be used only when *some* aspect of each of the four basic elements is present.

The four principal elements – planning intention, city design, urban order and planning instruments – are independent in the sense that one does not necessarily imply another. That said, they form a spectrum in which the upper tend to be 'ends' to which the lower can serve as 'means' – most obviously, planning instruments are means to the ends of planning intention.[20]

That said, while ordering can be thought of as to do with building blocks to support a design at a larger scale, a design could be a module or building-block used to form urban order at a larger scale. For example, a designed neighbourhood 'cell' could be multiplied up to give a macro-scale order – but without any design at the macro-scale. In other words, design and ordering can take place at different scales (Figure 2.8).

Overall, then, planning can be seen as independent of the nature of its component architecture, infrastructure, materials, and so on, but is, rather, the packaging, the combination of instruments, ordering and design to serve the intention. These four 'classic' elements of city planning will be interpreted and referred to during the course of the book. For now, let us see how we can interpret them with respect to the advent of Modernism.

2.7 • Four classic elements of city planning, expanded to show typical components.

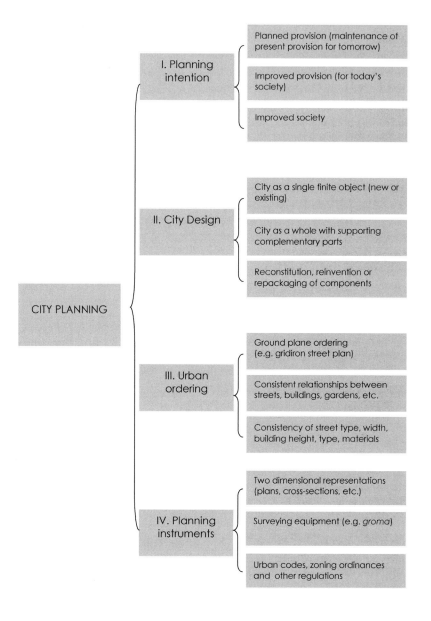

CITY PLANNING

I. Planning intention
- Planned provision (maintenance of present provision for tomorrow)
- Improved provision (for today's society)
- Improved society

II. City Design
- City as a single finite object (new or existing)
- City as a whole with supporting complementary parts
- Reconstitution, reinvention or repackaging of components

III. Urban ordering
- Ground plane ordering (e.g. gridiron street plan)
- Consistent relationships between streets, buildings, gardens, etc.
- Consistency of street type, width, building height, type, materials

IV. Planning instruments
- Two dimensional representations (plans, cross-sections, etc.)
- Surveying equipment (e.g. *groma*)
- Urban codes, zoning ordinances and other regulations

MODERNIST CITY PLANNING

Modernism is not just about concrete buildings and motorways on stilts. Modernism is an intellectual tradition that has been around for centuries: it is associated with ideals of the Renaissance and the Enlightenment, and these

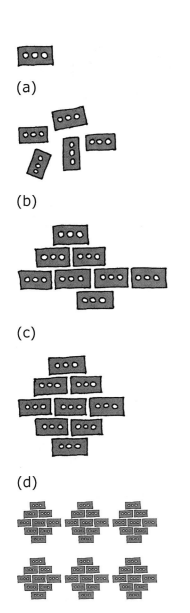

2.8 • Design versus ordering: (a) A designed unit; (b) Units deposited without order, the only consistency being that the units are the same; (c) Order: units deposited with ordered relationships to each other – whether or not there is any design of a finite whole; (d) Large-scale design composition of a finite whole: design plus order; (e) The designed whole of (d) becomes a unit of ordering for the next scale up.

ideas can also be traced back to ancient Greece. Indeed, in *The Politics*, Aristotle refers to Hippodamus' grid planning as 'modern'.[21]

In its broadest interpretation, Modernism can be regarded as a belief in the possibility of progress through rational action. This is as opposed to either a static worldview, in which there is no progress, or a passive worldview, in which any progress unfolds 'naturally', oblivious to human agency. Modernism has therefore been associated with idealism, innovation, rationalism, technological functionalism, mechanisation, rejection of tradition or historicism, abstraction and reinvention.[22] In a very broad sense, Modernism gave us democracy, reinforced concrete, Frankenstein's monster, movies, moon buggies, intercontinental ballistic missiles and the internet.[23]

The term 'modern' is also used in a second, everyday sense to refer to something contemporary or up-to-date. In this sense, we can still regard concrete and railways as 'modern', though they may have been around for centuries, since they are not superseded or outmoded in the way that more recent technologies are (e.g. the telegraph, or typewriter).[24]

A third sense of modern – Modern*ist* – is taken to mean the conscious pursuit of the modern instead of tradition.[25] This could be seen as the belief that 'new' equates with 'improved'; in effect, the assumption that things have to be modern (in the second sense) in order to realise the ideal city (modern in the first sense).

City planning is intrinsically modern in the sense of being a conscious action for the betterment of cities. So, in a sense, all of the kinds of planning seen in this chapter so far – Hippodamus, Vitruvius, and the rest – could be considered modern, even though these cases go back hundreds or thousands of years. To avoid 'modern planning' being a tautology, let us use the term 'modern' to refer to things that are contemporary, up-to-date methods (for example, using GIS or GPS), while using 'Modernist' to refer to the kind of planning that pursued the modern in conscious contradistinction to the traditional.

Modernist city planning, then, is the same as classical city planning except for being distinguished by its use of modern technology – railways, motorways, steel and reinforced concrete. As we shall see, these in turn lead to new formats (roads and free-standing buildings instead of street-grids) and larger-scale wholes and sub-components.[26]

Let us now track the rise and fall of Modernist city planning, interpreting cases in terms of city design and urban ordering.

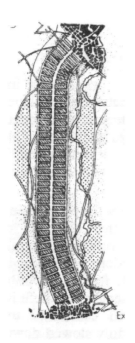

2.9 • *Ciudad Lineal*, a linear city capable of extension across the country – or continents.

Pioneers

Arturo Soria y Mata's proposal of 1892 for a linear city – *Ciudad Lineal* – based on a railway or tramway provides a useful point at which to mark the advent of Modernist city planning.[27] Although best known for its tramline spine, the *Ciudad Lineal* was addressing social and political issues, hygiene, and modern technology generally – including pneumatic tubes for letters and packages.

Ciudad Lineal had urban order in the sense of a consistent street-grid strung along a tramway spine that could be indefinitely extended across the countryside or even across continents – in principle, from Cadiz to St Petersburg, or Brussels to Beijing. This allowed the conception of cites to be extrapolated to an unprecedented scale (Figure 2.9).

Over and above the particulars of his *Ciudad Lineal* proposals, Soria y Mata was perhaps the first of the modern generation of town planning visionaries to articulate the idea of the whole city or town as being in need of planning or design like a building: 'An architecture of the cities is as necessary as the architecture that teaches how to construct buildings.'[28]

Even more explicitly, the theological Argument from Design is extrapolated to become an Argument for City Design:

> Most people find indispensable the existence of an Architect for the Universe, or a licensed architect for a house, and yet these same people do not recognize the need for an architect when constructing a city – which we believe to be more important than a house.[29]

So, Soria y Mata's extrapolatory thinking represents the application of both urban ordering and city design to modern planning.

In 1898, Ebenezer Howard published *Tomorrow: A Peaceful Path to Real Reform.*[30] In a curious cocktail of the mundane and arcane, with its railways sidings, allotments, homes for inebriates and crystal palaces, Howard's famous diagram of the Garden City is one of the most influential and memorable images in town planning history (Figure 2.10).

Ebenezer Howard's ideas can – like Soria y Mata's – also be seen as amounting to the case for City Design. Although Howard's plan included individual settlements that were meant to be more or less self-contained, it is surely significant that Howard's diagram shows a cluster of seven cities. In this, we could even interpret an instance of 'conurbation design' – that is, the set of seven cities is the whole unit, and individual garden cities are supporting sub-components. The countryside between settlements is not leftover space, but is part of the design, part of the whole.

2.10 • Ebenezer Howard's famous Garden City diagram.

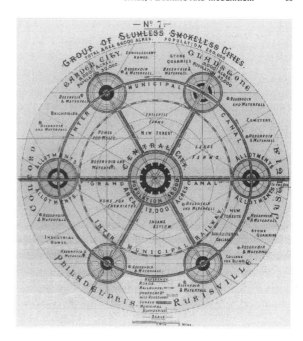

Howard's Garden Cities contained a whole package of modern features, including land use zoning, with industry at the edge, civic functions at the centre, and intermediate zones for housing and shopping. This functional separation relates to city design in the sense that these activities are traditionally interdependent, but by being separated they are in a sense made dependent on the whole.

Howard's Garden City would have a 'town centre' at the centre – not just a series of streets serving central (city-status) land uses. Places recognisable as 'town centres' were identifiable before, but the idea of a 'town centre' as a designed unit of a town, with a novel arrangement of town centre buildings, can be seen as a Modernist reinvention, or reconstitution of existing features. Rather than a web of traditional commercial streets meeting in a central crossroads, we have civic buildings arranged around the central junction, and shops in a separate 'crystal palace' format encircling these – an unprecedented combination.[31]

Between 1901 and 1917 Tony Garnier developed further crucial advances in modern planning in his model for a planned industrial city, *La Cité Industrielle*. This featured a functional separation of areas for living, work and social life; a separation of routes for traffic and pedestrians; and included buildings made from reinforced concrete.[32]

The creation of residential areas with complete separation of vehicles and traffic – with each house connecting to the road system on one side, and the path system on the other – was crystallised at Radburn, New Jersey, whereupon this form of urban ordering became known as the 'Radburn' layout. Meanwhile, Clarence Perry formalised the idea of the neighbourhood unit (hence, neighbourhood design), having communal facilities (park, school) at the centre, while shops lined the bounding main roads.[33]

Taken together, the elements of the Modern city identifiable in the work of those pioneers were combined to powerful effect, most significantly, by Le Corbusier.

The Corbusian revolution

Le Corbusier combined the earlier pioneers' ideas of linearity, extensibility, modern transport, regularity, rationality, zoning, and modern transport and construction technologies, and added in novel forms such as tower blocks on *pilotis*, grade-separated 'cloverleaf' intersections, interior streets and 'autoports'.[34] The results were as revolutionary as they were visionary. For example, Le Corbusier's *Ville Radieuse* (The Radiant City) is a radical departure from a traditional city, both in terms of its overall city design and its internal urban ordering (Figure 2.11).

Interpreted as a plan of a complete settlement, this would be an innovative case of City Design. The sense of reinvention or reconstitution can be seen here in the abnormal asymmetric layout, where, for example, the administrative centre, rather than being at the geographical centre of the city, is at the edge. This is reliant on the preconceived contrivance of the concept of the whole, and complementary parts – whose separation was enabled by fast transport accessibility – for it to work.[35]

The modern internal urban order can also be noted: the combination of stand-alone buildings, separated from vehicular routes (hence the dissolution of the street as an urban form); the segregation of transport modes themselves (particularly between fast vehicles and slow pedestrians); multi-level circulation (including buildings over roads).[36] This urban order is almost visually synonymous with Modernism – as depicted in Figure 1.2. That innovative format – which we may refer to as the Corbusian revolution – was consciously heralded and precipitated by Le Corbusier as a '*complete reversal* of the economy of streets, of the situation of houses and streets in respect to each other, of the hitherto interdependent function of house and street'.[37]

2.11 • Le Corbusier's *La Ville Radieuse* (1933).

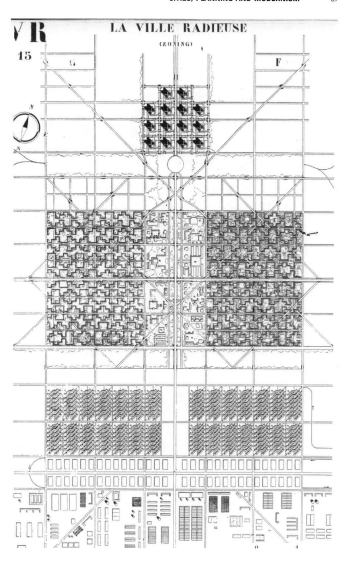

Le Corbusier's revolution in urban form was of an order perhaps unprecedented in urban history; perhaps since the invention of the street, and the emergence of the cities in the first place. Le Corbusier's new urban order made other modern visions look passé. Skyscrapers plugged into conventional street-grids; multi-lane traffic-ways with conventional building frontages; neighbourhood units embedded in the traditional urban fabric all came to look curiously anachronistic before their time.

Le Corbusier's theories effectively became the foundation for the dogma of the Modern Movement's Congres Internationaux d'Architecture Moderne (CIAM), embodied in the Charter of Athens. As Modernism moved from avant-garde movement to the mainstream, following the Second World War, CIAM planning principles could be regarded as forming the orthodoxy against which subsequent developments and alternatives may be compared and contrasted, which we can see both for the design of new cities, and the reconstruction of existing ones.

New cities and new towns

The full throttle of utopian Modernism was perhaps applied when it came to the creation of whole new settlements. Here city design was played out on a grand scale. The design for Brasilia – a new city that was to become home to millions of people – was based on a hand-drawn competition entry submitted at the last minute on 'five small pieces of paper', the winning entry chosen not for its functionality but its symbolism.[38] Under the spell of Modernist planning theorists, whole towns and cities were laid out according to the abstract ideas imagined by their creators. Never before had so much power for shaping the human habitat been invested in so few individuals.

More common than whole new cities were the postwar new towns – each with their new town centres, civic centres, residential areas, local centres, industrial estates, dual carriageways and roundabouts.

The new town of Cumbernauld, northeast of Glasgow, is a powerful example of an innovative, perhaps unprecedented urban form. The town has an almost organic looking arterial web of routes, with free-flowing grade-separated interchanges, and a system of pedestrian paths completely separate from the main roads (Figure 2.12a).

While the urban ordering was based on the familiar Radburn format of loop roads and cul-de-sacs, Cumbernauld was significant in moulding this order into a grand new form, an almost symmetrical town-scale composition, perhaps the ultimate expression of motor age planning. This could be interpreted as an exercise in city design optimised for motor travel, just as Soria y Mata's had been for trams – or Vitruvius' for the control of winds.[39]

Cumbernauld's town centre took the form of a single building complex, a megastructure sitting astride the central dual carriageway spine route. The combined effect of this and the Radburn layout was that people could walk to the town centre from any part of the town without having to cross a road, and once there, remain indoors (Figure 2.12 b).[40]

2.12 • Cumbernauld, Scotland: (a) Plan; (b) Town Centre in a building.

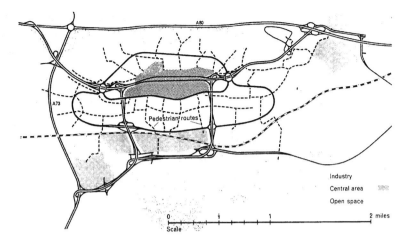

(a)

(b)

Those responsible for the design of Cumbernauld were conscious of the experimental nature: one designer declared that the New Towns should be considered as 'town-planning laboratories' – not just for new towns, indeed, but for restructuring *existing* cities.[41]

Reinventing existing cities

In his book *Rebuilding Cities*, Percy Johnson-Marshall presents a sketch of how an existing city could be replanned on Modernist lines (Figure 2.13). First, we see a generalised interpretation of an existing city (a), and secondly the city replanned (b). In effect, it is the recognition of the city as a single whole object, together with its sub-components – albeit at low resolution – that allows the whole to be reconstituted in a new form. The whole performs much as before – there is still a centre, suburbs and radial routes – but the individual constituent parts are *not* preserved. This diagram could be regarded as a graphic shorthand for Modernist city design, equivalent to that for Modernist urban ordering shown earlier in Figure 1.2.[42]

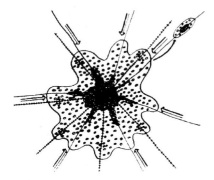

(a)

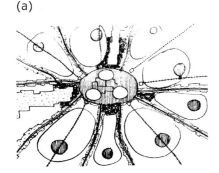

(b)

2.13 • The city reconstituted: simplistic conceptualisation (a) leading to simplistic design (b).

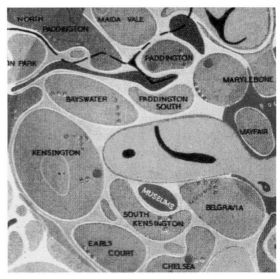

2.14 • The 'communities of London', interpreted in the Forshaw-Abercrombie plan of London, 1943.

This kind of reorganisation implied a *tabula rasa* approach: comprehensive clearance on the ground, followed by comprehensive reconstruction. This kind of approach was envisaged in an extreme form in the 'MARS plan' for London,[43] and in a more subtle form in the case of the Forshaw-Abercrombie plan of London (Figure 2.14).[44] In each case, the existing city form is interpreted in abstract terms of low-resolution sub-components, where those abstractions could be used as the units for onward design, with neighbourhood units being used as the modules of a new urban order.

Neither the MARS plan, nor widespread 'community restructuring' along the lines of the Forshaw-Abercrombie plan, were imposed on London. However, other cities were to take the plunge.

Glasgow provides a vivid illustration of how Modernism could seduce and grip an existing city. Plans for comprehensive redevelopment of the inner city were enacted, with the Modernist confidence that the new would be better than the old. An extensive motorway system was planned with multi-lane motorways penetrating the city centre. (By now, Hippodamus would be lost.) (Figure 2.15). The heart was ripped out of existing communities: Anderston Cross was demolished, replaced by the motorway spaghetti of the Kingston Bridge approaches, and the Anderston Cross Shopping Centre. The Townhead area was almost completely demolished. Dozens of streets were wiped from the map. This was *progress*.[45]

2.15 • Glasgow gets Modernism: the Townhead area, as envisaged in the *Highway Plan for Glasgow* (1965) – almost every building in the area was to be demolished and replaced.

On one level, the demolition of individual worn-out slum buildings could be seen as a necessary renewal – at the scale of architecture. But the justification for the demolition and reconstitution of whole areas such as Anderston and Townhead must be interpreted as a Modernistic act of *city planning*. More specifically, the rhetoric accompanying the roads programme – which went hand in glove with the comprehensive development – sounds like a justification for the creative destruction, in terms of Modernist *city design*:

> The very nature of this motorway will define the City into understandable units *each with its own identity* and from this it will be possible for the citizen to experience what the City means, how it functions and *what it symbolises*.[46] [emphases added]

So the demolition and erasure of Anderston and Townhead was partly done to help foster *identity*. And:

New housing, new services, new roads and new public transport are all needed to meet the changing needs of the city. If this change is to be both good in itself and to enhance what is to be retained, then everything must be *carefully planned* to form *a new and coherent whole*.[47] [emphases added]

Whereas the planning intention to provide new houses and improved roads was responding to genuine needs of the citizens of Glasgow, we need to be wary of additional planning intentions – for a 'new and coherent whole' – associated with the large-scale symbolism of city design, if these are to be used to justify carte blanche urban destruction.

Megastructures

Perhaps the creation of a whole new city in the form of a finite, whole, single building, designed and executed as a single architectural project, would represent the ultimate expression of 'new, coherent' city design.[48]

The 1960s bristled with images of futuristic cities, often featuring both monolithic megastructures and articulated urbanisms based on futuristic transport systems. Geoffrey Jellicoe's *Motopia* nearly encapsulates the concept of a 'utopia' for the motor age – a megastructural supergrid of housing blocks with free-flowing roads on the roofs. Elsewhere, the urban visions blended science fiction urbanism and space age technology. The Metabolists were inspired by organic interpretations of buildings and cities; Kisho Kurakawa's Helix City perhaps recalls the double helix of DNA. The Archigram group's Plug-In City and Walking Cities, with their novel forms, component parts and pseudo-organic extensibility, seemed to simultaneously fuse and challenge the concepts of the building and the city. These pushed out the frontiers of possible urbanism (Figure 2.16).[49]

Modernism in crisis

For all its successes in delivering modern homes and transport systems, the heady course of Modernist planning was not one of sustained progress. Things started going wrong on the ground. Some of the hastily created environments did not fit well with their surroundings, and failed to 'take'. Old areas half-demolished and never properly healed became blighted. New settlements suffered from a surfeit of 'sloap' (space left over after planning). 'New town blues' set in for some of their inhabitants, who found themselves isolated in bland 'prairie planning' or alienating tower block landscapes.[50]

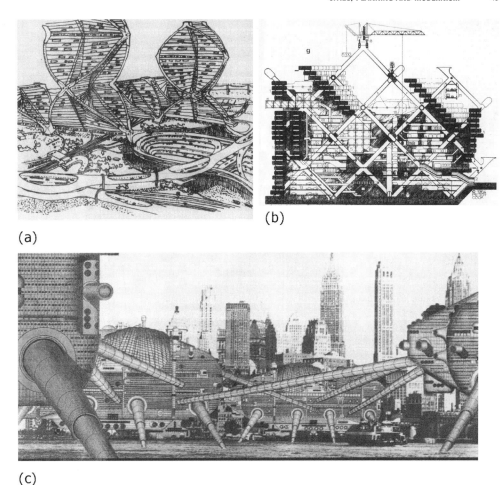

2.16 • Sixties' futurism – megastructural urbanism combining technology with organicity: (a) Kurakawa's Helix City; (b) Cook's Plug-in City; (c) Herron's Walking City – on a visit to New York.

In Glasgow, Anderston Cross shopping centre became a deserted concrete hulk; Cumbernauld town centre was voted one of Britain's worst buildings. If Cumbernauld could be considered a laboratory in town planning, the experience reminds us that we can learn from unsuccessful experiments: town planning students now visit the town as an example of what not to do.[51]

Housing estates once considered exemplary became the new urban problem, suffering from vandalism and premature dereliction. The brave new slab blocks that had replaced the bad old slums became slums themselves, and were demolished leaving communities to start all over again – within a

2.17 • Demolition of Hutchesontown 'E' blocks, Gorbals, Glasgow.

single generation (Figure 2.17). Comprehensive planning and Modernist architecture both became discredited. Bold but brutally built landscapes that pleased the professional elite but failed to deliver livable environments were no longer acceptable to the public. Charles Jencks proclaimed the demolition of the Pruitt-Igoe flats in St Louis on 15 July 1972 as the death of Modernist architecture.[52]

POST-MODERN URBANISM

The responses to the failures of Modernist planning were varied. For a start, there was a pragmatic response, a kind of instinctive recoil from the more destructive tendencies of Modernism: stop demolishing things, and start conserving them. This was as much thanks to people power as to planning theory.

Secondly, institutionally and professionally, planning changed: it became less 'physicalist' – less centred on the city plan as a blueprint, and less believing in physical solutions to society's needs.[53] Planning also became less top-down elitist and more concerned with citizens' needs (which were often to not have their homes demolished). Professionally, planning became not really about planning towns any more, but slipped into the more diffuse – or less physically specific – concept of 'spatial planning'; concerned with the allocation and organisation of goals, mediation of conflicting interests, closely tied to the fields of public administration and politics.[54] Planning often came to be seen as a mundane, regulatory and even negative enterprise – the profession that stopped you adding an extension to your house, or building a shed in your own garden. Rumours of the 'death' of town planning may be premature, but the idea of 'town planning' to mean actually planning towns, or creating planned towns, seems to be less prominent today than in the past.[55]

Thirdly, on the theoretical and academic fronts, there were a series of 'post-modern' assaults on Modernism and planning. These have ended up criticising town planning, 'physicalist' planning, 'Euclidean' planning, blueprint planning; and not only condemning Modernist town planning, but critiquing the whole Modernist project, questioning the value and validity of science, engineering, technology and even rationality.[56] Although some of these critiques score some useful points, many of the arguments end up creating more heat than light. They do not necessarily offer useful solutions to replace 'bad old Modernism'; in particular, they do not provide much that is constructive regarding the physical form and layout of the city that is the primary concern of this book. For all their faults, the old technocratic physicalist Euclidean rationalists at least got houses and roads built – things that the public seem to appreciate more tangibly than any number of 'critical postmodernist discourses'.[57]

Out of the debris of Modernism, however, new positive strands have gradually emerged, equated with new or reoriented planning intentions. These include the pursuit of environmentally friendly urbanism – or 'sustainable' settlements – with emphasis on walkable neighbourhoods and public transport, as well as 'eco-friendly' architecture and infrastructure.[58] Then there is 'neo-traditionalism', which aims to use the best from traditional urbanism – traditional architecture; and the traditional urban design format of streets and squares, which is directly counter to the Corbusian revolution (Figure 1.2).[59] The rise of urban design – promoting urban order at a level between the architectural and settlement planning scales – can also be seen as a response to the 'death of the street' and the 'lost space' of Modernism. Although in principle independent of style (at least in the architectural sense), urban design is typically concerned with relationships between buildings in a framework of streets and spaces and is hence traditional at least in the sense of a return to street-based urbanism. This morphs into what we might call design-led urbanism, of the sort championed by Richard Rogers.[60]

Finally, we have a distinctive new planning package that unites these various strands. More invasive of planning's traditional turf than urban design, and more dangerous to Modernism than a post-modernist discourse, is the latest movement to hit the scene: New Urbanism.

New Urbanism

Born in the USA, the 'New Urbanism' movement represents perhaps the most significant new school of thought in urban planning and design in decades. With its charter, annual congresses and peripatetic evangelism, the New Urbanists have grabbed the agenda, stirred up the urban debate, and forced those who believe otherwise to sharpen their arguments.

New Urbanism provides a combined package of neo-traditional architecture, urbanism and what might be termed neo-traditional transport provision (encouraging walking, cycling and public transport), combining attention to physical urban form with some aspects of 'town making', regional planning and sustainable development. It is consciously in opposition to Modernist planning, in particular to mono-use zoning and car-oriented sprawl (Figure 2.18).[61]

New Urbanism is significant on a number of fronts. First, it constitutes a clearly identifiable movement, with well-defined aims and methods, and principles set out in the Charter of the New Urbanism.[62] Secondly, New Urbanism transcends more than the narrow sectoral interests of any one built

(a)

(b)

(c)

2.18 • New Urbanist development: (a) Mixed-use development; (b) Formal modern; (c) Traditional residential.

environment profession; it embodies a comprehensive ideology which may be expressed through a variety of professional practices. Thirdly, it has a high profile in practice, academia and the media. Fourthly, New Urbanism has followers in many different countries, who apply, adapt and roll out their own versions of the movement's principles and practice, keeping in touch with but extending beyond the immediate ambit of the founding members of the movement. Finally, New Urbanism is not just a talking shop. New Urbanists are not just pontificating in print, but getting things built.[63]

In all these respects, New Urbanism has some resonance with the Modern movement (CIAM), and in a slightly different way, the original 'town planning' movement associated with the advocacy of the likes of Ebenezer Howard and Raymond Unwin. One does not need to agree with all the arguments or belong to any of these movements to appreciate their disarming positivity, passion and sense of purpose.[64]

New Urbanism is by no means the only approach to achieving sustainable settlements, street-based urban design, walkable neighbourhoods, or 'making towns', but in combining these contemporary approaches in a single recognisable package, it provides a convenient example to compare and contrast with Modernist city planning.

The neo-traditional counter-revolution

The clearest impact of post-modern or neo-traditional approach is seen in the case of urban ordering. This sees an almost complete reversal of the Corbusian urban ordering of the Modernist period, in the return to street-based urbanism. In terms of Figure 1.2 (page 3), the arrow goes back from 1 to 2. This is a reversal of sufficient scale that it could be called a counter-revolution.

It is clear that neo-traditionalist and neo-classical urban design effectively represent a return to the traditional order of grids of streets. In other words, this goes back to the pre-Modernist (pre-Corbusian) urban order. In this very obvious and well-understood way, then, contemporary planning and urbanism can be seen as a rejection of Corbusian Modernism and a return to pre-Corbusian urban order. Such a perspective – revolution plus counter-revolution and hence reinstatement of the older order – might see the Corbusian urban order in retrospect as a temporary aberration (even if we do keep segregated traffic ways for the busiest roads, separating pockets of more traditional urban fabric).

However, contemporary planning and urbanism is not a complete reversal of everything to do with Modernist urban planning. At the level of individual components – such as motor cars, motorways, interchanges, modern materials and building types, and so on – these are retained after all. And, perhaps significantly, we still keep aspects of Modernist city design.

Indeed, while the differences between contemporary urbanism and Modernist City Planning are well known – as are the aspired-to continuities between contemporary and traditional urbanism – the counter-revolution, such as it is, seems principally to do with urban ordering. On the city design, town design and neighbourhood design fronts, the Modernist project of city planning seems to be alive and well.[65]

Post-modernist city design

In an echo of Soria y Mata, a century on, Vincent Scully restates the role of architects as urban creators, in forming the city: 'It reclaims for architecture, and for architects, a whole realm of environmental shaping that has been usurped in recent generations.'[66]

While sometimes New Urbanism explicitly appreciates the piecemeal, evolutionary nature of urbanism, at other times elsewhere New Urbanism seems to be very much all about 'city design' or 'town design' – just like classic or Modernist town planning.[67]

For example, New Urbanism has embraced the idea of the whole settlement as the unit of design. New Urbanism recognises a hierarchy where neighbourhoods are designed as a whole, to fit into settlement as a whole, and where even the entire region should be 'designed'. The settlement, and the neighbourhood – the whole and sub-component – should each have a centre and an edge.[68]

Meanwhile, the more general contemporary quest for designing sustainable settlements also follows the Modernist tradition of city design. This includes, for example, the urban villages movement in the UK, which pursues the idea of settlements as bounded, self-contained entities.[69]

We can also see a resonance from Modernist city design in the redesign of existing settlements in the neo-traditional manner. For example, we can see the influence of the urge for 'reinvention' in the case of Gordon Cullen's proposals for Glasgow. At the urban design scale, the traditional townscape of streets and squares would be retained, unlike in the 1960s proposals. However, exactly like the 1960s proposals, Cullen was still aiming for a 'macro-scale' conceptualisation of a whole supported by parts. Cullen's proposals envisaged what has been described as a 'revolutionary yet sensitive restructuring of inner Glasgow with the object of giving the city a real centre'. This recalls uncannily the justification for the Inner Ring Road motorway, or the 'reconstitution' of the Johnson-Marshall diagrams (Figure 2.13).[70] Treating the inner city as a 'walled city', with abstract concepts such as 'axes', 'bastions' and 'gateways', was flying in the face of the real city: Glasgow was never a walled city; and as we have seen, it had an indefinitely extensible, Hippodamian-style grid. Yet the Cullen proposals choose to reinforce the barrier effect of the motorway. The 'gateways' over-emphasise boundaries and key monumental routes to the exclusion of general permeability on ordinary streets. Like any Modernist grand design, this is toying with form, at the urban scale (Figure 2.19), to the neglect of the existing intricate functional relationships at street level.

As with the commentary on the motorways and demolition of the 1970s, the intention here is not to criticise those specific proposals for Glasgow that ultimately helped contribute to the renaissance of the city centre. The point is to draw attention to the 'town planning ideas' that appear to be driving them, and the similarity between these and those of Modernism. Figure 2.19 (b) shows the abstraction and simplification, applied to the identifiable districts of Glasgow. The significance of these cases is not just about 'how a city is put together' in terms of component parts, but in the process by which they are put together, in a way that has distinct resonance with Modernism.

Neo-traditional déjà vu

If this all seems strangely familiar, it is because we have been here before. Both Jane Jacobs and Christopher Alexander are – rightly – hailed as pioneers of 'organic' approaches which have helped pave the way for neo-traditionalism, and New Urbanism. But, in significant ways, their lessons have not been learned. As noted in Chapter 1, Jacobs and Alexander were not simply criticising modern buildings or infrastructure, but the processes and perspectives of planning and city design.

Jacobs was dismissive of the 'pseudo-science of city planning and its

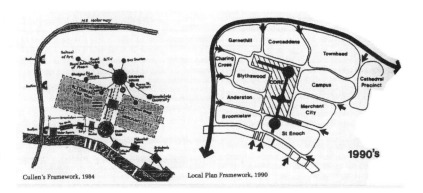

2.19 • Post-modern Glasgow: (a) Cullen's proposals; (b) Subsequent proposals. These look not so different from the Modernist interpretations of the city (Figures 2.13 and 2.14).

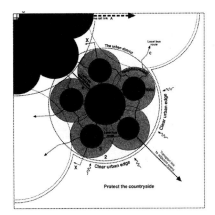

2.20 • The Urban Task Force plan. This looks like Modernist structuring: the city is still a 'tree'.

companion, the art of city design'. She was specifically dismissive of those urban professionals who 'like to think they deal in grand terms with the city as a whole, and that their value is great because they "grasp the whole picture" '. *They still do.*

Alexander warned that cities should not be imagined or designed as simplistic hierarchical systems, from the top down, with neighbourhoods neatly nested within towns. *They still are.*

All around, we see master plans with 'blob-like' neighbourhoods, sub-components of a grand design. We have already seen how Cullen's neo-traditional plans recall the Modernist reconstitution of the Johnson-Marshall plan (Figure 2.13) – or the Forshaw-Abercrombie plan (Figure 2.14). A similar effect is seen in Krier's Poundbury master plan. The Urban Task Force's 1999 report shows a city as a finite bounded area, constituted by clusters of component neighbourhoods, assembled in a hierarchy (Figure 2.20). This looks very much like the clusters of neighbourhoods of Reston new town, used to illustrate what not to do in Alexander's essay 'A City Is Not a Tree'.[71]

And so, while in principle neo-traditional urbanism intends to replicate the *forms* of traditional settlements, the *process* often appears more akin to the top-down master planning, town design and city design associated with the Modern movement that it is supposed to supplant. While in some cases neo-traditional urbanism may use design tools such as codes and context-sensitive design, in other cases neo-traditionalist master plans still bristle with abstract axes that owe more to the expression of abstract con-cepts and the geometric aesthetics of the drawing board than the existing site features. Neo-traditional urbanism appreciates and applauds sense of place and the organic growth of traditional towns, but its adherents still pro-pose master plans that have a resonance with their Modernist forebears. The operative Modernistic structure of city design seems to live on, albeit behind a neo-traditional façade.[72]

In short, cities are still, in a significant sense, being designed and churned out in the way that Jane Jacobs and Christopher Alexander argued they should not be, over forty years ago. This unfinished business represents a key challenge to be addressed in the following chapters.

CONCLUSIONS

This chapter has aimed to unpack the meaning of planning and Modernism, and to investigate manifestations of Modernist city planning and what came after it.

City planning can be interpreted as comprising four key elements: planning intention, city design, urban ordering and planning instruments.

Modernism has been equated with first, progress through rational action, second, the pursuit of contemporary methods, and third, the belief in improvement through modern rather than traditional solutions. Insofar as planning equates with the first of these kinds of Modernism, planning is intrinsically entwined with Modernism. In this sense, we can't discard Modernism, but keep city planning.

Having said that, the particular kind of Modernist planned environment – of concern in this and the opening chapter – is identifiable with Modernism in the third sense, in the pursuit of modern solutions at the expense of traditional formats. We can also note that the absence of a certain kind of city design or urban ordering need not mean a lack of planning intention – forward thinking for a better future. So we could yet keep some kind of proactive, rational planning, without implying this put the modern ahead of the traditional.

In the course of the last hundred years or so, we have seen the ascendancy of Modernist city planning, and its subsequent fall from grace, and fracturing into different alternatives: less 'physicalist' versions of planning, and post-modernism, and neo-traditionalism. These refute Modernist city planning – but only in part. Contemporary urbanism may offer the finest neo-traditional architecture, and the carefully crafted streets and piazzas – identifiable as a return to traditional urban ordering. But the process by which this urban fabric is generated perhaps has more in common with Modernism than with traditional urbanism. That is, while post-modernist and neo-traditional approaches have overturned Le Corbusier's revolution in *urban ordering* (Figure 1.2), it seems that they often pursue *city design* in a way similar to old Modernism (Figure 2.13).

City design is not, of itself, a problem. But Modernist city design could conceivably be a problem when cities get too large, when design for such a large whole is based on a limited number of objectives, and carried out by a very few remote from the needs of ordinary people. Or, when the design of a unified, coherent whole – or a certain kind of urban order – becomes the objective, an end rather than a means to an end. Or finally, the problem could be when objectives such as 'creating a coherent whole' – pursuit of city design – are put ahead of ensuring attractive functional urban order at street level. This implies that we need to be clear when and how to employ urban ordering and city design in the contemporary context.

We can do this by exploring in more detail what cities are made up of: what are their fundamental building-blocks, and their relationships, and their typical order. This is the subject of the next chapter.

Notes

1 The wording here is after Morris (1994: 43). See also Aristotle (1992: 133–134); Kostof (1991: 105).

2 Kriesis (1958: 48); Benevolo (1980: 107); Kostof (1991: 105); Morris (1994: 43,54). Hippodamus' system of division into public, private and sacred spaces is critiqued by Aristotle as a theoretical suggestion, not a description of an actual place (Aristotle, 1992: 133–134). Owens (1991: 6,149).

3 Hall (2002: 1–3); quotation is Hall (2002: 3).

4 Here the term city – in the context of this book – is primarily referring to the design and ordering of the physical city, and not (unless explicitly stated) the city as a community or political entity. Planning intentions and planning instruments are, of course, important to planning overall, but these are dealt with in general planning literature. The term 'city design' was used by Geddes ([1915] 1949: 138); Lynch (1990).

5 This echoes Daniel Dennett's placing of 'design' and 'order' lying midway up a 'cosmic pyramid', with God and Mind above, and Chaos and Nothing below (Dennett, 1996: 65).

6 On the social or political purpose of planning: Kostof (1992: 8); Fawcett (1944: 5,7).

7 A fourth kind of planning intention would be a case where one assumes that society will be better in some way, and where the planning is reliant on 'better' behaviour. In a 'utopian' society, where there is no crime, there would be no need for shops to have doors with locks, and no need for prisons or law courts. (However, normally the lack of such provision would be seen as a failure of planning.) Such Utopian cases are perhaps usually only found in fiction and satire, rather than in actual city planning. Thomas More's *Utopia* (2003, ed. Turner), a political satire, featured the fictitious city of Aircastle, planned by its founder, Utopos, complete with city walls, streets of terraced houses and gardens, designed for protection against the wind, and extramural suburbs (Manguel and Guadalupi, 1999; More, 2003: 53). Other Utopias: Berneri (1982).

8 On political purposes of planning, see, for example, Greed (2000), Thompson (2000), Tewdwr-Jones (2002).

9 What is a newly founded city, without the prior conception of a city as a whole entity? How can one have planned specialised subdivisions, without there being a 'whole' for these to add up to? Similarly, how can one have neighbourhood 'cells' unless these are part of a larger 'body' – otherwise, these would not be neighbourhoods, but a 'conurbation of villages'. The ability to optimise a town or city for a single variable implies it is for the good of the whole.

10 See, for example, Mumford (1938: 484); Gibberd (1967). On newly founded settlements: Benevolo (1980:220); Morris (1994: 119); 'New Jerusalems' (Hardy, 2006). The sub-units may sometimes be referred to as 'villages'; but 'villages' that are sub-units of the city designed as a whole are functionally no different from other sub-units such as neighbourhoods, industrial areas, and so on.

11 Vitruvius Pollio (1999); Holgate (1986: 157–158); Evers (2003: 6). Palmanova: Morris (1994: 172–173); Kostof (1991: 161). The principles of symmetry and

geometrical regularity were described as 'the new scientific school of thought' Benevolo (1980: 629, 639). For an in-depth treatment of ideal cities, see Eaton (2002).

12   Baines (1994: 118) describes Alexander Thomson's customary architectural elements as a 'kit of parts with the inherent capacity for multiple and incremental assembly in different combinations'.

13   And the grid itself can be further subdivided into different kinds, including orthogonal (non-rectangular), chequerboard (square), tartan grids, and so on. For a taxonomy of street patterns, see Marshall (2005).

14   While Mohenjo-Daro may represent one of the oldest cases of a planned city, it is likely that the planners of Mohenjo-Daro and other Harappan cities imported the idea from somewhere else, yet further back in time (Morris, 1994: 1). See also Morris (1994: 29) and Owens (1991: 51–53) regarding early gridiron planning. Hippodamus has sometimes been described as 'the father of town planning', but caution is required in interpreting what Hippodamus may himself have actually planned or built: Moholy-Nagy (1968); Morris (1994: 43); Owens (1991: 4, 51).

15   Glasgow: McKean (1996: 41), Walker (1996: 61); Thomson: Stamp and McKinstry (eds) (1994), Stamp (1999).

16   Reps (1965), Spreiregen (1968), Morris (1994: 344).

17   Hall (2002). See also Turner (1996) on plans and GIS. A plan depicts 'how things are organised' on a two-dimensional surface, even if – like a star map – the things depicted are not themselves 'organised on a two-dimensional surface'. A plan also depicts how urban things are 'organised on a two-dimensional surface' (Chapter 3), although – like a 3D model – it is not necessary to *be* a two-dimensional surface to do so.

18   Hill (1996:119). The *groma* passed to Greeks and Romans from the Egyptians (Kostof, 1991: 127). Kostof (1991) on Miletus. On ancient settlements laid out by marks on the ground, that is, without a 'plan-making' process (Turner, 1996); 'the ancients did not conceive their plans on drawing boards' (Sitte, 1945[1889]: 30).

19   Urban codes, and regulations for buildings and streets: Kostof (1992: 41; 200; 247, 217); Hakim (2001: 8); Kotkin (2005: 30); on Great Fire of London, Hebbert (1998a), Southworth and Ben-Joseph (2003), Ben-Joseph, (2005), Carmona *et al.* (2006), Carmona and Dann (2007).

20   This fits with Daniel Dennett's 'cosmic pyramid' in which historically design is seen as being 'above' order since it has a purpose: order is used to serve design (Dennett, 1996: 65).

21   LeGates and Stout (1998). From the ancient Greek perspective: Hall (1999: 26). Aristotle (1992: 422) refers to the 'modern or Hippodamean scheme of regularity'. Hippodamus could yet be the earliest person known to be considered *in his own day* as a modern city planner. Note: to be called modern contemporaneously would require the context of a society in which the idea of Modernity had meaning. Elsewhere, Aristotle (who must be comfortably situating himself in the modern world) refers perhaps disdainfully to 'scattered settlements, which were common in primitive times' (Aristotle, 1992: 58).

22 Bullock *et al.* (1988), Bloomsbury (1993, 1996), Abercrombie *et al.* (1994), Oxford University Press (1995); see also Turner (1996: 3), LeGates and Stout (1998), Allmendinger (2001: 12). In the context of modern art, Lavin (1993: 79) suggests 'The process of simplification and abstraction had been inherent in the Modernist enterprise'. Sorkin: 'Modernity invented nature and at the minute of its creation moved to civilize it' (2000: x).

23 In general, things *have* changed for the better, at least in the technical, functional sense that today's monsters, movies and missiles are functionally superior to yesterday's. That is, these modern products function better *in terms of what they are supposed to do*, even if we don't always like what they do.

24 The ancient Romans used mass concrete, such as in the Pantheon in Rome. The ancient Greeks had an early form of railway at Corinth.

25 'The modern movement in city planning and architecture rejected the traditional city as a foundation upon which to build and sought to replace it wholesale', Greenberg (2000: 173). See the various works of Le Corbusier, which collectively are like a rejection of the traditional city. The justification of using new site 'unencumbered by context' is given by Jellicoe (1961: 7–8).

26 Le Corbusier himself refers to the 'revolution in town-planning made possible by modern techniques' (1947a: 56). Higgott (2000: 153) refers to 'erasure and reinvention'.

27 Moreover, there are three specific and historical reasons that make the *Ciudad Lineal* a useful choice. First, Soria y Mata's vision was at least partly realised, in a linear suburb in Madrid: that is, this was not an unbuildable 'science fiction' city nor 'social science fiction' utopia, even if the most wildly imagined scale of potential extension remains unrealised. Secondly, there is an unbroken lineage of Modernist ideas from then till now. Thirdly, not only is the lineage there, but the ideas for transit-oriented linear cities are still extant; Soria y Mata (1892) *Ciudad Lineal* (Linear City). Appended to a small book entitled *Ferrocarril-Tranvia de Circunvalacion*, the *Linear City* was published in 1892, a rewriting of proposals made a decade earlier (Gonzalez, 1998: 2). Gold (1997: 14) remarks it is impossible to state the precise moment at which Modernism emerged. Shane (2005: 83) suggests the case for regarding Cerda as modern.

28 Soria y Mata (1892: 12).

29 Soria y Mata (1892: 24).

30 Garden Cities have had worldwide influence (Hall, 1988; Ward, 1998), and are still influential in debates across the world (Saiki, 2001). Howard's idea of the Garden City (Howard, 1904) was as much to do with rail freight and averting revolution as it was to do with gardens, and so for all the romantic associations of garden cities and suburbs, Howard's idea was radical and Modernist.

31 In the words of Michael Hebbert, 'the elements were familiar, the combination was unique'; Hebbert (1998b). The abstract nature of Howard's diagram is discussed by Steeley (1998).

32 Paul (2003: 680–682).

33   Perry: Hall (1988: 123); Radburn: Hall (1988: 127). Hall also points out precursors.

34   Le Corbusier ([1933] 1964: 39). Although known as an architect and planner, Le Corbusier's background was in the arts: he originally trained as an engraver and worked as a painter and lithographer (Johnson and Langmead, 1997); von Moos and Ruegg (2002).

35   Although interpreted here as a finite city design, alternatively the whole layout here could be seen as a module whose multiplication would create a conurbation-like linear city (extending from left to right) – a case where city design would support a larger-scale urban ordering (Korn, 1953: 86).

36   This Modernist landscape has been described as comprising buildings as stand-alone 'pavilions' (Martin *et al.*, 1972) or 'isolated monuments' (Oc and Tiesdell, 1997) forming 'still life' set-pieces (Southworth and Owens, 1993).

37   This has been described variously as a 'revolution' or 'cataclysm' – see for example Tripp ([1938] 1950, 1942), Colin Buchanan and Partners (1968), Llewelyn-Davies (1968). Discussed more fully in Marshall (2005). The Corbusian revolution is suggested as one specifically of urban ordering since the formats (1 and 2) shown in Figure 1.2 do not presuppose any ultimate urban unit such as city or town. Both forms might be extended indefinitely, without any overall settlement hierarchy to fit into. See also Panerai *et al.* (2004: 116). According to Panerai *et al.* (2004: 118) 'All relationships are inverted and contradicted'.

38   Deckker (2000). The master plan for Peterlee new town was based on an idea of abstract 'spatial vectors' (Allan, 2000).

39   Houghton-Evans (1978). Keeble describes Cumbernauld as being the first attempt 'to design a road system which would really work and to insist upon this as an essential and dominant consideration in the design of the town' (Keeble, 1969: 108). Note that the rationality traditionally associated with classical town planning never went away. Although the forms were not the same, in creating free-flowing motorways and 'organic' shaped superblocks, Modernist city planning was no less rational, but was simply adapting the rationality to deal with the logic of fast-moving streams of traffic, and buildings and blocks that need not interlock in a rectangular fashion on the ground plan.

40   Houghton-Evans (1975), Banham (1976), Houghton-Evans (1978). For recent discussion on the history of Cumbernauld, see Gold (2006).

41   Benevolo (1980: 940).

42   Johnson-Marshall (1966: 21)

43   The MARS (Modern Architecture Research Society) plan for London is perhaps a famous – or infamous – example of a 'plan' contemplating the replacement of almost all of an existing city with a new urban structure. Contemplating replace-ment of the existing urban fabric is not necessarily hubristic; it was perhaps quite reasonable in the wartime context in which it was conceived, with bombs falling around the team, and where the obliteration of the existing city was in full swing anyway (Gold, 2000).

44   Forshaw and Abercrombie (1943: 21–22, 28). The image has been described as being 'classic' (Gibberd, 1962: 30), 'famous' (Johnson-Marshall, 1966: 200;

Biddulph, 2000: 72), 'celebrated' (Hall, 1995: 230) and 'memorable' (Hebbert, 1998a); and indeed as 'the "egg-basket" diagram for which the plan is most famous' (Gold, 1997: 180). Although associated with Abercrombie, the image itself is attributed to Ling and others.

45 See, for example, Markus (1999).

46 Quoted from *Highway Plan for Glasgow* (Scott and Wilson, Kirkpatrick and Partners, 1965).

47 The Corporation of the City of Glasgow (1972: 4).

48 'The modern city, however, could be formed from much larger units, . . . each planned as a single architectural entity', Benevolo (1980: 881).

49 Walking City: Archigram <wwww.archigram.net>. Other futuristic schemes: see, for example, Richards (1969); Houghton-Evans (1975); Banham (1976); Barnett (1986). See also Nakamura (1989). For more recent discussion of Japanese megastructures and Metabolism, see also Shelton (1999: 166), Lin (2007).

50 Alex Marshall (2000) describes the effect for the city of Norfolk, Virginia. 'New town blues' – loneliness and isolation, especially for women as housewives (Clapson, 1998: 121); Wilson (1991: 101); Marshall (2006a); 'boring' modern landscapes (Parr, 1999).

51 Jordison and Kieran (2003). Cumbernauld town centre described as 'horrible' in Pearson (2006).

52 Coleman (1985). Demolitions: for example, Hutchesonstown, Glasgow; Hulme, Manchester. Jencks (1981). On problems with Modernism, see also, for example, Panerai *et al.* (2004: 116, 118, 156).

53 Taylor (1998); Hall (2002: 211–212). Hardy (1991: 311–312).

54 Tewdwr-Jones (2002: 7, 9).

55 Sorkin (2000) alludes in passing to the 'death of planning'. Turner (1996) refers to the 'death' of a particular kind of town planning. According to Allmendinger, 'While there was no death of planning *per se*, a strategic overview of planning did die' (2001: 116). The Royal Town Planning Institute's (RTPI) mission statement refers not to planning towns but to 'the mediation of space and making of place' <www.RTPI.org.uk>. Planning courses and planning textbooks have been known to drop the word 'town' from their titles (see, for example, Greed, 1993 and 2000).

56 See, for example, Campbell and Marshall (2002: 22); Friedmann (2003); Sandercock (1998, 2003), and commentaries by Taylor (1998); Allmendinger (2001).

57 Here, we are indebted to Philip Allmendinger for his comprehensive analysis and interpretation of post-modernism with respect to planning, in his book *Planning in Postmodern Times*: 'One looks in vain for a "postmodern planning" after wading through countless critiques that purport to reflect upon the postmodern (as new times and social theory) and planning'; 'I would contend that planning theorists have also been reticent in transforming ideas into practice because practice exposes the redundancy and impractical nature of their thinking', Allmendinger (2001: 155). Of Lyotard: 'His lack of engagement with detail in his analysis of science mean that it is difficult to tie down exactly what he is basing his

arguments on' (ibid., 33). 'Attempting to capture the essence of Foucault is a slippery and difficult business, not least because he deliberately attempted to evade capture' (ibid., 34). Of Baudrillard: 'It is difficult if not impossible to grasp anything concrete in his work' (ibid., 45). '[T]he problem with the analyses of Habermas and Harvey is that they are prisoners of their own position' (ibid., 78). Finally: 'Talk of whether the signifier produces the signified or vice versa, valuable though it doubtless is, is not quite what stormed the Winter Palace or brought down the Heath government' (Eagleton, 1996: 13, cited in Allmendinger, 2001: 87).

58   Sustainable settlements: see, for example, Barton *et al.* (1995); Williams *et al.* (2000); Barton *et al.* (2003); sustainable cities (Houghton and Hunter, 1994; Newman and Kenworthy, 1999); sustainable new towns (Battle and McCarthy, 1994); transit villages (Bernick and Cervero, 1997); restructuring the city for sustainability (Frey, 1999).

59   Collage city (Rowe and Koetter, 1978); post-modern architecture (Jencks, 1981, 1987); urban villages (Aldous, 1992; Neal, 2003); traditional urbanism (Hanson and Younés, 2001); neo-traditional settlements (Banai, 1996); post-modern urbanism (Ellin, 1996); 'Re-urbanism' (Campbell and Cowan, 2002). Some of this has a resonance with earlier approaches such as Cullen's *Townscape* (1961).

60   The emergence and establishment of urban design: Barnett (1982); Gosling and Maitland (1984); Bentley *et al.* (1985); Jacobs and Appleyard (1987); Moughtin (1992); Hayward and McGlynn (eds) (1993); Lang (1994); Parfect and Power (1997); Cowan (1997, 2002); Lloyd-Jones (1998); Schurch (1999); Llewelyn-Davies (2000); Urban Design Associates (2003); Madanipour (2006). Street-oriented urban design: Hebbert (2005a), Marshall (2005). The growth of the Urban Design Group (in the UK); new journals *Journal of Urban Design* and *Urban Design International* in the 1990s, and *The Journal of Urbanism* and *Urban Design and Planning* launching in 2008. Design-led urbanism and 'urban renaissance': Urban Task Force (1999); the design dimension of planning: Punter and Carmona (1997).

61   The terms neo-traditional urbanism and New Urbanism are often associated. The distinction or lack of distinction in a way mirrors the use of the terms 'modern architecture' and 'Modern Architecture'. In principle, 'modern architecture' could include anything contemporary, while 'Modern Architecture' might strictly be reserved for that associated with CIAM (Congres Internationaux d'Architecture Moderne) or the principles of the Charter of Athens (Le Corbusier, [1943] 1973). In practice, the terms are often used interchangeably. Key New Urbanist books include: Kreiger and Lennertz (1991); Calthorpe (1993); Katz (1994); Leccese and McCormick (2000); also see Duany and Talen on 'transect planning' (2002). For commentaries see Marshall (ed.) (2003), Garde (2006), Grant (2006).

62   Leccese and McCormick (2000); for discussion, see Hebbert (2003).

63   For details of New Urbanism and New Urbanist projects, see <www.cnu.org>. For commentaries and critiques of New Urbanism, see, for example, Robbins (2000), Marshall (2000), Hebbert (2003), Southworth (2003); Panerai *et al.* (2004: 179) on New Urbanism as part of the Modernist project.

64 This point is, however, perhaps hidden in a couple of the above points, to the extent that the town planning movement so successfully established town planning as a separate profession that its interdisciplinary roots are somewhat overlooked, and its establishment as a profession meant that its existence and practice outgrew association with any particular institution or set of aims. On resonance with Modernism: it remains to be seen if the New Urbanists' influence will be as deep-rooted, long-lasting and internationally broad as CIAM. That said, it must be remembered that CIAM took some time – a couple of decades at least – before it went from being avant garde to mainstream. On resonance with town planning: in the UK, the Town and Country Planning Association continues to operate its own agenda, separately from government or the town planning professional body RTPI.

65 Contemporary planning and urbanism share, with Modernist city planning, aspirations to creating a desired future state, and is as susceptible to praise or criticism for being utopian. It is therefore in this sense a continuation of the Modernist project (Panerai *et al.*, 2004: 179).

66 Scully (1994: 225).

67 'Cities are perpetually unfinished serial creations . . . The form of the city develops through a continuous reworking over the traces of what came before. This non-stop evolution of use and form is both inevitable and desirable'; 'This Charter principle affirms New Urbanism's respect for continuity and evolution in the built environment and in landscapes', Leccese and McCormick (2000: 173).

68 Kreiger and Lennertz (1991); Calthorpe (1994: xi); Duany and Plater-Zyberk (1994: xvii).

69 The urban villages movement in the UK has also come under criticism, not so much for the neo-traditional urban ordering, but for what in effect amounts to its city design. This city design aspect may be equated with what Mike Biddulph refers to as a 'macro-concept' (Biddulph, 2000). 'For planning and design professionals it seems that the search for a macro-concept can suggest an added level of legitimacy for their design' (Biddulph, 2000: 78). While Biddulph welcomes the commitment to good urban design (which would amount to good urban ordering, or good design at the scale of squares and blocks), he warns that 'the macro-concept must be more rigorously questioned', Biddulph (2000: 80).

70 Gosling (1996); Carmona (1998); Reed (1999d).

71 Alexander (1966); Krier (1993a, 1993b); Hardy (2006). Urban Task Force (1999: 52).

72 Katz (1994:19); Dutton (2000). For example, the arc of Calthorpe's Laguna West (Calthorpe, 1993) recalls the arc of Gibberd's Harlow (Gibberd, 1967) – looking at the master plan for Laguna West, it looks just as if a planner-God has 'struck an arc' from a central node, just like Harlow.

3 ARTICULATING URBAN ORDER

The metamorphosis of Glasgow into <u>the</u> tenement city proceeded by aggregation: of flat stacked vertically on flat around a close; of tenement added to tenement to line a street; of street intersecting with street to form a block; of block added to block to make a district.
Peter Reed, *Glasgow. The Forming of a City*[1]

Urban order is, on the face of it, in the eye of the beholder. In his book *Glasgow: The Forming of the City*, Peter Reed draws attention to two quite contrasting views of the order – or otherwise – of the city of Glasgow. On the one hand, George Blake looked at Glasgow and saw a 'sprawling' and 'chaotic' city, 'without plan and without regard for tradition'. On the other hand, Ian Nairn found 'probably the most dignified and *coherent*' of Britain's bigger cities.[2] As Reed points out, Glasgow's quality lay in the part rather than the whole: while the overall form of Glasgow may have appeared disorderly, the city had a coherence in the way its streets and blocks of tenements – of red or yellow sandstone of mostly three or four storeys – fitted together, in a way that 'gave to the piecemeal, fragmented development of the city a signal consistency and connectedess'. Glasgow, in other words, already had an urban order and coherence that was to be so grievously injured by the intervention of Modernist planning in search of a 'new coherent whole' (Chapter 2). If a city can be at once chaotic and coherent, ordered and disordered, how can we make sense of how to plan or design one?

If we wish to plan a city – or in the terms of Chapter 2, if we wish to undertake city design or urban ordering – then it will pay us to be able to understand the nature of this urban object, its component parts, and potential building-blocks, and the way the different parts relate to each other and to the whole.[3]

3.0 • Glasgow's tenemental urban order.

In other disciplines, the elemental units we work with are reasonably clear. Engineers' elemental units are things like beams and columns, and architects' elemental units include those solid, physical components plus enclosed volumes such as rooms and corridors. But what about planners? The task here is to identify the elemental units of settlements used by planners – the building-blocks and sub-components – and how these are put together, to constitute urban order.

This chapter, then, aims to articulate and hence help understand the urban order, and identify the elemental parts that may subsequently be used in urban ordering and city design. The focus here is on the physical structure, leaving aside the formation, function, intention and intervention for later chapters.

Let us first identify fundamental Urban Units (sub-components or building-blocks), interpreted in three dimensions. Secondly, we shall scrutinise the relationships between these elements, to understand the systematic order – or Urban Syntax – that may be recognised as the 'signature' order of cities. Finally, we shall reflect on The Nature of Urban Order, and how it has been applied in city planning.

This chapter is a little abstract in places, but never far from the simple urban things we encounter every day: rooms, buildings and streets.

URBAN UNITS

The universe is made up of many diverse constituent units, and we can recognise sub-units and, if we like, super-units, operating at many scales from the subatomic to the supergalactic. But this is not just a simple transition of scale, in terms of, for example, metric size measured in millimetres, metres and kilometres, nor temporal intervals, like quavers, semi-quavers, demi-semi-quavers, and hemi-demi-semi-quavers. While a spectrum of scale is identifiable, the relationships between units and sub-units *may* be the same at different scales, or they may be different. It is the difference in phenomena at different scales, after all, that makes chemistry different from complex physics, or biology different from complex chemistry. Our task here is to find out what the similarities and differences are at different scales, with respect to the *urban* context.

Our first task is to work out what fundamental urban units might be. What do we mean by an urban unit? It means something we can break down (decompose) larger things into, but does not necessarily mean the smallest possible constituent element. A unit implies something atomistic; that is not divisible: where, for example, cutting in half would destroy its integrity and

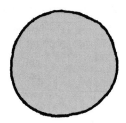

(a)

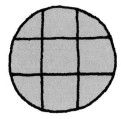

(b)

(c)

3.1 • Units, sub-units and super-units: (a) Unit; (b) Unit subdivided into nine sub-units; (c) Super-unit comprising nine units. Note that the unit is present in each case.

functionality. A unit is something that can stand alone, or could be combined into larger assemblies – like atoms forming molecules.

We can in principle recognise *units*, that are divided into *sub-units*, or aggregated into larger assemblies that might be identified as *super-units*.[4]

We can use an abstract graphic shorthand to illustrate this as follows. A unit is represented as a circle – a finite whole, where nothing can be added or taken away without disturbing its integrity (Figure 3.1a). A unit can of course be subdivided; and a partitioned circle represents a unit divided into sub-units. Here, the sub-units are segments that do not stand alone, but (like pizza slices) make most sense as complementary parts of a larger circular whole (Figure 3.1b). An array, assembly or aggregation of units – which could be identified as a super-unit – is represented by an array of circles (Figure 3.1c).

The term *sub-component* implies sub-unit. On the other hand, a *building-block* could best be regarded as a unit, perhaps especially a unit that forms part of a super-unit (the circles in Figure 3.1c), but that could also stand alone. The term *component* could be used generally to mean a part of something, whether a sub-unit, or a unit that is part of a super-unit.

What we take from the images in Figure 3.1 – which would not be discernible had these been drawn as squares – is that the relationship between unit and sub-unit (a:b) is different from that between super-unit and unit (c:a). Though very simple and abstract, this demonstration goes to the heart of the difference between buildings and cities, architecture and planning, people and society, city design and urban order – and hence is of significance to this book.

Let us scrutinise what are the fundamental units of cities, first in terms of three-dimensional forms, then two-dimensional patterns and finally linear structures.

Three-dimensional units

The urban world is not just three-dimensional in the abstract sense of Cartesian space, but is a world of reassuringly tangible objects such as cities, buildings, post-boxes, trees, dogs, and so on (Figure 3.2). Yet this three-dimensional world is not a three dimensional solid: in order to function, cities tend to be hollow, that is riddled with spaces, forming an interlocking solid and void. (The same may be said of dogs and postboxes.)[5]

Although the city forms in figure 3.2 are all three-dimensional, we can note that these tend not to be monolithic solid objects, but articulated into parts. Cities are made up of many individual buildings: this contributes to the sense of 'city-shapedness' that unites all sorts of actual cities, and even

3.2 • Three-dimensional forms recognisable as urban forms. However diverse, these are articulated into discrete buildings and voids. (a) Los Angeles; (b) Flying saucer city; (c) Registan, Samarkand; (d) Chongqing; (e) Singapore; (f) Viaduc-du-lac, St Quentin-en-Yvelines, France; (g) Bruges; (h) Hong Kong; (i) Terrace, London; (j) Chalets, Switzerland; (k) Taxco, Mexico; (l) El Fouar, Tunisia.

science fiction 'cities' that look distinctively like cities rather than science fiction 'something-elses' (Figure 3.2b).

The buildings themselves tend to be arranged in sub-units such as rooms. How do these building-blocks stack up? Let us consider different ways in which we can see a transition in scale from small to large, with reference to abstract three-dimensional units in Figure 3.3:

(a–b)   First an object may simply be scaled up – in other words, its dimensions are multiplied up.

(a–c)   Secondly, we may get something large from something small by repeating or multiplying an object many times. Here, there is no change in the 'design' of the object; simply, there are more objects.

(a–d)   Thirdly, the object may increase in complexity, by internal subdivision and differentiation, and multiplying itself in such a way that it gains a more complex structure as well as a greater scale or overall size. In this third case, the number of overall 'wholes' stays the same, but the number of cellular components increases; the size of the overall object increases but the size of the individual cells stays the same.[6]

Let us now interpret Figure 3.3 first in terms of units being rooms, then units as buildings.

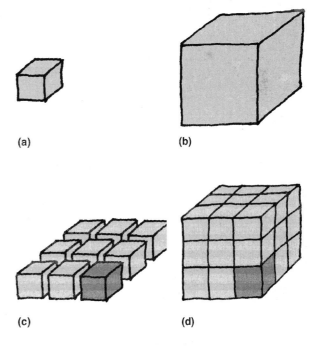

(a)   **(b)**

(c)   **(d)**

3.3 • Three-dimensional units: (a) Unit; (b) Large unit; (c) Array of units – possibly interpreted as a super-unit; (d) Large unit composed of sub-units.

When we interpret each unit as a room, then (a) is a single room or single-room building; (b) is a building comprising one very big room, like a hall or auditorium; (c) is like an array of single-room huts; and (d) is like a typical building comprising several normal-sized rooms.

When we interpret each unit as a building, then (a) is a single standard-sized building; (b) would represent a giant building; (c) would represent an array of buildings – a settlement, in effect; (d) does not really look like any normal urban configuration, unless some kind of strange megastructural complex, with buildings stacked on top of each other, packed closely together in a single mass.

Figure 3.3 graphically points out a basic distinction between a city and a building. The difference between a small building and a large building is normally that of complexity, represented by the difference between (a) and (d). The change from small city and a large city can be interpreted as one of multiplication of buildings, represented by the difference between (a) and (c), extrapolated upwards. This means that urban growth doesn't lead to a single 'megabuilding' that could house a 'giant' (b); nor a 'hive-like' megabuilding (b) that could house a city of hundreds of thousands of people.[7] Rather, we get a multiplication of individual buildings.

So, insofar as a city is an aggregation of buildings, the normal form of cities is like (c), not (d). (Or, like Figure 3.1c, not Figure 3.1b.) A settlement, in other words, is not a big building. Adding buildings multiplies floorspace, but the distinction between a building and a settlement is not primarily one of scale, size or floorspace. After all, a large building may contain more people and more floorspace than a small village. Rather, it is suggested that the primary – or most useful – distinction is based on structure.[8]

This structural difference is reflected in the normal tendency to say that a building is subdivided into rooms (Figure 3.1b); and a city an aggregation of buildings (Figure 3.1c); we tend not to say that a city is divided into buildings, nor that a building is an aggregation of rooms. So, a room is a sub-component of a building – it in a sense only exists in the context of being part of a building. In contrast, a building can stand alone, whether it forms part of a block, district or city. For example, the urban sub-unit 'hotel room' makes sense in only the context of a hotel, whereas a hotel is a unit that need not be part of a hotel district (or 'resort city') but could stand alone, in the 'middle of nowhere'. Hence we can say that a building is a unit or 'building-block' that may be aggregated to form those larger units, but need not do.

In sum, we can regard the building as the basic three-dimensional urban unit or building-block, in the sense that there are no particular three-dimensional units larger than the building that serve this purpose, while,

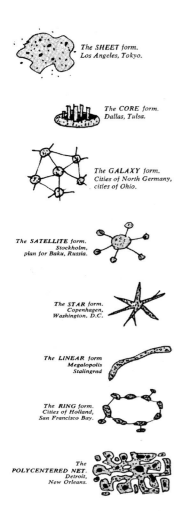

The SHEET form.
Los Angeles, Tokyo.

The CORE form.
Dallas, Tulsa.

The GALAXY form.
Cities of North Germany,
cities of Ohio.

The SATELLITE form.
Stockholm,
plan for Baku, Russia.

The STAR form.
Copenhagen,
Washington, D.C.

The LINEAR form
Megalopolis
Stalingrad

The RING form.
Cities of Holland,
San Francisco Bay.

The
POLYCENTERED NET.
Detroit,
New Orleans.

3.4 • Two-dimensional urban forms – Spreiregen's types.

smaller than the building, we don't have building-blocks so much as sub-components.

Two-dimensional units

Let us now contemplate various ways in which a two-dimensional structure may be organised. Figure 3.4 shows an example of a typology that has been used to characterise city form, in a more or less two-dimensional format. Here, we are not so concerned with either the overall geometry of the forms (linear or radial, for example), or the utility as a set of types – both issues dealt with elsewhere.[9] Rather, we are concerned with their topology: their internal structure. When trying to describe the structure of a city: is it possible to identify definite physical sub-components?

First let us look at the simplest most basic structural differentiation of parts of a city – what the first order of sub-components might be: basically, the kinds of thing that almost any city could be said to have.[10]

At a most basic level, we can recognise the presence of centres, and hence suburbs, and possibly suburban centres (or sub-centres). The eight types in Paul Spreiregen's typology could be reduced to six basic topologies (Figure 3.5).[11]

Incidentally, we can also recognise typical standard form-types – linear, radial or star, and 'beads-on-a-string' – as variants of the basic topologies (Figure 3.6). That is, although they are different shapes from their equivalents in Figure 3.5, they have the same topology in terms of units, sub-units and their relationships. At the same time, the basic six-type typology of Figure 3.5 could be extended and elaborated to as many new, different shapes or forms as desired (Figure 3.7).[12]

In effect, the point here is that if a settlement is regarded as a unit, then we could identify centres and sub-centres as sub-units. However, it looks rather too low-resolution to be considered an accurate picture of units. Not least, there is the undifferentiated mass of suburbia. We are tempted to probe further to see if we can't find smaller units or building-blocks.

At first sight, land use zones or neighbourhoods might make promising candidates for urban units. However, we do not tend to see a clear separation of functions into internally homogeneous zones at the city scale. We see it perhaps only in idealised city plans, like *La Ville Radieuse* (Figure 2.11), that significantly, do not look like real cities and were never built. Rather, we tend to find some mixing of land uses, so there are some shops within residential areas, and residences within commercial areas. But even if we allow that identifiable zones may contain a degree of heterogeneity, then what would we find?

3.5 • Six basic types: (a) Monolithic; (b) Core city with satellites; (c) Constellation; (d) Monocentric; (e) 'Hub and sub' – monocentric with sub-centres; (f) Polycentric (no single dominant centre).

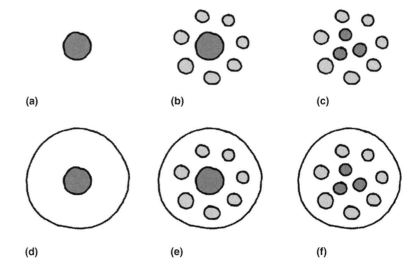

(a)   (b)   (c)

(d)   (e)   (f)

(a)

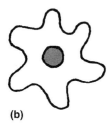

(b)

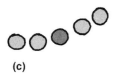

(c)

3.6 • Variations on the topologies of Figure 3.5: (a) Monolithic-linear; (b) Monocentric-radial; (c) Constellation-linear ('beads on a string').

For a start, the difference between one neighbourhood and another – unlike centres and sub-centres – is typically not so clearly differentiable. An observer from space might be able to distinguish a city's central business district from its suburbs, as a real, empirically measurable physical differentiation.[13] However, an observer looking down on London would not see something like the 'ravishing cellular vision' of a microscope slide (Figure 2.14). The neighbourhoods have no distinct, observable physical presence on the ground.[14] This is not to say that neighbourhoods or districts should be written off as figments of the imagination – after all, London's West End is a recognisable place, even if we cannot put our finger on a physical boundary. But the point is that at the neighbourhood level we find more of a continuum. If there are indeed identifiable districts, zones or neighbourhoods, these must be diffuse, fuzzy-edged and overlapping affairs. Indeed, the Forshaw-Abercrombie diagram is at its most convincing in the central area, where the ovoids are allowed to overlap.

In effect, the problem of trying to identify zones as urban building-blocks is that these are still too crude, low-resolution caricatures. While this might also be held against the simplest case of centres and sub-centres (Figure 3.5), these are sufficiently low-resolution to act as 'lowest common denominators' present in almost any city – in the same configuration. But for land use zones or neighbourhoods, these seem not general enough as consistent entities, in any consistent order, to be useful as fundamental units.

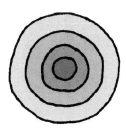

(a)

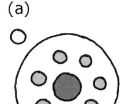

(b)

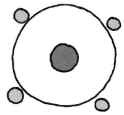

(c)

3.7 • Further elaborations: (a) Concentric; (b) Satellite; (c) External 'centres'.

(They are perhaps best seen as either sub-units of larger units, or aggregations of smaller units.)

This suggests that we need to look at urban features at a still higher resolution, at yet smaller component parts. But the more we try to disaggregate overlapping zones, it seems, the smaller units we find (Figure 3.8). This leads us, finally, to the level of individual plots and land parcels. These have clear boundaries – some with legal force – and a certain kind of homogeneity, such as being a distinct land use, or having a distinct physical character. And almost any settlement (surely, any city) will have distinct bounded plots or parcels of land – that can act as fundamental two-dimensional units.

Linear units

Finally, we can recognise linear units in the case of the components of transport networks. The units in linear structures such as transport networks are conventionally interpreted as links and nodes (where each link connects to a node at either end). Alternatively, the units could be interpreted as routes and joints, where a given route may be continuous through several joints. These routes may be added to the network like skeletal members added to an engineering structure.[15]

The distinction between links and routes is to some extent rather abstract, but on the other hand is effectively to do with breaking down larger things into smaller things, and in this sense is no more or less important than whether we aggregate or break down two-dimensional areas into zones or land parcels.

Conclusions on fundamental units: buildings, plots and routes

However diverse the city forms we see, they tend to have the same basic units in common. In effect, we can usefully divide up the urban fabric into basic units – associated with one, two and three dimensions – namely, routes, plots and buildings.[16]

Routes, plots and buildings form useful elements, for a number of inter-linked reasons. First, the elements are rather distinct entities, with their own distinctive geometric character. Secondly, they tend to be more clear-cut (than districts, neighbourhoods, and so on). Something is usually clearly either a route *or* a plot *or* a building. Thirdly, this is partly because they are made of different kinds of sub-component. Whereas different kinds of district – whether residential, university campus, or business park – are made up of the *same* mix of constituent elements (buildings *and* plots *and* routes), buildings, plots and roads are generally though not exclusively made up of *different* stuff (tarmac *or* landscaping *or* bricks and mortar).

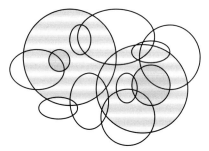

3.8 • Overlapping zones. There always seems to be a smaller unit of area that can be discerned.

This is why these are good *units*. Now, why are these good specifically as building-blocks? First, these are typically what we actually build, or actually use to build with. In contrast, a district – even a settlement – is not a necessary (definite, conscious) building-block for urban ordering, whereas, roads, plots and buildings are. A second reason why routes, plots and buildings may be usefully thought of as urban building-blocks is that they relate to each other in a systematic ordered manner, as we shall now see.

URBAN SYNTAX

We have seen how cities, however different-looking, have in common that they may be broken down into individual buildings, plots of land, and routes. This allows us to recognise objects that are 'city-shaped' when we see them. However, the commonality and recognisable order is not just due to their possessing similar constituent elements. It is also the way that these parts relate to each other in consistent ways.

This is a bit like the way that a piece of prose text has a recognisable order to it. This is not merely because of the use of words, but the way the words fit together to make larger units, such as sentences. In effect, a piece of prose is recognisable as being ordered because it obeys certain rules of *syntax*. It is not just a jumble of nouns, verbs and other parts of speech dumped together in an arbitrary pile; but there are rules that normally apply, that guide how nouns, verbs, adjectives and so on, should fit together. So, no matter how much a text may have a mix of long and short sentences of different styles, there is a basic consistency by which one type of word follows another.

Can we find a similar consistency – or syntax – in the urban case? We have the urban units; now, how do these fit together? How do three-dimensional building blocks, two-dimensional building-blocks and linear building-blocks fit together with each other, to create recognisable urban order?

3D enclosure

We have seen many three-dimensional forms – buildings separate or joined together in various ways to form terraces and building complexes. Generally speaking, buildings are not enclosed by other buildings. This means that a building is typically not 'boxed in' by having buildings tightly packed around it, nor enclosed by a whole other building – as might be the case if Figure 3.3 (d) were interpreted as a packing of buildings. This means that a building always has at least part of it facing the outside.

This spatial effect of three-dimensional enclosure goes to the scale of whole cities. We do not (yet) tend to find whole cities enclosed in an outer envelope or 'bubble', or cities with their districts and wards nested three-dimensionally inside like Russian dolls – although these can, of course, be imagined.[17]

This point is in one sense a rather obvious one; however, it is logically necessary to be able to account for the ways in which cities are structured, and has a resonance with other topological relationships, as we shall see.[18]

The order of the ground plan

Cities tend to be built on the ground surface of the Earth. This order is a simple response to the law of gravity, which tends to fix everything – buildings, streets, street furniture, dogs, fallen leaves, and so on – to the ground surface of the planet.[19]

While both cities and buildings may be regarded in common-sense terms as three-dimensional objects, cities may often be approximated to two-dimensional entities. This is, first and perhaps most obviously, because they tend to be 'flattish' – built out the way (laterally) rather than up the way; being much more spread out than they are tall (Figure 3.9).

But, secondly, cities are roughly two-dimensional because they tend to be *organised in two dimensions*. This is because of the way that everything plugs into the ground surface. A city is in some ways organised like an electronic circuit board, in the sense that while it is undeniably a three-dimensional object, the components are arranged on the two-dimensional plane of the motherboard (Figure 3.10).

So, rather than a city being simply a series of three-dimensional objects floating in space, or stuck together in some arbitrary way, a city tends to have a single significant surface – the ground surface – that all other components plug into (Figure 3.11). This situation is quite different from other kinds of organisational structure, such as the structure of the internet, for example, that has no such common datum or unifying surface – it simply straggles in all directions.

3.9 • Edinburgh skyline. Even a hilly city is much more extensive in its horizontal dimensions than in its vertical dimension.

3.10 • Circuit-board: a three-dimensional object, but one that is significantly organised on the two-dimensional motherboard.

The set of 'footprints' given by the buildings articulates what we recognise as the ground plan – a two-dimensional world. In Edwin Abbott's classic book *Flatland*, the narrator A. Square describes a two-dimensional world inhabited by flat shapes.[20] The Flatlanders would be quite at home in the world of city plans.

The point here is that although cities are three-dimensional objects – made from three-dimensional bricks and so on – their *organisation* is largely two-dimensional.[21] It is because of this that one could select a chunk of Chicago whose greatest dimension was in the vertical direction (Figure 3.12), but that urban chunk would still be more significantly represented as a two-dimensional organisation. It is for this reason that A. Square (the narrator of *Flatland*) could make sense of the geography and general layout of Chicago, even if he was spooked by the notion of soaring architecture, or got confused when getting out of the lift. This gives the city its signature three-dimensional form, as distinct from other possible three-dimensional forms. It is why the flying saucer city, however outlandish, still significantly looks like a city (Figure 3.2b).

This makes the ground plane the single most critical slice through the three-dimensional city. This gives the city plan its organisational potency, which explains the conventional degree of attention given by urban planning to the 'first two' dimensions of the ground, relative to the 'third', vertical dimension (even if architects and urban designers periodically implore planners to think in three dimensions).

The city plan dissected

Although famously three-dimensional, the Earth, for many practical purposes, may as well be flat. The Earth's surface can be divided successively into landmasses, nations, regions, city authority areas, districts, wards, blocks, individual plots of land, buildings and rooms. At first sight this seems a simple nesting of scale. But, things are more subtle than this. Figure 3.13 shows, in addition to a spectrum of scale, a distinction between two kinds of topological pattern, referred to here as 'archipelagos' and 'jigsaws'.

On the left-hand side of Figure 3.13 we see patterns described as 'archipelagos', where a series of areas of similar kind are all surrounded by – set within – another area of a different kind. At the Earth's surface, every landmass is surrounded by the all-encircling sea. At the urban level, plots form 'islands' which are ultimately surrounded by the street (public space) system. With an archipelago structure, the 'islands' (although similar in basic kind) may be quite different in detail – different in shape, size and character – and may be independent of the existence of one another.[22]

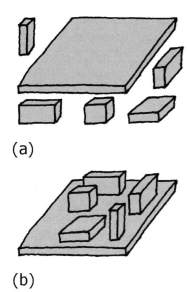

(a)

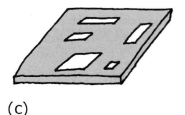

(b)

(c)

3.11 • Three-dimensional objects organised in two dimensions: (a) six cuboids in space; (b) five architectural objects + ground plan; (c) five building footprints on ground plan.

On the right-hand side of Figure 3.13 we see an alternative, where the structure takes the form of a 'jigsaw'. The term jigsaw is used here to mean that the sub-components are all similar, typically of a *roughly* similar order of magnitude, and add up to make an exact whole, with no leftover spaces, for example a nation divided into provinces, where there is no part of the nation that is not within one or other of the provinces; or a city authority area divided into wards. As with a jigsaw puzzle, the components are *designed* to be roughly the same size, and to interlock with no gaps. The jigsaw pieces form a complementary set, in the sense that a ward or province does not really make sense except in relation to a complete set of wards or provinces. In this sense, a jigsaw can be seen as a set of sub-components – rather than an aggregate of independent building-blocks.[23]

In Japan, an address starts with the largest geographical area and works its way down through wards to blocks and individual buildings.[24] This has an impeccably nested spatial logic, despite – or rather, because of – omitting the street or route as a geographical referent. This is because, in effect, the street or route system cuts across all the other land units. Streets are in effect the spaces left over after private territory has been parcelled off and developed – hence in Japan, it is normal for most streets to go without names.

But while in one sense streets are 'left over', from another perspective they are crucial in linking everything up. The street system is a single contiguous entity that unites other land uses: at the urban scale it converts the archipelago of land plots into a complete jigsaw of land units. In this sense the street system is the 'missing piece' in the jigsaw. This gives streets their significance for organising urban layout, precisely because the streets all connect whereas the land parcels don't (Figure 3.14).[25]

Just as Figure 3.11 gets us from three-dimensional objects to two-dimensional plan, Figure 3.14 gets us from two-dimensional plan to linear (skeletal) structure. In the end, a circuit-board, although in a sense organised on the two-dimensional plane of the motherboard, is even more significantly organised according to its linear connections.

The street system's contiguity is a kind of regularity, a kind of systematic urban order. We can also see a second kind of regularity on the ground plane, in that private plots of land tend to connect directly to the single contiguous public space or route network. This is the condition by which one tends to be able to get from one's own plot out on to a public road or street, without having to traipse through someone else's property (Figure 3.15).[26]

Just as the ground plane organisation of cities gives the city plan its potency, the fact that all land parcels or uses connect to the route system

3.12 • Chicago roofscape. Even 'vertically inclined' cities are organised most significantly on the horizontal plane.

gives the transport network its pivotal significance. This is why the street – outside Japan at least – can form the basic unit of any address. So how is the street system structured?

The order of route structures

Here, we need not restrict consideration of 'the linear' to entities that are single lines, but can consider any structure made up of discrete elements that are themselves linear. This equates with the route network – of routes, streets and public spaces, where these are represented as one-dimensional lines. These linear elements may be connected up in different ways – perhaps like a skeletal structure – to create an overall structure.

While there are many ways of connecting up routes of different types – defined in different ways[27] – there is one way by which routes tend to be connected up in a systematic way. Road networks are often arranged in a *hierarchy* where there are major, intermediate and minor roads. These are often arranged on a spectrum from more strategic to more local. The most strategic roads are typically national or international; the most local roads perhaps just serve the immediate buildings of plots of land adjoining them.

In one sense this distinction between strategic and local is a matter of geographical scale. But it can also be seen as a topological criterion, in the following sense. Strategic routes all connect up to form a single network; routes of a lower order connect up at least with another of their own level, or to a higher level. This leads to a fractal-like structure with more local sub-networks nested within more strategic networks (Figure 3.16). This topological property – known as arteriality – is in principle separable from geographical scale, though these typically coincide, for road networks.[28]

This structure of major roads and minor roads, strategic networks and sub-networks echoes the structure of centres and sub-centres we saw earlier with respect to two-dimensional structure (Figure 3.5). That is, the most strategic entity is a single contiguous entity, while the more local entities – as a class – form a discontiguous scatter.

In fact, we can see that this structure is coincident with – and an extension of – the structure that has all streets connect up, and that all plots connect to the street system. In other words, the street network has a strategic contiguity relative to land plots; land plots plug into the bottom of the structure that has strategic roads at the top and local roads at the bottom.[29] This does not mean that land uses and buildings should be regarded as somehow functionally subordinate to roads, but there is an undeniable structural asymmetry – just as with centres and suburbs – that

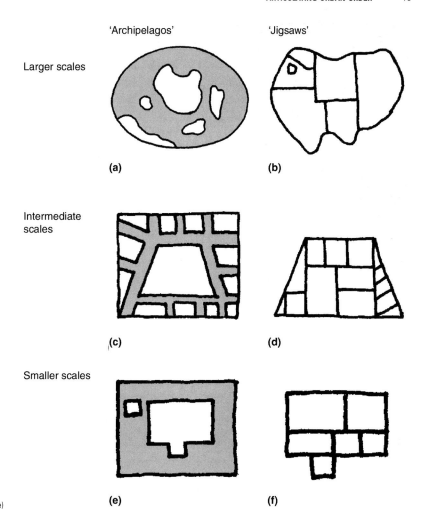

'Archipelagos'   'Jigsaws'

Larger scales

(a)   (b)

Intermediate scales

(c)   (d)

Smaller scales

(e)   (f)

3.13 • Two-dimensional configurations at different scales – 'archipelagos' and 'jigsaws': (a) Landmasses; (b) Nations on a continent, regions within a nation, districts within a region, districts within a city; (c) Urban blocks within continuum of public street space; (d) Plots of land within block; (e) Buildings within plot; (f) Rooms within building.

can't be simply wished away in the interests of trying to 'balance' transport and land use, or centre and periphery.

In fact, there is a structural resonance going on here – a systematic order – that we may call 'street syntax'.

Street syntax

The term street syntax relates to the way that the consistent elements of streets and the streets themselves connect up. The relationships are

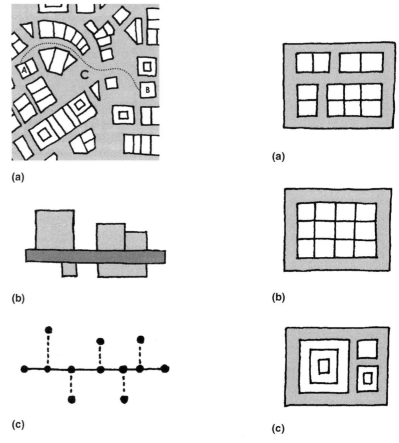

3.14 • Two-dimensional areas organised by the streets: (a) Public street space all connects up; (b) Streets connect every other land use to each other; (c) The same topology represented as a skeletal diagram.

3.15 • Private plots and public space: (a) Normal case; (b) 'Boxed in' plots; (c) Plots 'boxed in' by nesting.

considered systematic 'rules' in the way that linguistic syntax is considered systematic: it means this is how sentences are normally put together, without claiming that it applies in every single case. (Alternatively, rather than claiming these rules always apply, we could put it the other way round, and simply say that systematic urban order applies wherever the rules *are* followed.) The following rules are drawn from this chapter:

1.   The route system forms a single contiguous network. Within this, strategic routes all connect up (Figure 3.17a).

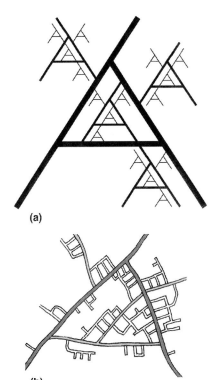

(a)

(b)

3.16 • Fractal structure of road network. At any scale, the strategic routes form a single contiguous network: (a) Abstract principle, emphasising repetition of structure at different scales; (b) Example interpreted at a local urban scale.

2. Plots of land (including those built-up) are accessed from the route network. Plots of private land may occasionally connect to each other directly without connection to the public circulation system; however, access to one plot that was only via another private plot would tend to be exceptional cases in the urban context (Figure 3.17b).
3. Buildings connect directly to the outdoor space. There is a single contiguous outdoor space; any new building newly encloses part of that which was outdoor space; no building encloses another building, therefore all buildings connect directly to the outdoor space. Buildings may connect to each other without having to go outside (Figure 3.17c).
4. All buildings plug into a plot on the ground. For any given landmass, there is a single contiguous ground surface onto which all buildings ultimately are founded on, and from which access is obtained. Buildings may occasionally connect to each other above ground level; however, these tend to be exceptional cases (Figure 3.17d).

Interestingly, the four rules have similar structures, in a general abstract sense – that is, to do with strategic contiguity (right-hand images, Figure 3.17). The 'single contiguous' part of each one is often the same space: that is, ground-level, outdoor, public circulation space. That said, in detail, there are differences: the strength of the connection between like elements, and the number of 'tiers' or 'storeys'.

It is suggested that these 'street syntax' rules are generally valid for terrestrial cities, but there are exceptions, or at least, complications. For example, the cases of 'sky bridges' linking buildings above the ground (Figure 3.18a); the ancient (neolithic) settlement of Çatalhöyük, where circulation is contiguous (only) on the roof, with trapdoors leading down to private interior ground floor spaces (Figure 3.18b); and buildings (though not yet whole cities) built over the sea, such as oil rigs or piers (Figure 3.18c). A Corbusian landscape of buildings on pilotis forming a new ground level would also be likely to break some of the rules of street syntax – not surprising, given Le Corbusier's intention to break away from a city of streets. Interior public streets could also be regarded as complicating the basic order of street syntax, if the routes are interpreted as passing within buildings. Alexander Thomson proposed for Glasgow a system of glazed-over residential streets that could have formed an innovative new urban order for the city (Figure 3.18d).[30]

These cases are notable precisely for being exceptional. The exceptions are nevertheless worthwhile acknowledging, and the rules are worth making despite the exceptions, because it shows how much of the built environment *is* actually systematically ordered. This is what gives cities their characteristic 'city-shapedness' – relative to other objects in a hypothetical 'catalogue of all possible forms'.

3.17 • Street syntax: (a) All strategic roads connect to form a single network; (b) All private spaces connect to the (single) public space; (c) All buildings have an interface with the (single) outside space; (d) All buildings connect to the (single) ground surface.

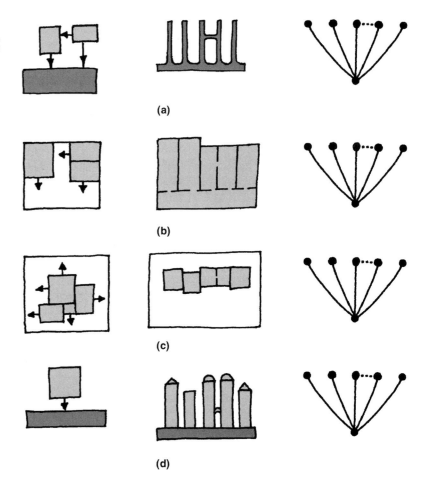

It must be clear that the traditional order of street syntax does not mean the architecture needs to be traditional (Figure 3.19a). We can have modern architecture that still fits the traditional street syntax (Figure 3.19b). However, some modern urban layouts break or bend the rules, or take them to their logical limit. In the case shown in Figure 3.19c, the rules are twisted a bit, as the ground surface appears to form a continuum – with no discrete private plots – and the space used for vehicles penetrates into the interiors of the buildings.

The effect of street syntax is that however superficially irregular an urban pattern – such as an asymmetrical straggling village shape – if it is ordered according to street syntax it is more structured than some random

3.18 • 'Exceptional' cases: (a) Sky bridges – Fuji TV building, Tokyo; (b) Çatalhöyök – circulation on the roof; (c) Pier building – not on the ground; (d) Interior public street, proposed by Alexander Thomson.

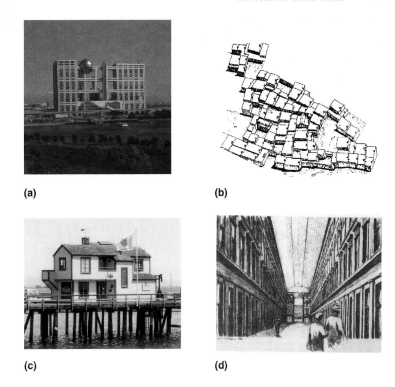

(a)

(b)

(c)

(d)

arrangement of objects in space. Hence Glasgow could be recognised as being ordered at the scale of plots and blocks and streets, even if a higher level order is not discernible at the scale of the whole city.

A significant consequence of the systematic order of street syntax is that not only do the different units – routes, plots, buildings – fit together in systematic ways, but the basic units can be recognised as such partly *because* they fit together in systematic ways. For example, a building can be identified as a distinct entity partly because it can be identified by its footprint; if buildings were locked together in a three-dimensional megastructural jigsaw (Figure 3.3d), it would be harder to make sense of a building as a discrete unit in the first place.[31]

A consequence: the street as building-block

Since all buildings and plots ultimately are connected up to all routes (and attached to the ground), then the system of streets and their appendages, multiplied up, can contain everything urban. That is, due to the rules of street

(a)

(b)

(c)

3.19 • Street syntax in action: (a) Traditional urban fabric, Cellardyke, Scotland; (b) Modern architecture, but with traditional street syntax, Cumbernauld, Scotland; (c) Modern urban fabric, but with bending of street syntax rules, Cumbernauld, Scotland.

syntax, if we were to try to detach a route from the fabric, it would 'bring with it' a series of attached land parcels and plots, and with those, all the buildings. Indeed, the streets – each with its own local 'hinterland' of plots and buildings – can be the two-dimensional jigsaw pieces that fit together to form a complete city plan. This is why the street can form a significant comprehensive address system.

The street, in combining, route, adjoining plots and associated buildings, can therefore become a building-block in its own right, a composite unit. Streets have a built-in connective interface – the contiguity of their routes, that allow them to easily plug together to create structure. As building blocks, streets can be multiplied up, to get whole cities. Street syntax becomes *urban* syntax.

THE NATURE OF URBAN ORDER

We have seen examples of urban order in the way that buildings systematically plug into plots and plots plug into routes, and also in the rougher order at the scale of whole settlements, where, for example, settlements characteristically have a roughly concentric pattern. These are both recognisably kinds of order, to be sure, but they are not the *same* kind of order. Rather, we can distinguish two kinds of order: one that can be referred to as systematic order, and the other as characteristic order. This distinction is not just something to do with the theoretical nature of order itself, but as we shall see has practical implications to do with the scale of urban building-blocks or planned units, and the difference between 'planned' and 'unplanned' cities.

Systematic and characteristic order

The order seen in the case of the rules of 'street syntax' (between buildings, routes and plots) can be regarded as *systematic order*, in the sense that it applies consistently and systematically to all routes, plots, buildings, more or less (any that does not is considered exceptional or aberrational). This is like the systematic way that nouns, verbs, and so on, fit together within sentences: in almost every sentence, the rules of syntax are followed. With systematic order, for a given set of objects, or sample of the urban fabric, the same units (sub-units and super-units) have the same relationships with respect to each other.

Zooming out to look at the city as a whole, we tend to see a different kind of order. The most persistent form recognisable as order is perhaps the concentric form, where some higher-order functions, land uses, building types, higher-rise or higher-density forms are found in the inner

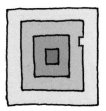

(a)

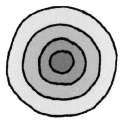

(b)

3.20 • Systematic order and characteristic order: (a) Pyramid (plan view) – any brick out of place is disorder; (b) Sand pile (plan view). The contours are concentric but not exactly circular.

areas, and lower-order functions and lower-rise and lower-density forms in the outer areas. But this is only a general tendency, and when we look more closely we will persistently find exceptions all over the place. The concentric effect is not as systematic or predictable as with the case of street syntax.

In effect, the concentric effect and the presence of centres and sub-centres can be seen as another kind of order, that may be referred to as *characteristic order*. This refers to the recognisable rough kind of order that typically applies in the absence of conscious planning. This applies in the case of the rough 'city-shapedness' that we can recognise in a city even if there is no systematic order in common. The equivalent of characteristic order in a piece of text might be the number of words per sentence, or sentences per paragraph. There will tend to be typical pervasive tendencies, within any given text, but this does not rule out exceptionally long or short sentences or paragraphs.

Systematic order is like a red brick wall where all the bricks should be red. A yellow brick in a red brick wall is an erroneous brick. Or, it is like a stepped pyramid, where all the stone blocks need to be in a particular arrangement in order to create the macro-scale pyramid (Figure 3.20a). In contrast, characteristic order is like the roughly conic shape of a sand pile. The not-quite-conic pile is not an imperfect approximation of a perfect cone of theory. The 'rules' that make the roughly conic shape are to do with gravity and frictional resistance of the sand grains; there is no rule saying the pile ought to be precisely conic – although it may be statistically predictable as an approximate cone. The characteristic order one sees in a sand pile – the roughly conic shape whose contours are roughly circular – lies in the constancy of the physical laws that create the sand pile, not the detailed geometric profile of the pile itself.

In a sense, characteristic order refers to something outside of itself – the laws that are common across all sand piles, even if each one is different (and differently disordered) in detail. In contrast, with systematic order, the order is self-contained within the whole (or a given sample in which systematic order is discernible) (Figure 3.21).

We can also see the distinction with respect to street-grids. Figure 3.22 (a) shows a street-grid that has a simple, systematic order, while (b) has a similar order except for one area where the order is 'broken' or 'imperfect'. In contrast, Figure 3.22 (c) shows a case of characteristic order. In one sense, Figure 3.22 (c) is irregular and disordered, and in some ways less ordered than (b). But (c) also has a consistent degree of order to it. First, it has a localised systematic order, where there is consistent use of right

(a)

(b)

(c)

(d)

3.21 • Characteristic order and systematic order. The planned city (c) has systematic internal order (seven more or less equal components), while the unplanned cities (a, b, d) are each irregular and roughly ordered. Within the 'population' of all cities, however, the unplanned ones show a characteristic order, while the planned city could be seen as a deviation from *this* order.

angles, rectangles, formed through bisections of rectangles. However, this consistency does not extend to having a regular tiling of identical squares, like (a). Secondly, (c) possesses characteristic order in the consistency with which a multitude or 'population' of such street-grid excerpts will have a similar degree of order (or disorder) as found in the individual grid.

In a sense, then, characteristic order is recognisable at the 'next scale up'. The characteristic 'street pattern shape' of Figure 3.22 (c) is recognisable as the kind of semi-regular, semi-irregular pattern that is notable for the consistency with which it is found 'naturally' across many urban contexts, that is, in the absence of overall planning otherwise.

Relation to city design and urban ordering

We can relate systematic and characteristic order to city design and urban ordering through a linguistic analogy. City design creates a finite product – like a poem – typically with regular subdivisions; but like a poem, it could also be deliberately contrived to be irregular. Urban order is equivalent to syntax. So urban order in the absence of city design is like the equivalent of prose – it is open-ended, without a regular overall form or subdivisions, although it does follow rules of syntax. Systematic order is seen in the case of street syntax (which might be the only kind of order in an otherwise 'unplanned' settlement); also in the case of urban ordering (e.g. a city based on a modular grid); and also might be seen in the case of a city design, where a finite design has sub-components (such as neighbourhoods) organised in a systematic way relative to each other and the whole. Characteristic order would be seen in the case of streets being aggregated in such a way as to give rise to characteristic street-pattern-shape (Figure 3.22c); or land uses forming a concentric pattern in the absence of overall planning or design.

At the scale of whole cities, we tend not to see any systematic order (except in case of planned cities with city design), but rather what has been termed characteristic order: the typical tendency for cities to have concentric rings of growth, development along main roads, street patterns that are often a rather irregular mix of long and short streets at different angles, and so on.

These observations refer to typical cases in 'unplanned' situations, where places have grown up incrementally, organically, left to their own devices. In 'planned' situations, however, then we can see any sort of pattern wilfully set down with any kind of geometric order, or for that matter contrived irregularity. This means one can create systematic order at the city

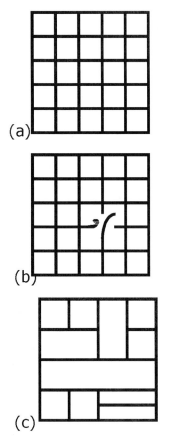

3.22 • Interpretations of order: (a) Systematic order; (b) Imperfect or broken systematic order; (c) Characteristic order.

scale – in effect, systematic order observed at the city scale is a hallmark of city design. Or, more generally, we can say that systematic order at any given scale is a hallmark of design at that scale.

Relation to planned and 'unplanned' cities

The difference between a planned city and an 'unplanned' one is not so much that one has foresighted intention and the other does not. Rather, they may be distinguished by the scale at which they are designed, or the *scale over which systematic order applies*.

In a traditional 'unplanned' city, the city's urban order is no different from the degree of order found in a straggling village or smallest hamlet worthy of the name: this is the order of street syntax, which simply amounts to the systematic way that buildings and plots connect to routes and routes connect up in a single system. In other words, the traditional 'unplanned' city has systematic order at the scale of streets, while having characteristic order at the scale of the whole city. In contrast, the planned city may have systematic order at the scale of streets *and* at the scale of the city (and scales in between). Systematic order at the scale of the whole city means, for example, a planned new town with the cluster of similar-sized, similar-functioning units – neighbourhoods, each with its park, its local centre – relating in the same way to the whole.

In effect, street syntax is a kind of urban ordering that is present in both traditional unplanned and planned cities. That is, urban ordering is not an indicator of planning or planned cities *per se* – any more than the presence of a plan representation is – since systematic urban ordering is found in 'unplanned' cities. The difference is that in planned towns or cities, urban ordering is at the level of whole blocks (for example, a grid of rectangular blocks), or neighbourhoods (for example, a distinct set of neighbourhoods clustered round the town centre).

CONCLUSIONS

This chapter set out to articulate the urban order found in cities (and other scales of settlements) – identifying building-blocks and their relationships – in such a way that might inform their onward design and planning.

In the course of the chapter we have seen how urban order can be unpacked on a dimensional basis: the three-dimensional city is ordered to a significant extent by the ground plan, and the two-dimensional ground plan is in turn ordered to a significant extent by the linear structure of the route system. Buildings, plots and routes have been identified as significant building-blocks of urban form and structure. These are clearly definable and relate to each other in systematic ways. Buildings plug into plots, plots plug into routes, and routes all connect up to form a single system. This set of rules can be referred to as 'street syntax', with the street syntax being a significant contributor to urban ordering overall. In addition to this systematic order, we have also seen the characteristic order, as in characteristic street pattern shapes, and concentric urban patterns.

A planned city, then, is a city with planned order at the scale of the whole city; an 'unplanned' city also has planning forethought and design intention, but at the scale of smaller-scale units such as streets and buildings.

When it comes to Modernist city design, it is curious the extent to which planners and urban designers have attempted to capture and replicate the overall macro-scale form, and larger sub-units of the city (central business districts, neighbourhoods, and so on).[32] These are forms which are characteristic of traditional unplanned settlements, but were not systematically created. In effect, Modernists often treated the characteristic order as if it were imperfect systematic order, and attempted to 'rectify' it – make it better by reconstituting the units (such as zones, neighbourhoods and town centres), and relating them in systematic ways (Figure 2.13). This is like trying to 'rectify' a sand pile by making it into a perfect cone, when the roughly conic shape comes naturally, according to laws that apply to every sand pile.

Meanwhile, when it came to urban ordering, Modernist planners were happy to meddle with or rip up the traditional systematic order of the city at the micro-scale – the traditional 'street syntax' of routes fronted by buildings. The 'Corbusian revolution' after all (Figure 1.2) tore up the idea of the traditional street, put public streets (and shops) above ground, put buildings above rather than on the ground – as well as putting the 'back' of buildings to the underside, and so on. Hence we should not be surprised that it did not work in the way traditional urbanism did.

So, here we see part of the answer to the question of how it is that Modernist planned urbanism is not necessarily better than traditional unplanned urbanism. First, Modernist urban ordering overturned the 'natural' order of traditional urbanism. Secondly, Modernist city design tried to apply systematic order to macro-scale features such as centres, neighbourhoods and whole cities, that are more naturally possessing characteristic order. In other words, rather than seeing unplanned cities as imperfectly irregular, and planned cities as regularised improvements or rectifications, we can see unplanned cities have a natural characteristic order, and planned ones are artificial contrivances (that, if incompletely imposed, may create a result that is *more* disordered than the original rough order).

It was, after all, the pursuit of a 'new coherent whole' – supported by a system of ring and radial motorways – that led to the destruction of the fabric of inner Glasgow. And although the slum clearance most directly amounted to urban destruction, it was arguably the tampering with the traditional syntax of local streets (systematic order) that led to a kind of disurban creation, such that the urban communities could not regenerate themselves along traditional lines.

But why should overturning the traditional order of streets be destructive? Or put another way, why does the traditional urban order work in the first place? Where does the systematic order of street syntax come from? To answer these questions, we would need to have an effective understanding of why the typical urban order is the way it is.

This chapter has mainly looked upon the city from an outsider's perspective, but taking human agency for granted. This is perhaps a bit like an extra-terrestrial observer studying urban form, or a human observer studying the form of a wasp's nest, whether from the outside or dissecting the individual parts, but without studying the means or motives of those who constructed them. This serves the purposes of description; but when it comes to explanation, it is now time to explore the human factors behind the urban forms and structures.

Notes

1   Reed (1999c: 106). The chapter is entitled *The Tenement City*.
2   Reed (1999a: 1,6). The italics are Reed's. Blake's view was in 1934, while Nairn's was in 1960; but as Reed points out, they were looking at substantially the same city. If anything, one might add, the city of 1960 with disparate additions would surely be more incoherent than the city of 1934.
3   This is like 'urban anatomy' – to do with component parts and structure, rather than 'urban morphology' to do with form. 'Urban anatomy' is not an established term like urban morphology, which is traditionally associated with high-resolution examination of the urban fabric – such as patterns of street blocks and land plots (Conzen, 1969; Whitehand, 1981; Gordon, 1984; Larkham and Jones, 1991; Moudon, 1994, 1997; Larkham, 2006). That said, morphology can also refer to the science of all possible form, and we can use the term urban morphology to include this wider sense (Steadman, 1983; also Thompson, [1917] 1948: 1026). In the urban context, anatomy is used figuratively from time to time, for example, Spreiregen (1965: 59), MacCormac (1996).
4   There are implicit questions here about whether super-units are themselves units. If they are, then we don't need the term super-unit, since unit and sub-unit will suffice to cover any frame of reference. If they aren't, then we could identify them as a super-unit in contradistinction to unit, but again, it is not essential. A building-block could be the 'sub-unit of a super-unit'.

5   Stephen Hawking's *Brief History of Time* (original edition) has a curious image of a two-dimensional dog divided by its digestive tract (Hawking, 1988: 181).

6   Note other possible operations. From (b) to (d) by subdivision. From (d) to (b) by amalgamation. From (c) to (d) by fusion. From (d) to (c) by fission.

7   NASA's Vertical Assembly Building is a 'giant' building with a large interior space that is like a single room – a building so large that clouds form inside it (Banham, 1976; Holgate, 1986). Note that in a 'megahouse', not everyone can have direct access to light and air – this may be fine for bees and termites, but no so great for humans.

8   Steadman (1983: 241) 'no very distinct line of demarcation can be drawn between the architectural and settlement scales: indeed the size of many a single building can approach that of a village, with an organization along covered "streets" or around internal courts. The real distinction is between enclosed space within buildings, and open spaces between buildings.' See also Steadman *et al.* (2000) for a classification of built forms.

9   See, for example, Lynch (1981), Frey (1999), Jacobs (2000), Marshall (2005) for discussion of classification of urban structure.

10 This would be, very loosely speaking, like being able to identify the head, body and limbs of an animal – and hence awareness of looking at an animal in the first place – irrespective of overall shape or size, and before looking in detail at organs. In other words, this scrutiny is not to do with the overall shape or form of cities (like linear versus compact), but a look at what the first order of sub-components might be.

11 The detailed correspondence would depend on the detail of definition, but could be, for example: (a) Star and Linear; (b) Satellite; (c) Galaxy and Ring; (d) Core; (e) and (f) Sheet and/or Polycentred Net.

12 Note that with the models at this simple level, there is a significant asymmetry between some different things (core and periphery), and a sense of hierarchy between similar things (centre and sub-centre). In effect, there is a structural significance to the pattern, something to do with the position in the configuration and the urban function being related.

13 Or a human geographer, researching 'town-centredness' (Thurstain-Goodwin and Batty, 2001: 263).

14 For example, different observers who did not know London would be unlikely to make the same divisions into units, whereas they might agree on the basic distinctions between centres and suburbs.

15 See Marshall (2005) for interpretation of routes and joints as opposed to links and nodes.

16 These basic morphological elements are related to the traditions of urban morphology. Whitehand (1981); Kostof (1991: 25/26). Moudon (1997: 7) puts it this way: 'Urban form is defined by three fundamental physical elements: buildings and their related open spaces, plots or lots, and streets.' Panerai *et al.* (2004: 158) suggest the three key elements are the logic of roads, the logic of plot sub-divisions and the logic of buildings.

17 Archigram: 'Housing is a crust around a shopping area'; see Archigram at <http://www.archigram.net/projects_pages/plug_in_city_6.html 29.04.07>.

18 This 3D enclosure effect would not necessarily be expected to hold for space-stations – depending how 'buildings' were interpreted with respect to the space-station whole or parts.

19 This generalisation that cities are built on the surface of the Earth applies to all known cities on this planet, and excludes parts of cities lying underground, house-boats, other floating or undersea constructions, oil rigs, or aircraft or spacecraft, none of which could usefully be described fully as 'cities'. In general, this book addresses human-built cities on Earth; other rules could apply to human-built cities in space, or non-human-built cities. 'In architecture, gravity is always a constraint' (Aldersey-Williams, 2003: 14).

20 Abbott (2006 [1884]). The citizens can move around each other but not above or below. Their buildings are partial enclosures in two dimensions. The Flatlanders are surprised by the entrance on their dimension of alien objects in three dimensions (such as spheres), who appear as two-dimensional cross-sections (such as circles). The Flatlanders are also surprised to find that these otherworldly 3D characters can see inside them – the interior of A. Square is neither accessible nor visible to the Flatlanders.

21 This also applies to a lesser extent to architecture, where a building can be seen as a three-dimensional arrangement of two-dimensional plots or floorplans (Shelton, 1999: 47, 98; Unwin, 1997).

22 In Latin, blocks were *insulae*; in French, blocks are *îlots* (Panerai *et al.*, 2004: 152)

23 The term jigsaw is preferred to tiling or tessellation, since tiling or tessellation may imply that the component pieces are of the same shape and size.

24 An address will typically start with the nation (in this case Japan), then the pre-fecture (*ken*), then the city (*shi*), then the ward (*machi*), then the (numbered) ward division (*chome*), then the housing block (if applicable), then the house or flat number. (The house is further divisible into smaller areas, rooms and finally *tatami* mats, the smallest areal unit) (Shelton, 1999: 180). The Japanese address system has a clear spatial logic, and in a way is more consistent than the more familiar system that includes a street name, because the street system is not nested in the way the other components are.

25 On streets and the transport network more generally acting as key organising elements of urban settlement structure, see Hilberseimer (1944: 104); Smithson and Smithson (1967; 1968: 42); Trancik (1986: 106); Brett (1994: 71); Friedman (1998); Roberts *et al.* (1999: 55); Roberts and Lloyd-Jones (2001); Erickson (2001); Lillebye (2001: 5).

26 This is not necessarily universally the case. It is quite possible in principle and in practice to have a plot of land 'boxed in' by other private plots. This may especially be the case with fields of different ownership. However, it is generally the case that plots are *not* boxed in in this way; or that where they are, it is the case that there is some kind of access provided to them, possibly and especially if the private plots have the same owner (Figure 3.16b).

27 There are many ways of defining route or street type. For some kinds of street or route type – for example, street types defined by physical characteristics or by their use, such as by traffic volume, or land use – these do not necessarily connect up in any systematic way. That is, there is no particular way in which we would expect a 'park avenue' to connect up systematically with, say, a 'shopping street', or a 'residential street' (Marshall, 2005).

28 The issue of street type and network structure is treated in detail in *Streets and Patterns* (Marshall, 2005).

29 This does not necessarily mean that land plots cannot be directly accessed from main roads, any more than a road hierarchy necessarily disallows connection between the most local and most strategic roads – though in each case, this could be so.

30 Çatal Höyük: Kostof (1992); Hodder (2005). Thomson's glazed streets: McKean (1994); Edwards (1994). The Walled City of Kowloon is a case where an 'organic' agglomeration of buildings had a labyrinth of passages through it that allowed one to traverse the interior of the urban form without going down to street level. The Walled City of Kowloon was demolished around 1993 (Girard and Lambot, 1999).

31 Note that this works with respect to the idea of a suburban ring surrounding a town centre (this arises in planned and unplanned cases), but not, generally, a configuration of individual zones or neighbourhoods.

32 Neighbourhood as building-block: see, for example, Mumford (1938); Forshaw and Abercrombie (1943); Fawcett (1944), who used the term 'vill'; Osborn and Whittick (1969); Hauman (1984); Hall (1988); Duany and Plater-Zyberk (1994). Biddulph (2000) on the pursuit of the 'macro-concept' as a legitimisation of the role of the planner.

4 THE SOCIAL LOGIC OF URBAN ORDER

Man is an animal who lives or whose nature is to live in a <u>polis</u>.
Aristotle, *The Politics*[1]

When surveying urban places over space and time, we may discern a diversity of urban forms, from ancient camel-trod walled cities to modern car-treaded suburbs. But despite the differences in climate and culture, technology or economies, our built environments seem to make sense, from a common human point of view. The human motives for walled private gardens and fountains of stone-built sun-baked cities of antiquity, and the walled private gardens and sprinklers and swimming pools of the sunny suburbs of today are not so different. Cities may be all different insofar as their contexts are different; they are similar insofar as human beings are similar.

The same kind of structure of streets, separating building blocs divided into cellular rooms, can be seen in diverse cases across time and space in the ancient world (Figure 4.1). The Indus valley settlement of Mohenjo-Daro had planned grids of streets, 'dual carriageways', shops and houses with two storeys, connected by brick stairways, most with running water – surely a 'modern' city of the third millennium BC. The houses, as Lewis Mumford pointed out, were 'about the same size as a modest house in Greek Priene about 200 BC . . . Neither would have seemed out of place in the East End of London in the eighteenth century' – nor, one might add, many urban contexts of today.[2] One could say this constancy is because humans are essentially the same creatures now as they were then and roughly the same size, and have the same disinclination for climbing too far upstairs, cleaning too large a house or tending too large a garden. That said, the urban order is not only to do with humans as physical organisms and their individual inclinations; as we

(a)

(b)

(c)

4.1 • Similarities of urban form and structure across time and space: (a) Mohenjo-Daro, India; (b) Gournia, Crete; (c) Ur.

shall see, it is also to do with *social* considerations. As Spiro Kostof put it, 'Urban form is never innocent of social content'.[3]

The last chapter has suggested typical urban units such as routes, plots and buildings, and suggested the recognition of a systematic urban order, by which these combine in various ways to create composite units such as streets, squares, and so on. These units and relationships have so far been taken as given. But why do they have this order in the first place? Why do we have buildings nested within plots, nested within public spaces? Why do we have buildings, rooms and settlements in the first place, rather than having, say, settlements in the form of giant city-sized buildings?

Urban order is not just about the creation and manipulation of abstract topologies (Chapter 3), but deals with topologies that have a definite human purpose. In effect, cities, streets, buildings are the way they are because they are 'human-shaped' on the inside, and moreover 'socially constructed' in their relationships. This chapter looks at some of the human and social purposes behind the abstractions.

In this chapter, we first look at the social logic of Buildings, and how the accommodation of humans as individuals and in social units helps explain why we have buildings and rooms. Then, we see how larger social structures are organised as arrays of buildings; this helps explain why we have Cities and other kinds of settlements. Finally we look at how distinctions between different kinds of people lead to a public–private gradient which relates the inside of private buildings to outdoor public space; this helps explain the significance of The Streets as basic building-blocks of urban structure. This investigation helps explain the typical systematic order we see in any city, planned or 'unplanned'.

The interpretation of this chapter is necessarily selective with respect to architectural and social theory; it is not the only possible interpretation of the relationships between people, buildings, streets and cities, but it is one that is relevant to this book's treatment of articulating urban order.

BUILDINGS

Buildings provide for some of the most fundamental human – indeed, animal – needs. And so, many kinds of organism create their own built environment to live in; in *Animal Architecture*, Mike Hansell sets out the varied functions of the built dwellings of a variety of mammals, birds, insects, arachnids and molluscs, among others. These functions include control of the physical environment, in factors such as temperature, oxygen and respiration, humidity control and water management; and control of the biological environment, in terms of defence against predators and parasites, food storage and cultivation.[4]

If the environment is an all-encompassing container, we can see the built environment as a sort of specialised sub-container for various human activities, offering protection from the more harmful elements of nature (Figure 4.2). But nature can be nice as well as nasty. We can also see the creation of built structures as a means of *filtering the environment*, that is, not only shutting out nature, but letting through or 'connecting back to' favourable aspects (for example, light, air, and generally the friendlier aspects of nature). The result is to create a new artificial or internal environment, that the organism is better suited to than the pre-existing natural or external one.

For humans, therefore, a dwelling can be seen as a purpose-built habitat, a sort of artificial Eden of itself: bright, airy, temperate; with running water, on demand, all *inside*; even tame animals and singing birds, and an abundant stock of food and wine, and a place to relax and pass time in good company. This artificial, interior Eden – 'better than nature', in effect – is what we create when we build a building to separate us from the wider environment.[5]

To explore why we have buildings in the forms we have, we first briefly look at the general nature of the building, appropriate for the individual human. Then we note how buildings change according to the needs of accommodating people collectively, and finally how they change in complexity according to the kind of social structure, or social unit, they are to house.

4.2 • Eden project, Cornwall: an environmental container, and environmental filter.

4.3 • Adam's primitive hut: a rudimentary human container, and environmental filter.

The human being and building

Architectural theorists from Vitruvius onwards have been drawn to consider a hypothetical early human, and in particular, a 'first human' in the form of the biblical Adam, as the first architect, and a 'primitive hut' as the first building, or first work of architecture. The primitive hut signifies the most elemental unit of built environment, the most basic form of 'human container' (Figure 4.3).[6]

A building creates a new interior environment that acts as a filter on the external environment, providing physical and psychological security; peace and quiet; a temperate climate.[7] Broadly speaking, the exclusion of harmful environmental factors is a basic reason for 'why we have buildings'; while the desired condition of the new internal environment is influential on 'why buildings have the forms they have'.

The need to let light and air in means that buildings tend not to be too enclosed – buried in the Earth, or otherwise with deep interiors – like a termite's nest. Buildings tend to be punctuated by openings – windows and doors set in walls, skylights in roofs, courtyards and lightwells that appear as if 'carved' from the solid mass.[8] So there is a constraint on how large an area (or rather, how 'deep') a building can be. Large buildings tend to be articulated into discrete sections that allow in air and daylight. Windows, as well as allowing lighting of the interior, also afford views in and out, and help create a 'feeling of space'. The desire to be close to nature – or at least, an unthreatening, aesthetically and psychologically pleasing part of it – leads to the cultivation of houseplants, and the creation of gardens next to and around buildings. Buildings are also often designed to take care of water supply, water storage and sanitation. While this plumbing apparatus may often be hidden, features such as water tanks can affect the external form of buildings. The need to provide outlets for smoke from fires and to keep water out leads to pitched roofs with chimneys.

The needs of the human being as an organism influence the design of interior spaces of buildings in a variety of ways. Vitruvius, Leonardo da Vinci and Le Corbusier all used the human form and human dimensions as the basic units for analysis and design.[9] The size of the human frame, and the upright posture, affects the minimum dimensions of internal spaces such as rooms and corridors. A room usually must be big enough to hold at least one whole adult human, usually in a way that allows one to stand up and sit or lie down. A Japanese 'capsule hotel' – where the user lies horizontally – is a clear exception (Figure 4.4).[10]

The speed and range of the human – since movement takes effort and energy – influences the maximum dimensions of buildings, especially in the

4.4 • A capsule hotel, Tokyo: a 'cell' for male 'worker bees' (*sararimen*).

vertical dimension, in the absence of mechanical locomotion. Not only do buildings not float in the air but humans tend to access everything on horizontal surfaces, whether the ground surface, or artificial horizontal surfaces above or below ground: stairs, floors, roof terraces, and so on (Chapter 3).[11] Also, even though we may have vertical transportation to assist high-rise living, some people simply prefer being situated closer to the ground.

The form and structure of buildings is also affected by the objects a building is to house. This includes items like furniture, any machinery or equipment, and also things like food storage (and cultivation of plants or keeping of pets) which may require their own specialised micro-environments.

The form of a building will also be influenced by practical considerations about how it is designed and built – some forms will be more favoured than others due to ease of conception and construction. And finally, the form of a building will be affected by factors that are closely related to the art of architecture: the provision of beauty and delight, the generation and expression of feeling, identity and meaning.[12]

So the form of the buildings we see is influenced not just by the physical nature of the organism to be housed, but the wider psychological and intellectual character of human needs (Figure 4.5). These considerations would apply to any building for an individual human. But what happens when we multiply up from a lone 'Adam' to house a number of humans?

Buildings for people

When we move from building a hut for a lone individual to building for many people, some of the factors we saw earlier (for a lone human) will not change much, if at all. Buildings for many people – rather than a single individual – will still be built on the ground, even if rising to the sky; the need for light, air and water supply, and security and so on, will still apply. However, some factors will change as rooms or buildings accommodate more than one person. These relate to size, form and configuration (recall Figure 3.3).

With regard to room size, if a room is to accommodate more people, then the dimensions of the rooms will be expected to increase. In turn, the minimum building size must automatically increase if the minimum room size does. A primitive hut for 'Adam' could be extremely compact, a single cell (cf. capsule hotel). But if a building is to house more people, it is likely to be bigger, whether because of having more rooms, or bigger rooms, or a combination of both.

So far we have simply assumed the distinction between rooms and buildings. But where does this distinction come from? Why are arrays of

4.5 • Different-shaped buildings for different reasons; note that each has slightly different relationships between indoors and outdoors: (a) Blue Mosque, Istanbul; (b) Church, Moscow; (c) 'Beehive' dwelling, Ireland; (d) BedZed housing, London; (e) House with garages, London; (f) Castle, Athenry; (g) Opera House, Sydney; (h) Supermarket, London; (i) Department store, Houston; (j) Hotel, Kalgoorlie; (k) Factory, Welwyn Garden City; (l) Multi-storey garage, Austin.

rooms assembled in buildings, or, why are buildings subdivided into rooms? As numbers of people increase, why don't we just get bigger and bigger rooms, or bigger and bigger buildings? Or alternatively, why do we not just get an upward multiplication of primitive huts, each a singe cell housing a lone 'Adam'?

The answer is that humanity is not just lots of lone 'Adams', but lots of *different* kinds of people: people of different gender, generation, age, marital status, social status, economic role, and so on. This is, of course, to do with what we call society.

Human society

Thomas Hobbes in his classic work *Leviathan* invites the reader to contemplate a 'state of nature' – a hypothetical original state in which there is no human society, but just individual persons. Here, the individual primordial human is alone in the wilderness, fending for himself or herself. While this might be considered a pure state, it is not a romantic one, as Hobbes spells out in a famous passage. A state of nature would mean:

> no place for Industry, . . . no commodious Building; . . . no Knowledge of the face of the Earth; no account of Time; no Arts; no Letters; no Society; and which is worst of all, continuall feare, and danger of violent death; And the life of man, solitary, poore, nasty, brutish, and short.[13]

Anyone finding themselves in this hypothetical state would wish to get out of it if they could.[14] Accordingly, instead of a state of nature, people tend to abide by a 'social contract', where people agree to limit some of their freedom to do as they will (which might include causing harm to others) in return for others agreeing to do the same. This results in what we call society. In effect, to explain urban form we need to consider not only the presence of human individuals, but also human societies.[15]

Let us briefly consider social organisation; and then the consequences of buildings being used to contain different kinds of social groupings of different kinds of people.

Social groups and social units

The identity, motivation and behaviour of individuals is often very much bound up with the needs and expectations of the social groups to which they belong – their family, circle of friends, work colleagues, and any number of religious, political or cultural affiliations. Human behaviour cannot therefore be reduced to the satisfaction of the bodily and mental needs of individual persons, but must also take account of their social context.

While there are many ways of dividing a population into different groupings – for example, by where a person lives, what a person does for a living, and so on – it will be useful here to recognise a particular, tightly focused kind of social group, that may be referred to as a *social unit*. A social unit could be a couple, a family, a business, a club or society. We can define a social unit as one which is a single decision-making entity. A social unit will typically have a leader or decision-making executive acting on behalf of the whole unit. In a social unit, the needs of the individual are to some extent subordinated to the needs of the group. A social unit will typically have a differentiation of roles within it. And finally, it will typically have some sort of hierarchy of control, rights and privileges, and so on. In a social unit, no one is autonomous.

For example, a family consisting of mother, father and children may be regarded as a social unit. Typically the parents will subordinate at least some of their individual needs to the needs of the family. Typically one or both parents will form the decision-making executive. Mother, father and children play different roles. The children may not volunteer to subordinate their needs to the needs of the whole, but may be persuaded, cajoled or ordered to do so. A family is not normally a democracy.[16]

It is a similar story for a workplace: a differentiation of roles between bosses and ordinary employees, where the needs of the whole company are nominally put ahead of any one individual, and so on. A workplace is not normally a democracy.

In effect, a social unit can form a building-block of a society – this equates with social order (analogous to urban order), whether or not there is any societal 'design' (analogous to city design). So, how might social units be related to the urban units of Chapter 3?

Social and spatial structures

The form and internal structure of buildings will tend to reflect their social organisation. Here, we now shift from the perspective of a hut for a lone individual in a state of nature, to one where a building is housing a social unit. As Alexander and colleagues assert in *A Pattern Langauge*: 'Structure follows social spaces'; and 'A building is a visible, concrete manifestation of a social group or social institution.' This social aspect will influence size, form and structure of rooms, buildings and settlements.[17]

Room size, as stated earlier, will relate to the number of people using a room at any time. This number will depend on social units and relationships. For example, in a family dwelling, there is typically at least one room big enough to accommodate – comfortably or otherwise – the whole family at a time (even if it is but a single room).[18]

Building size will be influenced by size of rooms, and by the number of types of room. A family home will contain enough rooms, of the right type and size, to house a family engaged in the requisite range of domestic activities. The overall building size will then depend on how many are in the family, cohabiting at any one time.

A building for different types of people implies different types of room. At first we might imagine that 'Adam', having first built himself a primitive single-room hut, could then expand it into a house with a kitchen, bathroom, bedroom, and so on. However, this scenario begs the question as to why 'Adam' would need all these different kinds of room in the first place. Why would a lone male – whether a first human in a state of nature, or a lone hunter-gatherer – bother with a separate kitchen, when he can just bring home his food and eat it in bed? The prerogative to eat separately from sleeping is surely a result of being part of a social context, where one doesn't sleep with everyone one eats with.[19]

Compared with a primitive hut – a nominal single-room enclosure, for a single person – a building to house a social group or unit is therefore likely to require bigger rooms, more rooms and more *types* of room. Building design therefore requires taking account of how these rooms are organised in relation to each other, differentiated by different functions and different social associations. This is noted, for example, with regard to domestic dwellings, as Julienne Hanson points out in *Decoding Homes and Homes*:

> Homes may reflect many differences between cultural categories, including greater divisions between men and women, power relations between hosts and guests, patrons and clients or householders and servants, generational differences between adults and children, differences in how people and household objects or domestic animals are accommodated in the home, lifestyle differences between the home as a locus for family life or as a place of work and so on.[20]

Internal structuring can help minimise socially aggravated nuisances – in other words, noises, possibly smells, and so on, that arise directly as a result of occupying space in close proximity, within the same building. So, for example, cooking smells isolated by having a separate kitchen; partition between living room and study, to keep noise at bay; and privacy (of different kinds) for the bathroom and bedroom.[21]

Julienne Hanson describes a series of cases where increased social complexity in dwellings produces 'increased segmentation and partitioning' within the home; different domestic space arrangements relating to different kinds of family structure; or in the case of a country house, reflecting social differentiation between gentry and servants. In the last case, the country house is, of course, both a dwelling and a workplace – and might include separate areas and even separate circulation routes (such as stairways) for the different kinds of people.[22]

This structuring according to social role also applies outside the domestic setting. For example, the form of the Greek amphitheatre relates to the relationship between performers and audience; a parliament building may be organised spatially to reflect the binary distinction between government and opposition. Consider also a courtroom, where there may be separate entrances and division of space for the judge; the jury; the accused; the court staff; the public; witnesses, and so on.[23]

The internal structure of buildings, then, is strongly related to the social organisation and social units they contain. So far we have seen the correspondence between increasing size and complexity of social units and increasing size and complexity of buildings. But this increase does not go on indefinitely. Instead, we tend to see another kind of social container at the upper scale: cities and other kinds of settlements.

CITIES

The city, as the largest and most complex human construction, could be regarded as the signature artefact of the species, like the web of a spider, or the hive of a bee. The city is also inextricable from the human's status as social – and indeed political – animal; cities are strongly associated with citizenship and civilisation. The emergence of cities and the emergence of modern complex societies seems to have gone hand in hand. It almost goes without saying that the urban order of cities, their physical form and layout, reflects their people, their social organisation, their way of life. With hindsight, it seems only natural that, having invented buildings and architecture, humanity should graduate to the larger scale, and master the art of city planning and design.[24]

And yet, there is perhaps a question here, that normally goes without asking, as to why we have settlements like cities, villages and towns to house our urban populations in the first place. That is, why do we not just see buildings get indefinitely larger and larger, so that we have city-scale populations living in mega-sized buildings – like the 'skyscrapers' of social insects, housing thousands of individuals – growing inexorably upwards and outwards like ever-expanding Towers of Babel?

Let us consider a variety of different reasons for why we tend to have cities (rather than city-sized buildings), before going on to focus on the social logic of cities, as social containers.

On growth and form

Let us briefly consider some reasons why buildings, as they grow in size, don't just go on growing to become city-sized or society-sized constructions, as might be whimsically portrayed in the cartoon in Figure 4.6.

First, there are technical factors to do with the building itself. From an engineering point of view, it is relatively more difficult to build larger

4.6 • Why don't we see city-sized buildings?

buildings, especially in the sense of vertically upwards (recall the horizontality of cities, discussed in the last chapter). Building a monolithic city-building may also be discouraged for fire safety reasons, or due to vulnerability to attack.

Secondly, it may be disproportionately costly to build large buildings – this relates to the first point. It may also be considered an expensive luxury to pay to enclose circulation spaces that could otherwise be had for free if they were simply exterior voids.

Thirdly, and partly contributing to the first two reasons, there are factors relating to the organisation of the construction. A city-sized building would imply the need for a substantial sum of collective will, forethought and coordination.

Fourthly, there may be reasons concerning internal circulation: vertical circulation between storeys not only means more effort for the inhabitants, but becomes positively problematic for large animals such as horses, and vehicles. Historically, then, there have been good reasons for keeping settlements on the level.

Fifthly, there are environmental factors. As buildings get larger, their interiors lack natural light and fresh air. This is not an absolute constraint on building size, but becomes one of configuration. As Philip Steadman points out:

> the forms of day-lit and naturally ventilated buildings must, as they grow, become flattened and attenuated into blocks that are made progressively longer, or progressively taller, or both longer and taller at once. Alternatively their forms may become more convoluted, changing perhaps from simple parallelepipeds into forms with branching wings or enclosed courtyards.[25]

There is a parallel here with the changes in the form of organisms, as they alter in size. As Philip Steadman says:

> larger animals have different forms from smaller ones, in part precisely so that surface area can keep pace with volume and body mass. The stomach and gut are lengthened and looped back and forth, again to increase their surface area.

This echoes the way that the urban fabric is typically crinkled or crenellated into punctured blocks or tentacled terraces – rather than a city being a large monolith like a mammoth building.[26]

(a)

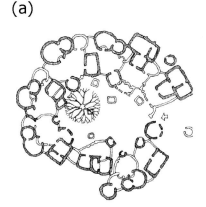

(b)

(c)

4.7 • Different urban units and structures reflecting different social units and structures: (a) House; (b) Compound; (c) Village.

Having said all that, even if large buildings were technically and economically feasible, organisationally simple, and adapted for vertical circulation and environmental conditioning, there are, finally, social factors why we might not see cities as coherent integrated 'unities'. These relate to the way that a society is typically not a single homogeneous mass of people, nor a rigidly organised single large social unit, but consists of different kinds of people and different social units, that operate often independently, even if ultimately interdependently. It is these social factors that are the principal focus for discussion here.

Let us look at the social reasons for why we find settlements and cities structured the way they are – as arrays of buildings – and not structured like large buildings subdivided into discrete rooms.

Large complex buildings

Large complex buildings, or building complexes, or compounds can be regarded as intermediate forms between individual buildings and settlements (Figure 4.7). As such, they can give an insight into relationships between social units and urban units.

In *The Social Logic of Space*, Bill Hillier and Julienne Hanson give examples of building compounds which could almost be said to be transitional, in size, form and structure, between being buildings and settlements. For example, an Ashanti 'Palace' houses an extended family, its building-like character depending on everyone fitting into the allotted hierarchy. It is also partly urban in its morphology, which could suggest it is, figuratively speaking, straining to break out into being a settlement. In the case of the Tallensi tribe of Africa, the compound has no streets. It is a cluster form, not a linear (street-like) form. It is more like a house (with a single entrance) than a neighbourhood or street. The same could be said of the case of a Mongolian yurt, which looks almost like a diagram of an idealised circular settlement, with its subdivision into different 'land uses' (Figure 4.8).[27]

The size of such a dwelling unit is partly to do with the size and the structure of an extended family. Even a large extended family still has only a few generational layers at any one time, and only a limited number of offspring per generation. Some Native American societies have lived in longhouses (in some cases over 100 metres long) that accommodated the whole extended family.[28]

If humans routinely had families of a hundred or more offspring, then dwelling types could be expected to be significantly different from the conventional family house. This is not a completely idle speculation; we

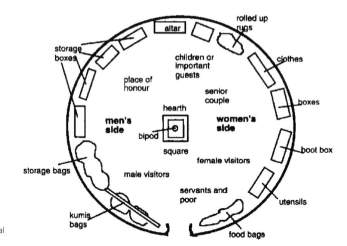

4.8 • Mongolian Yurt: 'land uses' within a communal building.

can see the potential consequences with reference to other species. For example, a beehive houses a whole 'family' – all offspring of the queen. In other words, if humans had families of hundreds of members, then settlements might be more hive-like – contained in one building, for a start. Such a hypothetical building would need to be adapted for humans' environmental preferences – for light and air, for example – so a thin floorplan building would do the trick. A tower block might do nicely – Le Corbusier's Unité d'Habitation, perhaps?[29]

A city is not a hive

Le Corbusier liked to think that a city apartment should be designed to provide the comfort and modern conveniences of an ocean liner. It could even be serviced in a way that would liberate its occupants from household drudgery. In realising the image of the ocean liner, the Unité d'Habitation perhaps connotes the freedom of being at sea while providing the convenience of a hotel (Figure 4.9).[30]

However, an ocean liner – besides, obviously, being a ship – is not like a city or even an apartment block because of its social-political structure. This is very rigid, with clear demarcation lines between passengers and crew, and what they can and cannot do, and where they may or may not go. A ship, in short, is not a democracy. So a city's structure is – normally – quite different from a ship's. It is not just a matter of crew versus passengers, but communal areas (such as for eating), the absence of 'workplaces' for the citizens, the small berths (cf. bedrooms) being cells connecting directly to the

4.9 • (a) Ship as 'floating city'; (b) Unité arrives at Nantes.

communal corridor (cells that might favour singles or couples, who could afford room service and no need to cook, and eat in bed, and so on). Even in an apartment block, residents are not 'passengers' who have to obey the orders of a captain or crew.

In effect, city design is inclined towards the autocratic, paternalistic or 'nanny state' design, where the citizens are children and the ruling elite are the parents in control. The attempt to 'design' a city – as a unit – only works if the citizens are well behaved like children, knowing their place and doing what they are expected to.[31]

To live in a city – or Unité – that was a single building like a large hive, then we might expect a rigid social structure for it to work, where the individuals are subordinated to the whole. But a human society is – contrary to the cartoon in Figure 4.6 – not like a beehive in that it does not form a single social unit. Members of society may perform roles not determined by birth; those roles can change. People make their own decisions about where to live, and so on. In contrast, a bee colony, with its strict gender roles, has been described as an 'ovarian police state'.[32]

So, the form of a settlement – an array of buildings housing individual social units – can be seen as a reflection of the structure of society: that is, not one single social unit like a big family or big workplace.

The spatial order of cities

In Chapter 3, it was suggested that there are local systematic relationships between buildings, plots and routes, but overall city form does not possess systematic order so much as characteristic order. That is, overall city form tends to have certain very general aspects – such as a distinction between core and periphery – but these are not clear-cut units, and are not arranged systematically in this way. For example, although there may often be a civic zone next to the retail core, one would not say this applied 'as a rule'.

And when we turn to the social structure, we can find a roughly parallel story. That is, we have systematic 'local' relationships between parent and child, wife and husband, teacher and pupil, boss and employee, staff member and customer, judge and defendant. But when we look at a whole city – the city community or citizenry – we do not normally see groups organised in a systematic way as units. That is, we do not systematically have a class or bloc of gentry, servants, artisans, clergy, cyclists, and so on, each forming social *units*, that need to be housed in appropriate urban units.

For example, a city may be composed of business owners, managers, employees, and others. But the city does not have discrete quarters for those, or rights of access to different areas according to status. Unlike a building, which may have separate corridors for employees, and separate rooms accessible only by the management, the city does not have separate circulation systems for different types of person – city employee, city resident, visitor, and so on. There are no 'staff only' signs at the urban level.

Instead, we may tend to see areas *roughly* identifiable with more affluent people, or people of a certain ethnicity. But these relationships are – in terms of Chapter 3 – indicative of characteristic order, not systematic order. We expect things to be a bit mixed up, not segregated into homogeneous zones. That is to say, people tend to be free to locate themselves and their organisations where they wish to. These are basically according to individual requirements, but without reference to relations between social groups as wholes. Indeed, it is only in exceptional, often dysfunctional cases – such as ghettos, or foreigners' quarters – that whole social groups live in distinct bounded enclaves.[33]

This relates directly to the identification of 'communities' or 'neighbourhoods', and the use of a neighbourhood (in a physical sense) as a building-block of urban form. Let us recall the Forshaw-Abercrombie plan of London, and the classic image showing London 'communities' (Figure 2.14). The image is deliberately a caricature, but nevertheless reflects the intention to plan using this conception of the 'communities':

> The proposal is to emphasise the identity of the existing communities, to increase their degree of segregation, and where necessary to reorganise them as separate and definite entities.[34]

Note how, almost as if by sleight of hand, within one sentence the Modernist rhetoric slides from acknowledging the existence of identifiable

(a)

(b)

(c)

4.10 • Streets as public spaces, social places, cultural loci, political arenas, 'outdoor rooms': (a) Pavement café, Richmond; (b) Commerce and sightseeing, Chinatown, Shanghai; (c) Pro-Soviet demonstrators in Red Square, Moscow, 2002.

communities, to presuming licence to 'reorganise' them as separate entities. But since when did residents ever call for distinctive segregation? Since when did the residents of Kensington clamour to be separated from those of Bayswater? Here, the 'rectified' order seems to become the objective, rather than a means to an end.[35]

In other words, this diagram (Figure 2.14) begs the question as to whether 'communities' or neighbourhoods – and never mind simplified representations of them – are legitimate building-blocks for the future design or reorganisational design of cities.

In this sense a city is *not* like a building full of rooms, where a district or neighbourhood is equivalent to a room (Chapter 3). That is, there is no *systematic* distinction at the settlement scale. For example, while an hotel might contain a room operating as a restaurant, and another as a shop, we tend not to see settlements with a whole homogeneous restaurant quarter here, and homogeneous shop district there. Rather, cities tend to be 'permeable', with all sorts of people all over the place. It is only at the level of the individual private plot that the barriers go up, and a kind of social filtering takes place; and generally only within buildings that systematic allocation of space takes place, where relations between different people of different types really bites.

A city, then, is not a big building. But neither is it a cluster of separate compounds each housing village-sized social units, like loose scatters of tents, individual farmsteads or isolated tribal compounds on a plain; or, for that matter, a scatter of Corbusian Unités – or beehives – set in a garden-like landscape. Rather, a city is a large array of buildings housing different kinds of social units, that are simultaneously separated and joined by the system of public streets. This system of public street space is not just a 'void' separating different urban units (Chapter 3), but must be seen as an urban unit in its own right, part of the *social* fabric of cities. In a sense, we need streets – as much as buildings – to explain the social logic of cities.

THE STREETS

Urban planners and designers, human geographers, sociologists and anthropologists are used to appreciating the social aspect of streets: in their role as 'people places' and 'public spaces'; as settings for political expression and struggle, and loci of cultural identity. This stance is often a conscious rejection of a common twentieth-century view, traditionally attributed variously to traffic engineers, municipal authorities, and the motoring public, that 'streets are for traffic'. As we saw in Chapters 1 and 2, the renaissance of the street is at the heart of contemporary urbanism and the 'neo-traditional counter-revolution'. Certainly, there is a rich diversity of street life to study, the street as 'land use', the street as 'communications artefact', or 'locus of significa-tion', the street as a cultural context, as an ecology or environment. All these can conveniently be summed up as the premise that a street is an 'outdoor room' (Figure 4.10).[36]

To treat the street as an 'outdoor room' is fine. But, in this chapter, we have been asking why we have rooms in the first place. We have explored how and why rooms relate to buildings; now we explore how streets – as 'outdoor rooms' or otherwise – relate to buildings, and to cities; indeed how do they relate *between* buildings and cities?[37]

The street is not just 'given' as a contiguous publicly accessible space that links different social places, but is part of the social fabric of cities. Even more strongly, it is arguably this role as part of the social fabric that helps make cities what they are, in the first place.

As we saw in Chapter 3, cities have an intricate and complex urban order that is to do with how buildings relate to plots and routes, and how public and private spaces link up in an 'archipelago' structure. This can be seen as not just a physical structure, but is a 'socially constructed' one. What might be the reasons behind this spatial order?

Let us now take a closer look at how social topologies and spatial topolo-gies are related, how buildings relate to the public space of streets – and hence the systematic order of 'street syntax' that we saw in Chapter 3. As we shall see, the key to this is to do with social hierarchies, and inclusive and exclusive social groupings that translate into inclusive and exclusive spaces.

Social hierarchies

Within a social context, we may identify hierarchies to do with power rela-tions, for example, between people or social units. In some social groups, each individual may be considered as nominal or actual equal. For example, each voter in an electorate or each pupil in a school is nominally equal. But, especially within social units viewed as a whole, there may be asymmetries, and those asymmetries may imply definite hierarchies, for example between the government and governed, teachers and taught, and so on (Figure 4.11).

In any particular circumstance, the hierarchical ordering may be related to the granting or withholding of certain rights and privileges, and related to the extent to which people are excluded from certain groups, activities or locations. As such this may be purely a non-physical state – such as a subset of a group of friends between whom certain information circulates to

Religious hierarchy
1. Deity or deities, angels, immortal spirits
2. Religious officials
3. Ordinary believers
4. Visiting non-believers
5. Animals, being with no soul

Legal rights hierarchy
1. Adult
2. Teenager
3. Incapacitated adult (prisoner, patient)
4. Child
5. Non-persons (non-living persons, unborn, human body parts, artificial intelligences, animals)

Political hierarchy
1. Political leadership
2. Elected representatives (or party members)
3. Ordinary citizens
4. Legal immigrants and visitors
5. 'Unsolicited'

Shop, café, hotel
1. Management
2. Ordinary staff
3. Customers
4. Bona fide visitors
5. 'Unsolicited'

Workplace
1. Management
2. Employees
3. Visitors – clients, suppliers, etc.
4. Other visitors
5. 'Unsolicited'

Hospital
1. Management
2. Staff
3. Patients
4. Visitors
5. 'Unsolicited'

University
1. Management
2. Ordinary staff
3. Students
4. Visitors
5. 'Unsolicited'

4.11 • Examples of socially distinguished hierarchies. In each case, the higher are more exclusive with more rights. In each case, 'unsolicited' will often imply downright unwelcome visitors: beggars, spies, competitors, outsiders preying on customers, parasites, thieves, people undertaking unauthorised business, illegal immigrants, unaccompanied animals, and so on.

the exclusion of others. However, these may also imply spatial topological relationships.

Spatial topologies

Social organisation and hierarchy are a reflection of distinctions and asymmetries between different people and social groups. These are in turn converted into spatial topological distinctions that may be manifested in physical entities such as partitions, connections, nesting of enclosures.

Figure 4.12 shows some examples of possible spatial topologies corresponding to the social topologies. As soon as these topologies are expressed as Venn diagrams (especially rectangular Venn diagrams) the topologies (and ultimately geometries) of actual physical buildings and spaces seems to suggest themselves.

In the first case there are two mutually exclusive domains (two domains with no social unit in common), hence mutually inaccessible domains. This could represent the partition between sacred and profane areas, male-only and female-only areas, and so on. This is like a 'jigsaw'; in this case, one with two pieces (Figure 4.12a).

However in the second case, the all-encompassing public space is, crucially, all-inclusive. This creates an 'archipelago' (Figure 4.12b). This is crucial for the structure to function: it means that, if A represents a private

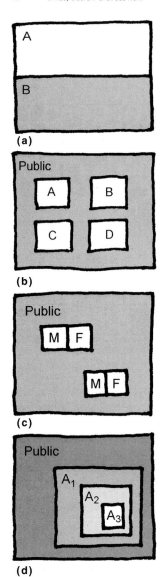

(a)

(b)

(c)

(d)

4.12 • Socially constructed topologies: (a) Single subdivision or partition between mutually exclusive realms; (b) Single contiguous public space, within which private spaces A–D are located; (c) Two nested private spaces partitioned into two mutually exclusive sub-domains, M and F (male and female); (d) Successive enclosures reflecting increasing exclusivity from A_3 to A_1. This is identifiable with a public–private spectrum.

house and B represents a 'public house' (or other public building), then a member of the public (also known as a 'private individual') may happily pass from A to B, since the intervening space is accessible to 'anyone and every-one'. If this intervening space had represented 'public building staff only' then the territory would be impassable to the ordinary member of the public.[38]

In Figure 4.12 (c) we see nested areas further subdivided or partitioned into mutually exclusive domains (male and female toilets, for example). Again, the system works because all areas accessible to males are contiguous and all areas accessible to females are contiguous.

Finally, we have a nested hierarchy of areas – subsets within subsets (Figure 4.12d). This is asymmetric; and this is where a hierarchy of insiders and outsiders really bites. The hierarchy could relate to any of the hierarchies referred to previously (Figure 4.11). For example, a religious hierarchy can translate into the topology of a religious *building*, with most sacred space reserved for (representation of) the deity (A_1), then an area for religious officials (A_2), then an area for the ordinary worshippers (A_3). This area may exclude non-worshippers, non-believers, and other 'outsiders'. Or, a shop might have private offices of the management (A_1), areas for ordinary employees (staff only) (A_2), and customers (A_3).

Note that 'deepest' spaces tend to be the most privileged and exclusive locations – a bit like the Forbidden City of Beijing, perhaps. But this is also seen in everyday cases, such as religious or university precincts (Figure 4.13).[39]

In fact, we can see that this gradient – of enclosed exclusivity (for those 'included') and residual inclusivity (for those 'excluded') – is, in effect, what we recognise as the familiar public–private gradient.

Public and private

There are various subtle complexities of interpretation of privacy, and not a single simple linear public–private gradient. A lot comes down to who is allowed to do what, with – or in proximity to – whom.[40] The repeated action of local specialisation and control of space, reserving certain areas for use by certain groups, gives rise to an overall pattern of distinction between public and private, a key socially constructed distinction that manifests itself across the urban environment. It is related to where strangers mix; privacy and intimacy; public demonstration; what may be done where. Public space implies space where anyone may go, where strangers are free to meet and mix, and interact. They still do so, nevertheless, according to social conventions.[41]

(a)

(b)

(c)

(d)

4.13 • Private spaces used by the public; hierarchical nesting of more exclusive spaces: (a) Political: Forbidden City, Beijing; (b) Religious: Hindu temple complex, London; (c) Institutional: University College London; (d) Commercial: Venus Fort shopping mall, Tokyo. This 'public' space is iniside a building (complete with artificial sky).

Private space is in some way controlled: one may only go there if explicitly or implicitly invited, and once there behave according to rules and conventions that are more particular than those for public space. Conversely, once inside, one may do private things considered unacceptable in public.

In general, public places are the most inclusive places – anyone can go there, including all sorts of 'outsiders' and 'undesirables'.[42] Different parts of cities may be divided off for specialist or private use only. Usually, when one steps from public to private space, one undergoes a subtle change in status. One either becomes identified as an 'insider': with more privileges, relative to outsiders, when inside, this being a more advantageous situation than when outside. Or one becomes an 'outsider': with fewer privileges, relative to insiders, when inside; this being a less advantageous situation than when outside. The gradient means often you only go into the more privileged, exclusive space when invited, whereas an insider can invite themselves outside any time. A worker, in going to the workplace, agrees to be controlled by management, in return for the privileges of being an employee, and more of an 'insider' than the general public.

It hardly needs saying that Figure 4.12 interpreted as two-dimensional floor plans can easily be converted into three-dimensional built forms. Enclosure can be marked by vertical barriers around the area to be enclosed – fences, walls, and so on – hence creating an inside and an outside. Alternatively a similar effect could be achieved by a raised platform or podium.[43]

An important point here is that public–private can be seen to arise from social distinctions that need not have physical expression in the built infrastructure. This suggests that it is not the volumetric enclosure that determines the public–private divide, but the other way around. While external circulation space is generally public, this is effectively a consequence of certain private areas being cordoned off for specific uses, and the leftover space being used for circulation. The result is the archipelago effect, where a 'sea' of public streets joins – or separates – the 'islands' of private space (Figure 4.14). This equates with the normal order of city structure – privately enclosed buildings fronting public streets.

Note that this links back to Chapter 3 as explaining the 'meaning' of public and private space, which was then simply noted as being an observable distinction – associated with public circulation routes and spaces, linking private plots and buildings. In other words, the visible regularities – the urban order – observed in Chapter 3 may be related to invisible relationships between people.

This public–private distinction and urban structuring by streets is deeply ingrained in our urban fabrics. It was seen, for example, five thousand years

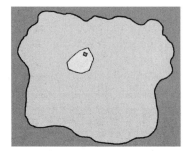

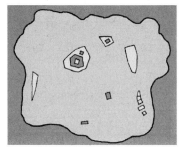

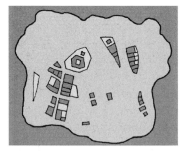

4.14 • Urban development can be seen as successive subdivision of the surface of the Earth, into different land use units. The street network can be seen as a kind of residual public commons – or space left over after privatisation of land.

ago in the case of Mohenjo-Daro (recall Figure 4.1a)[44] – over and above the familiarity of the shapes and sizes and interior structure of the buildings. This public–private distinction is perhaps best seen as a spectrum rather than as a polarisation: the distinction between rooms, buildings and settlements is not necessarily an inevitable difference in kind (like between, say, the solid structure of a building and the void of circulation space), but a matter of degree. The way the public–private spectrum connects the insides and outsides of buildings is seen in the cellular urban structures of Figure 4.1.

Figure 4.15 shows the classic case of Nolli's plan of Rome, depicting something half-way between a public street system and the cellular urban structure that includes building interiors already seen earlier in the cases (Figure 4.1). Nolli's plan shows the interiors of (only) public buildings. This graphically demonstrates how the more public space of the interiors of public buildings merges seamlessly with the public space of the streets; and also, how a public building is intermediate between a private building and public street.

In effect, just as the built fabric of cities, that encloses rooms and buildings, filters the environment, the spatial structure of public and private, sometimes enforced by barriers, gates, walls, or invisible boundaries, acts as a *social* filter on what aspects of the external social environment are allowed in and which are kept out. Just as the external physical environment is a single contiguous space off of which interior environments are enclosed, the social space of streets is the single contiguous public space off of which private spaces are carved.

The way that cities are laid out with public streets and private plots and buildings allows the right mix of surveillance, anonymity, personal control of own space, and so on, that make this structure suitable for accommodating people who do not know each other. Basically, it allows a city to exist as a container for strangers. As Joel Kotkin has remarked, the earliest city dwellers 'found themselves confronting vastly different problems from those faced in prehistoric nomadic communities and agricultural villages. Urbanites had to learn how to coexist and interact with strangers from outside their clan or tribe'.[45]

In this sense, the public–private filtering of the building–plot–street system enables settlements (as containers of strangers) to exist – they enable large agglomeration of humans to coexist in a limited area. This is why streets are not merely voids between blocks of buildings, but must be seen as integral to the concept and fabric of a city. Just as the arrangement of a supermarket in 'public' aisles is not just about physical circulation, but is inextricable from the very concept of a supermarket, the arrangement of

4.15 • Nolli's plan of Rome.

cities in streets is not just about physical circulation, but is inextricable from the very concept of a city.

CONCLUSIONS

This chapter sought to explore the human and social reasons behind the physical urban order and units examined in Chapter 3. In the course of the chapter, we have seen in particular how social considerations give rise to the basic units of the urban built environment: why we have rooms, buildings, streets and settlements. We have seen how the form, size and internal structure of a building is related to its social structure. Similarly, the reasons cities exist and have the structure they do are also significantly to do with social structure: we do not see city-sized buildings, to a significant extent, because the population is not a unified social unit, like one big family or one big workplace. Rather, a city is a heterogeneous mix of different kinds of people – a container of strangers – and this works by a kind of social filtering, that is realised through the street system of public circulation spaces and private plots and buildings.

In short, buildings and cities are different kinds of social container, reflecting their differences in social structure. A city is not just a big building, but is articulated into different buildings, mediated by a social fabric of public streets. A building is an environmental container and filter; the building–plot–street system is both a social container and a social filter.

Overall, these findings have two significant implications for understanding the structure of cities: the first relating to urban ordering, and the second to city design.

First, it reinforces the importance of public streets as being not voids, but as integral to the notion of a city, a kind of mortar binding between social units. Without this system of public spaces, a city would not be a city. Moreover, it is the systematic relationship between social units housed in private buildings and the exterior public realm that gives rise to the 'archipelago' structure of public streets and private plots, the systematic order of 'street syntax', demonstrated in Chapter 3. This is the basic kind of urban ordering found even in 'unplanned' cities.

This intricate urban order has been around for thousands of years, perhaps as long as there have been cities with streets. It is this order that was to be swept away by the Corbusian revolution (Chapter 2). In proclaiming the 'death of the street', Le Corbusier was not merely messing with the traffic, but was overturning millennia of *social* order.

This hasty upheaval must be seen as one of the reasons why Modern planned environments could turn out worse than more traditional ones that have stood the test of time: while a new technology (whether motorway, piloti or tower block) could be introduced overnight, it takes time for social organisation to adapt (if indeed it is inclined to adapt), hence the problem with Le Corbusier's Unités requiring an upheaval or reversal of personal life for them to work. This partly explains why the new spatial arrangements appear, in the words of Hillier and Hanson, 'at best, as no improvement and, at worst, as socially damaging'.[46]

The second significant implication concerns the rationale for city design. From Chapter 2, it was suggested that city design was based on the premise that the city is a finite designable object, a whole with supporting subcomponents. But the argument of this chapter has cast doubt on the city being a cohesive whole unit, in the way a building is. For example, a city or neighbourhood typically does not correspond with a social unit. While a city or neighbourhood may have an overall public authority, this does not direct where people live or what people do when, in the way that a head of a household or workplace controls the activities of members of household or workplace. Hence, cities and neighbourhoods typically do not have the internal structure of buildings. As noted in Chapter 3, a city is not 'divided into' buildings in the way a building is 'divided into' rooms (and only in planned cases might cities be said to be 'divided into' neighbourhoods, and even then, normally this means only in a superficial physical sense, and not in the sense of social units like buildings).

This implies that we need to have a closer scrutiny of the city as a whole, and how the city structure has been interpreted, in terms of how the parts should fit with the whole, and the nature of the whole city as an object of city design. To address this, we need to take a closer look at the kind of thing a city is.

Notes

1   Aristotle (1992: 58). This version of Aristotle's famous phrase is slightly awkward, but somehow more subtle and satisfying for purposes here, in combining the more biological or ecological interpretation 'Man is an animal that lives in cities' (Hacking, 1983: 132) and the more socio-political interpretation: 'Man is a political creature.' We can also infer the latent connections between city, political organisation, organism and environment.

2   Morris (1994: 33); Kenoyer (2005: 29) refers *inter alia* to major avenues having 'central dividers that may have regulated two-way bullock cart traffic'; Mumford (1961: 62).

3   Kostof (1992: 8). 'As one geographer put it, "Few social values and actions are so abstract that they fail to be reflected in material forms" (Kostof, 1991: 25).

4   'The ultimate adaptation to the physical environment is control of the environment' (Seeley and Heinrich, cited in Camazine *et al.*, 2001: 285). A house can be regarded as a defence against predation (Vermeij, 2004: 64). Homes, along with prey traps and communication devices, form the three predominant kinds of animal-built structure. 'Homes . . . vary greatly from a simple protective wall to a *complex differentiated residence*' [emphasis added] Hansell (2005: 1); see also Hansell (2007), Gould and Gould (2007).

5   Joseph Rykwert infers the existence of wine, hence cups and hence sideboards and ultimately a house in Eden, while acknowledging that a house is not expressly referred to in Genesis (Rykwert, 1981: 13).

6   Vitruvius, also Alberti, Blondel, Filarete, Laugier, and others: see *Architectural Theory* (Biermann, 2003: 31; Freigang, 2003a: 261, 2003b; Gronert, 2003: 187; Ruhl, 2003: 448; Zimmer, 2003: 482). See Rykwert (1981) for detailed scrutiny of

Adam and his hut. Rykwert's book includes an image of Adam getting wet in the 'first rain'.

7   This might also be noted for whole cities – recall Vitruvius' ideal city planned to control the winds (Chapter 2; Morris, 1994: 22–23). Some of these objectives may be in conflict. Underground dwellings have peace, quiet and temperate climate (Golany and Ojima, 1996), but may lack natural light and ventilation.

8   After Panerai *et al.* (2004: 23).

9   Vitruvius: Zimmer (2003: 482). Leonardo: Nicholl (2005: 246–247). Modulor: Le Corbusier (1951).

10 The capsule is interesting as: (1) minimalist 'human container'; (2) reminds one of a 'beehive'; (3) has a vertical aspect to it (i.e. the capsules are stacked up on top of each other, to create a 'façade' of cell openings, but not really with a floor plan as such. A capsule hotel in a Japanese city is geared to catering for *sararimen* – a bit like a 'hive' for male 'worker bees' – plus the occasional anthropological or architectural tourist.

11 As various architectural writers note from time to time, humans don't fly. 'Human architecture would no doubt be different if we could fly freely in three dimensions. Because we walk and are held down by gravity, our lives mainly take place on flat surfaces, and architecture is concerned with the planning of floors' (Unwin, 1997: 149); see also Hanson (1998: 54; 271).

12 So architecture is part art, part interior–landscape–architecture, part interior–ecosystem–engineering, part urban design. See Hillier (1996) on discussion of architecture in contradistinction to building. Hansell (2005) refers to intra-specific communication as one of the three main types of structure built by animals.

13 Hobbes (1651). Diamond (1998) stresses that this is a hypothetical state.

14 Macpherson (1968). And, as Dr Johnson pointed out to Boswell, in addition to their presumed cultural poverty, 'The savages have no bodily advantages beyond those of civilised men'. Quoted in Rykwert (1981: 75).

15 Social contract: see also, for example, Dennett (1996: 454); Diamond (1998: 283); Fernández-Armesto (2000). The advantages of social over solitary living are, of course, exploited not only by humans, but also by ants, bees, termites, thrips, aphids, dogs, and naked mole rats (Vermeij, 2004: 20).

16 Julienne Hanson draws attention to 'governance' within a household: the link between the head of a household, or authority in domestic setting, paralleling a ruler's relationship with his or her subjects (1998: 74).

17 Alexander *et al.* (1977: 940–945, 469). It is interesting that these two statements come at the two pivotal points separating the three major divisions of *A Pattern Language* (corresponding to the book's subtitle: *Towns. Buildings. Construction*). The associated patterns each represent the 'bottleneck through which all languages pass' (1977: 469, 945). 'Social geometry conditions the sizes and the layout of the spaces' (Unwin, 1997: 117).

18 For examples of families living in a single room – such as the 'single end' tenement flat – see Reed (1999c: 114).

19 However, a home for a single individual who is 'socialised' or living within the context of a society will tend to reflect the norms of that society, and hence differ from the kind of home for a single individual in a state of nature. Hence a modern bachelor in a bedsit, or capsule hotel guest, may have separate kitchen and dining areas, even if they still end up eating in bed.

20 Hanson (1998: 286).

21 Hanson (1998: 145).

22 Hanson (1998: 48; 54; 74).

23 Unwin (1997: 115, 129); Hillier (1996). Hillier (1996) also discusses educational establishments, hospitals, newspaper offices.

24 If singling out a construction like a city – rather than things more social, cultural or moral – as the achievements of humanity, this is doing no more or less than judging ourselves as we judge spiders and bees. On cities being the largest, most complex human constructions: see Hillier (1996). On matters of cities or physical organisation reflecting their social organisation, in early urban settlements, see, for example, Stone and Zemansky (2005: 62); settlements as a product of successive social choices: Pumain (2004: 231); 'Townscape . . . is the true reflection of the way of living and the attitude to life of its inhabitants' (Kriesis, cited in Morris, 1994: 35).

25 Steadman (2005: 11).

26 Another strategy is to have a large, open, exposed interface. Sports stadia, for example, are typically not fully enclosed, but spectators are exposed to light and air (and sometimes rain). See also Steadman (1979). An exceptional form would be that of the Walled City of Kowloon (Girard and Lambot, 1999) which was subjected to a very dark interior.

27 Hillier and Hanson (1984: 243). The yurt's interior structure is said to reflect an image of the global structure of society, or the structure of the cosmos (Hanson, 1998: 12).

28 Fernández-Armesto (2000: 153).

29 Ramírez suggests that Le Corbusier was inspired by beehives (Ramírez, 2000). Le Corbusier (1947a). The society-in-a-building also may be related to Fourier's 'Phalanstere' (Vidler, 1968: 235; Houghton-Evans, 1975; Vidler, 1978: 51; Hillier and Hanson, 1984: 266). The Hutterite community of Canada acts in some ways like a bee colony, promoting communal, selfless behaviour. The community – like a bee colony – grows to a certain size then splits and forms a new colony elsewhere (Dennett, 1996: 473). Social insects also have a division of labour, that has been expressly related to economic behaviour (Jones, 1999: 202; see also a quotation from Geddes, cited in Boardman, 1978: 65; and Vermeij, 2004).

30 In *La Ville Radieuse,* Le Corbusier shows a cross-section of an ocean liner, and asks 'Why should a city apartment house not attempt to provide us with the same comfort as a ship?' Le Corbusier ([1933] 1964: 39; 118). Servicing apartments like an ocean liner or hotel's 'room service' would mean having other people cook food for you, and clean for you. Hence Le Corbusier explicitly links the 'town-planning

revolution' to the 'art of housekeeping', heralding the 'Liberation of the Mistress of the House' – through modern technology allied to building design (Le Corbusier, 1947a: 72–74).

31   The sociologist Setsuko Hai has referred to 'the idea or consciousness of the house', where, in the Japanese context, 'asserting the hierarchy of the "house" had the effect of reinforcing the authority of parents, firm owners, military and political leaders, and, ultimately, the emperor'. This was as if the nation – and one could apply the same to a city – had 'one mind', or rather, as if a nation or city were a single social unit, a single decision-making authority (Kotkin, 2005: 101). See also Hanson (1998: 74).

32   City as united social and political entity: Benevolo (1980: 60, 72); ovarian police state: Hrdy (1999: 60).

33   In the past, cities were more strictly organised according to social hierarchies, where only people of certain types could access certain areas – such as the historic case of the 'Forbidden City' in Beijing, a city 'nested' within a city. Or, in some rigidly organised societies, we might have specific artisans' quarters and religious quarters, where people of a certain type are supposed to live and work. See also Benevolo (1980). For a stark illustration of enforced segregation of circulation routes, see Kostof (1992: 108).

34   Forshaw and Abercrombie (1943: 28).

35   In *The Napoleon of Notting Hill*, G. K. Chesterton imagines the separate localities of Notting Hill and Bayswater having separate identities so strong and politically charged that they end up with their own armies, fighting each other (Chesterton, [1904] 1996).

36   For references on streets as public spaces, see, for example, Anderson (ed.) (1978); Moudon (ed.) (1987); Fyfe (ed.) (1998); Engwicht (1999); Carmona *et al.* (2003); Jefferson *et al.* (eds) (2001); Marshall, (2005). Jacobs refers to the political and ceremonial roles of streets (1993: 3); Czarnowski refers to the street as a 'communications artefact' (1978: 207); Levitas refers to the street as a 'cultural artefact' (1978: 228).

37   Campbell and Cowan (2002).

38   The public and private domains are sometimes equated with the male and female spheres of activity (see, for example, Dench, 1998).

39   In some contexts, the same gradient of enclosure and exclusivity applies, but the sense of privileged is reversed, as with the detention of prisoners or segregation of communities in ghettos. For other discussions on this kind of inversion, 'inhabitant – visitor' relationships and other social topologies, see Hillier and Hanson (1984: 183, 184).

40   Julienne Hanson rejects a 'clearly expressed hierarchy', Hanson (1998: 117). See also Unwin (1997: 159) for examples of public, semi-public, semi-private and private. In effect there are different dimensions, that may override or overlap. For example, in a private house, bedroom and bathroom have different kinds of privacy applying to different people in different circumstances.

41 On the social use of public space, see for example, Rapoport (1977, 1987); Appleyard (1981); Moudon (ed.) (1987); Gehl (2001); Madanipour (1996); Fyfe (ed.) (1998), Hebbert (2005b). Kostof (1992: 194) refers to the struggle between public and private interests.

42 This includes animals. These are not just kept outside for physical reasons (large, unhygienic, harmful), but they are in a sense 'social outsiders'. Outside is 'their place' – except for some domesticated animals or pets.

43 As Barrie Shelton points out, this is the case in the Japanese tradition of stepping up from the 'common earth' when entering a building; and seen in the case of a temple as a raised platform, the sacred elevated above the profane. The Venn diagram is the same – and the purpose to distinguish 'inner private' and 'outer public' is the same but the physical means is different (Shelton, 1999: 28).

44 Kenoyer refers to the architecture and street layout being organised to segregate public and private areas (2005: 29).

45 Kotkin (2005: 158).

46 Hillier and Hanson (1984: 262).

5 THE KIND OF THING A CITY IS

Town and Country Planning seeks to proffer a guiding hand to the trend of natural evolution . . . The result . . . should be a social organism and a work of art.
Patrick Abercrombie, Town and Country Planning[1]

The price of metaphor is eternal vigilance.
Rosenblueth and Wiener[2]

A city may be conceptualised as a work of art, a product of technology, or something organic – or all three, like Salvador Dalí's Lobster Telephone (opening image). More than an intellectual curiosity, the question as to what kind of thing we think a city is will affect how – and if – we design or plan it. If we are to successfully plan or design a city as a whole, rather than just churning out lots of streets of houses, we need to get to grips with the nature of the complex, multi-faceted object that is the city. We know well enough modern theories for designing modern buildings and modern roads. But what about modern cities? What theories or paradigms guide us here?

A paradigm is an overarching frame of reference within which 'normal business' is conducted. For example, it is normal business to assume there are such things as nature, humanity and society, and not just lots of individual things and persons. Or, it is normal business within city planning to treat the city as an object or definite place that can and should be studied and planned.

The term paradigm is perhaps most closely associated with scientific understanding. In *The Structure of Scientific Revolutions*, Thomas Kuhn proposed that science advanced not in a steady, cumulative manner, but by means of a series of scientific 'revolutions' marking shifts between different

5.0 • Lobster Telephone (Salvador Dalí).

'paradigms'. A classic example of a paradigm shift is that of the Copernican Revolution, in which the heliocentric universe replaced the geocentric one. Another significant shift in understanding might be that from an organism-centred perspective to a gene-centred perspective on biology and evolution, as articulated by Richard Dawkins.[3]

A paradigm shift has three features of interest that distinguish it from other kinds of change or 'revolution'. First, the new paradigm may represent a new simplicity, whose recognition may be as much about getting rid of old theories, as generating new ones. (Copernicus' theory removed the need for epicycles and pericycles, which are now almost proverbial in their redundancy.)

Secondly, the new paradigm often 'clicks into place' so effortlessly that it seems counterintuitive to go back to the old way of thinking. (Once one has visualised the configuration of the solar system, it is hard to go back to imagining the Sun and planets going round the Earth.)

Thirdly, however ground-breaking the change in understanding, the paradigm shift does not necessarily alter the veracity of existing observations – only their interpretation – nor make life significantly different to the person in the street. (The post-Copernican sun still 'rises' and 'sets' as normal.)[4]

This chapter aims to explore 'the kind of thing a city is', to try to identify how different models for what the city is affect the way we design them. In doing so, it will come up against what are conventional paradigms and to what extent they may be challenged by new, emerging ones, coming from contemporary science.

In this chapter let us first look at conventional Metaphors and Models for understanding the city that have inspired ways of planning and designing them: the city as a work of art, the city as machine, and city as organic entity. Secondly, we shall consider the Emerging Perspectives of the city as a complex dynamic entity. This captures the sense of a city being organic, but not necessarily in the conventional interpretation of a city as an organism. Thirdly, we shall consider a 'new' perspective – The City as Ecosystem – in which we can recognise the complex dynamic *collective* entity. These perspectives will provide keys to understanding the kind of thing a city is, in ways that will advance our methods of planning or designing cities.

METAPHORS AND MODELS

In his book *The Evolution of Designs*, Philip Steadman draws attention to the ways in which organisms, mechanisms and works of applied art can be seen to be related to each other (Figure 5.1 a).[5] For example, a work of art can be inspired by or superficially reflect nature, or may be designed in a more

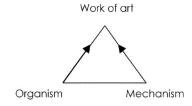

(a)

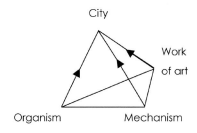

(b)

5.1 • Metaphors: (a) Work of art as an organism or mechanism (simplified, after Steadman); (b) City as work of art, organism or mechanism.

profound way to embody a variety of biological characteristics or principles. Or, a work of art may be inspired by machines or mechanisms, use mechanical metaphors, or literally embody machines or mechanisms in their physical fabric (in an artistic installation, for example).

While Dalí's chimerical creation combines representations of a lobster and a telephone, the 'Lobster Telephone' is nevertheless ultimately a work of art, and functions as such whether or not it works as a communication mechanism or crustacean.

The city, in turn, is sometimes treated as a mixed metaphor – part machine, part organism, and part work of art. But a city, while it may have partial aspects of machine, organism and work of art, must additionally – indeed essentially and primarily – function as a city. This, in effect, adds an extra dimension (Figure 5.1b), since a city may be considered in contra-distinction to works of art, as well as to organisms and mechanisms. Indeed, these correspond to three key metaphors that recur in the city planning and design thought: the city as a work of art, the city as a functional machine, and the city as an organic entity.[6]

These three metaphors seen in Figure 5.1(b) are significant as they go beyond wordplay or figures of speech for describing cities – unlike some other metaphors, like declaring that 'a city is a chimera' or 'a city is a palimpsest' – but convert into actual *models* for future design and planning. They are therefore worth exploring in more detail, as they provide models for packaging parts to create a coherent whole, and hence help explain thinking behind city design.[7]

The city as a work of art

A city, its plan or its whole fabric, may be considered a work of art, an artistic creation, an expressive object, diagram or symbol. The symbolism may be religious or cultural, or ultimately 'cosmic' in significance; in some cases the city plan is intended to reflect the wider order of the universe, such that the 'earthly city' mirrors the 'heavenly city' above.[8]

The form of Brasilia has been interpreted as symbolic of a bird in flight or crucifix. An early proposal for the New Town of Edinburgh was for the streets to be laid out in the shape of the Union flag, symbolising the political union of Scotland and England.[9]

In each case here, while the individual elements have to be functional in their own right (as streets and squares, for example), their overall configuration is arranged in a way to support the creation of a higher-order entity. This is typically to suit the desires of the city rulers who commission such urban-scale symbolism. In terms of the elements of city planning in

Chapter 2, the city design itself – the designed plan layout, for example – becomes part of the planning intention.

The idea of a city as a work of art – or an artistic medium – goes back at least to the Renaissance. Leonardo Benevolo says of Renaissance Florence: 'it was believed that any sculptor or painter, skilled in modelling or drawing visual forms, was able to deal in any formal medium, even on the scale of designing buildings or laying our whole cities'.[10]

Early pioneers of town planning also saw their profession as an art. Raymond Unwin referred to town planning as an art, considering the urban designer as an 'artist' and the town plan as a canvas. Even the classic Modernist planners – perhaps more immediately associated with functionalism – saw things from an artistic perspective: Percy Johnson-Marshall described town planning as a 'branch of artistic expression'; Arthur Korn asserted that the town should be 'a work of art both as a whole and throughout the whole order of units'. Frederick Gibberd similarly refers to the 'art of town design' and alludes to painting on a large canvas and lightly sketching in the future details. In the terminology of Chapter 2, this is 'city design' as art.[11]

Overall, with the city as a work of art, we can identify the following connotations: a designed object, the product of its creator's will; a composition of definite form and fixed extent; a single overriding purpose (the artistic expression) to which the purposes of component parts are subordinated (individual buildings or streets are placed as they are first and foremost to make up their particular contribution to the overall composition). The work of art also implies something finite and indivisible – that cannot be added to or subtracted from; a finished state (when the artwork is completed and ready for public exposure). Finally, a work of art is often expected to be beautiful, inspirational, enriching or otherwise expressing meaning.[12]

Although in principle cities may often be regarded figuratively as works of art, in practice artistic expression is not normally set out – explicitly, at least – as a purpose of planning intervention. This is not to say that individual buildings or streets should not be designed with suitable artistry, nor that the outcome should not be aesthetically pleasing. Rather, it is to say that the individual parts of the city are not normally designed primarily *as subordinate components* of a larger artistic vision.

The city as a machine

The term 'city as a machine' is intended to convey the idea of a city as primarily a functional construct, where the component parts and their overall arrangement are devised to maximise functionality, whatever the resulting overall form. Here, the city plan could be like a circuit-board, where the important thing is the functional connections, not the resulting visual effect. The city designer here is more like an engineer than an artist.

As with the 'city as a work of art', the 'city as a machine' is clearly a consciously designed object, with a single overriding purpose to which the purposes of component parts are subordinated. The machine metaphor adds more explicitly the idea of the functional specialisation of parts (cogs, gears, springs, and so on), which might be replaced with other parts. A machine is normally interpreted as having a definite final form (as with the work of art), although it could potentially be extensible.[13]

The machine may be regarded as indivisible in the sense that half a machine may be useless – or at least, does not serve the same function as the whole. That said, a machine is yet divisible in the sense that its parts could still potentially function in their specialist roles in some other context. For example, a car engine could still function as an engine outside the context of the car, although neither the engine nor the engineless car would perform the function of the car. Similarly, a car mirror, fan, seat and glovebox would all function outside the car, not doing what a car does as a whole, of course, but functioning respectively for reflecting, cooling, seating and containing gloves. This is different from the holistic nature of the work of art, where, for example, the whole and the individual parts lose their meaning if dis-assembled (imagine the Lobster Telephone without the lobster).[14] Unlike the city as work of art, the city as a machine is not required or even expected to be beautiful, inspirational or otherwise enriching.[15]

The machine metaphor gained some following in the twentieth century – Le Corbusier positively heralded the 'Machine-Age Civilization'. However, the machine metaphor's negative connotations came to outweigh its positive ones, on at least three fronts. First, rather than being seen as an intricate artifice of magical functionality, the machine came to be regarded as something rigid, inflexible and hence ultimately dysfunctional. Secondly, rather than being seen as liberating humans from toil, the machine came to be seen as something brutish threatening to harm humans, with its awesome but amoral power. Finally, the machine might threaten people's very humanity, if somehow becoming 'mechanised' themselves, as part of a new mechanistic order. In this last connection, Richard Sennett has argued against the anti-urban unity of the machine, whose parts are devised towards a single func-tion: 'any conflict between the parts, or even the existence of parts working independently of the whole, would defeat the purpose of the machine'.[16]

The machine metaphor fell out of favour, perhaps like Modernist city planning itself, in the last quarter of the twentieth century; and one scarcely hears today of anyone saying a city should be designed as if a machine.

The organic metaphor

Imagine a city as an organism having a civic centre for a heart, roads for arteries, neighbourhoods for cells, a railway as a spine, parks for lungs, a sewer system for an intestine, and suburban extensions for limbs, fingers or tentacles. This conjures up a Frankenstein's monster of a mixed metaphor for a city as an organism.

Organic interpretations of the city are not, however, limited to anatomical analogies of form and function between city parts and body parts – that may further extend down to the level of organs, tissues, cells and genetic units. Organic interpretations include more general associations to do with dynamic aspects of a living system.[17] There is the ongoing self-regulation and maintenance of equilibrium. There is the life-cycle of birth, growth, maturity and decay.[18] And there are the notions of adaptation and evolution.[19]

These organic interpretations are pervasive in the urban literature. They are not just found in the writings of the 'Organic Family Tree'[20] of Ebenezer Howard, Patrick Geddes, Lewis Mumford, Jane Jacobs and Christopher Alexander; but the writings of classic Modernists like Frank Lloyd Wright and Le Corbusier; plus mainstream – even establishment – planners and architects such as Sir Patrick Abercrombie, Sir Frederick Gibberd and Lord Rogers of Riverside.[21] Moreover, organic metaphors are routinely used in common language in everyday phrases such as urban vitality, urban growth, urban development, renaissance and regeneration.

The organic metaphor (if we call it a single metaphor) distinguishes itself from the artistic and machine metaphors – and hence finds favour – because it captures the sense of a city as somehow flexible, sensitive and responsive, perhaps somehow in tune with its environment; something that is dynamic, subject to rhythms and cumulative adaptive change; and perhaps with additional comforting overtones of being 'natural' and hence wholesome and somehow right or fitting.

The particular case of the 'city as organism' – as opposed to the city simply being vaguely organic – additionally has a series of connotations relating to the idea of optimum size, homeostatic equilibrium (e.g. self-regulation of temperature)[22] and a characteristic life-cycle (birth, maturity, decay, death). The 'city as organism' also has some connotations that directly parallel the city as machine metaphor: the idea of having a definite boundary, functional specialisation of parts, and also the idea that the parts function for the benefit of the whole. An organism is usually interpreted[23] as 'indivisible' like a machine or work of art.

While a city is not alive in the sense that an organism is, there nevertheless seems to be something organic about a city that separates it from the inanimate nature of a machine: monofunctional, deterministically and designedly mechanical, with no sense of self or self-purpose.

While organic metaphors continue to be popular, particular features have been questioned or criticised. For example, why should one emphasise a city's indivisibility, when it is clearly assembled from component parts, and when a city 'whole' is a transient entity, a snapshot in time? Why emphasise a definite boundary, when in fact it is often very hard to define exactly where a city stops, especially when its indivisible whole sprawls across administrative boundaries?

Spiro Kostof rejected the idea that cities were analogous to organisms in terms of having an optimum size and fixed development, concluding that 'The confusion stems from the fundamental inaptitude of the organic analogy'. Kevin Lynch also criticises the organic metaphor's treatment of infections and suppression of competing centres.[24] He nevertheless concludes: 'Although it has been repeatedly attacked and partially discredited, no other generally accepted theory has appeared to take its place.'

The city as mixed metaphor

That cities could be likened to works of art, machines or organic entities is perhaps no more and no less than a reflection of the way that these three entities themselves may be likened to each other. When we look at certain kinds of complicated industrial installations, such as machinery, blast furnaces or water towers, we can recognise that these are clearly technological. They also have a kind of strange, alien beauty to them; and could be interpreted as being artistic objects in their own right, as seen in the photography of Bernd and Hilla Becher (Figure 5.2).[25] But as well as being machine-like and perhaps works of art, do these have something organic about them? These appear almost 'biological' perhaps in the sense they are coherent objects, and they are functional – all pipes and struts and apertures, and so on. Form appears to follow function in a natural, direct and unadorned way.[26]

And so if these objects can be artistic and mechanical and organic at the same time, it is not surprising that cities might also be considered artistic, mechanical *and* organic. And so, although we have looked at the three metaphors for cities separately, a city might – like Dalí's Lobster Telephone – be interpreted as a hybrid, chimera or mixed metaphor. Indeed, on closer inspection, several interpretations of cities have combined all three metaphorical associations, to varying degrees.

The city of Venice could be described as an urban masterpiece, a work of art. Even Le Corbusier was seduced, equating Venice with poetry and describing it as a 'symphony of majesty and delicacy'. However, elsewhere

(a)

(b)

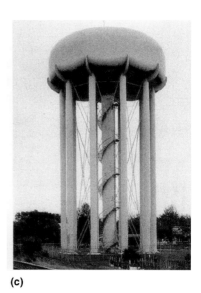

(c)

5.2 • Bernd and Hiller Becher's industrial photography. Buildings, machines or 'the perfect biology'? (a) Machine installation; (b) Blast furnace; (c) Water tower.

he describes the city as 'a magnificently functional machine'. And finally, Le Corbusier contemplates Venice's different circulation systems, reflecting 'Doesn't it look like the perfect biology – the circulation of blood in a living thing?' So Venice seems to be a machine *and* like an organism, and a work of art.[27]

The mixed metaphor carries across into city planning and design. Le Corbusier's *Ville Radieuse* (Figure 2.11) looks at first sight like a typical 'mechanistic Modernist' creation: it presents an ordered diagram of routes and functionally articulated components, rationally assembled in a logical order quite unlike the chaotic mass of unplanned cities. That said, the city plan's somewhat eccentric shape has been likened to an anthropomorphic affectation, where the city has an administrative 'head', residential 'body' and industrial 'feet' – and as such may be regarded as an artistic expression. Then again, Le Corbusier himself emphasised the *organic* sense of its extensibility: the *Ville* represented was actually an 'organism', a segment of what could be a laterally extensible linear city.[28]

Ludwig Hilberseimer's *New City* might look like mechanistic Modernism, especially in the rectilinear sections seen close up. That said, when seen as a larger curvilinear whole, it looks more organic, as it was supposed to be – where the repetition was of a biological rather than

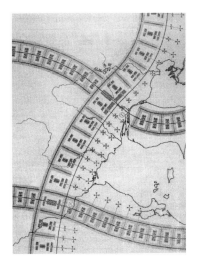

5.3 • Hilberseimer's New City. From a distance, it looks organic; up close, mechanistic.

mechanical nature (Figure 5.3). Then again, Hilberseimer refers to the 'art of city planning', and asserts that 'the idea of planning is at the base of all art'.[29]

Similarly, Arturo Soria y Mata's *Ciudad Lineal* (Figure 2.9), although superficially mechanistic, is similarly infused with biological analogy and rhetoric. Soria regarded the linear city as a 'vertebrate or higher form' compared with the garden city, regarded as a 'lower or vegetable form'. Yet, as we saw in Chapter 2, he also considered that this vertebrate creation needed an Architect. Finally, let us contemplate Herron's Walking City (Figure 2.16c), which most obviously looks 'insectile' and organic, but which would literally be a mechanical construction; and yet, to date, actually exists only as an artistic creation.[30]

From metaphors to models

The point of discussing metaphors is because it gives insights into models for city design. While a metaphor can help represent, describe and explain 'the kind of thing a city is', a model not only does this, but may also be used to prescribe the kind of thing a city should be, and how it should be designed or planned.

All three of the foregoing metaphors seem to have some sort of legitimacy, but also some sort of deficiency, that makes them not completely appropriate as a general metaphor for representing, describing or explaining cities. That is, they are only partially applicable, and cannot on their own completely encapsulate the kind of thing a city is.

Certainly, Jane Jacobs was dismissive of almost all the models and metaphors used for describing cities. She expressly insisted that *a city cannot be a work of art*; she also rejected mechanistic or organic interpretations of city formation, arguing that a city is 'not put together like a mammal or a steel-frame building – or even like a honeycomb or a coral'.[31]

Part of the problem indeed is to do with 'how it is put together' in terms of process. If a city is a work of art or machine, then it is a designed object, but is not expected to grow or change. On the other hand, if a city is an organism, then it may grow and change, but an organism is not designed.

This may lead us to question whether these metaphors have any value, as models for future design or planning. It was suggested in Chapter 2 that the planning of cities seems to be to do with the packaging of components. It seems that for a model to be useful, it should provide a means of generating a coherent package. If we have to resort to a mixed metaphor of organs, cogs and brush strokes, why bother with metaphors and models at all? Why not simply assemble buildings, streets and parks in an ad hoc manner?

Perhaps it is because cities are so complex that we are tempted to use metaphors and analogies to help clarify what city design is actually doing. After all, the designer of a cup or a kettle does not need to use figures of speech – needing to conceive of the cup as a work of art, or a kettle as organism – to help decide how best to approach design. There seems little need to think of those objects – the cup or kettle – in terms of other than what the object actually is. But with cities, it seems that somehow metaphors and analogies help us think about how they work and how they are – or might be – put together.

Perhaps we need an alternative metaphor or model, that explicitly acknowledges the complexity of the city, beyond being a simple object of design?

EMERGING PERSPECTIVES

City planning is in effect founded on the premise that 'unplanned' settlements are more disordered and dysfunctional than planned ones. However, just as contemporary urbanism now challenges the premise that traditional 'unplanned' settlements are not necessarily dysfunctional (Chapter 1), contemporary science now challenges the premise that traditional 'unplanned' settlements are disordered in the first place. Could this be a paradigm shift in understanding of 'the kind of thing a city is'?

In science, a paradigm shift is a significant occurrence in the sense that it potentially affects how a whole range of things in the world is interpreted, even if the shift itself is not proverbially Earth-shattering, and is achieved by a relatively simple mental switch or change in point of view.

That said, in the sphere of urban design and planning, significant changes are usually associated with acts of will or changes in practice, rather than changes in scientific understanding. These significant changes are therefore better regarded as transformations or revolutions than paradigm shifts. Hence we may identify the adoption of Corbusian-style urban ordering as an 'urban revolution' in terms of its historical significance and its impact on cities (Figure 1.2). But this Corbusian revolution was not a paradigm shift: it was a revolution in aspiration and application, not one of scientific understanding.[32]

The twentieth century did, however, see the start of a new understanding that could be come to be seen as a new paradigm, in the urban context: this regards the complex, dynamic, organic nature of cities.

Organic order

Patrick Geddes was one of the most extraordinary thinkers of the late nineteenth and early twentieth centuries: a polymath who published on topics as diverse as art, biology, economics, geography, history, planning and sociology – including cross-cutting topics such as sex, cities and evolution.[33] Originally trained in the life sciences, he was one of the foremost thinkers to draw insights from biology for understanding and planning cities. Geddes recognised the intricate complexity of urbanism and the parallels with nature:

> This octopus of London, polypus rather, is something curious exceedingly, a vast irregular growth without previous parallel in the world of life – perhaps likest to the spreadings of a great coral reef. Like this, it has a strong skeleton, and living polyps – call it, then, a 'man-reef' if you will.[34]

Referring to the 'inseparably interwoven structure' of traditional towns, Geddes realised – in the words of Spiro Kostof – that 'the seeming chaos was of our imagining – the product of the Western addiction to mechanical order'. Instead, Geddes recognised 'the order of life in development'.[35]

With his organic sensibility, Geddes inveighed against town planning as a technical 'art of compass and rule' or 'pompous imperial art'.[36] Instead, Geddes pioneered what we would recognise as an ecological perspective on urbanism; advocated the value of undertaking surveys to understand cities before proceeding to plan them; and recommended a gradualist approach to urban intervention – 'conservative surgery'. This is in effect based on seeing urban areas as having an organic kind of order, rather than just being disordered. The idea of cities being organic in time became an influential strand of town planning thought.

Organic complexity

Geddes' recognition of this complex or organic order was later crystallised more explicitly by Jane Jacobs' recognition of cities as problems in organised complexity.

In doing so, Jane Jacobs was building on Warren Weaver's identification of three kinds of scientific problem. The first kind of problem was that of simplicity, such as the motion of a planetary body relative to another. The second kind was that of disorganised complexity, such as the behaviour of gas particles – where the individual trajectories are not known, but the whole mass can be treated relatively simply, statistically. The third kind of problem was that of organised complexity, as dealt with in biological sciences.

Weaver's insight was to suggest the scientific framework; Jacobs' insight was to recognise the city as falling into the third category alongside biology, and not the first or second, as city planning had typically presumed. The significance of this to urban design and planning is that one cannot hope to solve the problem of the city if one is framing the wrong problem in the first place.[37]

Christopher Alexander also contributed to understanding cities as having a kind of complex organic nature. Alexander has emphasised that the structure cities have is inextricable from the way they are put together. In *A City is Not a Tree*, Alexander suggests in effect that cities have a complex order that equates with their functionality; he argues in effect that 'artificial' (planned) settlements are dysfunctional due to their simplicity.

In *A Timeless Way of Building* and its companion volume *A Pattern Language* Alexander sets out a system capable of creating a great variety of urban forms and relationships from the scale of furniture to whole settlements, and how these may be put together. In this, the overlapping interconnectedness of the city is clear; and moreover the kind of complexity found in cities comes from the interaction and relationships between the different parts at different scales, and over time. This relates to the idea that a city is complex, but not just a complicated, designable object.[38]

Cities and complexity

As noted in Chapter 1, there is now an increasing contemporary recognition of the significance of the sciences of complexity, and their potential application to urbanism. A variety of urban theorists and analysts have made links between complexity and cities. The crossover between science and urbanism is seen, not least, in the appearance of work on urbanism in scientific journals such as *Nature, Science* and *Complexity*.[39]

Perhaps foremost among these contemporary urban theorists is Michael Batty, whose book *Cities and Complexity* draws together a variety of perspectives on complexity and urbanism, and presents the application of models and methods for exploring this field. These illustrate the 'philosophy that cities should be treated as emergent structures, built from the bottom up, whose processes are intrinsic to the form and structure that ultimately develops'. These result in hierarchically differentiated structures that might suggest central planning: 'But central planning there is not; there are only the actions of individual elements whose coordination results from the remorseless processes of competition and adaptation.' Batty explicitly identifies complexity theory as a 'new paradigm'.[40]

Applied to cities, this can be interpreted as meaning that we now tend to recognise the complex, organic kind of order that cities possess,

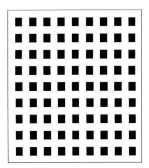

(a)

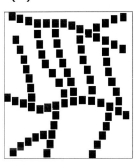

(b)

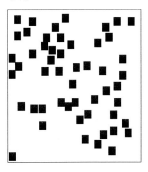

(c)

5.4 • Different kinds of order: (a) Simple order; (b) Complex order; (c) Disorder.

that is different from either the simplistic order of planned settlements or complete disorder (Figure 5.4). This recognition of complex order can be related to the recognition of characteristic order as a kind of order, not disorder, nor imperfect regularity (Chapter 3). Cities, therefore, seem to be complex in an organic kind of way that sets them apart from works of art and machines.[41]

Complex and dynamic entities

Complex here is taken to mean something different from complicated. A complicated object could be something where every single element was deliberately and knowingly positioned with respect to each other and the whole – like the complicated wiring of a circuit-board, or the complicated structure of a large building, or aircraft. In order for the wiring or the structure to function, all the elements and connections must be known. In contrast, the term complex is taken to refer to something with many parts that are not pre-specified, and may be unknown to any one person, or to each other – even if each individual part was consciously put there by someone. In this sense, the structure of the World Wide Web is complex, whereas the internal circuitry in a computer is complicated. Similarly, a city or organism can be described as complex, whereas a machine or work of art would be more likely to be interpreted as complicated.[42]

The complexity arises partly out of the dynamic way the city is put together. Dynamic here is taken to mean that a city changes over time, in a way that is not simply prompted by an external agency (like a human operator altering a machine), nor simply predictable from its current state (a mechanism that goes 'like clockwork'). In the conventional sense a work of fine art – like a painting or sculpture – is not dynamic, nor is a machine. Although clearly cities change in large part due to human agency, the humans are in effect part of the city, and therefore can be thought of as an internal part of the city that itself is changing, rather than being like a machine passively altered by an external agency. So an organism is complex and dynamic, but in a way that is not just complicated and dynamic like the clockwork of a machine. This implies a distinction opening up between the city and organism on the one hand, and the machine and work of art on the other.

And yet, we also know that the idea of city-as-organism is not quite right. So we need to revisit the organic metaphor to see which parts work, and which don't. This should ideally mean not just a better-functioning metaphor (or paradigm) for ordering information about cities, but as a model that is useful for onward planning and design.

What is sought here is a conception of the city that goes beyond being a complex dynamic object – something that could be said of organisms – that can be a useful way of understanding cities and useful as a basis for city planning and design. To be a useful model for understanding cities, it should be able to accommodate the complex dynamic nature of cities. To be useful as a model for planning or designing cities, it should be able to point to the kind of building-blocks or components from which cities are made, and the coherence that a city has as a whole, and the way that parts relate to the whole.

Otherwise, one could say: 'a city is complex and dynamic, so is an organism, so a city is an organism, let us build a city with the characteristics of an organism – a finite unified entity with subordinate, complementary parts'. This would be like designing a new town in the 1960s, and is not, of itself building on any of the most recent understanding of complexity theory. It would, indeed, be exactly like what Christopher Alexander argued against doing, in *A City is Not a Tree*.[43]

A city is not an organism

The problem with the organic metaphor is that a crucial part of it is misleading: a city is not an organism. That is, most or all of the criticisms of 'the' organic metaphor are actually directed at that part that says a city is an organism: the definite boundary, the optimum size, the sense of striving to maintain 'balance' (homeostatic equilibrium), the life-cycle (birth, maturity, death). A city is not like these, or it is not helpful to think of cities this way, and just because a city is 'like' an organism in one of these ways does not mean that a city should be treated like an organism in other senses.[44]

A city is not an organism in a variety of senses. A city is not 'put together' like an organism in the way the parts are composed with respect to the whole. The parts of a city do not serve the interests of the whole, in the way that the organs of an organism's body contribute systematically to the well-being of the whole body, or the way the parts are complementary and cooperative. In contrast, in a city the parts are often in competition, and at the very least, the individual components tend to have their own agendas, which may or may not coincide with those of the city as a whole.

In this sense, then, the city-as-organism metaphor is no more useful as an indication of the structure of a city than the city-as-machine or city-as-work-of-art metaphors. Indeed in treating the city as an organism, as a model, planners were arguably treating it as if it were an organism *of machine-like simplicity*. The interpretation of neighbourhoods as cells or organs was little more than identification of crude sub-components with the simplistic specialism of machine parts – such as the heart as 'pump'. This implies that cities planned in this way were crude and simplistic, lacking the intricate functionality of a natural organism, but more like Dr Frankenstein's monster, cobbled together from a variety of existing organs. The city-as-an-organism is surely as artificial as a machine, but not necessarily as functional as a machine, or a real organism.[45]

Then again, perhaps the problem is that we have too simplistic a conception of what an organism is in the first place – as if the organism were simply like a robot, with discrete moving parts, all supporting the functioning of the whole. This is perhaps what our urban caricatures of organisms are like. But a real organism is more complex than this.

The organism revisited

A city *could* be like an organism, in at least three ways not normally considered in the urban literature. First, a city might be like *some* kinds of organism. For example, a sponge aggregates itself in a way that means it cooperates to create a whole, but internally the components are competitive (Figure 5.5 a). The ringed marine worm *Syllis ramosa* is an 'almost bush-like compound organism' with more than one head (Figure 5.5 b); while a siphonophore 'colony' (Figure 5.5 c) is a compound organism that sometimes

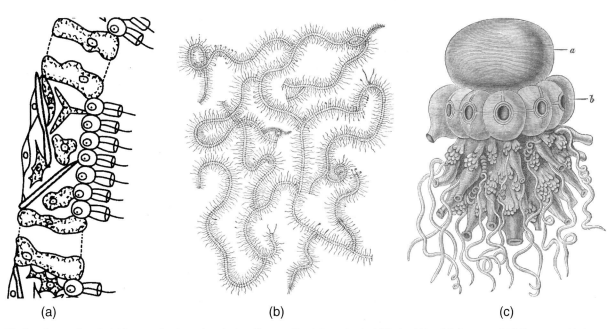

(a)   (b)   (c)

5.5 • Complex organisms that defy conventional organic analogies with respect to wholes and parts: (a) The 'sociable cells' of a sponge; (b) *Syllis ramosa*, a kind of marine worm, with many heads and tails; (c) A siphonophore 'colony'.

behaves as a single whole; at other times its detachable parts behave independently – as noted by Geddes, in the biological context. In the urban context, as we have seen, Geddes suggested that a city could be likened to a 'man-reef'. More recently, Charles Jencks has suggested that a city could be like a slime-mould that behaves sometimes like a single entity and sometimes like a collection of independent parts.[46]

Secondly, even for familiar kinds of organism, there is more to an organism than meets the eye. A complex organism like a human has millions of organisms inside: parasites and symbionts including various kinds of worms, fungi, bacteria and viruses. Insofar as a city is a collective of many individuals – partly cooperating, and partly competing – a human body and its community of organisms could be said to be like a city.[47]

Thirdly, we can actually make use of the gene-centred paradigm and apply it to cities – unexpectedly directly, as it turns out, however loosely and superficially. An organism is composed of many self-interested genes, who use the body as a 'vehicle' for survival. The genes are 'selfish' in the sense they are (as it were) looking out for themselves, and only 'care' about the fate of the host body as long as it affects their own survival and opportunity for reproduction. The parallel here is that people tend to care about the fate of their city or society insofar as it affects their own quality of life and prospects (for survival, reproduction, and so on).[48]

Now, we would surely be taking things too far if we held up the sponge or slime-mould or genome as a metaphor for a city, and then tried to use the detailed mechanisms of sponges or slime-moulds or the structure of DNA as a model for how to plan cities. Indeed, we would reasonably be concerned about the theoretical validity of such propositions, never mind their practicability, if an urban planning model required a detailed knowledge of zoology or genetics for it to be made to work. We must be wary of pushing organic analogies too far – like Lewis Mumford getting bogged down with amoebas and chromosomes – in case it discredits the organic interpretation of cities in general.[49]

In the end, as to whether a city is or is not like an organism, the jury is in a sense still out, and always will be, as long as our knowledge of organisms is incomplete. In the end, it seems more likely to be zoologists or geneticists, rather than urban analysts, who could settle the argument as to what extent a city is like an organism.

While possibly interesting interpretations, these latest organic analogies do not seem to take us any further than saying 'a city is like a collection of different component entities with their own agendas'. Then again, perhaps this is the point: perhaps that *is* exactly 'the kind of thing a city is'.

THE CITY AS ECOSYSTEM

The key difference that separates cities on the one hand, and works of art, machines or organisms (in their conventional interpretation) on the other, is that the city is a collective of parts with their own agendas. Here we may usefully distinguish between what can be called a corporate object and a collective entity (Figure 5.6).

A corporate object is a unitary whole composed of complementary sub-units (Figure 3.1 b). In a corporate object, the component sub-units are subordinate to the whole and support the whole – the purpose or object of the whole. This is like the proverbial cog in the machine, or an individual feature in a painting, or an individual cell or organ in the body of an organism.[50]

A collective entity, by contrast, is a super-unit: an aggregate of many individual components; the aggregation may be simple (a stack of palettes) or complex (the World Wide Web). The distinction between corporate and collective echoes the distinction between central intelligence and collective or distributed intelligence (Chapter 1), or unit and super-unit (Figure 3.1 c).[51]

A city, then, is a complex collective dynamic entity: a super-unit, composed of components that are themselves units, rather than a corporate unit comprising sub-units (Chapter 3). As a collective entity, a city is simultaneously one thing and several things (like a chess set or bunch of bananas); being a collective entity does not deny that the city can be a 'thing'; it just suggests the *kind* of thing a city is.

The distinction between a corporate and collective entity can usefully distinguish and clarify separate things that this book has been concerned with up till now.

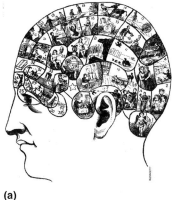

5.6 • Corporate versus collective: (a) A person or brain is a corporate unit: the components (appear to) work together to support the whole; (b) A society, super-organism, or 'body' of people is a collective entity. Recall also sub-units and super-units (Figure 3.1 b, c), and the British beehive (Figure 4.6).

(a)   **(b)**

A city is not a building

The idea that a city is not a building is so obvious that it normally does not require stating.[52] A city is, at the very least, a collection of buildings, and more properly includes other physical infrastructures – roads, parks, and so on – and may also be taken to include the people and human systems. But the distinction being pursued here is that a building is normally a corporate object, whereas a city is normally a collective entity.

That is to say: a building is a corporate entity, whose component parts (such as rooms) are complementary and serve to support the function of the whole.[53] On the other hand, a city, town, village or neighbourhood is more like a collective entity. It consists of units such as buildings that could stand alone; the parts in a sense come before the whole. Indeed, a city has competing as well as cooperating components. This makes its form and structure different from that of a building (Figure 5.7).[54]

And while it may be obvious that a city is not a building, this has not stopped us frequently using analogies and metaphors that are much more appropriately applied to buildings than cities. In effect, we can recognise that the ways in which a city is not put together like a work of art, machine or organism is just like the way that a city is not put together like a building.

It is the building that perhaps better fits all three of the classic urban metaphors (Figure 5.8). A building, as an architectural object, is readily and

(a)   **(b)**

5.7 • A city is not a building: (a) Lloyds of London, a completed composition from a preconceived design; (b) Skyline of Lucca (Italy), with competing components, that may change over time.

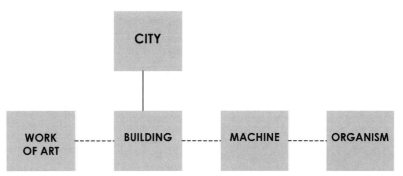

5.8 • A city is not a building; a building is more like a work of art, machine or organism than a city is.

routinely interpreted as a work of art. A building could be said to be like a machine in some respects – it is a designed object, for a start, it has an overall purpose, it has parts designed to fulfil the function of the whole, and so on. Le Corbusier famously – notoriously – described a house as a machine for living in. We can imagine machinery morphing into architecture in the sequence of Becher's images in Figure 5.2 (from *a* to *b* to *c*).

From the logic of Figure 5.8, rather than a work of art or machine, a city would be more like a *collection* of works of art or machines. For example, in an exhibition of artworks or machines, each exhibit is (as it were) expressing is own agenda, each competes for attention with others, yet each benefits from being part of the collective display. And rather than an individual organism, a city is more like a whole species, or in the human context, a whole society.

A city is like a society

A city is a collective entity – in the way that a society is. Hobbes' diagram (Figure 5.6 b) could here be interpreted not (only) in terms of society as a 'body' of people – a super-organism; but as an organism composed of self-interested or selfish citizens, like genes who use the body as a 'survival vehicle'. Therefore, the organism while perhaps conventionally regarded as a corporate object – a complete coherent whole, with an overall function, and overall decision-making executive, with sub-components like cells and organs that support the functioning of the whole – could alternatively be interpreted as a collective entity.

If it seems so simple as to almost be a truism that a city is not a building, it seems almost as much a truism to say a city is like a society. But, like the notion that a city is not a building, it seems that cities are not commonly described as being like societies (as opposed to coral reefs or machines or

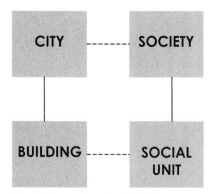

5.9 • A city is to society what a building is to an individual person or social unit; a city is to a building as a society is to an individual person or social unit.

works of art). But, nevertheless, the simple correspondence seems to work; and despite the danger of looking too simple to bother illustrating, this is preferable to more complex analogies that don't work so clearly (Figure 5.9).

Figure 5.9 suggests first that a city is to a building as a society is to a social unit. Secondly, a city is to society as a building is to a social unit.[55] From this simple perspective, it can be seen that we do not need an organic model at all; we do not need biology – except insofar as people and societies are biological – to understand the complex nature of a city.

The city as ecosystem

If we *did* wish to use an organic analogy to express the paradigm of the city as a collective entity, then perhaps the simplest way is this. Let us agree, with Alexander, that a city is not a tree (a corporate, finite, if dynamic object). A city is more like a forest of trees – a collective entity – something that may grow indefinitely as long as there are resources and land to support it.

Better even than a forest, perhaps, a city is like a whole ecosystem: not only the collection of trees, but the lichens and fungi that live on the trees, the birds and insects that eat their fruits and seeds, and the living and deceased organisms that contribute the nutrients to the soil – and the insects and worms and bacteria that live in the soil . . . (Figure 5.10).[56]

The city as ecosystem seems to work usefully as metaphor and with respect to analogous relationships. An ecosystem contains the forest plus all the other stuff that makes the forest work. An individual building would be analogous to an individual tree. A city is no more or less like an organism than an ecosystem is.

So, a city (ecosystem) contains the building stock (forest) comprising all the individual buildings (trees) plus all the other visible and invisible things that make the whole thing work. This helps us see what kind of a 'whole' a city is, and how its parts are related. That is, not so much like cogs or organs, but more like different individual organisms and species interlocking in dynamic competitive and symbiotic relationships. It also shows how even the individual tree is not an autonomous unit after all: it reminds us that a building is not an isolated object either, but its existence and functioning depends on the urban context it is inserted into. And, the ecosystem or environment contains the sum of all the organisms in it. The individual is dependent on the environment, and is also part of other individuals' environments.[57]

Not only is the city like an ecosystem, but it *is* an ecosystem. A city besides supporting human life supports all manner of other species, in all

5.10 • A city is more like an ecosystem than an individual organism.

manner of exploitative and symbiotic relationships. The built environment is itself no less an environment to the creatures it accommodates than any 'natural' environment – to the barn owl in the barn, or the cockroaches in the bricks or the woodworm in the sideboard or moths in the wardrobes, or bookworms in books.

Saying that a city is literally an ecosystem could be seen as a perhaps another truism – like saying that a room is literally an environment. But what is potentially interesting here is that in recognising a city actually as an eco-system it naturally accommodates the biological and non-biological in the same thing: not simply a city being analogous to a forest, but being as much an ecosystem as a forest is, complete with plants, animals *and* human constructions.[58]

The use of the term ecosystem seems fitting, since the word originally comes from the Greek *oikos* meaning house. So, saying that a city is an ecosystem is no more than returning what was originally a figure of speech of natural science borrowing from urbanism. A city as 'eco' system – a system of houses – provides a fitting built environment for its human inhabitants.[59]

CONCLUSIONS

This chapter set out to explore various ways in which a city has been con-ceptualised *as a whole*, in order to understand how this has in the past influenced, and might in the future influence, the package that is city design.

It has been suggested that city planning is effectively premised on the idea of the unplanned city as disordered and dysfunctional. Moreover, we can also now add that city design has historically been premised on the idea of a *city as an object* in the first place. This could yet mean an intricate, functional, complicated corporate object, comprising subordinate parts that support the functioning of the whole; and potentially an object with moving parts or that could be added to or subtracted to from time to time. We can see how this is in effect a *paradigm* for the kind of thing a city is; and we can see how three classic models of the city – city as work of art, city as machine and city as organism – all fit with this paradigm. They are to some extent indeed inter-changeable – since a work of art could be a machine (installation), a machine could be a work of art, an organism could be a machine, and so on. They all, indeed, may as well be equivalent to saying that *a city is a building*.

But, it is argued here that a city is not a building – or, as Christopher Alexander had it, a city is not a tree. Rather, it has been suggested that a city is a complex, dynamic, collective entity. This means that while it may be organic, it is more like a forest or ecosystem rather than an individual tree; more like a society than an individual person or organism. It is more like the complex, collective, ever-changing entity that is the internet, rather than an individual computer. It is more like an exhibition of surreal art installations than an individual Lobster Telephone.

Even if it seems rather simple to say a city is like a society, or a city is not a building, nevertheless these statements by their simplicity seem clearer and more useful ways of thinking about the city as a whole and in its parts, than to consider a city as a work of art, machine or organism. Those conventional metaphors and analogies were perhaps on the wrong track because they misrepresent or muddle the nature of the part–whole relationship. This is to do with the difference between units, sub-units and super-units (Chapter 3). In effect, the analysis of this chapter suggests that while a building is an urban unit, and a room a sub-unit, it may be better to think of a city as a super-unit – a collection of components that are themselves units – rather than a unitary whole, like a building.

So is the new perspective here – the idea of the city as a complex, dynamic, collective entity, like an ecosystem – a new paradigm? Not particularly: to suggest that a city is a collection of buildings rather than a big building is not particularly new nor particularly profound. It is perhaps not so much a new paradigm as the undoing of an old paradigm: that of treating a city as a corporate, unitary, designable object in the first place.[60]

At first sight, a potential problem of the suggestion that a city is like a society or ecosystem is that it seems not to offer useful suggestions for the design of a city, in the way that the city-as-machine, or city-as-work-of-art models do. But perhaps the problem is not in the model, but in the assumption that a city is any more designable than a society or ecosystem in the first place.

In effect, the history of the 'city design' part of city planning has been the recognition and reinforcement of the city as a single whole corporate object, a designable object, whose parts should be systematically and supportively related. In effect, city design may be associated with the attempt to design a city as if it were a large complicated building. Insofar as Modernist city planning did this on an unprecedented scale, this perhaps helps explain why it risked being dysfunctional. The larger the exercise in city design or town design, the more likely that the thing being housed – a citizenry – would depart from being the kind of social unit for which building-design is appropriate.

If, on the other hand, we accept the city instead as a complex, dynamic, collective entity – like a society, or ecosystem – then a city is more like an *objet trouvée* that could be recognised in retrospect as a work of art, but is not created like a conventional work of art.

What, then, does this mean for planning and design? How, in the end, might an ecosystem be designed, or at least planned? Not like designing an artificial organism – sewing or bolting together different organs, as if it were a machine. Put another way, how does complex urban order come about, without city design? To answer these questions, we need to see how complex things themselves, and other features of the natural world, come into existence; how complex organic order is created in nature, in the absence of any 'designer'.

Notes

1   Abercrombie (1933: 27).
2   Rosenblueth and Wiener (1951), in 'Purposeful and non-purposeful behavior', in *Philosophy of Science*, 18; cited in Lewontin (2000: 4).
3   Kuhn (1970). A paradigm provides an overarching frame of reference within which 'normal science' takes place – hence there is a cycle of normal science, crisis, revolution, new normal science (Hacking, 1983: 7; Young, 1988). The idea of a paradigm shift often implies something relatively infrequent and extreme. The new paradigm replaces the old; therefore, some of the old theories and methods are cast aside. Although paradigm shifts are sometimes associated with particular individuals, their true realisation requires adoption and application by many people (Taylor, 1998; Ladyman, 2002: 102). Some have argued that paradigm shifts are relatively rare and less significant than Kuhn makes out (F. Dyson, 1998: 124; see also Young, 1988: 151–152). A paradigm shift might equate with a shift in perspective, where a change of point of view reveals a new way of thinking about things. See Dawkins ([1982] 1999: 1); also Dawkins ([1976] 2006: xv) on the gene-centred perspective.
4   A paradigm shift is best regarded as a change in scientific understanding, rather than a revolution in aspiration or action. For example, a political revolution is not a paradigm shift, in the sense that no change in understanding is necessary to replace a monarchy with a republic – just a change in will – and one could as easily change back from a republic to a monarchy. Secondly, in a political revolution, things definitely do change on the ground, for the person in the street – that is one of their purposes, after all.
5   For simplicity, an extra part of Steadman's original diagram is omitted here. The extra part is the interpretation of organisms as machines, and the interpretation of machines as organisms (this is returned to later in this chapter, and in Chapter 10).
6   In *Good City Form* Kevin Lynch (1981) describes three broad normative models of city form: the cosmic, the machine and the organic. Lynch's cosmic model may be regarded as a subset of a more general model, that of city as a diagram (Kostof, 1991), and in turn the city as a work of art. Kostof (1991) and Shane (2005) reflect on and analyse further these models.
7   'Whatever words we employ, field or atom or something as yet unnamed, they will help shape our city, for the kind of metaphors we choose will influence the

kind of city we see' (Sharpe and Wallock, 1987: 38). A palimpsest is a document that has been overwritten, implying that old text is replaced by new, although perhaps some old prevails in places. The word seems to be used mostly today as a metaphor – for things such as cities.

8   Unwin (1920: 9,16); Mumford (1938: 480); Korn, (1953: 101); Gibberd (1962: 16,20); Moholy-Nagy (1968); Rykwert (1976: 202); Lynch (1981) on 'cosmic' model; Cherry (1988: 2); Kostof (1991: 162); Kostof (1992: 232); Elliott (1998) on 'earthly city'; Rossi (2003: 285).

9   Deckker (2000); McKean (1996).

10 Benevolo (1980: 473) on the city as artistic medium; Benevolo also refers to the 'mysterious art of designing a town' (1980: 478).

11 Unwin also sees the communities themselves as 'artists of their own cities, portraying on a gigantic canvas the expression of their life' ([1909] 1920: 9); Geddes ([1915] 1949); Gibberd (1962: 14); Gibberd (1962: 20); Korn (1953: 101); Kostof also refers to town planner as artist (1991: 128); Spreiregen (1968) on the art of designing cities; Keeble (1969: 1) on town planning as an art and science; Rossi (1982: 32–33) on the urban artefacts as works of art; Prince of Wales (1989: 85); Butina Watson (1993) on the art of building cities.

12 It is acknowledged that there are many kinds of artistic expression, many of which challenge conventional assumptions such as that the artist is in control, that the artwork has a fixed point of completion, and so on. However, a simplified, if stereotypical, view of art is here expressed, in order to provide a readily grasped contrast with the other two city models.

13 According to Lynch, a machine is made up of 'small, autonomous, undifferentiated parts', Lynch (1981: 83). He says a city (as a machine) grows by addition (Lynch, 1981: 81). See also Barnett (1986).

14 If that is too easy, try imagining Dalí's *Fried egg on a plate, without the plate*, without the fried egg – or with the plate.

15 However, this is not to deny the possibility of machines, or engineering structures, being beautiful or being created with conscious artistic intent. See, for example, Billington (1983), Holgate (1986).

16 Trancik (1986: 230).

17 Cities as living, growing or evolving entities: Geddes (1915); Unwin (1920: 16); Thompson ([1917] 1948: 1020); Rossi (1982); Sharpe and Wallock (1987: 37); Vickers (1998); Woolley and Johns (2001: 211). Settlements as organisms: Geddes, P. ([1915] 1949: 11); Korn (1953: 89); Benevolo (1980: 60); Gibberd (1967: 27, 28); Smith (1974); Smith (1983: 17); Sohn (2003: 125). City as organism: Soria y Mata (1892: 7); Choay (1969: 17,109); Tunnard (1970: 46); Batty (1995c: 478); Tsui (1999); Caves (2005: xxi). Sohn (2003: 127) *Stadtorganismus* – urban organism. Mould on a jam-pot, 'fungus-city' (Geddes, 1949 [1915]: 26). Anatomy: backbone and artery (Hilberseimer, 1944: 14); skeleton (Jacobs, 1962; Soria y Mata, 1892); veins and arteries, blood, bile, sewer system as intestine, flesh and muscles,

embryo (Soria y Mata, 1892: 6,7,13); cellular morphology (Morris, 1994: 9); life-blood and arteries (Roberts and Lloyd-Jones, 2001). Mumford thought that Rome suffered from a 'megalopolitan elephantiasis' (Kotkin, 2005); 'diseased extensions of tentacled cities' (Le Corbusier, 1947a: 115); 'monstrous cancer' (Kostof, 1992: 58); 'the city as a sort of giant human being'; 'city as a wen, a cancer, a polyp', 'diseased urban body' (Sharpe and Wallock, 1987: 35–37) needing surgery (Gold, 1997: 44); Mumford (1961: 510); Mumford (1938: 472), Mumford (1938: 249; 1961: 93); 'fungus-like growth' (Porter, 1994: 372); society as an organism (Hobbes, 1651; Wojtowicz, 1996: 14, after Geddes). Evolution and descent of civilisations (Morris, 1994: 1); Aristotle (1992: 60–61) – individual to state as limbs are to body.

18 Mumford (1961: 496); Gibberd (1967: 27); Osborn and Whittick (1969: 414); cities 'still-born' or born 'ab ovo' (Kostof, 1991: 40); Lock (1994). Cities being born and growing (Soria y Mata, 1892: 13); Tunnard (1970: 44). Bacon (1975: 301) refers to evolving, growth, development and organism.

19 Venturi (1966: 49) asserts that 'Architecture is evolutionary as well as revolutionary'. Also: 'evolution of urban structure' (Jo, 1998: 288); 'city centre blocks and their evolution' (Siksna, 1998); 'evolution' of the street system (Erickson and Lloyd-Jones, 1997: 909); the 'slowly evolved husks of existing cities' (Kostof, 1991: 154; after CIAM); evolving New Town plans (Lock, 1994: 87). Unwin ([1909] 1920: 16) refers to the 'different types of plan which have been evolved in the course of natural growth or have been designed at different periods by human art'.

20 Newman and Kenworthy (1999: 291).

21 Influential writers such as Lewis Mumford, who drew many parallels between cities and organisms, insisted that cities therefore had to be designed whole – where the unit of design was no less than the city itself. Mumford (1938: 484). Frank Lloyd Wright has been associated with 'organic architecture' (Johnson and Langmead (1997). Although Hilberseimer's *New City* plan (1944) looks about as mechanistic as it is possible for a city plan to be, Hilberseimer himself stressed the need for organic city structure. Le Corbusier, although a leading proponent of the 'Machine-Age Civilisation', simultaneously embraced the idea of the biological organisation of the city. 'Towns are biological phenomena' – Le Corbusier (1947a: 48); Le Corbusier ([1933] 1964: 168); 'BIOLOGY! The great new word in architecture and planning' (Le Corbusier, 1960). See, for example, Rogers (1998) on the 'evolution' of cities.

22 The homeostatic equilibrium is also described as the 'rhythmic behaviour that seeks, in the face of inevitable change, to maintain a balanced state' (Kostof, 1991: 15).

23 Note that this is very dependent on what kind of 'organism' is envisaged. See later in this chapter.

24 Lynch (1981: 94).

25 Becher and Becher (2004).

26 Perhaps the Becher subjects look 'biological' not because they have some mystical or vitalistic essence to them, but because – or to the extent that – organisms themselves are mechanistic. In other words, perhaps one could recognise there is a very general class of objects – whose form follows function, that have moving parts, that have some overall functional capability, and so on – to which both machines and organisms belong. This is returned to in Chapter 10.

27 Benevolo (1980: 336); Le Corbusier ([1933] 1964: 268); Le Corbusier (1947a: 41).

28 Machine: Le Corbusier ([1933] 1964); anthropomorphic expression: Barnett (1986); Gold (1997: 45); organic: Korn (1953: 86) 'Corbusier's plan forms an organic group of zones . . . the plan is capable of lateral extension in one or both directions'.

29 Hilberseimer (1944: 167,170, 191).

30 Soria y Mata (1892). Elsewhere, Paolo Soleri mixes biological and technical metaphors when describing his Arcosanti development – a kind of city in a building, in Arizona (Soleri, 1969; also Lima 2003). Sohn (2003: 119) refers to *Organische Stadtbaukunst* – the organic art of building towns. 'Insectile' – Barnett (1986).

31 Jacobs (1965: 386; 390).

32 Nigel Taylor (1998) discusses possible interpretations of paradigm shifts in planning theory in the fifty-year period since the Second World War.

33 Geddes' biographies describe him variously as 'The Interpreter' (Defries, 1928); 'Pioneer of Sociology' (Mairet, 1957), 'Biologist. Town Planner. Re-educator, Peace-warrior' (Boardman, 1978), 'Social Evolutionist and City Planner' (Meller, 1990) and simply 'Maker of the Future' (Boardman, 1944). Geddes' wide range of publications have been categorised under the following headings: Biology-Botany (38 references); Sociology (38); Town and Regional Planning (23); Education (24); Art (10); Economics (7); Geography (3); History (3); Classification of the Sciences (1); Exhibitions (1); Religion and Philosophy (1); and finally 'Miscellaneous' (3) (Strathclyde University Geddes Archive, <www.strath.ac.uk/archives/ua/pg/index/d/indextothepapersofsirpatrickgeddes-subjectlisting/indextothepapersofsirpatrickgeddes-publishedmaterial/>). Among other things, Geddes studied under T. H. Huxley and at the Sorbonne, met Charles Darwin while a demonstrator at University College London, and became Professor of Botany at Dundee University. He advanced his own theories of life and evolution, before becoming a pioneer of the town planning movement, personally applying himself to various urban regeneration schemes, town plans and garden designs. See also Kitchen (1975: 53); Welter (2002).

34 Geddes ([1915] 1949: 9).

35 Cited in Kostof (1991: 86). Indeed, Geddes seemed to anticipate today's fascination with complexity: 'The patterns here seem simple, there intricate, often mazy beyond our unravelling, and all well-nigh are changing, even day by day, as we watch. Nay, these very webs are themselves anew caught up to serve as threads again, within new and vaster combinations' Geddes ([1915] 1949: 2). According to Meller (1980: 203), Geddes understood 'the totality of modern city life in all its complexity'.

36 Geddes ([1915] 1949: 71, 80).

37 Jacobs (1965: 442–443, 445); Jacobs (1965: 448). The link between Jacobs' organised complexity and contemporary complexity science has been noted by Charles Jencks (for example, 1995) and Michael Batty (for example, 2005) – a point to be returned to in Chapter 6. Perhaps cities also can still be related to the first and second kinds of problem, as well as the third, where the latter build upon the former.

38 This also relates to the idea that intricate complex urbanism can be achieved not (only) by skilled professionals designing complicated urban products in the abstract, but can be achieved by the combination of many relatively simple acts of construction, of the kind that can be handled by individuals (Alexander, 1979; Alexander *et al.*, 1977).

39 The sciences of complexity have been linked to urbanism, for example, with regard to fractal geometry at different urban scales (Batty and Longley, 1994; Bovill, 1996; Frankhauser and Tannier, 2005); the generation of complex emergent patterns from simple rule systems (Batty, 1995a, 2000; Batty and Xie, 1997; Erickson and Lloyd-Jones, 1997; Xie, 1996;); social networks and complex adaptive systems (Green, 1999); interpretations of the complexity of architectural form (Salingaros, 1997); 'new science and new architecture' (Jencks (ed.), 1997b); emergence and cities (Johnson, 2001; Peterlin, 2005a, 2005b). See also Batty (1995b, 1995c); Diappi (ed.) (2004); Batty (2005, 2008b).

40 Batty (2005: 107; 457); Batty (2005: 5).

41 This parallels the recognition of the 'characteristic structure' of street patterns (Marshall, 2005).

42 Kostof (1991: 13) remarks that urban form is not a finite complicated object.

43 Chapters 1, 2; Alexander (1966).

44 This is not to say that a city could not or should not be planned or designed to be in some aspect 'like an organism'. It would be quite possible to advocate, say, that a city should have a definite limit of growth and optimum size, for example. But the argument here is that it is not a good description of naturally growing cities; and while there may be good reason to limit settlement size, it is an illogical argument to say that a city should have a maximum size *because* an organism has one. In any case, as Thomson and Geddes pointed out, 'some fishes and reptiles continue growing as long as they live, just like many trees; and this shows that a limit of size is not fundamentally insisted on by nature' (1931: 17).

45 An organism and a city both have functionally specialised parts, but in an organism the parts are subordinate and in effect work together to support the functioning of the whole body; whereas in a city, the parts may complement each other to some extent – or be cooperative to some extent – but they are also partly in competition. The Architext group were opposed to the 'incipient totalitarianism' of Modernism and Metabolism (Curl, 2005: 33) – which we could interpret as being against the city as organism–machine.

46 Characteristics of sponge: Jenkins (1999: 55); *Syllis ramosa*: Geddes and

Thomson (1889: 196–197); siphonophore colony: Geddes and Thomson (1889: 194); 'Man-reef': Geddes ([1915] 1949: 9). Slime-mould: Jencks (1995: 36); specific analogy between city and slime-mould made by Jencks at Cities of Tomorrow lecture, Bartlett School of Planning, 1998.

47   Vermeij (2004: 20) on composite organisms.

48   Dawkins ([1976] 2006, [1982] 1999). Another analogy: a snail, its shell, and its genes. This could be a society, its inorganic physical containment (such as a city), and its components citizens with their own agendas.

49   Mumford refers to 'amoeboid growth' and 'social chromosomes' (1938: 233–234); Marshall (2001); Green (2005); Vermeij (2004: 146) 'Metaphors can be at once illuminating and misleading. We must tread carefully in extracting insights from them lest these revelations emanate from parts of the metaphor that do not accurately represent the abstract phenomena we are trying to understand.'

50   As Resnick (1997: 134) has pointed out, a flock of birds may behave sometimes as if a whole, but this does not mean it behaves like an individual bird: 'A flock isn't a big bird.'

51   Vermeij (2004: 144) on distinction between central and collective intelligence; also Resnick, centralised and decentralised (1997: 4–5).

52   However, see Choay (1997: 74, 82, 107) on the building–city 'homology'.

53   The rooms house different people in different roles doing different activities. A building is a corporate entity because it houses a social unit (Chapter 4). Wojtowicz (1996: 76) on building as organism.

54   Relationships will vary between cultures. Barrie Shelton points out the 'tendency for western buildings to be designed whole, complete, and not necessarily easily extendible, whereas Japanese buildings are more modular' (Shelton, 1999: 31–33). Also Japanese cities are more like collectives of autonomous parts rather than corporate wholes (Shelton, 1999: 175). Both Japanese houses and cities are more 'collective' than 'corporate' compared to their western counterparts.

55   Indeed, a city accommodates a society (the citizenry) in the way a building accommodates a social unit (such as a household or firm). That is to say, there is not a one-to-one relationship between individuals in a social unit and the rooms in a building; nor is there a one-to-one relationship between social units in a society and the buildings in a city.

56   According to Shane, the term ecosystem was coined to mean a self-organizing system of relationships, a 'community of organisms and their physical environment as an ecological unit' (2005: 52).

57   This has a resonance with *A Pattern Language*: 'In short, no pattern is an isolated entity . . . when you build a thing you cannot merely build that thing in isolation . . . the thing which you make takes its place in the web of nature, as you make it' (Alexander *et al.*, 1977: xiii).

58   To a swallow, as Daniel Dennett points out, a barn *is* its environment (1996). And, a termite nest, which we consider as part of the natural environment, is a

mini-ecosystem or microclimate constructed by the termites in a directly analogous way to our own urban constructions.

59   In another urban analogy used in biology, the biological cell has been called a 'vast, teeming metropolis' (Bryson, 2003: 333). The biological cell was originally named – by Robert Hooke – after the cell in the sense of a small enclosed room (Bennett *et al.*, 2003). Hooke proposed rebuilding London after the Great Fire by means of a 'cellular' plan (March and Steadman, 1971).

60   In the distant past, one could imagine, any city or settlement could be regarded as simply a collection or array of buildings. One could add another building, to get an array with more units (Figure 3.3 c). However, somewhere down the line, people got to thinking of the city as a single object. This is seen in the way we talk of a city *growing* or *developing* (Figure 3.3 b or d). City 'growth' or 'development' is perhaps the oldest organic analogy in urbanism. It implies that the city is something singular and capable of growth or development like an organism This is so ingrained that we hardly notice it as a metaphor or analogy. Hence, recognition of a city as a complex, collective entity is perhaps just removing the assumption of being a corporate object, however complex or dynamic.

6 EMERGENCE AND EVOLUTION

Natural selection is the blind watchmaker, blind because it does not see ahead, does not plan consequences, has no purpose in view. Yet the living results of natural selection overwhelmingly impress us with the appearance of design as if by a master watchmaker, impress us with the illusion of design and planning.
Richard Dawkins, *The Blind Watchmaker*[1]

The creation of complex functional 'architecture' is not limited to the human world. Termites create the world's tallest non-human structures, nests that have been described as 'air-conditioned skyscrapers that are immensely larger and arguably more sophisticated than the vast majority of human buildings'. Termites create complex architectures with intricate interior features such as stacked chambers connected by helix-shaped vertical passages like spiral staircases. Compass termites create 'tower blocks' that are aligned north–south, in such a way that they have minimum exposure to the fierce midday sun (image opposite).[2]

Because of their sophistication and fitness for purpose, these insect structures look as if they have been deliberately designed or planned. For example, the compass termites' mounds look as if they were designed for the same temperature-regulating purpose for which some of Le Corbusier's blocks of flats were expressly designed on a north–south axis. However, unlike the blocks of flats, the termite 'skyscrapers' were not purposively designed in this way. As far as we know, there is no termite 'master architect' or 'master planner' preconceiving the design or supervising construction. Everywhere in the natural world we see this 'illusion of design and planning', or 'design without a designer'.[3]

In the urban world, we can recognise some parallels. While most

6.0 • Termite 'skyscrapers' aligned north–south (Australia).

buildings are designed in the sense that they are preconceived as a whole before construction, we sometimes have cases of 'architecture without architects'. More significantly, we can recognise the cases of 'unplanned' cities – collective entities – where individual buildings or streets may be deliberately designed, but there is no overall planning. And yet these traditional settlements (like Arbil in Mesopotamia, Chapter 1) seem to have a coherent order and functionality about them.

Can we learn from our understanding of insect 'cities' – how they came to be the way they are – to help understand how human cities can be 'unplanned', and yet ordered and functional?

The form of the termite skyscrapers is not designed but may be said to be *emergent*. The emergent order – or 'design' – came out of, or emerged from, the interactions of individual termites doing simple individual actions, like picking up, carrying and depositing things. Having said that, this order cannot wholly be explained by trial and error or random chance occurring *during* the emergence of an individual mound, but must be seen to result from this inherited building behaviour being repeated and adapted over the course of successive iterations of mound-building over countless generations of termites. This amounts to saying that the functional 'design' of the termite mounds is a product of evolution – just like the 'functional design' of the termites' bodies themselves.[4]

This chapter sets out to explore and explain the concepts of emergence and evolution, and interpret their effects as manifested in a variety of biological and non-biological contexts. In the first half of this chapter, we shall look at the phenomenon of Emergence, and how simple generative processes can create large-scale complex order. In the second half of the chapter, we turn to Evolution, in which we see how generative processes, in tandem with iterative feedback from the environment, can create what we recognise as functional order. Together, the concepts of emergence and evolution can help explain the 'illusion of design and planning' in the natural world, and ultimately, can help explain the functional order in humans' 'unplanned' cities.

This chapter touches on a number of issues – fractals, self-organisation, animal 'architecture', adaptation, evolution, and so on – whose full understanding would require reference to works in those specific disciplines. The treatment here is not a comprehensive synopsis, but should be seen as a selection of highlights – a series of appetisers, perhaps – which the reader may wish to follow up by reference to more specialist works. The chapter is to a large extent a review and synthesis of findings from other disciplines, but with some new interpretations developed in particular in the latter part of the chapter, that develop a perspective on emergence and evolution that is suitable for application to cities and urbanism.

EMERGENCE

An emergent effect is one that arises from the interaction of individual actions, which may have their own rules, but there is no overarching blueprint. As a result, an emergent effect is one whose overall form or outcome is in some way surprising – that is, unanticipated from the (rules of) assembly of individual parts. Jack Cohen and Ian Stewart have described emergent phenomena as 'regularities of behaviour that somehow seem to transcend their own ingredients'.[5]

To explore and explain emergence, we shall first consider the phenomenon of emergence, in a simple abstract way, and then illustrate it with more elaborate examples from computer simulations, the natural world and finally the human context.

Abstract patterns

Let us start by considering as simple an example as possible. Suppose you are given the following rule-set:

(1)   Move forward 10 metres, marking out a line
(2)   Turn to face 90 degrees to the left
(3)   Repeat steps (1) and (2) three times.

What you will end up with is four lines that make up a square (Figure 6.1a).[6] Here, the square is technically emergent (though in this very simple case, not exactly unanticipated), in the sense that the rules nowhere specify 'create a square'. In effect, from what was ostensibly an exercise in linear extension and rotation, a two-dimensional figure has suddenly popped into existence. That is emergence.

In terms of Chapter 2, we have created geometric *order*, without necessarily any planning *intention*, or the use of a prescription by *plan*. In effect, emergent order arises through aggregation and application of consistent rules or repeated actions. In this sense, we say that a square is ordered because (for example) its sides and angles are the same, not because there is an 'essence of squareness' that is intrinsically 'ordered'.

As another example, let us now assume that the unit of generation is the square itself. Add one square to another, and, if overlapping in a certain way, shown in Figure 6.1 (b), you will get two squares, plus another smaller square (their overlap), plus two L-shaped hexagons, plus an octagon (the overall outline shape). The combined figure – which is complex compared with the

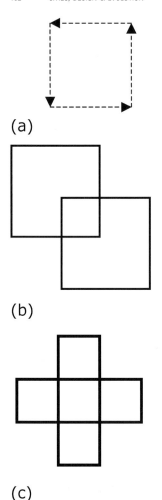

(a)

(b)

(c)

6.1 • Emergent shapes: (a) Four lines added creating a square; (b) Two squares added creating at least six shapes; (c) Two rectangles added creating at least 20 shapes.

two original squares – contains six figures instead of two, including two new *types* of shape (L-shaped hexagon, and octagon). The whole, in other words, is greater than the sum of the parts – a characteristic indicator of emergence.[7]

A third example is shown in Figure 6.1 (c), where two rectangles are added together to generate at least twenty shapes, including a cross (the overall outline), five small squares, and a variety of small rectangles, T shapes and L shapes.[8]

A practical consequence of this is that the complex geometric order need not be generated by a complicated blueprint, but by a simple rule-set: take two simple shapes and add them together. In other words, complex order need not be generated by painstakingly preconceiving and drafting out complicated shapes.

Put another way, if Figure 6.1 (c) were a cross-shaped city layout, this could have been designed consciously as a cross on plan (city design) or it could be achieved by aggregating a series of squares (urban order without city design); or simply setting out a series of orthogonal lines – such as using a Roman *groma* (Chapter 2).

The facility to create complex shapes from simple rules is also seen in the case of fractals.[9] For example, the 'H-fractal' in Figure 6.2 (a) was generated by a simple branching algorithm, iterated several times. The 'diamond-cross tapestry' shape (b) was created by simply adding four small squares to each square present at each stage, and repeating. Figure 6.2 (c) and (d) show the difference between tweaking the rule of generation slightly. In (c), each successive set of circles has a diameter of a third of the previous; in (d) the figure is 45 per cent. Seemingly out of nowhere, a 'tartan' grid pattern emerges.

Each of the Figures in Figure 6.2 displays order, but the order is obtained by application of a programme (rule), not by setting out a blueprint where the exact position of each element is determined in advance. Figure 6.2 (b) *could* be a blueprint for a 'Diamond-cross tapestry city' (city design), but the same layout could result from applying urban ordering through repeated application of the 'square → 5 square' rule.

Figure 6.3 shows a fractal known as the Lévy curve.[10] The overall figure (a) was generated by making a perpendicular kink in each straight-line segment, iterating 12 times (b). The result is a curly, croissant-like object – but there is no blueprint for curly croissants; only the 'kink-link' rule.

Note that the complex form (that is nevertheless clearly regular and symmetrical seen as a whole) includes parts that locally look irregular, and look like a labyrinthine tessellation of rectilinear polygons that resemble neither the whole (croissant) nor the original generator (kinked link).

6.2 • Four fractals with their generative rules: (a) H-fractal; (b) Diamond-cross tapestry; (c) Circles at 33 per cent diameter reduction per iteration; (d) Circles at 45 per cent.

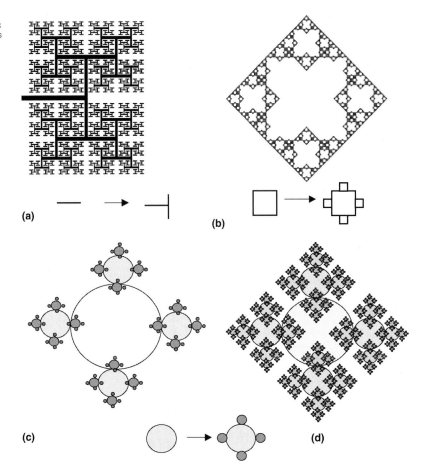

(a)

(b)

(c)

(d)

In each case, in the fractals of Figure 6.2 and 6.3, the generative parts here really are simple, and are *not* simplifications of the whole, that is, not like the superficial simplified representations of cities we saw in Chapter 2 (Johnson-Marshall, Figure 2.13; Forshaw-Abercrombie, Figure 2.14). Here, the line and square are true generators of the final complex form.

These examples demonstrate the difference between a 'recipe' and a 'blueprint' as a generator of form. A blueprint specifies the complete product; whereas a recipe tells of the steps required to make it. One could issue the three instructions for making a square verbally, without the need for any two-dimensional representation or blueprint. This points to the 'compact' or 'concise' nature of construction instructions in the form of a recipe – which is useful when actually generating forms.

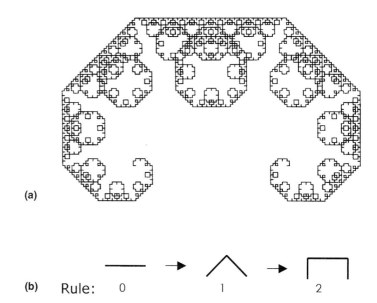

(a)

6.3 • Lévy curve (a) 'Croissant', $i = 12$ (b) Rule ($i = 0$, 1, 2).

(b)   Rule: 0   1   2

The examples we have seen, and the discussion so far, have focused mainly on the idea that a given starting position and known programme would generate a given kind of output (final pattern). The outcome is in principle predictable, simply dependent on the number of iterations. Next, we look at a case where the starting position may be unknown or random, but once started, the outcome is deterministic.

Cellular automata and artificial life

A simple example of the dynamic aspect of emergence can be taken from the classic Game of Life, a cellular automaton application originally devised by John Conway. Put briefly, a cellular automaton is a grid of cells, where each cell may take one of a number of states, according to a rule-set relating to the state of neighbouring cells.[11] In the Game of Life, the grid is square, there are only two states (alive and dead) and only three rules. A dead cell stays dead and a live cell stays alive unless:

(1)   If a dead cell has exactly three live neighbours, it comes alive.
(2)   If a live cell has more than three live neighbours, it 'dies of overcrowding'.
(3)   If a live cell has less than two live neighbours, it 'dies of exposure'.

The Game of Life can be played out on paper (or across the floor of a building . . . and down the corridor), but is much more effectively done by computer.

What happens when this is run is a surprising array of shapes and dynamic phenomena, including blinking rectangles, blooming florescences and bursting fireworks. The effect is kaleidoscopic, sometimes chaotic, sometimes like colliding particles, and sometimes lifelike – like a 'zoo' of microbes, perhaps. Some phenomena continue dynamically and unpredictably for some considerable time but eventually settle down to an equilibrium where everything is permanently dead, alive, or simply oscillating between the two (Figure 6.4).

Of particular note, there is the phenomenon of the 'glider' (or 'walker'), a shape that walks across the screen, two shapes alternating one after the other (but moved on one 'step') (Figure 6.4 d; Figure 6.5). This looks almost as if it is a single entity that has been programmed to glide. For example, one may imagine a programmer using the whole glider as the fundamental generative unit, and programming it to move as a whole. For example, the rule-set:

(1)   Make 'glider shape' out of pixels;
(2)   Move all pixels constituting 'glider shape' one pixel diagonally to the lower right;
(3)   Repeat step (2).

would move the shape directly from Figure 6.5 (a) to (e), and onwards.

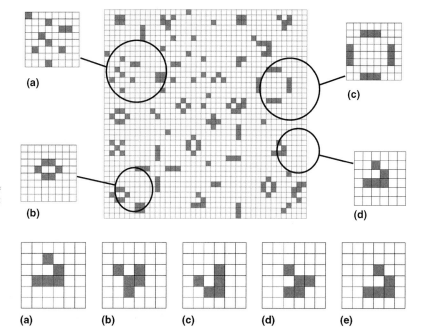

6.4 • Examples from the Game of Life: (a) Will die of exposure in next iteration; (b) Stays fixed in position; (c) Alternates between horizontal and vertical; (d) Moves across the screen (see Figure 6.5).

6.5 • Emergent behaviour: a 'glider' walks across the grid (a) to (e). The apparent behaviour of the whole – the 'glider' – is entirely a product of the behaviour of the individual cells.

(a)   (b)   (c)   (d)   (e)

But in the Game of Life things have not been programmed like this at all. The only rules being followed are the three rules given earlier, that are enacted by individual cells. The glider as a whole unit is not following any rules – only the individual cells are. So the glider is not a fundamental unit at all, simply a by-product of the on–off behaviour of individual pixels. The same rules are being followed by *all* the pixels, simply doing their own thing, oblivious to the existence of gliders. This is what we mean by saying the rules are local, but the effects are unanticipated from those rules. So the 'glider' can be seen as the way a higher-order phenomenon may emerge from a lower-order system – in a very simple and most rudimentary way, almost as one might imagine the emergence of a living thing from non-living material.

Emergent patterns in living things

Self-organisation and emergent patterns are not just limited to computer models, but are clearly interpretable in (real, biological) living systems. In self-organising systems in nature, order is created through internal interactions and feedback, but without intervention by external directing influences: 'No architect or foreman holds the blueprint or has a preconceived idea about what patterns will evolve.' The rules are local, applying to each individual transformation. So the constructor need not have a grand vision of a whole, but simply add a branch here or a kink there.[12]

Cellular automata have also been used to create patterns that have intriguing resemblances to living creatures, for example, the patterns on shells or zebras (Figure 6.6). Whatever the biochemical details, the common point here is that simple local rules create complex global patterns. The intricate natural pattern we see on a shell (Figure 1.8(d) need not have been created by any conscious will – like an anthropomorphic 'Nature' painting her pretty striped patterns. Rather, the pattern is simply encoded in a short logical rule-set (or chemical 'code') for dark and light, and mechanistically cranked out as the organism grows.[13]

The ability to generate complexity from a small amount of information is clearly extremely useful for concise instruction-making, for packaging instructions, such as when an organism reproduces the instructions to create another organism. For example, the information that would be required to specify the location of all the parts of the human body – indeed, the connections in the brain alone – is more than the information encoded in a human cell, that is used to specify development of a new organism. (In this sense, an organism is not a 'building' with a 'blueprint'.)[14]

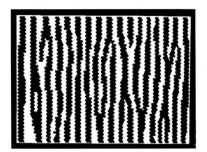

6.6 • Zebra stripes pattern generated by cellular automata; compare Figure 1.8.

Beehive 'planning'

Bees and beehives have often provided inspiration for metaphors about societies, architectural forms and city-building.[15] Bee 'architecture' is impressive in its intricate functionality, its fitness for purpose, its efficiency, and the marvel as to how small simple-minded creatures can create such large and complex constructions – as an alien observer might say of human cities.

Bees' hives can be revealing in the way they are 'designed'. For a start, the bees build the hive in a way that need not involve a grand plan, a blueprint inside the head of any particular bee, but rather through incremental application of local rules for forming cells. The idea of a beehive designed collectively without a single 'architect' clearly has a parallel with Rudofsky's *Architecture without Architects*. But we can also see the two-dimensional equivalent of 'land use planning without land use planners' in the pattern of cells in the hive comb.[16]

A typical honey bee colony has some 100,000 hexagonal cells. In the hive comb of the honey bee, there is an array of practically identical hexagonal cells, each of which can have one of three 'land uses': each cell can be a 'brood' cell (occupied by an egg, pupa or larva), a cell filled with honey; or cell filled with pollen. Additionally, a cell can be empty: this represents the fourth state.[17]

Starting from an empty comb, the cells are then deposited with eggs, pollen or honey. The pattern of cells in the comb turns out to be a kind of concentric pattern, where the innermost part is filled with eggs (brood cells); then in the middle there is a layer of pollen cells, and finally an outer zone of honey cells. This almost looks like a classic urban concentric pattern. At first sight one might imagine that the bees planned the comb this way, with a 'brood zone' on the inside and 'honey zone' on the outside (Figure 6.7).

6.7 • The concentric pattern of three 'land use zones' in a hive comb: brood cells in the middle, then a concentric ring of pollen, then honey on the outside. Note that not all cells conform with this 'zoning' pattern.

However, this is not a fixed pattern – there is an ongoing turnover of 'land uses' between cells, but despite periodic deposition and removal of different kinds of cell content, overall a concentric pattern prevails.[18]

It turns out, indeed, that we do not need to imagine a bee 'planner' planning a concentric land use pattern. The pattern can be readily generated by simple rules as follows.

(1) The queen lays eggs in an 'unsystematic, zig-zagging' path, but where there is a tendency for these to be in cells close to each other.
(2) The workers deposit honey and pollen at random.
(3) Honey and pollen are removed preferentially from cells near the brood cells.
(4) Pollen (used to feed the brood) is used up faster than honey.[19]

What happens is that as the queen wanders across the comb, crossing and recrossing the surface, the central cells tend to fill up with brood. The pollen and honey are used to feed the developing larvae, but they are used up at differential rates – the pollen is used up at ten times the rate of honey. This means that the pollen is more likely to be used up close to the brood cells. The result is the concentric 'zoning' pattern.[20]

The first important point here is that – like the case of the glider in the Game of Life – the pattern looks as if it were 'designed', but it is not. Scott Camazine and colleagues have shown that it is possible for the pattern to emerge simply from those local rules and simple behaviours (Figure 6.8): 'In the self-organization hypothesis, there is no need to invoke a blueprint that specifies locations for brood, pollen, and honey, since the dynamic relationships among the component processes of deposition and removal are sufficient to organize a pattern on the combs.' This means the bees need not have any 'grand plan', nor 'omniscient architect', but they just keep doing simple things. As Steve Jones points out, for the concentric pattern to emerge, no more organisation is needed than the ability for a bee to test the contents of what is in a neighbouring cell.[21]

A second important point should also be noted, to do with the nature of the emergent order. Where there are cells of one type in the 'wrong zone' (for example, a honey cell inside the central 'pollen zone') these are emphatically *not* 'anomalies', or 'locational errors' or 'imperfections in the plan'. That is to say, they are not imperfect systematic order (Chapter 3). They are not like a yellow brick erroneously placed in what should be a red brick wall. Rather, it is simply that cells of a given type are more likely to be found in some locations than others, and those occupying less likely locations are simply the result of faithfully executing the rule-set.

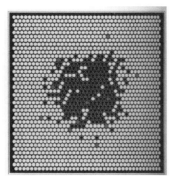
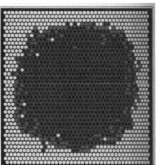

6.8 • Hexagonal cellular automaton simulation of hive comb concentric pattern formation.

In effect, this illustrates a case of characteristic order overlain on systematic order: in effect, the hexagonal cells represent a systematic order, while the pattern of 'land uses' overlain on it exhibits characteristic order. The characteristic order is identifiable when a roughly concentric hive comb pattern is formed, even if the central zone has occasional honey or pollen cells instead of brood cells. The characteristic order – the order part – is explained by the consistency of rules; so it is not completely random (even though random processes are involved). Also seen is the difference between 'concentric design' and 'comb ordering' – echoing city design and urban ordering – and echoing the difference between an overall composition and internal order – except that the concentric pattern was not the product of design, only ordering working itself out.[22]

Emergence in human affairs

Emergent effects can also be seen in the case of human behaviour and systems. These have the distinguishing feature that individual actions may be known to be conscious and intentional, even if the aggregate outcomes are not. Most familiar is perhaps market behaviour, applying to all sorts of markets in all kinds of goods and services – as argued by Adam Smith.[23]

A direct vivid example of emergence is the phenomenon of a 'Mexican wave' at a sports stadium, where the wave's apparent movement round the stadium is the result of individual spectators leaping up and down in succession. Here, the wave – like the glider in the Game of Life – is not a fundamental unit; rather, it is a by-product or emergent effect of actions of individual people standing up and sitting down. That is, the wave's transverse movement round the stadium is not a macro-scale version of the spectators' vertical movements.[24]

In this case the macro-effect is impersonal – the wave itself is not consciously propagating itself – even if the individual crowd members are consciously and intentionally leaping up and down. As it happens, the Mexican wave is an unusual case in that the members of the crowd are usually deliberately standing up and down precisely in order to create the wave. But more normally, the macro-effects are unanticipated, perhaps unknown and unheeded – like the 'pattern' formed by, say, the components of the pin-manufacturing industry, or distribution of wealth in a society.

Lessons from emergence

We can pause here briefly to draw attention to five key aspects of emergence that will help us better understand evolution and ultimately urban change.

First – and this was the main point of studying emergence in the first place – emergence shows how we can have the creation of recognisable order, even if there is no design, planning, forethought or conscious intention. There was no master artist preconceiving the form of the Lévy 'croissant', no master engineer creating a blueprint for a 'glider', no bee master-planner setting out concentric zones for brood, pollen and honey. Rather, in each case, the ordered-looking patterns arose out of the interactions of individual actors (or programmes) doing individually simple (and not necessarily conscious) things, many times and in combination.

Secondly, however, the individual actions *may* be conscious and purposeful, but this does not mean that the emergent effect is necessarily intended or anticipated (far less, that it itself has consciousness or purpose). So, even if the bees were conscious of the rules by which they are intentionally depositing eggs, pollen and honey, this does not mean they are intentionally creating a concentric pattern. In other words, it does *not* require the micro-action to be 'blind' or 'unconscious' for the macro-effect (large-scale or long-term) to be unconscious and unanticipated.

Thirdly, we see that the 'global' order or patterns emerge from the behaviour of actors following local rules. These actors may only have local knowledge – what is happening in the immediately neighbouring cells, stadium seats, and so on. They may not be aware of the wider consequences of their actions – the emergent patterns that may be created at the larger scale.

Fourthly, it is not the local actors or actions that are doing the emerging. Emergence is rather the indirect effect of the individual actions, observed from a suitably zoomed-out spatial or temporal scale. In the case of the emergent stadium wave, for example, the wave sweeps round the stadium, but the individual spectators are themselves neither sweeping nor emerging. They are just standing up and sitting down. Similarly, in the Game of Life, the gliders may glide emergently, but the pixels are neither gliding nor emerging, but simply toggling on and off.

Fifthly and finally, it is clear that these emergent effects can be seen in both biological and non-biological contexts. Just because emergence may be interpreted in patterns on shells or hive combs does not mean that it is an exclusively biological phenomenon. Rather, emergence is a generic, abstract concept, that only requires us to identify components and their rules of interaction at one scale, and to identify emergent patterns at another scale. It does not matter if either the local components are individually alive, or the emergent effect is alive. The fact that gliders emerge in the Game of Life does not mean the gliders or the pixels are alive in a biological sense, any more than a tree-like fractal, administrative hierarchy or road layout structure is alive, for being tree-like. In the living world, it is just that the generic logical operation of repeated branching – that creates a tree-like structure – is one 'discovered' and exploited by Nature, in the form of trees, lungs, and other branching structures.

Emergence, then, gives the illusion of planning and design through ordered appearance. However, planning and design are not just about creating order. When it comes to biology and urban planning and design, the significance of the order is that it is associated with functionality and fitness for purpose. While emergence can explain order, we don't yet have an explanation for why a particular order has come about. For this, we need to turn to another phenomenon: evolution.

EVOLUTION

So far, we have seen how order may arise through various generative processes. In a limitless environment, one could imagine going on to create more and more forms, growing and then expanding to fill the universe with pixels, 'gliders', bees, hives, people, stadia and cities. But the world, as we know, doesn't work that way. The Earth is finite, resources are limited, and different life-forms, businesses and cities have to compete to survive. Clearly some things are better able to maintain and propagate themselves than others – we could say some things are fitter to survive than others. This fitness is significantly to do with adaptation to the environment. This adaptation comes through feedback from the environment. This is, of course, to do with evolution – or as Darwin had it, 'descent with modification through natural selection'.[25]

In this chapter so far, we have seen how order can be created in the absence of design and planning. But, over and above order, we need to understand how we can get *functional* order, and hence fitness for purpose. Therefore we turn to evolution to help understand parts of the complex functional ordered world that are not simply a result of emergence.

Evolution has a variety of definitions, of varying degrees of specificity, emphasising different aspects, and for use in different contexts.[26] For the purposes of this book, we shall explore to what extent evolution may be regarded as a generic concept, like emergence, that may be interpreted in biological and non-biological contexts. Can the human artefacts like tools and books and vehicles be said to evolve? Can evolution be used in a way that is more than 'just' an analogy, in the sense that a city is 'sort of' like an organism? Or is the essence of the meaning of evolution something that is common to both biological and non-biological cases?

In applying the concept of evolution outside biology, we have to tread carefully through a minefield of disciplinary sensitivities, ambiguities and controversies. But, given the potential promise of an evolutionary perspective, let us have faith that the effort will be worth it.[27]

First let us look at biological evolution, and then interpret what could be the evolution of artefacts. Then, we ask in what ways the latter kind of evolution differs from biological evolution, and explore how evolution might be said to apply to intentionally designed, culturally transmitted, non-living artefacts. Finally we shall see how evolution can be interpreted as an emergent effect, that, like emergence, can be interpreted outside the biological context.

Biological evolution

Biological evolution arises as a result of cumulative change in a population from generation to generation. This involves three key mechanisms: inheritance (replication and reproduction); variation (such as mutation) and natural selection (non-random elimination). Change arises from variation – mutations – in the genetic material of an organism. These are passed on to the next generation if an organism reproduces. Natural selection is the process whereby influences external to an organism favour the differential survival and reproduction of some organisms over others. Natural selection feeds back, then, to influence which organisms survive and reproduce, which species flourish and multiply and which go extinct.[28]

Over many generations this combination of reproduction, variation and selection can lead to what we recognise as *adaptation*: a good 'fit' with the environment. Ultimately, this gives rise to a long-term transformation in the form of organisms. This long-term transformation by descent is what we recognise as *evolution*.

Because organisms may have several offspring, family trees branch, and lineages diverge, according to variations in the population and in the environment. In the long term, this branching can lead to *speciation* – divergence of species. Over evolutionary timescales, this creates a spectacular diversity of forms. Multiple cases of speciation gives rise to a pattern of adaptive radiation, or divergence from a common origin. This creates the structure known as the 'tree of life', by which every living thing is related to every other in one giant 'family tree'.[29]

Overall, the combination of diverse environments and common descent helps explain the combination of diversity and 'family resemblance' seen among different species (Figure 6.9).

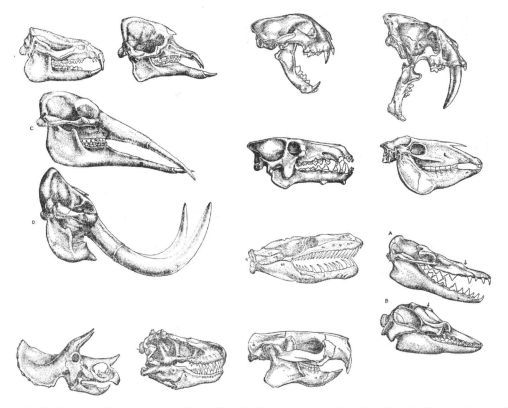

6.9 • Vertebrate skulls. The divergence of form is due to adaptation to different habitats and ways of making a living. The similarities are family resemblances, due to a common evolutionary origin. (This is a subset of the Museum of All Possible Animals.)

Evolution of artefacts

The term evolution has been regularly applied in non-biological contexts, where a variety of human systems and artefacts may be said to evolve in an open-ended, adaptive sense. These include the evolution of languages, the evolution of social customs and organisations, the evolution of institutions, the evolution of economic systems, the evolution of technological products. These cultural or technological products include things like medieval manuscripts (copied by hand, not always without error or emendation), technological products such as tools, weapons, vehicles, cutlery, office stationery, and computer hardware and software, to name just a few.[30] In each case, something useful, valued or simply something successful at getting itself retained or copied (whether intentionally or otherwise) is transmitted to the next generation. Some graphic examples are shown in Figures 6.10 to 6.12.

First, Figure 6.10 shows lineages of vehicles: (a) from horse and carriage to 'horseless carriage' and hence the private motor vehicle, and (b) from horse-drawn carriage to horse-drawn omnibus to a standard motor bus. This demonstrates that modern vehicles retained features of – or were copied from – predecessors that were different. The lineage could be extended back through time to the first wagon attached to an animal, with the wagon going back to the invention of the wheel, rollers, and so on.

Although Figure 6.10 shows what appear to be two parallel lineages, these are in effect joined, since the horse-drawn carriage led to both the car and bus. Taking this 'speciation' further, we end up with 'adaptive radiation'. Figure 6.11 shows a case of adaptive radiation, or divergence from a common origin, first in the case of the evolution of boomerangs and other weapons, and secondly in the case of Chaucerian manuscripts

Finally, Figure 6.12 shows a series of winding towers from Bernd and Hilla Becher's *Typologies*. When we look at the set of winding towers – and all the other sets in *Typologie*s, of water towers, grain silos, blast furnaces, and so on – we can interpret the similarities being due to the forms serving

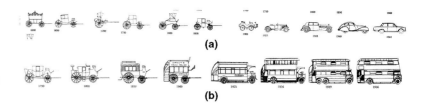

6.10 • Examples of evolution of lineages: (a) Private transport, from horse-drawn carriage to family saloon car; (b) Public transport, from horse-drawn carriage to bus.

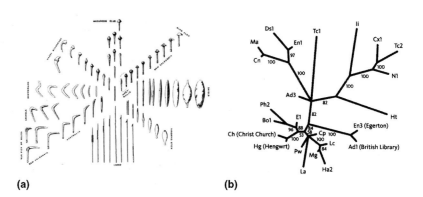

6.11 • Examples of adaptive radiation: (a) Weapons; (b) Chaucerian manuscripts.

the same functions: solving the same problems; while the differences may relate to different local contexts or circumstances (including incidental or accidental factors). The similarities could also be due to the designs being all related – all deriving from a preceding design, or set of related designs. This is what gives Figure 6.12 a resonance with the vertebrate skulls of Figure 6.9. This resonance is in effect an evolutionary resonance. This is perhaps what gives the set of industrial images a feel of the biological, even if the individual objects are not particularly biological, in the sense that winding towers do not particularly resemble organisms.

From Figures 6.10 to 6.12 we can infer variation, reproduction (copying from preceding design or model), form relating to functionality (in a

6.12 • Winding towers, by Bernd and Hilla Becher.

competitive, selective environment), and adaptation to different circumstances. It is hoped that the real, non-trivial nature of the relationships between each of the artefacts through time is understood, whether we regard this as amounting to 'evolution' or not. In all these cases, there is, at the very least, a clear resonance with biological evolution.

The question then arises as to how fundamental or essential is the relation between biological and non-biological cases. Can the term evolution reasonably be applied to these artefacts?

While there are many ways of exploring the evolution of artefacts, and many complex and subtle stories to be told, here we shall focus on just three key questions.[31] First, can evolution be applied to inanimate objects, that do not maintain or reproduce themselves? Secondly, can evolution apply to things that involve human purpose or design? And finally, can evolution apply to things that inherit characteristics from predecessors by cultural rather than genetic transmission?

Non-biological evolution

In his book *Darwin's Dangerous Idea*, Daniel Dennett suggests an abstract definition of evolution, based on a combination of variation, inheritance and selection. Dennett notes that this definition 'though drawn from biology, says nothing specific about organic molecules, nutrition, or even life'. This gives us encouragement to accept the possibility that evolution and certain of its component mechanisms may be applied to non-living contexts.[32]

When organisms reproduce, they pass on instructions not only for building bodies, but also for certain kinds of behaviour. So, along with the evolution of physical forms of species, we have the evolution of organisms' behaviour, their social systems and artefacts. In this sense, termite 'skyscrapers', beehives, wasp pots, beavers' dams and spiders' webs can be seen as products of evolution. In turn, the successful functioning of these artefacts helps the organisms that make them survive and reproduce, and are therefore part and parcel of their evolution.[33]

Today's termites' nest is not just the creation of some instantly inventive termite architect, nor of an improbably fortuitous piling up of material by unthinking termite operatives, but is the latest product in an historic lineage going back to the most rudimentary piling of material identifiable as a proto-nest. If we focus simply on the 'architecture' – ignoring for the moment the termites and their genealogy – what we see is a lineage of physical objects, that has arisen through iterations of reproduction, variation and selection. Hence, can we not say that this 'architecture' has *evolved*?

To say that a modern termite nest is a product of evolution does not imply that a nest is itself alive; nor that the 'design' of the nest was reproduced in the way that the termites themselves reproduce. But nevertheless, in their own fashion, termite nests can be said to have evolved.[34]

In this sense, it seems that a reasonable case can be made for saying that non-living things can evolve, where evolution means a long-term adaptive transformation. Put another way, a reasonable case can be made for saying that evolution is a generic concept that can be applied to both living and non-living cases.

A generic concept can be something altogether abstract, and yet still specifically and unambiguously the same concept applied in different contexts. For example, in everyday language, we talk of competition between two firms, and competition between two organisms. One does not say that when firms compete this is an analogy of the competition we see in biology, any more than we say that competition between two organisms is an analogy of human economics. We quite naturally, effortlessly and unremarkably regard these as the same concept, albeit applied in different contexts.[35]

We can recognise many such relatively abstract generic concepts, where the word is the same even if the physical process or context is different: as well as competition, we have cooperation, construction, organisation, function, locomotion, propulsion, exploitation, defence; as well as words associated with evolution, like reproduction, variation, adaptation and specialisation. In all these cases, the same word is used in both biological and non-biological contexts in the same essential way.

Patrick Geddes made a similar point, with respect to specialisation of role observed in ants: 'the "specialisation of functions" in *Formica* and the "division of labour" in *Homo* are not merely "analogues between man and nature" . . . but are absolutely identical.' While it is not claimed here that specialising mechanisms and intentions are themselves identical in ants and humans, it is suggested that the word 'specialisation', in its essential meaning, is being identically applied in the two contexts. The same is what is here being suggested for the term evolution.[36]

Therefore, if we say that a language, a manuscript or type of vehicle evolves, it means simply that it has gone through a kind of change that we recognise as amounting to evolution in biology. To say it is the same effect does *not* mean that they are done using the same internal processes: to say that a language or religion or type of technology evolves does *not* mean that we need to identify equivalents of sex or genes or biochemical bases, any more than to say that firms and plants both compete means we have to find analogies for photosynthesis in the business world, or boardrooms in the plant kingdom.

Artificial evolution

The second noted barrier to regarding the evolution of artefacts 'really' as evolution is that artefacts involve deliberate design intention. While a termite 'skyscraper' is, as far as we know, not a designed artefact, human artefacts do involve deliberate design intention: a preconception of a target designed object. There are two different ways in which this issue can be addressed.

First, we have the case of any artificial intervention. Artificial selection is when humans deliberately intervene in the reproduction of other species to produce some benefit, for example, to breed faster horses or fatter cattle. Here, only the 'best' (for human purposes) are allowed to breed, hence ensuring the next generation are full of the best of the last generation. Over many generations, humans have progressively created a diversity of domesticated forms fitter for a diversity of purposes – for example, faster racehorses, fatter cattle, friendlier dogs, juicier fruit – compared with their wild ancestors.

While evolution by artificial selection is clearly different from Darwinian evolution by natural selection – in the sense of human purpose entering the equation – it can still arguably be called a kind of evolution. After all, artificial selection is, from the selected organism's point of view, no different from natural selection. It is only 'artificial' in the sense that the human has purposely become the controlling external influence on selection, and considers this process one that is apart from nature.[37] Therefore, the presence of human intentionality *of itself* should not bar something from being called evolutionary (though it may bar it from being called Darwinian). This would apply whether the artificial intervention was through selection or through genetically engineered variation.

Artificial evolution means that a human could in principle selectively breed or genetically engineer termites, for interesting constructional behaviours, and hence evolve a succession of ever more fantastic skyscraping architectures. Here, it would seem reasonable to regard the artificially steered architectures as having evolved, even though there was conscious human steering, and although the mounds were of course not alive.

Note that *all* of the concepts suggested earlier as being generic enough to apply to both biological and non-biological contexts – such as competition, cooperation, specialisation and so on – could be said to differ between the human and natural world contexts on this point of intention. In this respect, evolution is arguably no more or less applicable to contexts in which conscious will is involved than in these other cases.[38]

Having said this, a second problem with intentionality is that it seems that in order to be meaningful, evolution has to be somehow kept as separate from intentional design or invention, where a particular target form is deliberately preconceived and constructed for some purpose.[39] The design of a new kind of car could be described as involving targeted innovation – and hence not of itself a product of evolution. But, this is no more problematic than saying that an organism reproducing is not evolving: this does not mean that reproduction cannot be part of evolution. Here the car designer's purpose is local; directed only towards the immediate next step. The aggregate outcome in the long term is still impersonal and undirected.

So, in common-sense terms, if we say that the 'railway train evolved from the ox-cart', then what we mean is that the latter is a transformed (but directly descended) version of the earlier one, not through a single complete purposive leap, but rather through a series of incremental changes, each of which had no foresight or intention with respect to the future long-term outcome (Figure 6.13). Curiously, Erasmus Darwin – grandfather of Charles – proposed several improvements to horse-drawn carriages, and had a vision of a steam-driven 'fiery chariot' that would some day replace the horse. Erasmus was no more consciously aiming for a modern 'bullet train' than was the first person to hook an ox to a wagon, but both contributed to the eventual evolution of today's model.[40]

6.13 • Transitional forms; the carriages can be interpreted as transitional adaptations between road carriages and railway carriages. But this is viewed in retrospect: at the time, those present would not necessarily regard these as transitional, and could not possibly know what they would be transitions *to*.

Overall, a case can be made for saying that evolution *can* include design as a component process; where design is of each individual iteration in a sequence, but where the design is targeted at only the immediate next step. Clearly this is different from Darwinian evolution; especially since one of the main revolutionary implications of Darwin's theory was that purposive design need not be involved anywhere in the evolution of species. However, we could nevertheless allow for a definition of evolution in which we say design *need not* be present in any stage of evolution; but yet *could* be involved in any immediate stage. This parallels the sense in which emergence may include individual acts of conscious will, but without the overall outcome having been intended.

In allowing the term evolution to include a purposive element (lest this sound heretical) this is no more or less the case than the word adaptation where – like evolution – there is no purposive element in nature. In its original sense, the word adapt meant to make apt, or make fit. It implies varying something (or oneself) so that it (or oneself) is more functional or fit for an existing purpose, or is fit for a new purpose, or is functional in a new context. In evolutionary biology, the term adaptation has come to mean better fit, but without the designed purpose. In a sense, biology has stripped the original purposive element out of the meaning of adaptation, to leave adaptation as an *effect* of processes or operations that are not purposive towards that effect.[41] Be that as it may, the result is that the term adaptation can be interpreted as referring in the most general sense to something 'changed in such a way as to become fit or fitter', where in the biological context there is no purposive element, while in the human context of systems and artefacts the purpose may be present (it may alternatively be accidental). The same, it is suggested, can be said for evolution.

Cultural evolution

In the earlier examples of the termite's nest, the nest architecture was considered part and parcel of evolution – whether arising from natural or artificial selection. But is it necessary that the evolution of the nests takes place so directly in step with the life-cycles of the termites? Is it necessary that termites and humans evolved for termites' and humans' skyscrapers to be considered evolutionary? Is it necessary that the designed is so intimately connected with the mortal fate of the designer?

For the termites, the 'design' (or structure-creating behaviour) is embodied in the termites themselves, and hence transmitted genetically from one generation to the next – the conventional case of evolutionary descent. But for humans, skyscraper designs exist independently of human genetics. Designs can be devised, stored, reproduced, varied, selected and constructed, all without any change in human genetics or generational change. After all, a single human designer, for example, could create a series of designs that could be said to evolve, from one to the next. Can this case be called evolution, when the transmission is not genetic?

This is a more difficult case to answer, not least since there is a clear difference of kind between cultural and genetic transmission, whereas the natural–artificial and even biological–non-biological boundaries are at least somewhat arbitrarily drawn. With cultural evolution, the units of transmission are in dispute, or in any case behave differently from genetic information; cultural transmission may arise from any number of disparate kinds of influence (not a single pair of complementary parents), and indeed the antecedents may be remote, with no continuous chain of viable artefacts. With cultural transmission, there is no single traceable path for ideas to follow; and there may be blurring between the reproductive, varying and selective processes within a design process. There is a case for seeing cultural transmission as being 'just an analogy' with biological evolution, even though we may allow that the long-term adaptive transformation of termite-nest architectures by humans' artificial selection is 'really' evolution.[42]

Then again, if ongoing human evolution is indeed counted as evolution – if we as a species are considered to still be evolving – then our onward evolution surely involves a combination of genetic and cultural transmission. That is, if the way the human population continues to change – which must include the influence of cultural and not just genetic advantages and inheritance on fitness – is allowed to be called evolution, then cultural transmission must surely be allowed in principle to form part of evolution.[43]

The interpretation of whether the evolution of termites' nests, artificially selected or human evolution including a culturally transmitted element are 'really' evolution in a biological sense is, in the end, in the hands of biologists. But the way that evolution may be interpreted with respect to artefacts and urbanism is something that can be further pursued in this book, whatever the biological verdict. In particular, it is possible to avoid problems of cultural transmission – and indeed of purposive design in individual increments of artificial evolution – if we consider evolution not as a *process*, but as an *effect*.

Evolution as a generic effect

The term evolution may be used to refer to the *process* by which populations transform themselves adaptively over time. The process is really a *set* of operations, such as reproduction (with the transmission of genetic information), variation (such as mutation) and selection. Alternatively, evolution can be seen as the long-term *effect* of those processes, those many generations of adaptive change. Lobe-finned fish evolved to become four-legged land animals and finally humans. When we say evolution happened, we mean that there was a transformation, via successive intermediates, or descent with modification.

If we use the term evolution to mean the effect, this has a direct parallel with the way we use the terms adaptation and emergence. Adaptation is the effect of processes (whether purposive or not). For adaptation to have its biological meaning, it must refer to the effect, since adaptation is something we recognise after the event, not before or during. Something similar can be said for emergence. Individual actors do not emerge, but their actions may lead to effects later recognised as emergence.[44]

Hence, we can say that no individual evolves, or participates in evolutionary activity *per se*. Individuals breathe, eat, and mate, but the long-term evolutionary effects – such as 'acquiring' lungs and legs or 'losing' gills and tails are of a quite different kind (referring to a population over time). Moreover, different lineages of individuals breathing, eating and mating in their own different ways and circumstances end up evolving in quite different ways.

An advantage of regarding evolution as an effect is that it is a more definite thing. If evolution is a process, it is really a set of processes, including reproduction, variation, selection, and intermediate processes or effects such as adaptation, specialisation and speciation. This set is a rather disparate collection of things ranging from internal genetic (and biochemical) processes to factors such as natural selection that are external to the organism (and, arguably, environmental rather than intrinsically biological). Rather than regarding this as a super-process or meta-process (called evolution) that explains the transformative effect, one could simply regard the transformative effect, resulting from these processes, as evolution. This effect is seen in the patterns of long-term transformation of lineages, speciation and adaptive radiation. In other words, we could say that evolution refers to the outcome of patterns of relationships over time in Figures 6.10 to 6.12, irrespective of what process caused them.[45]

If the use of the term evolution in this way offends biologists, we could give a different name to what happens in the more general, non-biological cases.[46] However, it is felt justifiable to use the term evolution as an effect, in the same way that adaptation and emergence can be applied to both biological and non-biological cases as effects: in a way that is independent of the individual transmission processes, that may or may not include increments of intention.

The effect of long-term adaptive change – from ancestral fish to ox, or ox-cart to steam-chariot – is real and equivalent, whether called evolution or 'evolution'. When using the term evolution in non-biological contexts, then, the intention is to draw attention to the reality of the phenomenon in its own context, not the proximity to biology. Today's bullet train is not just a 'creation' out of thin air, but is derived from designs of predecessors; nor is it an unchanging model, stamped out over time from an ancestral template.

Intriguingly, Patrick Geddes used the evolution of technology to help explain Darwinian evolution in biology – being 'an analogy derived from an age of mechanical progress, which gives us the watch, or sewing-machine, or tricycle' – and the express locomotive and flying-machine. Whereas Darwin's explanation of evolution – 'descent with modification by natural selection' – alluded to genealogy and animal husbandry, Geddes the biologist styled Darwinian evolution as 'cumulative patenting . . . of useful improvements in detail'.[47]

To sum up: if we allow that evolution can cover what happens to a lineage of termite nests; to the creation of dogs from wolves (through cumulative artificial selection); and to mean that it applies to the effects (adaptation, speciation) rather than processes (reproduction, variation, selection), then this amounts to saying that evolution can be non-biological, artificial and include cases of cultural transmission. In these circumstances, we could allow that populations of human-made artefacts – watches and locomotives, manuscripts, weapons and winding towers – could be said to evolve. These artefacts can, in other words, be seen as products of design *and* of evolution.

With evolution regarded as a generic concept, meaning long-term adaptive transformation, then Darwinian evolution becomes a special case in which the subjects are self-reproducing living things, with random variation and genetic transmission, and there is no conscious intention or purpose anywhere. But other versions of evolution could include non-living things, constructed by external agencies, cultural transmission, genetic-engineered variation and artificial selection, where purpose could enter individual actions, but still with no long-term purpose. Intermediate cases would include termite architecture (non-living, no intention, but genetic transmission), and traditional craft evolution (non-living, cultural transmission), where the intention is to make faithful copies of artefacts, but accidental variations arise, and these are selected by impersonal market forces.

Evolution as adaptive emergence

Recall that emergence is an effect when individual actions of one kind give rise to an outcome or product of kind that is different from – and not predictable from – the component actions. Evolution can also be seen as an emergent effect, where there is adaptive feedback from the environment. In short, evolution can be interpreted as *adaptive emergence*. This interpretation could apply to the adaptive emergence of designed objects, systems, or populations of living things.

Recall that we can recognise emergence as a generic effect, whether this happens in a stadium wave or a pixel 'glider'. That is, it is the equivalent effect in the different contexts, even if the processes (spectators leaping; or pixels toggling) is different. We can also recognise evolution as an emergent effect, recognisable as such in different contexts, even if the contributory processes (reproduction, variation and selection) are different in detail, in the different contexts.

As an emergent effect, then, evolution is independent of the nature of individual local actions – whether or not these include design intention. In nature, we can have the illusion of design of the resulting organisms, even though there is not the slightest scintilla of purpose in any individual biochemical or genetic process. Conversely, in the world of artefacts, we can refer to the evolution of wristwatches and winding towers, even if individual increments of design *are* involved.

In effect, Darwin sliced up the increments of change (required for evolution to happen) so small that they could be effectively random, without the need for any design or purpose to direct them. In the case of evolution of human artefacts and systems, however, we can say that the increments are sufficiently small that they *could* be designed, while the overall effect is still unknowably emergent in the long term, and that we can recognise this kind of long-term emergence – involving adaptive transformation – as evolution.[48]

An integrated perspective of emergence and evolution

We can now crystallise the significance of emergence and evolution through considering an historical series of assumptions, illustrated in Figures 6.14 to 6.16. First, there is a conventional assumption that a lack of design implies disorder (I); while conversely, the presence of functional order implies purposive intervention (II) – the argument from design in biology (or the original argument for town planning) (Figure 6.14).

Adam Smith showed that an overall ordered market could arise without an overall purposive agency, but simply due to the actions of individuals acting in self-interest (III), while Darwin showed that, in nature, functional

6.14 • Traditional assumptions: (I) Random forces creating disorder; (II) Direct design of an artefact – such as a machine.

order did not imply design or purposive intervention (IV) (Figure 6.15). More recently, contemporary science (complexity, artificial life, and so on) has drawn attention to the significance of emergence, and that emergent order does not imply design, at the overall level – though it does not rule out local purposive intervention (path V).

Finally, this chapter is drawing attention to the recognition of evolution as an emergent effect that, like emergence, *may* include local purposive intervention as well as non-purposive interactions. And hence, we can have functional order without *overall* design; but *with* individual design increments (path VI, Figure 6.16).

While the meaning of 'functional' and 'intentional' may be interpreted differently in different contexts, and whatever the difference between biological and non-biological evolution, the main point being argued here is the reality of the 'evolutionary' path that includes local increments of design:

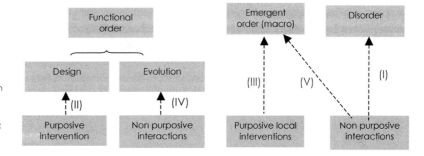

6.15 • Five paths: with the contributions of (III) Smith – individual rational consumer behaviour shapes aggregate order of the market; (IV) Darwin – biological evolution – with feedback from the environment; (V) Contemporary science: emergent effects of cellular automata, patterns of cracks, termite architecture, etc.

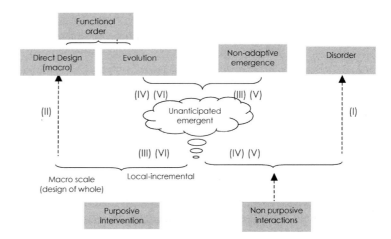

6.16 • The framework proposed here draws attention to a sixth path: (VI) Evolution of artefacts – such as machines, or buildings – over the long term. Design at micro-scale can yet lead to evolutionary effects. Functional order can be obtained directly by overall design, or can emerge through a 'fog' of unanticipated intermediate effects.

represented by path VI in Figure 6.16, but not accounted for explicitly in Figures 6.14 or 6.15. Therefore, even if there were no such thing as biological evolution (path IV), we still need a word to use for path (VI) in the cultural, technological and urban contexts to refer to the long-term transformative effect through a series of iterations (of variation, reproduction and selection) that, while they *may* be individually purposive, are not directed to any final outcome – whether or not this is labelled evolution (or 'evolution').

CONCLUSIONS

This chapter has explored the concepts of emergence and evolution in case they may help us better understand how functional order can arise in the absence of design or planning.

First, we have seen the phenomenon of emergence, where ordered patterns can arise from the interactions between simple local rules; or, a higher-level order emerges that is not specified in the rules. This shows the possibility of creating order by a rule-set, programme or recipe, rather than a blueprint or preconceived plan. This allows insects such as termites to build extraordinarily complex structures without any termite having to hold a 'blueprint' in its tiny head.

Secondly, we have seen how evolution can be regarded as the long-term adaptive transformation through successive iterative changes. Evolution also can be seen to apply to many non-biological contexts, even though the processes differ in detail. Evolution teaches us how iterative reproduction and variation with feedback from the environment can lead to adaptive fit, or functional order. This explains the functional order seen in nature, such as termite 'architecture', or the 'designs' of the termites themselves.

In the end, evolution can be seen as an emergent effect – as adaptive emergence. This chapter has drawn explicit attention to a combination in which local inputs may include intentional design, but the outcome is still emergent, unknowable in advance. This is path (VI) in Figure 6.16; and here it has been called simply evolution, although the main point is the phenomenon, rather than the label.

That said, if we do recognise it as evolution, then this formulation in effect treats evolution as a generic effect, recognisable in a variety of contexts, of which biological evolution is a specialist branch. If we accept this, then this makes the appeal to regarding urban change in evolutionary terms if anything *less* wilfully exotic (or naturalistically contrived) than if we were to insist that evolution is quintessentially biological, and a special appeal that cities are therefore 'organic entities'. Indeed, if anything it can avoid the contrivance of spurious organic analogies, because it does *not* insist that in order to accept and make use of the evolutionary nature of cities, we *also* have to assume cities are living organisms that 'naturally' reproduce themselves via some kind of genetic process.[49]

Instead, we have a perspective, of emergence and evolution, in which things are happening on at least two levels: immediate local actions, and long-term, large-scale effects. We can have functional order in the absence of overall design, but that might yet include purposive action at the micro-scale.

Although evolution is being used to refer to a generic effect, it is not so general that it can't be distinguished from other kinds of 'change with continuity over time' – it is clearly different from growth, development, reproduction, and so on. It is also different from (non-adaptive) emergence, since evolution involves environmental feedback, that changes the 'code' in an open-ended way over time. An individual termite skyscraper emerges, whereas a lineage of termite skyscrapers may be said to evolve.

The perspective here could in effect be seen as an alternative paradigm within which to treat design and evolution. Rather than a paradigm in which design and evolution are different, opposing things, we have a paradigm in which design can be part of evolution, and evolution part of design. That is to say: we can recognise evolution as emergent, where some increments may be locally purposive; while a 'design' – like nature's 'design' of a termite – can also be seen as an end-product of an evolutionary lineage or predecessor products.[50]

This paradigm – of evolution as adaptive emergence which allows local increments of design – relies on the recognition of 'path VI' in Figure 6.16. Path VI is well enough known in terms of technological and cultural evolution, including architecture, whether dealing with individual populations of buses or books or boomerangs or buildings (Figures 6.10–6.12). But it is not well developed in terms of an urban equivalent – the city as a complex dynamic collective entity – dealing with the combined populations of those artefacts and their coevolution. There still seems to be a latent assumption that things like buildings and books are simply objects taken for granted as the given contents of cities, things to be contained and organised in space; a latent assumption that functional order logically requires planning or design (perhaps especially in terms of city design) and that lack of planning leads to disorder and dysfunctional urbanism (Chapter 1). Yet the framework presented here suggests the possibility of functional order via an alternative path, that has an emergent, evolutionary aspect.

We are now ready to see how the concepts of emergence and evolution can be applied in the urban context. This we shall do first in terms of emergence (Chapter 7) and then evolution (Chapter 8).

Notes

1 Dawkins (1991: 21).

2 Tsui (1999: 87); Camazine *et al.* (2001: 377). *Apicotermes* termites (Theraulaz *et al.*, 2003: 1263, 1265); compass termite mounds (Dawkins, 1997. 13), see also Abe *et al.* (2000), Ozeki *et al.* (2007). For detailed treatment of 'animal architecture' (including animal behaviour, cognition, design, construction and evolution), see Hansell (2005, 2007) and Gould and Gould (2007).

3 Le Corbusier's Unités 'rigorously north-south oriented' (Panerai *et al.*, 2004: 116). What with 'mason' bees and 'potter' wasps – who create buildings of stones and mortar, or round pots that look as if they could be human-designed – we would be justified in calling these as 'technological' insects rather than merely 'social' insects. 'No termite need serve as overseer with blueprint in hand': Chris Langton, quoted in Levy (1993: 105). 'There was no central intelligence holding a blueprint and directing traffic': E. O. Wilson, quoted in Levy (1993: 105). The concept of 'design without a designer': see Jones (1999: 91); Ayala (2007).

4 Richard Dawkins makes an equivalent point with reference to wasps (Dawkins, 1997: 13).

5 Cohen and Stewart (1994: 232); see also Batty (2005: 51).

6 This assumes that you are on a flat plane. If you are on a sphere, you will create a curvy figure. If you are at the equator of a sphere with a circumference of 40 metres, and you start by heading north, you will arrive back where you started after three steps, having created a curvy 'triangle'. This demonstrates that if a recipe is inserted in the 'wrong' environment, one will get the 'wrong' result.

7 Overlapping squares: after Mitchell (1990: 103–104). Sum greater than parts; linear system: Saunders (1997: 52). Complex system: Herbert Simon (Batty, 2005: 65).

8 The number of shapes recognised depends on whether one includes non-contiguous shapes, or shapes joined only diagonally at their apexes.

9 The word 'fractal' was coined by Benoît Mandelbrot (1983).

10 Lauwerier (1991: 46). Technically the Lévy curve itself would be the limit of this process.

11 Levy (1993). The grid is conventionally one of squares, but could be other shapes. What constitutes a 'neighbouring' cell may vary. Here, it is assumed to be the set of eight surrounding cells (the Moore neighbourhood).

12 See, for example, a range of cases in Camazine *et al.* (2001). Camazine *et al.* (2001: 7); Camazine (2003: 36); Theraulaz *et al.* (2003: 1269).

13 Whether or not this enhances or diminishes one's wonder of nature is up to personal taste or inclination – Keats lamented Newton's stealing away of the mystery of the rainbow (Carey, 1995: 33). Biochemical details: Gribbin (2005).

14 Camazine (2005). DNA as 'recipe' rather than 'blueprint' – see, for example, Wolpert (1998: 31); Dawkins (2004: 190); Gribbin (2005: 89).

15 Jones (1999) on Shakespeare and Marx on bees. Ramírez (2000) on a variety of architects, notably Gaudí and Le Corbusier. Ramírez suggests that Le Corbusier

was more or less consciously replicating beehive architectures in some of his writings and building designs.

16   Rudofsky (1965).

17   Camazine *et al.* (2001: 310).

18   Camazine *et al.* (2001: 310). 'Despite the constant turnover in which cells are often refilled with something different, the stability of the pattern is maintained.'

19   Camazine *et al.* (2001: 310, 316, 324).

20   Jones (1999: 203).

21   Camazine *et al.* (2001: 313–15). It is not essential that the hypothesis is correct with respect to bees; it is sufficient that a set of simple local rules could generate the concentric 'zones' in the absence of deliberate 'zoning'. This case is instructive, in other words, not because 'bees do it', but because it reveals a mechanism that could create a concentric pattern without central planning. Camazine *et al.* (2001: 309); Jones (1999: 203).

22   The case of bees shows that the agents need not be sophisticated, nor their motives knowable, for the emergent pattern formation to work. Whereas with cities we might never be sure if a pattern was a result of deliberate planning intention or not, with hives it is reasonable to infer that no master-planning took place, yet the concentric structure still appeared. Emergent effects are also seen in the case of ants' 'land use zoning'; also fishes' territory. Johnson (2001: 33); Camazine *et al.* (2001).

23   Smith (1999 [1776]).

24   Farkas *et al.* (2002). The Mexican wave illustrates the distinction between the overall pattern (the wave) and the programme (standing up – sitting down) that created it. See also Hansell (2007: 129, 131); Ozeki *et al.* (2007).

25   Thomas Malthus' analysis of world population growth – and the tendency for exponential growth in offspring and descendants if unchecked – inspired the thinking of Charles Darwin and Wallace to come up with the idea of evolution by natural selection (Dawkins, 2006 [1976]; Carey, 1995: 57). 'Descent with modification' Darwin (1859: 435). Darwin used the word 'evolved' once in *Origin of Species* – the last word in the book (1859: 460). The word 'evolution' also appears in the title of another work, Charles Darwin and Alfred Russel Wallace, *Evolution by Natural Selection*.

26   Some recent definitions of evolution from biological texts. 'Biological evolution entails inherited changes in populations of organisms, over time, that lead to differences among them' (Strickberger, 2000: 3); 'change over time via descent with modification' (Hamilton, cited in Ridley (2004: 5); 'The gradual process by which the living world has been developing following the origin of life' (Mayr, 2001: 286); '*Evolution* means change, change in the form and behavior of organisms between generations' (Ridley (2004: 4); 'Biological (or organic) evolution . . . is change in the properties of groups of organisms over the course of generations' (Futuyma, 2005: 2); 'Evolution is a population genetic process' (Lynch, 2007: 370). The term evolution comes from the Latin *evolvere*, which means to unfold. In

biology, the term evolution has 'evolved'; it used to mean an unfolding like a developing embryo – or 'something more like what we mean by development' (Ridley, 2004: 7); see also Ingold (1998: 79–81). The term evolution is also applied to stars, galaxies, geological formations, chemical reactions, mathematical curves (so, even among sciences, biology does not have a monopoly on the use of the word). In this book, we concentrate on those meanings of evolution having the open-ended, adaptive connotations shared with biological evolution.

27   Jones warns against misappropriation of biological or evolutionary concepts (1999: xxiv–xxv); Mindell (2006: 195, 247) and Lynch (2007: 366, 389) are cautious applying evolutionary metaphors or evolutionary theory outside biology; while Vermeij (2004) makes the case for attempting this hazardous journey between disciplines.

28   Jones (1999: 201) 'variation, inheritance and natural selection'. Vermeij (2004: 24) refers to 'nonrandom elimination' of which natural selection is the biological manifestation. Jenkins (1999: 194) defines natural selection as 'an evolutionary mechanism by which the *total environment* selects those forms that are best suited to survive and breed' [emphasis added].

29   Cracraft and Donoghue (2004). 'In one of the most breathtaking ideas in the history of science, Charles Darwin proposed that "all the organic beings which have ever lived on this earth have descended from some one primordial form." ' (Futuyma, 2005: 1).

30   Social and cultural evolution (Young, 1988; Runciman, 1989: 34–36,44; Wheeler *et al.*, 2002; Mindell, 2006); evolution of languages (Young, 1988; after Barricelli: F. Dyson, 1998: 120; Mindell, 2006); evolution of manuscripts – 'for it really is an evolutionary process' (Dawkins, 2004: 133); evolution of artefacts and applied arts (Kubler, 1962; Steadman, 1979); evolution of the telegraph system (G. Dyson, 1998: 131–143); evolution of farm wagons (Turner, 1996: 12); the evolution of forks from knives, and paper clips from pins (Carroll, 2006: 167–169); the evolution of computer programming languages (Bolter, 1993); evolution of software: 'teeming software ecosystem' (Pincock, 2006: 20); spam and anti-spam coevolution and arms races (Goodman *et al.*, 2005: 25); evolution of viruses (Levy, 1993: 332–335; Jones, 1999); artificial software 'creatures' in the field of artificial life (Levy, 1993: 105; G. Dyson, 1998: 121–123). Note that even religions can evolve, as attitudes to morals and rituals (such as attitudes to idolatry, clothing, customs, diet, sex, suicide, and so on) gradually change over the decades and centuries; also there are schisms between different branches of religion (Hopkins, 1999; Mindell, 2006).

31   Darwin was able to usefully set out the key concepts of evolution, even without reference to detailed mechanisms of genetics (Jablonka, 2000: 28). In non-biological evolution – as with biological evolution – much effort and energy has gone into trying to establish what the units of evolution, transmission or selection actually are. This is an ongoing field of inquiry; there is no scope here to go into all the details of the different mechanisms and the precise ways in which they may be said to differ from Darwinian evolution. For detailed treatment of this topic, see,

for example, Steadman (1979); Runciman (1989); Dennett (1996); Ziman (2000a); Jablonka and Ziman (2000); Loasby (2002); Wheeler *et al.* (2002).

32 Dennett (1996: 343) continues: 'This maximally abstract definition of evolution by natural selection has been formulated *in many roughly equivalent versions*' [emphasis added]. Geerat Vermeij is quite explicit in stating that evolution – descent with modification – is 'an expected and universal historical process in economic systems' and that the fundamental processes 'work regardless of the particulars of how performance-related characteristics are introduced, inherited, modified, or eliminated' (Vermeij, 2004: 2, 3). See also Ziman (2000b: 41–42); Ziman (2002: 1–2).

33 These could be seen as part of the 'extended phenotype' of an organism – or the 'long reach of the gene' – as suggested by Richard Dawkins (1999). Dawkins elsewhere explicitly describes animal artefacts – such as potter wasps' pots – as being products of the same process as created their own bodies: 'The wasp pot gets its elegance and fitness to its task from . . . exactly the same process, indeed, as gave elegance and fitness to the wasp's own body' (Dawkins, 1997: 13).

34 'Termite nest architecture *evolved* . . .' (Noirot and Darlington, 2000: 121); 'Comparing the *evolution* of the nests with the phylogeny of the termites could be of great interest' (ibid.: 126); 'Soldier morphology and behaviour, worker defensive behaviour . . . and the detailed structure of the nest . . . all *evolve* together in a coordinated fashion' (ibid.: 137). Emphases added.

35 A bird's wing and a bee's wing are said to be analogous: they both perform the function of flight, although they fly in different ways, and were evolved by different routes. The same may be said for an aeroplane's wing. That is, we say that an aeroplane flies (whether by propeller or jet propulsion) even though its wings don't move like birds' or bees'. We tend not to regard saying that an aeroplane flies is an analogy, or a figure of speech borrowing from biology. If to fly means 'to propel oneself through the air in a controlled manner' then we can say this is a general enough definition to cover birds, bees and aeroplanes (while excluding wind-blown leaves or ballistic lava-bombs), *without* the association implying that aeroplanes must be 'alive' or 'biological' in any other sense.

36 Geddes, cited in Boardman (1978: 65). Samuel Butler made a similar point, with respect to reproduction: 'Surely if a machine is able to reproduce another machine systematically, we may say that it has a reproductive system. What is a reproductive system if it is not a system for reproduction?', Butler, cited in G Dyson (1998: 71). Here we might change the last line to 'system that reproduces', to avoid implying purpose. Vermeij (2004: 45) suggests that the division of labour underlies the ecological concept of a species and the economic concept of an occupation. Also, meaning and interpretation of 'organization' and functional specialisation (Vermeij, 2004: 138–139).

37 Besides, human influence wittingly or otherwise contributes to the 'total environment' (Jenkins, 1999: 194) that does the 'natural' selection.

38 That is, one of the objections to using terms like evolution to apply to human

products is that the evolution of human products often involves a deliberate design element (whether in variation or selection), whereas nature does not. But this objection could be levelled against using the same word 'competition' for meaning both firms consciously competing, and firms or plants unconsciously competing. The same may be said of defence, construction, division of labour, and so on. Note that a firm may not even know it is competing with another firm – the choice between the services may only be in the mind of the consumer who is aware of the choice. Even then, the consumer may not be aware of all the choices.

39   Steadman (1979).

40   G. Dyson (1998: 21–22).

41   Darwinism could be seen as a kind of inversion of the original meaning of adaptation – seeing the adaptation as an effect of fitness, rather than a cause of fitness (Steadman, 1979: 77).

42   That said, Geerat Vermeij makes the case for regarding cultural evolution as another kind of evolution. '*Regardless of how variants arise or how information is transmitted*, selection occurs through differential culling of variants according to the performance of entities in which these variants are expressed.' [Emphases added] (Vermeij, 2004: 24). See also Vermeij (2004: 25; 39).

43   On ongoing human evolution, see, for example, Douglas (2006), Holzman (2007). See also Major Transition Theory (Maynard Smith and Szathmáry, 1997).

44   We usefully talk of emergent effects rather than emergent processes. That is because the processes themselves are not directly or intrinsically associated with the effects, except with hindsight; they are fundamentally different in kind. The same may be said of evolution in the sense suggested here. Interpreting evolution as an effect rather than process is compatible with Mindell's suggestion that 'The limits of evolutionary metaphor are reached prior to identifying mechanisms of change' (2006: 247).

45   This use of the term to mean effect rather than process has a resonance with the way we use the term 'architecture'. Architecture can refer to both the art of designing buildings and the resulting physical product. Either biologists or architects might object to regarding termites' nests as being designed by a *process* of architecture, but they both seem quite comfortable in describing the *effects* or *products* – the finished nests with their spiral ramps and soaring cooling towers – as architecture (see, for example, Tsui, 1999; Noirot and Darlington, 2000; Hansell, 2005, 2007; Gould and Gould, 2007). A similar point may be made about animals' feats of 'engineering'; or genomic 'architecture' (Lynch, 2007).

46   We could say, for example, that artefacts are 'evolvent', and – at the risk of gratuitous neologism – the long-term effect is 'evolvence' (in parallel with emergence).

47   Geddes and Thomson (1889: 315); also Geddes and Thomson (1911: xii, 214). In fact, equating Darwinian evolution with the evolution of bicycles and railway locomotives was not entirely complimentary: Geddes was critical of Darwinian evolution as being *too* mechanistic, too much like an economic theory, dependent

on competitive struggle, selection and extinction. Geddes' own interpretation of evolution was somewhat more exclusively biological, more vitalistic and neo-Lamarckian. A century on, Geddes' 'cumulative patenting' is echoed by Kauffman's characterisation of Darwinian theory as a 'genealogy of contraptions' (1993: 643); and Geddes' reluctance to give selection so much credit for explaining evolution is echoed by both Kauffman and Lynch (2007). If it turns out that selection and adaptation are significantly less influential in biological evolution than is conventionally thought, then we have the intriguing prospect that the evolution of machines and other artefacts might turn out to be *more* Darwinian – in the sense of being more influenced by selection and adaptation – than biological evolution.

48   Here long-term means an unknowably large succession of increments or iterations, that makes a convergent solution impossible to target, that puts the ultimate outcome beyond the ability to influence the immediate actions.

49   This means that we need not be concerned with the details of biological repro-duction, variation, genetics, sex, chromosomes, DNA, and indeed the difference between Darwinian and neo-Darwinian evolution (or between the Darwinism of Charles and Erasmus). Those are of course significant to biological evolution, but may distract or only confuse us if we try to attach them to the other kinds of evolution. So, those seeking to understand the city in evolutionary terms need not become amateur biologists, any more than economists need to, in order to study competition or the division of labour. This conclusion appears to accord with one of the collective conclusions of Ziman *et al.* (2000: 313), despite their conclusions also being cautious about how general or abstract a level is useful to regard evolution (2000: 312).

50   This also means that as an alternative to having a distinction between planned and 'unplanned', we have a distinction between designed and 'evolvent' (Chapter 8).

7 EMERGENT URBAN ORDER

The Greeks, who used the word <u>polis</u> for city, used the very same word for a dice-and-board game that, rather like backgammon, depends upon interplay of chance and rule.

Joseph Rykwert, *The Seduction of Place*[1]

A city is like a game of chess, in that the location of each piece is the product of a rational decision, but the overall effect may look chaotic, and is unpredictable in advance. A city plan – like the plan of a chess game in progress – is a snapshot of a continuously changing process. Two cities – or two chess games – may have different distributions of pieces, but those distributions often have systematic local relationships, that give them a recognisable order. Hence cities and chess games are all different, but can all look the same.[2]

Urban forms and patterns, then, seem familiar and persistent, even as they are ever-changing. City planners, urban morphologists and geographers have traditionally studied these patterns, as if those were definite urban 'objects' for classification, like pressed flower specimens.[3] But, from the perspective of the Game of Life, this would be like the equivalent of fixing on the form of the 'glider' as an object, and studying that object's change in form over time (Figure 6.5).[4] As we saw in the last chapter, however, the glider is in a sense not a cohesive object at all, and in a sense it is not doing the behaving; rather, it is the individual pixels that are the essential units doing the behaving. In real life, as in the Game of Life, if we wish to understand the 'behaviour' of the whole, it will pay us to observe the rationale and behaviour of the parts.

In the urban context, this means thinking about what people do when they locate themselves somewhere, build something somewhere, undertake

7.0 • Snapshot of a dynamic order.

some activity (land use) somewhere. We have already seen how people's social organisation may be related to the basic elements of the built environment, such as buildings and streets (Chapter 4). These help explain the systematic order of 'street syntax' (Chapter 3). But what about the forms that arise, or indeed emerge, in the aggregate, in the absence of overall design or planning?

This chapter is about unpacking the characteristic order of 'unplanned' urbanism. This is done through looking at individual rationales and rule-sets, or programmes, that create patterns. The demonstrations relate to cities as collective entities, to the extent that – like the pixels in the Game of Life – they are composed of lots of individual things 'doing their own thing'. This chapter aims to apply the concept of emergence (in the last chapter) to urban change, and in doing so can perhaps illuminate the nature and significance of some of the concepts in earlier chapters, such as the paradigm that sees the city as a complex dynamic collective entity – and how complex, dynamic and collective are linked. The purpose is to explore and demonstrate general relationships between programmes and patterns; to see examples of how characteristic order can arise in the absence of city design – in effect, in the absence of systematic order being imposed at the city scale.

In this chapter, we shall first look at some examples of Urban Emergence, from previously published research, exploring how different patterns are created by different programmes. Then we shall develop and demonstrate how simple programmes based on formation by routes, plots and buildings can give rise to characteristic Street Patterns. Thirdly, we shall look at how individual acts of location can lead to the emergent City Forms – such as the characteristic concentric urban order at the settlement scale.

This chapter presents a series of demonstrations relating different programmes to patterns. There is a probabilistic element to this: in the absence of overall design or planning, some patterns are more likely than others, and this probabilistic tendency will affect what we see on the ground. To get a grasp of the significance of this probabilistic aspect, this chapter – alone in this book – has some quantification of the phenomena.[5]

URBAN EMERGENCE

Here we shall explore how emergent urban patterns can arise, from individual decisions of location or increments of design. First, we shall look at the emergence of concentric rings of different land uses in and around a city; secondly we shall look at the patterns of settlement in a region; thirdly, we shall see how purely local rules relating to elements such as buildings and roads and gardens give rise to the characteristic 'organic order' of traditional settlements, and finally we shall see the case of self-segregation, a potentially negative emergent outcome.

Concentric settlements

A classic model of concentric urban formation is that of von Thünen's Isolated State. Von Thünen showed how concentric rings of land uses could form due to the different prices of agricultural products located at different distances from a central market (Figure 7.1). This is based on the differential propensity, between different land uses, to try to be as accessible as possible to an urban centre. Land uses which are prepared to pay higher rent in order to be closer to the centre outbid those that are prepared to pay lower rent, for location in the innermost locations. A spectrum of different bid prices leads to a theoretical concentric distribution around the centre. This relates not only to different urban land uses, but, as von Thünen showed, also to different rural land uses, with market gardens closest to the urban area and other uses like forestry further out.[6]

While concentric land use patterns are very familiar to urban scholars and geographers, the point to be emphasised here is that these patterns form spontaneously. It is not that some city mayor or town and country planner knew or just decided that the optimal distribution was to have shops in the centre, and houses further out, and then market gardens, then pasture and finally forestry. Rather, the pattern formed spontaneously as a result of individual citizens, shop-owners and farmers and foresters acting in their own self-interests, with no regard for what the overall (or optimal) pattern would be.

This spontaneous effect is familiar enough to those studying 'unplanned' settlements, in the interest of understanding and explaining observed patterns. But what would tend to happen historically with the advent of town planning was to interpret the roughly concentric pattern as if it is the right and fitting and natural form that a city *should* have – noting, indeed, that the pattern does after all work, with shops in the most accessible location in the centre, and so on. The town planner would then tend to use this as a model for what a future settlement *should* be like. Hence, whereas a traditional 'unplanned' settlement might have a roughly concentric pattern, modern planned towns would be given a centre and a ring of suburbs or neighbourhoods, from the start. This is fine; but it is the equivalent of paying attention to the form of the 'glider' (Figure 6.6), and fitting pixels to create that shape, rather than paying attention to what the pixels are doing.

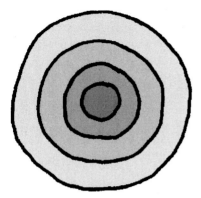

7.1 • Von Thünen's concentric land use model. Nearest the urban centre are market gardens, then arable, then pasture then forestry.

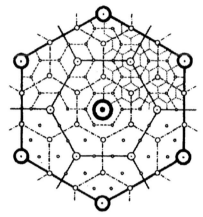

7.2 • Christaller's central place theory, resulting in a theoretical hexagonal distribution of settlements.

Distributions of settlements

A second classic example from urban geography is that of Christaller's central place theory. Here, the distribution of different kinds of shops or services, markets and market towns, for example, can be seen to form a reasonably orderly distribution generated simply by the locational choices and trading decisions of individual consumers and suppliers, with no coordination or central planning. Christaller showed that in the theoretical case of a homogeneous plain, towns would be expected to arrange themselves in an almost hexagonal hierarchical formation (Figure 7.2), not because any central authority is dictating a hexagonal pattern, but simply due to people exercising their individual locational decisions.[7]

While in reality the distribution is not as neatly hexagonal as this, the general principle tends to hold, that higher-order functions are further away from any individual, and higher-order settlements fewer and further between, than lower-order ones. Urban theory has also been applied to the distribution of settlements of different sizes.[8]

Traditional 'organic' urban forms

The foregoing examples dealt with broad distributions of land uses or settlements at low resolution. Here, we take a much higher resolution look at urban structure, at the scale of individual built and unbuilt plots of land. This third demonstration now looks at an urban simulation CA (cellular automata) model developed by Paul Coates, originally for exploring the form of the medina (old city core) of San'a, Yemen.[9]

Coates' model uses a four-state cellular automata: one unbuilt state (0), and three built states: (1) road; (2) house; (3) garden. The simulation allows changes from unoccupied to either garden, house or road; or a change from any of the occupied types to any other. There are five local rules, such as: 'If a cell is empty and there is at least one road cell *and* less than two garden cells among the four bordering cells, then make the cell a road, with 50% probability, otherwise a house.'[10]

Here, we are not so concerned with the details of the rules or the extent to which they may be said to simulate the actual morphology or morphogenetics of San'a. The point is to note how this *kind* of programme can create that *kind* of recognisable urban order. A typical result of running the simulation is shown in Figure 7.3.

We can note four points here. First, this very simple rule-set has yet generated something rather complex (cf. Chapter 6). Secondly, this somewhat mechanistic programme has yet created something rather organic-looking. Thirdly, this incremental partly random process has managed

7.3 • Typical simulation using Coates' San'a CA model.

to create something that has a coherence or order about it. Finally, something based on individual acts of construction (buildings, roads, and so on) creates something recognisably *urban* (that is, town-like or city-like).

The pattern is created only by the five local rules. These are local in the sense that there is only knowledge of what is in the immediately adjacent cells; also, there is (as before) no prescription of the overall form. For example, the creation of a scatter of enclosed *bostans* (garden surrounded by houses) was not achieved through specification of a 'scatter of green spaces'. There is no rule saying 'green space should be 25% of total space, distributed in pockets of such and such a size', never mind an outright specification of particular locations. Neither was it a case of 'stuff just dumped down anywhere'. It shows how local rules (systematically applied) can create a recognisably urban order, without a blueprint.

The bostans were (in this simulation) simply created by individual acts of construction of houses and gardens, not by a city-level decree for bostans. This is just like in the Game of Life, where there are only pixels doing their thing, and not specification of 'build a glider here'.

The above demonstration amounted to a combination of systematic 'ground rules' overlain by randomised acts of construction. We can now demonstrate two further kinds of variation: first, we can change the starting conditions, and secondly we can change the programme.

Figure 7.4 shows three arrays showing different outcomes for the same programme under different starting conditions: where the first cells representing 'road' are set down, from which everything else grows. In Figure 7.4 (a), the simulation is seeded by four locations representing 'town gates'; in (b), a contiguous set of road cells is used to create four roads meeting at a central crossroads; in (c), a scatter of 'seed' locations is chosen. Here, the resulting patterns (on the right hand side of Figure 7.4) all have a 'family resemblance' because they are generated from the same 'genetic code'.

As a final demonstration of Coates' model, we can tweak the parameters, to vary or 'mutate' the code, and hence get even more varied kinds of pattern. Figure 7.5 shows the result of changing the part of the code – the 'gene', perhaps – that controls the probability of an unoccupied cell becoming a road or a house, under certain circumstances. In the previous diagrams the probability of becoming a road rather than a house was 50 per cent. Figure 7.5 shows this changed to a range of different percentages.

What we now see is rather different outcomes. The first case, Figure 7.5(a), shows a rather granular pattern with hardly any garden space. As the probability for 'road' increases, then the overall morphology becomes more street-like and the area of garden increases.

7.4 • Application of the San'a programme from different 'seeding' points:(a) Four 'town gates'; (b) Four routes meeting at central square; (c) Scatter of seed points (small white points).

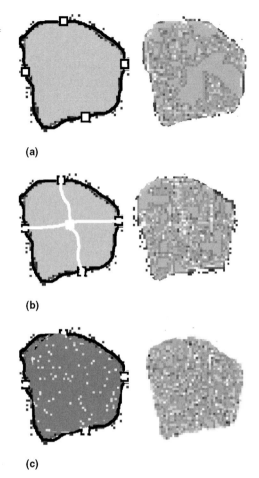

(a)

(b)

(c)

So this particular programme is not just about simulating the particular case of San'a; indeed, this *kind* of programme (CA with house, garden and road states) is not only suitable for generating medina-like morphologies in general, but it can also, by simply retuning the parameters, produce more streetgrid-like or even suburban street-like layouts (Figure 7.5d) – such as found in traditional European (non medina-like) cities or suburbs; or possibly in the more recent outer suburbs of cities of any origin.

This says something interesting about the 'San'a CA' as a tool, but it also surely tells us something interesting about real-life processes, real people and places. It tells us that rather similar – only slightly dissimilar – processes

(a)

(b)

(c)

(d)

7.5 • The code changed. The 'gene' that specifies the probability of an unoccupied cell becoming a road rather than a house was set as 50 per cent. Here we see this set at (a) 20 per cent; (b) 40 per cent; (c) 70 per cent; (d) 90 per cent.

could be at work giving rise to what are conventionally regarded as rather dissimilar forms. For example, rather than seeing the San'a medina as a completely different type of urban form from, say, suburban London (and this is a quite reasonable and sometimes useful assumption), we can see the forms as related, but where one is just 'tuned' differently from the other. So, just as the 'medina-like' form of San'a can be seen as closely related to that of, say, Tunis, or old Seville, it is much more distantly related – but still related – to the form of traditional cities such as London: especially the old City of London, but also its suburbs. The forms are related because the programmes are related; and the programmes are related because and to the extent that the needs of the people are similar: houses fronting roads, privacy, some garden space, and so on (the kinds of thing that could be codified in a 'street syntax' rule-set). It's just that these are achieved in different proportions.[11]

Finally, it is implicit that we can change the code: not just between cities, but in a single city as it grows, from inner core to outer suburbs, whether San'a, Seville or London. This aspect will be picked up later in this chapter and Chapter 8.

Emergent ghettos

In the San'a case we have just seen, the emergent features – the enclosed communal bostans – were benign, perhaps fortuitous community-beneficent by-products of individuals simply building themselves individual houses and gardens that ended up joining up. But life is not always so charmed; emergence is not intrinsically benign, and in general cannot be relied upon to deliver 'planning solutions without planning'. Or, put another way, the sum of individually favourable actions does not always add up to a gross benefit.

A clear example of this is shown graphically by Michael Batty in *Cities and Complexity*, in a simulation following the work of Schelling (Figure 7.6). Basically, the model is simulating the behaviour of individuals who are happy to live in mixed communities but who do not wish to be in a significant minority. This preference could be satisfied in principle by a completely heterogeneous spatial solution – say, where everyone is surrounded by an equal mix of all groups of people (for example, a chessboard pattern). But what we find in the process of individual people adjusting to an initial random distribution is that people end up segregating themselves into completely homogeneous blocs, with only a small minority of people – at the boundaries between blocs – living in mixed company. The nub of the matter is described in Batty's sub-caption: 'emergence of extreme segregation from local cellular automata rules implying a mild preference for living amongst one's own kind'.[12]

7.6 • Spontaneous self-segregation: 'Emergence of Extreme Segregation from Local Cellular Automata Rules Implying a Mild Preference for Living Amongst One's Own Kind.'

The point here is that, first, the segregated pattern emerged spontaneously, with each person simply reacting to the composition of their own immediate neighbours. There was no higher level of allocation to 'zones', or even any awareness by any individual of the pattern being formed. The effect is almost like a chess game in reverse, with a mix of black and white pieces spontaneously self-segregating (back) into the ordered pattern of two separate homogeneous zones.

Secondly, the outcome here can be considered negative, and happened despite being something that no individual explicitly sought. So this is a case of problematic or malign emergence, where it might have been preferable if there were some overall rules preventing this from happening. But it is nevertheless a consequence of people acting out their individual free will, without regard to any wider consequences.

A conclusion here is that we have now seen four cases of emergent urban order, showing how the same kinds of emergent effects that we saw in the last chapter – applied to beehive comb patterns, or cellular 'gliders' – can be interpreted in the urban context. The fact that we already know that such spontaneous order in the non-human cases arise with no conscious 'planning' (or no living thinking intention at all) should reinforce the idea that no overall planning is needed (and no 'hidden' planning intentions need be suspected) to create the order in the urban cases.

STREET PATTERNS

We now turn to look at 'morphogenetic' (form-generating) processes involved with the emergence of typical street-pattern shapes. In Chapter 4 we saw social reasons for the rules of street syntax. Here, let us explore the effects of growing structure in the absence of higher-level ordering above the level of streets. That is, given the basic building-blocks of routes, plots and buildings, and given the rules of street syntax that link these together (Chapter 3), what street-pattern shapes would we expect to see in the absence of overall street-plan design?

To answer this, let us first consider what programmes of growth or change we should expect to find. Then we shall see how these converge on typical characteristic street-pattern structures. Then we shall investigate the probability of these structures arising, hence helping explain the typical structure of 'unplanned' street patterns.

Programmes of structural formation

Three kinds of programme (or morphological operation) are suggested, based on the deposition of buildings (footprint formation), plot formation (subdivision) and route formation (propagation). Let us look at each of these in turn and see what patterns emerge.

With *footprint formation*, buildings are built or 'deposited' on the ground one after another, either on to public space or within private plots, with the spaces in between used for circulation (hence becoming the street pattern) or used for any other purposes (Figure 7.7).

With *plot subdivision*, a plot is divided up into subdivisions, creating new plots (either one at a time or several simultaneously). The pattern of plots may form a contiguous parcel of plots, for example with a perimeter road round the original plot boundary, or the subdivisions could themselves correspond with roads hence forming a new portion of street pattern directly (Figure 7.8).

With *route propagation*, we start with a single linear element, and add further linear elements to create a skeletal structure. This results in a branching pattern, and often one route will join up or intersect with an existing route, hence creating a connective street pattern (Figure 7.9).

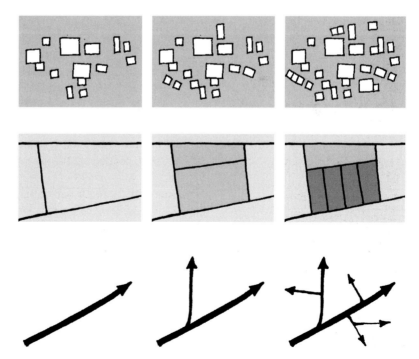

7.7 • Footprint formation.

7.8 • Plot subdivision.

7.9 • Route propagation.

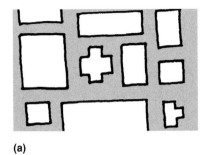

(a)

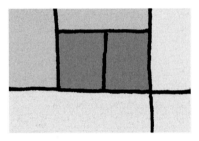

(b)

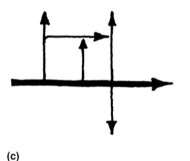

(c)

7.10 • Different processes of formation may yet give rise to or converge on the same characteristic structure: (a) Via footprint formation; (b) Via plot subdivision; (c) Via route propagation.

Convergence on characteristic structure

The different kinds of structural formation – route formation, plot subdivision and building footprint formation – often give rise to distinct patterns that are typical of that kind of means of formation (Figures 7.7 to 7.9). This having been said, any of these three kinds of formation can generate the characteristic street-pattern structure identified in Chapter 3.[13] Put another way, the different means of formation when added together *converge* on the same characteristic structure – semi-regular, semi-complex rectilinear grid-like patterns – seen in Figure 7.10.

Probabilistic emergence of characteristic street-pattern shapes

At this point we now introduce a new dimension to affairs: that of probability. In situations involving random actions or interactions, some outcomes are more likely than others. That is, although a situation may be random, this does not mean that all outcomes are equally likely – a natural level playing field of probability. Rather, there is a varying 'landscape of probability', in which some outcomes are more likely than others. Here, we shall see how there are probabilistic – or entropic – effects that lead to the kinds of familiar characteristic street patterns we see: first for footprint formation, then plot subdivision and then route propagation.[14]

Footprint formation

As an example demonstration, let us apply a programme with the following rule:

> Deposit buildings one at a time, such that each deposition is either: (a) a stand-alone building (creating a new footprint); or (b) an addition to an existing building (creating an enlarged footprint); where (a) and (b) have equal (50 per cent) probability.

Here, we are not concerned with the overall shape of the footprints – for simplicity, these are assumed to form terraces where each building adds on at one or other end. What is of interest here is the size of each building footprint (measured in number of buildings), and the distribution of sizes. The possible sets of buildings created are shown to the fifth generation in Figure 7.11.

At the third generation, note that although there are three outcomes, one of these (3B) is more likely than the others – it is twice as likely as either 3A or 3C. This represents the start of a probabilistic effect that underpins the patterns of development we see in many 'unplanned' urban contexts. That is,

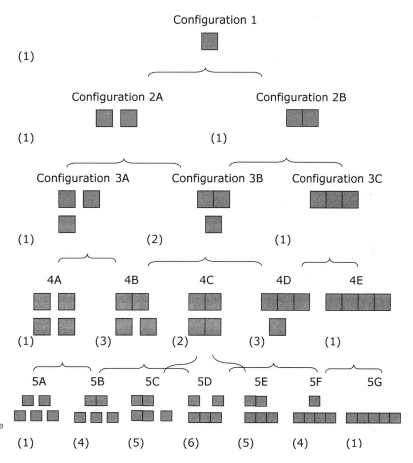

7.11 • Random-incremental generation of urban structure through footprint formation; a mix of size of footprints is likely. Numbers in parentheses indicate frequency of each configuration.

in the absence of a deliberate intention to create clusters of a given size, or more or fewer terraces, there is a probabilistic tendency at work.

At one extreme, then, the outcome is one where each footprint is a stand-alone building; at the other, all footprints are joined up in a single terrace. Notably, these extreme cases are the least likely (at the fifth generation, 5A and 5G each has a 1 in 26 chance, or the chance of picking a red or black ace from a pack of playing cards). For this random incremental programme, we are most likely to get a mix of larger and smaller units. We can, of course, quantify this probability, because we can work out all possibilities arising from a known programme. Here, the most likely pattern (5D) is six times as likely as the least likely.

Table 7.1 The distribution of building footprints predicted in Figure 7.11–26 outcomes of sets of five buildings arranged in clusters of up to five buildings (130 buildings in 73 footprints)

No. of buildings per footprint	No. of footprints	No. of buildings
1	38	38
2	19	38
3	11	33
4	4	16
5	1	5
Total	73	130

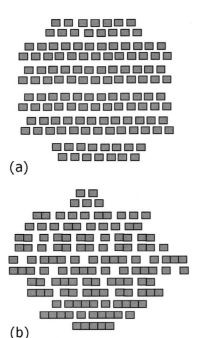

(a)

(b)

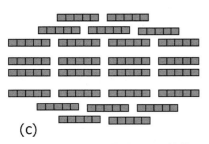

(c)

7.12 • 130 buildings arranged in three ways: (a) All stand-alone; (b) Distribution of building footprints predicted in Figure 7.11 and set out in Table 7.1; (c) All in terraces of five buildings. The programme giving rise to (b) could also give rise to (a) or (c), but those would be extremely unlikely.

As a result, we would expect to see a given distribution of buildings of different footprints as given in Table 7.1, and arranged in a notional settlement pattern for visual comparsion in Figure 7.12. The 'invisible hand' of entropy is much more likely to select something *roughly like* (b) out of all possible outcomes, than (a) or (c). So, when we see a straggling village with a mix of larger and smaller arrays of buildings in ones and twos, with fewer in threes, fewer still in fours and fives, and so on, then this is a typical outcome for a given random-incremental process, in the absence of planning; it could be interpreted as disorder, or alternatively a sort of predictable, characteristic order. The point here is that characteristic distributions appear – because of the way the programme is set up – even when no one is expressly setting out to create such a distribution.

Plot subdivision

Now, let us apply a programme where at each generation, an existing plot is selected at random and then bisected either horizontally or vertically. The resulting distribution is seen in Figure 7.13.

This outcome suggests that the most regular forms are less likely to happen by chance than a more irregular mix of parcels of different sizes and shapes (squares and oblongs). In particular, those with all four parcels identical (bottom row) occur in only a sixth of the cases – hence the probability of getting four equal subdivisions would be like throwing a dice and getting a six. Hence, when we see many same-size plots, this implies that these are more likely to be planned that way – subdivided simultaneously – to get intentional regularity, rather than arising from a random incremental process.

7.13 • Set of patterns generated by successive plot bisections. For the final set (fourth generation) there are 48 outcomes (each comprising 4 parcels).

1st generation:-

2nd generation:-

3rd generation:-

4th generation:-

Route propagation

Let us now consider a programme that generates simple 'tree' structures. Here the rule-set is:

(1)   Start with a single route;
(2)   Add routes one at a time to join the existing structure;
(3)   Each route may connect to the existing structure at one end only;
(4)   The point of connection is chosen at random, with equal probability given to (a) any existing route (at a point not already a connection, nor the end of a route); (b) any existing connection.

This programme generates a contiguous tree structure, hence giving rise to a structure compatible with the first 'street syntax' rule, the rule of contiguity of the public street network (Chapter 3). This includes T-junctions, crossroads, and junctions with more numbers of arms (Figure 7.14).

As with the buildings and plots, some structures are more probable than others, and we can quantify this probabilistic effect. For example, the chances of making the comb-shaped specimen labelled 4A is 1 in 15. In

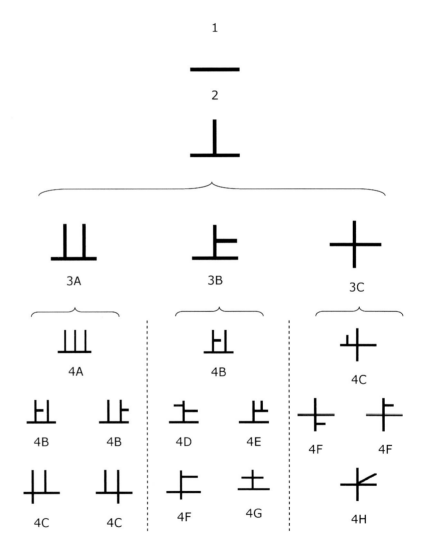

7.14 • All possible patterns generated by a T-structure route propagation programme, run to the fourth generation. At the fourth generation, there are 14 outcomes, represented by 8 distinct topologies (A–H).

contrast, shape 4B has a probability of 1 in 5, that is, it is three times as likely (to be generated by the given programme) as shape 4A.

While these patterns could be said to look all similarly tree-like or all differently tree-like, some are seen to be more distinctive shapes than others – for example, the comb shape (4A), the 'fractal fern' shape (4E) and the star shape (4H). These, indeed, are perhaps distinct precisely because they have a particular regularity about them – a consistent kind of branching. We can also see that these more regular structures (comb, fractal fern, star) are less likely; or, the types we distinguish as regular definite shapes are singular and less likely, whereas those that we lump together as 'irregular' are naturally more likely since there are more of them in the first place.

A further point here is to do with size. The different forms are easily extensible: we could have a comb with any number of teeth, or a fractal fern with any number of branches, and a star with any number of arms. But the probability of this regularity being maintained will become increasingly smaller with each generation – that is, with each random increment. This is exactly like the way that, if flipping a coin repeatedly, the chances of getting all heads or all tails becomes increasingly small for a larger number of flips. The same may be said of the chance of a family containing all girls or all boys. A mixed distribution is increasingly likely.[15]

Probability, regularity and urban order

The foregoing demonstrations show how some patterns are more likely to happen 'by chance' than others. We can draw some immediate conclusions for explaining patterns.

We can see that the most likely patterns are irregular – containing a mix of elements; or they might be said to have a consistent heterogeneity. The more regular are more unlikely (to be generated by the given programmes), and the most regular are the most unlikely; this improbability increases with size (number of elements, that is, number of random increments). So if we saw a long 'comb' shape of routes, or a long terrace of buildings stretching across the land, we would suspect this was a planned formation, and not a result of random deposition of routes or buildings.

That said, it is not necessarily the case that the more irregular patterns are more likely, nor that the more unlikely are necessarily more regular: irregular structures can also be unlikely.

What makes a given structure unlikely is that only a few paths lead to it, by means of the programme given. A regular structure is unlikely not because it is regular as such, but because to create the regularity one must not deviate from a given path, or limited set of paths. (This is like the case of only one path leading to all heads, or to all tails, when repeatedly tossing a coin.)

What makes a given class of structures unlikely also relates to how tightly defined it is. To count as regular, a pattern probably requires no deviation from a target form – for a 'fractal fern' to be fractal, it cannot afford any branch to be out of place. However, the set of 'irregular, roughly street-pattern-shaped structures' will be more likely because there are more of them in the first place. When it comes to street patterns, the irregular, 'street-pattern shape' is so common that its pervasive presence may be interpreted as characteristic *order*. (This is, in effect, a regularity in the population of all street patterns, Chapter 3.)

This means in effect that if we do see a regular pattern on the ground, it is more likely to have been designed or contrived that way. Or, alternatively, perhaps a different programme is operating, where the unit of design is at a higher level. So, for example, while a hexagonal pattern may be less likely to form from a branching route programme, it would automatically form if the unit of generation is a hexagon to start with – that is, it relates to which scale the unit of design is at (Figure 2.8). Or, one could have a dedicated 'comb' programme, that only made combs, rather than the more generic 'tree' programme, which might produce a comb, regular fractal or star (only) by chance.

Ways in which the 'characteristic' structure is more likely to arise – and prevail – than a 'contrived' geometric structure are laid out in Table 7.2. This table partly explains why cities like London are not full of hexagons.[16]

CITY FORMS

So far, we have seen programmes for relationships between routes, plots and buildings, and how these can give rise to emergent structures with characteristic order. Now we wish to see what happens where there is a differentiation of land uses, and how this plays out at a wider urban scale – albeit at a lower resolution – all in the absence of overall planning.

The most familiar 'unplanned' urban structure is perhaps the concentric city, where there is a central core, usually with civic and commercial land uses, surrounded by annular rings of residential suburbs. This structure has arisen again and again, without necessarily any planning, but simply through an aggregate of individuals making independent and often local decisions about location.[17]

Traditionally this has been explained with respect to *accessibility*: relating to how easy it is to get between different locations, in particular to an

Table 7.2 Influences on characteristic versus contrived patterns

Influence	'Characteristic' pattern	Hexagonal pattern
Route propagation	A structure based on major straight-through streets, with branches off, roughly 90°, forming blocks, is naturally formed from incremental route formation.	Routes forming junctions with equal 120° angles are rare. Layouts with no straight-through routes are rare. Routes where each section is same length are rare.
Plot subdivision	Rectangular plots are convenient for parcelling out land. Rectangles pack well together. Rectangles can be cut to form more rectangles.	Subdividing hexagons does not give hexagons; multiplying hexagons does not give hexagons.
Footprint formation	Rectangular buildings are the most common type of building footprint. Aggregating rectangles creates the typical characteristic structure.	Hexagonal buildings are uncommon in the first place.
Interpretation	If we see this pattern it is likely to imply unplanned.	If we see this pattern it is likely to be planned.

urban centre (as discussed earlier, in the case of the von Thünen model, Figure 7.1). However, this is only part of the story. It does not necessarily explain the centre to which things appear to be gravitating in the first place. Therefore, while accessibility is indeed an important generator of compact concentric urban forms, it is not the only factor. Here, we shall focus on programmes based on *adjacency*, and see how far this can account for the macro-patterns we see, before considering accessibility effects.[18]

With programmes of growth based on immediate adjacency, each new 'cell' of development is laid down taking into account only the current state of a given plot of land, and that of its immediate neighbours, irrespective of location in a wider sense. This is instructive, since it means that it is based only on truly local considerations (like CA or beehive). The development does not 'know' where it is within a settlement or even if it is in a settlement of any size; only whether it is next to another developed piece of land. This is useful to this chapter since it simulates well the absence of any sort of strategic planning, or awareness of what 'urban wholes' may be created.

Here, we shall first look at the emergence of compact forms, and then the emergence of concentric patterns. Finally, we shall see how retuning parameters can create the emergence of more dispersed twenty-first-century forms.[19]

Compact city form

Here we do a first experiment based wholly on adjacency, for two land uses (one urban and one rural). The programme here is:

(1)   Land use A. 'Agricultural': Assumed already covers the whole area under consideration;
(2)   Land use B. 'Built-up': Set down development of type B, incrementally and randomly, on any undeveloped cell (type A) such that it is adjacent to any currently developed cell (type B).

This process generates what we recognise as built-up areas – settlements – contiguous bounded areas with outsides and insides. This is simply by specifying adjacency, without the specification referring to the existence of a settlement or bounded built-up area. Figure 7.15 shows possible outcomes after each 'generation' of land use formation; while Figure 7.16 shows the outcome probabilities of each of the possible shapes.

Overall, what we see is that the more compact shapes are more likely. As the number of built-up cells increases, and the whole shape grows over time, assuming that each new increment is equally likely to be placed randomly to north, south, east or west, then cumulatively the whole is most likely to grow 'all around' rather than 'in any particular direction'.[20]

There is even a kind of compact 'correction' going on, or 'smoothing-out effect'. As the shape grows, even if it temporarily becomes elongated or branchy then the cumulative weight of additional layers all around is likely to give rise to a compact shape over time. Again this is not to say that the outline is likely to be evenly compact: it is still likely to be irregular, but overall not extending in one particular direction or another (Figure 7.17).

Finally we can see how this probabilistic compactness works for a larger, already-compact structure. Figure 7.18 (a) shows a built-up area comprising 37 contiguous cells. Figure 7.18 (b) shows the twenty possible adjacent cells to expand into. This time, we assume for simplicity that there is a one in twenty chance of any cell being filled. So, there are 20 possibilities for a 38-cell city.[21]

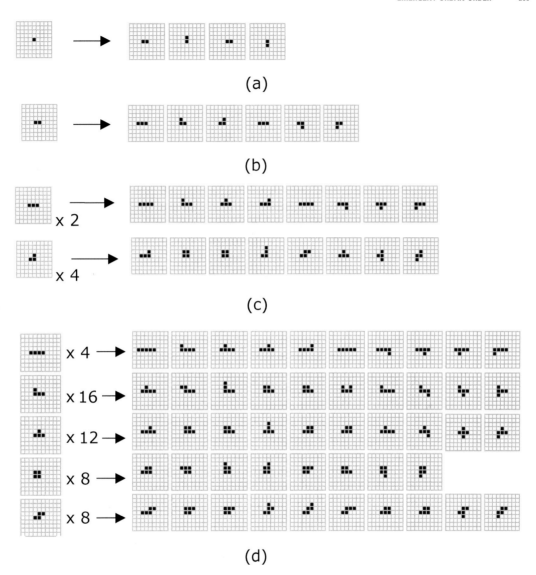

7.15 • Urban formation based on adjacency programme, to fifth generation: A (agricultural) is white; B (built-up) is black; (a) to (d) show the generation of different shapes, which have different probabilities of arising from the random incremental growth according to the adjacency rule stated. At the fifth generation, there are 12 unique shapes. These occur in different proportions (see Figure 7.16 below). The multipliers indicated are as a result of some shapes being more likely than others, from preceding generations.

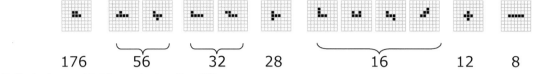

7.16 • Twelve shapes and their frequencies, from Figure 7.15.

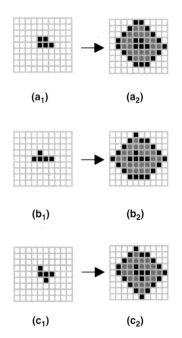

7.17 • The 'smoothing-out' effect. Take a five-cell shape and 'encase' it in three layers of new cells all round. The shapes that look different when small look similar when large.

Now Figure 7.19 shows four possible outcomes for a 41-cell city. These have different probabilities of being generated by the specified rule-set. Now while it may be intuitively obvious which configurations are more likely to arise by chance, it is not intuitively obvious what the *magnitude* of the difference in probability would be (hence why, in this chapter, it is worthwhile to quantify things).

The least likely is (a), since it can only be created by one path (each position must be occupied in the right order). Configuration (b) is more likely than (a), since there are twelve different ways in which four cells could be added to get configuration (b), whereas there is only one way of getting configuration (a).[22]

Configuration (c) is even more likely than either (a) or (b), since its four cells can be laid down in any order. In fact, there are 24 paths for reaching this outcome, that is, twice as many as (b), and 24 times as many as (a).

Finally we come to layout (d), which is intended to represent a 'typical irregular roughly compact' form. Now the *particular* configuration shown in Figure 7.19 (d) has exactly the same probability as (c). However, when we interpret city form, we would tend to regard (d) as similar to most other configurations where four 'random' boundary cells were filled in (i.e. all four occupy an outlined cell as shown in Figure 7.18b).

Now the total number of paths to reaching any of those combinations will be a very large number indeed. It turns out that the probability of the four new cells of development all lying 'tight' against the current boundary (i.e. as in Figure 7.19d) is not 100 times more likely than (a), not a 1,000 times more likely than (a), but *over 100,000* times more likely than (a).[23]

This makes roughly compact forms *much* more likely than any other specific forms, such as linear forms, spirals, fractal ferns, and so on – for the given rule-set. This explains why if we saw a very large regular structure like a '*Ciudad Lineal*' from Cádiz to St Petersburg, it would be overwhelmingly likely to have been planned this way, or based on modules with a programme that directs linear growth along a spine route, rather than to have arisen by, say, adding modules in random directions around the suburbs of Madrid, that all happen to line up in a single band from Atlantic to Baltic.[24]

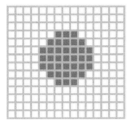

(a)

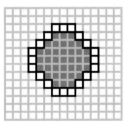

(b)

7.18 • (a) City of 37 cells; (b) 20 cells for future development.

Here, the combination of a consistent code with a random element leads to a rough order: a *roughly* compact form. While this may to some extent approximate a circle, it is important to be clear that the form is the way it is without reference to circularity: there is no aspiration to the ideal compactness of the circle; it is not an 'imperfect expression' of perfect compactness (cf. conic sand pile, Chapter 3). It is, rather, a true expression of a roughly compact form generated from an adjacency programme.

Finally, it is worth noting here that in the urban context the quest for compactness is often associated with minimising radius, or minimising perimeter relative to area. For example, we may often think of compactness implying buildings huddled as closely as possible to some central point, or implying the desire to minimise perimeter (minimise length and cost of defensive wall relative to area enclosed). However, while these may well be factors in creating compact forms, they need not be. We have seen here compactness arising probabilistically solely through adjacency rules – increments of development locating next to earlier increments. 'Centres' and 'perimeters' simply don't come into it.

Concentric city form

Here we do a second experiment, based as before wholly on adjacency, but this time distinguishing two urban land uses, giving three land uses in total. The programme this time is:

(1) Land use A. 'Agricultural': Assumed already covers the whole area under consideration (as before);

(2) Land use B. 'Built-up': Set down development of type B, incrementally and randomly, on any undeveloped cell (type A) such that it is adjacent to any currently urban cell (either type B or C);

(3) Land use C. 'Civic / commercial': Set down development of type C, incrementally and randomly, on any cell of type B, adjacent to any existing development of type C. (This simulates people converting private dwelling into a shop, for example.)

As it stands this programme is meant to simulate the formation of a new land use, labelled 'civic/commercial'. The operative detail here is that C simply wants to be near other Cs.[25]

What this does is to ensure that there will be a single contiguous core area C, and zooming out, a single contiguous area of (B+C), and of course (A + B + C) is also a single contiguous area. This is effectively a hierarchically nested formation.[26] One possible outcome is to create a concentric pattern Figure 7.20 (a). However, other possibilities may be generated (b), (c) – these are drawn in such a way as to look rather different from the familiar concentric topology, while still obeying the given programme.

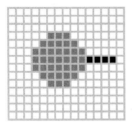

(a)

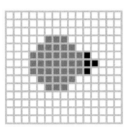

(b)

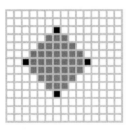

(c)

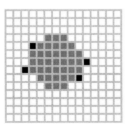

(d)

7.19 • Four alternative outcomes for adding four new cells of development.

Now, which pattern we see will depend on things probabilistic. We know from earlier that the core area (C) is more likely to be compact (as per the core shape of the 'bull's-eye' case, Figure 7.20a) than linear (as per the zig-zag core shape of Figure 7.20b) – eleven times likelier (according to Figure 7.16). And we know that subsequent extensions are much more likely to be compacting than linear (from Figure 7.17, 7.19). So, the concentric 'bull's-eye' (Figure 7.20a) is more likely than the 'stringy' shape (Figure 7.20b).

Another factor is the rate of generation of land use C relative to land use B. In Figure 7.20 (a) and (b) the ratio of B to C is 40:5, or 8:1. However, for the third case – the 'mask' shape of Figure 7.20 (c) – the ratio is 30:15 or 2:1. (This ratio is perhaps less likely in the first place, in practice, for land uses defined as above.) So, the programme itself can generate different forms but if we add in the rate of generation, then concentric is more likely. The concentric is more likely for a high ratio of B to C, due to the 'smoothing-out' effect: before the core C has a chance to throw out a 'limb', it is likely to be enveloped by an outer layer of B, hence creating or maintaining what we recognise as the concentric formation, with C a single bloc nested wholly within B, nested wholly within A. All that is needed to create such a concentric pattern is a set of different land uses with different preferences as to what other land uses they must locate next to.

While this demonstration has been very simple, it can be seen that it could easily be extended by including more land uses, which with the same logic for adjacency would give the same concentric results;[27] also, to be more realistic, clearly a grid of cells that was made up of higher-resolution land parcels of different shapes. But the overall results in terms of emergent contiguity and probable concentric patterns would be the same, characteristic order.

Adjacency effects for traditional cities

We have now seen how programmes that involve only adjacency rules can create the following: first, discretely bounded, contiguously built-up settlements, that are secondly, highly probably roughly compact, and thirdly, highly probably monoconcentric: that is, concentric, with a single contiguous core area.

There are four significant points here. First, the overall urban and suburban formations arising do so purely as a result of *individual* actions: independent acts of construction or locational choice. There is no coordinated action or planning foresight. Secondly, these are purely *local* actions. They are made without knowledge of what is happening outside the immediately neighbouring cells; or their position relative to the overall configuration of land

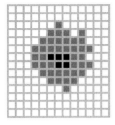

(a)

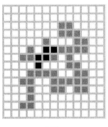

(b)

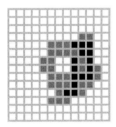

(c)

7.20 • Three land uses: (a) 'Bull's-eye' shape; (b) 'Spindly' shape; (c) 'Mask' shape.

uses. Thirdly, the programme includes a *random* element. There is no knowing at the start what particular pattern will form. Finally, this classic urban form – a contiguous bounded settlement with identifiable central core and annular suburbs – has formed without any explicit preference for or specification of the concept of settlement: boundedness, compactness, concentricity, centrality or suburbs.

Now, it is not being claimed that adjacency rules are the only influences on location, or even need be present at all. But the purpose here is to draw attention to the fact that these results *could* be achieved by developing this way, in the absence of any sort of overall planning or even in the absence of individuals calculating their optimal location with respect to the current land use distribution. This echoes the way in which the concentric distribution of 'land uses' in a hive comb can arise without any overall planning, with nothing more than a combination of random deposition, the queen checking what is in the next cell, and a given rate of one land use being deposited relative to the others.

Emergent twenty-first-century forms

Now, so far, we have accounted for the typical structure of traditional cities that tend to be roughly compact and concentric, with an inner core and suburbs. But, as we know, many late twentieth- and early twenty-first-century cities are *not* neatly contiguous concentric bounded settlements, but have all sorts of land uses all over the place. How do we account for the apparently 'amorphous form' of the post-modern urban sprawl and scatter? Has the centripetal pull of cities been replaced by the centrifugal push of dispersal? Have we switched from the apparently centripetal monocentric concentric model to the apparently centrifugal, polycentric model? Have we replaced the 'monocentripetal' city with 'polycentrifugal' sprawl?

No, not necessarily. We can test this by seeing if we can account for these post-modern forms, by retuning parameters – rather like the way that we retuned the parameters of the San'a model and ended up with suburbs (Figure 7.5). A difference in degree – in the input programme – led to a difference in kind, in terms of the pattern on the ground. If we retune some parameters, can we create programmes for twenty-first-century suburbs and sprawl?

For a start, we could loosen the adjacency requirements, such as those which state that commercial land uses locate next to each other. This can help lead to a more random scatter. This always happened, of course, with respect to any 'traditional' settlement developing suburban sub-centres.

The dispersal effect would, however, be seen perhaps most strongly in retuning accessibility. When saying retuning accessibility, it does not mean that a centripetal attraction is replaced by a centrifugal dispersion. All it requires is that the degree of resistance to distance is reduced: travel becomes easier or cheaper or both; this is simply a difference in degree; not a change in kind, nor a reversal of behaviour.

In effect, accessibility can be retuned due to the logistics of fast, cheap transport, where increased distance is tolerated to the extent that greater speed overcomes the time barrier. This is particularly seen for the private car or goods vehicle, which can go quickly in any direction. It may also be retuned according to the availability of telecommunications, which allows instant non-physical access that is insensitive to distance. The twentieth century saw huge leaps in accessibility on these fronts.[28]

The ability, on acquiring a car, to suddenly go anywhere in any direction could be likened to a game of chess when a pawn (once a plodding piece with limited influence) becomes a queen, and suddenly can sweep across the board in any direction, simultaneously altering its own accessibility but also the logistical rationale of all other carefully huddled chess pieces. The telecommunications effect is perhaps like turning into a knight that can penetrate the interior of a physically bounded formation (with the difference from real chess being that it would, like the queen, be unlimited in distance or direction). The combined effect is that circumstances change not only for the newly mobile 'actor' (the ex-pawn), but the logic of the whole extant city formation changes – some parts no longer make sense, and will have to adapt swiftly or be replaced by something else.

The result is that instead of being attracted to one centre, land uses are attracted to different centres, or rather, different locations of accessibility (whether central or not), which may be a motorway interchange on the urban periphery, rather than a bridge, dockside or railway station in the historic centre. Recall the San'a diagram with different 'seed points' (Figure 7.4) – the seed point is no longer the centre, but scattered around. There is still 'gravitational attraction', of course: but this gravitation operates in any direction, not focused on a single centre. So things like distance do not stop applying, but the distances tolerated become greater, and can apply in almost any direction. So, we get out-of-town stores on the periphery, industrial parks, leisure centres: all those commercial functions now distributed round all those 'most accessible' locations, now skewed towards orbital motorways and interchanges in addition to the traditional centre.

This latest wave of urbanisation to some extent undoes the apparent centripetality of the traditional city, as if it is the antithesis of previous urbanism. But in reality the logic of the car-mobility city is in effect not much different from the all-directions-accessible mobility of the historic city of the pedestrian, but just played out at a much larger scale, operating at higher speeds and over longer distances (this is in contrast to the logic of public transport). As far as the individual citizen or land use locating somewhere is concerned, there is the same set of decisions to be made, and time budgets to be juggled (close to workplace or workforce, market or customers, civic facilities or constituents).[29]

So it is the *same set of mechanisms* that caused the suburban to emerge from the urban, as caused the urban to emerge from the agricultural state in the first place. In other words, there is no need for this pattern to be explained by an historical 'reversal' where a centripetal era of urbanisation and city formation is supplanted by a centrifugal era of suburbanisation and fraying urbanity. This result is a bit like the way that in the San'a model, retuning one of the parameters gives rise to a more spacious urban form; a difference in *degree* (in terms of input or process) results in an outcome or pattern that is apparently or superficially different in *kind*.[30] This suggests that the outer suburbs do not represent a 'new organisational model', or that any such suburban model is a 'radical break with the evolution of cities', but rather is part of a continuous process of urban emergence, but just with the parameters retuned by automobile and telecommunications technologies.[31]

Overall, then, the application of adjacency and accessibility seems to be able to generate both traditional compact concentric forms, and the late twentieth- and early twentieth-century phenomena of outer suburbs, edge cities and 'silicon savannahs', where any of these could emerge in the absence of any explicit desire to create cities or centres or suburbs *per se*.

Here, we can see that urban growth and change can be better understood as being more like a 'live' cellular automata display (Figure 6.4), where individual pixels may change, leading to overall macro-patterns that – like 'gliders' in the Game of Life – may change or persist over time according to individual behaviours; rather than the city as something like a bull's-eye-like specimen pinned to a map, a unitary entity that adds outer layers or swells as a whole over time.

CONCLUSIONS

This chapter has explored a variety of ways in which different urban programmes can give rise to emergent order in the absence of overall design or planning. We have seen that some patterns are more likely than others to arise spontaneously. The absence of design and planning does not just mean some plain neutral or random scatter, but definite directions in which urban structure would go left to its own devices (exactly what happens when we get traditional compact concentric cities).

Cities again and again look similar, even though no one planned or colluded this way; simply they are similar to the extent people have similar desires to be near or next to some things and apart from others. So, we like buildings that have sufficient light and air, plots of a given shape and size, with access to the public street (Chapter 4); and in a democracy we like the freedom of where to locate, and so an aggregation of these individual decisions creates the typical city form.

The demonstration has shown that simple rules, relating to individual independent locational decisions – both with respect to the placement of individual streets or plots, or location within an urban area – can give rise to the characteristic complex order of street patterns and concentric urban forms, all in the absence of any express intention to create characteristic complex street patterns or concentric cities.

Therefore, although town planning has traditionally identified cities, centres, suburbs and boundaries as features to be replicated in planned towns – these being the units of *city design*, in terms of Chapter 2 – it is not (or at least *was* not) necessary to explicitly plan for them, to get them. Three land uses linked by adjacency or accessibility rules could be sufficient to create this order.

Yet, Modernist planning tended to use those emergent features (cities as whole units, centres and suburbs) as components of city design – systematic ordering at the city scale. Instead of being emergent effects of urbanisation and urbanism, they become ends in themselves. Consider this statement by Le Corbusier:

> Statistics show us that business is conducted in the centre. This means that wide avenues must be driven through the centres of our towns. Therefore the existing centres must come down. To save itself, every city must rebuild its centre.[32]

Here, Le Corbusier presumes the role of the centre is fixed. However, if we said: 'business is conducted where things are most accessible' then we would draw a completely different conclusion.

In effect, if we assume that cities and centres are the operational building-blocks, we may be misled into recreating (or dismantling) cities and centres for their own sakes. This could be a case of wrong diagnosis, hence wrong treatment; or 'operation successful, patient dead'. But if cities and centres are seen as emergent, these need not feature as part of the problem – nor part of the solution.

We shall consider the implications for planning and design in Chapter 9. But before that, we have some further explanation to do. This chapter has demonstrated the emergent patterns arising from given programmes. The programmes or rule-sets themselves arise from basic human preferences, and relational factors to do with adjacency, public and private space, and so on (Chapter 4). These may be codified in planning regulations. This chapter has mainly shown a given code applied progressively over time, to create a reasonably predictable unfolding urban pattern. However, in reality, codes and programmes themselves change over time, in unpredictable ways: as people's preferences change, as people's ability to exercise their preference changes, as planning regulations or other external influences kick in to alter what is allowed to happen where, when or how. Historically this change has typically been stimulated by external factors, such as changes in technology or wealth, or perhaps constraints on resources or climate change. The change in code means that later development will have a different form or spatial logic from earlier development. We already saw in the case of San'a, how the slight change in one parameter led to (what appeared to be) a radical change – a qualitative change – in the urban structure. This change in the 'code for development' is effectively due to 'feedback from the environment'. This combination amounts to evolution: the subject of the next chapter.

Notes

1   Rykwert (2000: 5).
2   A key difference between a city and a game of chess is, of course, that with a city, citizens tend to act in their own self-interest, rather than being 'pawns' in someone else's strategic game. If there is a hand moving the pieces, it is an Adam Smith-style figurative (and invisible) hand, that is no more than the resultant of the individual pieces' own actions. (Also, of course, cities do not normally have two teams forming competitive opposition). For a modern computer game, see Sim City 2000 (Dargahi and Bremer, 1995).
3   Of course, it is well known that cities change in time, and that these forms are only pages in a temporally changing atlas of all patterns. This is perhaps because planners, especially, have a target outcome or design in mind, that is typically fixed in form, even if understood to be part of a dynamic process. Lynch notes in passing (in a footnote) that 'It is interesting to see how many of our ideal forms are rationalizations of what are only momentary stages in evolving urban landscapes. It is difficult for us to conceive of form-in-process as a prototype model' (Lynch,

1981: 381). This seems important, since a city is an ever-changing entity (phenomenon, object or collection of objects) and a form is only one snapshot in time.

4   In effect, Modernist city design (Chapter 2) tried to capture and replicate the form of the whole city, as if trying to capture and replicate the form of the glider – albeit regularising or rectifying it (Figure 2.13).

5   This quantification – in the form of probability calculations – is necessary to convince the reader that when it is claimed that a certain pattern is 'likely' to arise (in the absence of definite design or planning intervention), we have a definite idea of how strong this likelihood really is. The quantitative difference between something being 'quite likely' and 'very likely' is like the difference between a village and a city: on one level merely a difference in degree, but such a strong one that one could say there is a step change involved, or even a difference in kind: more than the difference between a 'smaller town' and a 'larger town'.

6   Von Thünen (1966). See also Krugman (1996).

7   Christaller (1966).

8   Zipf (1949); Batty (2006).

9   The figures in this section are from Coates (2006).

10 The actual programme is: (1) If a cell is empty and there is at least one road cell *and* less than two garden cells among the four bordering cells, then make the cell a road, with 50 per cent probability, otherwise a house. (2) If a cell is empty and has exactly one house *or* more than one garden in the four bordering cells *and* there are no roads in the surrounding eight cells, then turn the cell into a garden. (3) If a cell is empty and there are more than two garden cells in the eight surrounding cells, then turn the cell into a garden. (4) If a cell is a house with one road but no houses bordering it, and less than four of the surrounding eight cells are garden, then turn the house into a road. (5) If a cell is a garden with two houses bordering and a road then turn garden into a house.

11 D'Arcy Thompson showed that different animal skulls could be seen as being related, through applying different numerical proportions to different parameters ([1917] 1948); see also Steadman (1998).

12 Batty (2005, 2007).

13 Marshall (2005).

14 For discussion of probability of different geometric configurations, see March (1998: 16).

15 For example, a two-tooth comb is one in three of the third-generation set; a three-tooth comb becomes only one out of five in the fourth-generation set (hence 1/15 overall), and so on. In this way, we see that regular forms are less and less likely to persist, over successive generations of random increments, or with growth of a settlement (Figure 7.14). Sooner or later, irregularity will kick in, and we end up with something more like the characteristic street-pattern structure. This helps explain why street patterns typically lie in a small interior region of the possible 'solution space' of structures (Marshall, 2005: 143, 284).

16 Hexagonal planning: Ben-Joseph and Gordon (2000). Steadman on why most buildings are rectangular (2006a).

17 While things are more complex than this, this is felt to be the only level – in the manner of a 'lowest common denominator' – in which cities are consistently structured (Chapter 3).

18 Accessibility does not fully explain the compact concentric form, because although it generates distance-minimising and therefore centralising tendencies, it does not necessarily lead to the generation of a contiguous core area; a settlement or centre in the first place, around which concentric rings would form. It could simply lead to a scatter of land uses, a polycentric accessibility field with 'gravitational attraction' pulling in all directions, with 'centres of gravity' diffusely spread.

19 How this differentiation comes about will be considered in Chapter 8.

20 Or, if we were extending a city in six directions, incrementally, with the growth each time determined by throwing a six-sided dice, we can see that the probability of extending continuously in any one direction is as unlikely as throwing an unbroken sequence of sixes.

21 As the city size increases, the number of possibilities increases (since the perimeter gets greater); a city of four additional cells would have at least $20 \times 20 \times 20 \times 20 = 160,000$ possibilities; that is, 160,000 possible arrays of 41-cell cities given the starting position of Figure 7.18b and the rule for growth.

22 The probability of getting (b) is slightly more than thirteen times as likely as getting (a). This is because the intermediate stages thrown up have different numbers of ways of *not* getting the target pattern.

23 The number of configurations where each of the four new cells occupies one of the twenty 'immediately bordering' cells (Figure 7.18b) is ($20 \times 19 \times 18 \times 17 / 1 \times 2 \times 3 \times 4$) or 4,845. However, since there are 24 (= $1 \times 2 \times 3 \times 4$) ways in which any of these could come about, the total number of permutations is 116,280 (= $20 \times 19 \times 18 \times 17$). The likelihood of getting a 'limb out to the east' as shown in Figure 7.19 (a) is as unlikely, compared with getting one 'like' Figure 7.19(d), as picking a particular card out of a novelty pack of cards where each suit has numbers going up to 29,070 – say, picking specifically the 'twenty nine thousand and ten of hearts' from a pack of over a hundred thousand (not 52) cards. Even if we compare 'one like b' with 'one like a', there are only three other configurations 'like' a, that is, limbs out to north, south and west. So the probability differential would only be cut by four; the differential still 29,070. So this would be like picking the 'twenty-nine thousand and ten' of *any* suit (clubs, diamonds, spades or hearts) – still a very tall order indeed.

24 Elongated shapes like the linear bar shape, or any specific shape (such as the cross) are relatively unlikely, because they require more specific arrangement for them to happen (recall Figure 7.14).

25 Note that this could easily be extended to include further urban land uses, where each time a land use type (D, E, . . .) is progressively more particular about what it lies next to, and less particular about what it displaces.

26 This relates to arteriality, or strategic contiguity (Chapter 3).

27 I.e. we could add land uses D and E, that extended the logic that relates B to A, and C to B and A.

28 See, for example, Clark (1958), Brotchie (1984), Banister (ed.) (1995), Graham and Marvin (1996) on telecommunications, Cooke (2000) on motor car and 'disurbanisation', Banister (2002), Brandon (2002); Marshall (2003).

29 Logic of public transport: Marshall (2005). Same logic of accessibility: Marshall (2006b).

30 Marshall (2006b).

31 Palen (1995: 92); Kotkin (2005: 113).

32 Le Corbusier (1929: 128).

8 CITIES IN EVOLUTION

In the marble columns and architraves of a Greek temple we still trace the timbers of its wooden prototype, and see beyond these the tree-trunks of a primeval sacred grove; roof and eaves of a pagoda recall the sagging mats which roofed an earlier edifice; Anglo-Saxon land-tenure influences the planning of our streets, and the cliff dwelling and the cave dwelling linger on in the construction of our homes!

D'Arcy Wentworth Thompson, *On Growth and Form*[1]

An organism is both a product of development and a product of evolution. In Chapter 6 we saw that an artefact such as a machine or a building may be regarded as a long-term product of technological evolution as well as an immediate product of design. It is now time to turn our attention to the evolution of cities. Do cities evolve? If so, we must ask, after Patrick Geddes, '*Whence*?' and '*How*?' What exactly is it that evolves? What are the mechanisms? And if cities evolve, what did they evolve from? And are they still evolving?[2]

The purpose of studying evolution is not so much to explore how closely urban evolution parallels biological evolution. Rather, the intention here is to see if an evolutionary perspective can help understand urban change and hence inform future planning and design, in part by answering the urban conundrum posed at the outset of the book: how it is that some traditional urbanism can have functional order *without* planning (Figure 1.6, 1.7) while some Modernist planned urbanism is dysfunctional *despite* planning (Figure 1.1)?

The issue of functional order without planning seems to require a 'special explanation', equivalent to the need for a special explanation for

8.0 • A built environment evolves from a primeval sacred grove . . .? Coba, Mexico.

functional order in nature in the absence of design (Chapter 1). Meanwhile, the issue of dysfunctional urbanism despite planning is perhaps what is special about the problem of *urban*-scale design or planning – as opposed to the design of cars or computers or individual buildings, where their functionality is routinely associated with their being designed and purpose-built.

This chapter therefore sets out an interpretation and analysis of evolution in the urban context. To do this, first let us look at the historical Evolution of Cities – the equivalent of the 'fossil record' of urbanism. This explores the basic ways in which which we can interpret cities in evolutionary terms. Secondly, we turn to see how Modernist planning and design may also be interpreted as part of evolution. Rather than Modernism supplanting traditional evolutionary urbanism, we can interpret Modernism in Evolution. Finally, we turn to the continuing courses of Twenty-First-Century Evolving Urbanism. This will help show how understanding of evolution is not just about explaining the urbanism of the past, but how things are currently operating and may continue to work in the future. The progression of historic, Modernist and contemporary phases in this chapter echoes the treatment with respect to planning in Chapter 2. While in Chapter 2 we tended to notice what was new at each stage, here we are just as interested in what was retained from the past. This combination of continuity and change, innovation and tradition, is the stuff of evolution.

THE EVOLUTION OF CITIES

As Aristotle understood, humans are animals; and as modern science has understood since Darwin, humans along with other living creatures are all related, through evolution. Evolution influences our physical features and needs as organisms, and also our mental and psychological features and needs as sentient ones. Therefore, ultimately – albeit indirectly – there are evolutionary explanations behind the ergonomic and social explanations for the human built environment of rooms, buildings, streets and cities, discussed in Chapter 4. So there may be good evolutionary reasons why humans feel particularly at home in the 'prospect and refuge' of the savannah-like suburbia of individual houses, gardens, trees and vistas, while being alienated by the almost diametrically opposite Modernist landscape of looming buildings and exposed empty spaces.[3]

As applied to the urban context of this chapter, the term evolution is taken to refer to long-term transformation over successive iterations of adaptive change, which may include increments of purposive design. As we shall see, urban evolution involves a combination of variation, reproduction and selection; these apply to the designs, plans, codes or other processes for creating buildings or cities. First, let us consider the origin of cities. Then we shall look at the evolution of urban components in cities in general; and then the evolution of planned cities (or city plans); looking at a variety of cases with a variety of evolutionary interpretations.

On the origin of cities

The search for urban origins is a bit like looking for the first society, or the first human, or the first organism. There always seems to be an earlier version, and the question becomes not so simply one of 'where' and 'when' to locate the first 'something', but specification of what qualifies as a 'something' in the first place. This becomes a matter of definition or conceptual classification, over and above empirical evidence.[4]

It should suffice for present purposes to make use of a simple thought experiment. We can imagine cities evolving from earlier kinds of settlement, going back to the simplest imaginable settlement – say a ring of huts or tents around a central fire. Figure 8.1 shows two types of dwelling from the same prehistoric site, Mount Sandel. These could be seen as the evolutionary ancestors of buildings and cities. But in what senses?

First and most obviously, the 'big tent' of the upper diagram could be interpreted as the evolutionary ancestor of the modern dwelling. One

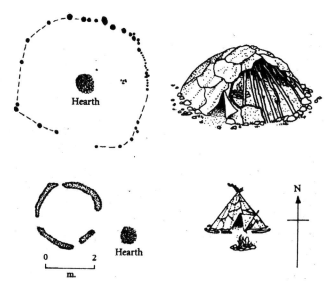

8.1 • Early domestic structures at Mount Sandel, County Antrim, dated around 9,000 years ago. The upper is a hoop-framed house with an internal hearth; the lower is a smaller tent-like structure with an external hearth. The dawn of the schism between buildings and cities?

can imagine the single interior space being progressively subdivided into specialised rooms, with the hearth becoming either the living room or kitchen or dining room, according to circumstances.

Meanwhile, in the lower arrangement, we have a 'small tent' next to an exterior hearth. We could imagine a cluster of such 'small tents' round a single central hearth being an ancestor of an urban settlement. This central hearth could then evolve into the equivalent of the town square or 'central business district' of a modern city, while the small tents would evolve into big tents (dwellings with their own internal hearths) and hence modern dwellings, as per the interpretation above.

In this interpretation, the first settlement would obviously come after the first building, since the settlement is an aggregation of buildings. However, this begs the question as to how the buildings would come to be aggregated in the first place. A group of tents arranged round a hearth could imply a series of 'lone Adams' or Hobbesian individuals who each have their own tents and then later assemble together to share a hearth and hence create a communal settlement.

However, an alternative explanation is that a social group is already in place – complete with hearth – prior to the construction of any tents. This could imply that each individual small tent is not so much a proto-building, as a proto-*room*, such as a private enclosure for sleeping; while the kitchen, dining and living room functions remain outside in the central communal space. In other words, the collective arrangement in the lower part of Figure 8.1, as well as being a possible ancestor of the urban settlement, could also be a possible ancestor of the modern composite *building*, that is, a building that combines cooking, eating, living *and* sleeping (in which case the upper arrangement in Figure 8.1 could be derived from the lower arrangement as a whole). In this latter interpretation, settlements (and hence cities) would not be derivative of buildings, but both modern (composite) buildings and cities would be descended from an earlier proto-arrangement.[5]

This suggests that a settlement is not just an accidental by-product of buildings that happen to be placed in proximity, in the way that a conurbation could be regarded as an accidental by-product of settlements happening to grow into each other. Rather, it is suggested that settlements are inextricably woven into the evolutionary fabric of society. This potential connectedness should not be any more surprising than the idea that the urban settlement might be derived from the fission of an existing large composite dwelling or compound.[6] Either way, cities and buildings share the same sense of public – private spectrum, which percolates through the urban fabric and into the interiors of buildings (Chapter 4). Either way, Figure 8.1 could represent the start of an emerging schism between the evolutionary paths of buildings and cities. And either way, urban roots run deep: the urban configuration could be said to be descended from a pre-urban – and possibly pre-human – social configuration.[7]

The discussion here implies that the differences between buildings and cities, and between corporate compounds and collective settlements, go back a long way and are bound up with societal considerations. While this thought experiment is by its nature conjectural about the distant past, it serves to prepare us for the idea that buildings and cities, though both may be interpreted in evolutionary terms, may be said to evolve in different ways.

Indeed, we can start to see how planned and 'unplanned' settlements may be said to evolve in different ways. In effect, we have two different kinds of 'thing' that is evolving. On the one hand, we have an 'unplanned' city that is a collective entity: this evolves not as a whole, but as a collection of partly competing, partly cooperating, or co-evolving parts: buildings, streets, land uses, and so on. On the other hand, we can have a planned city, that in its extreme form is like a building, designed by blueprint. This design or blueprint can form part of the evolution of planned settlements. Let us look first at 'unplanned' urban evolution, and then the evolution of city designs.

Evolution of urban components

The advent of agriculture gave rise to fixed settlements, a division of labour and a centralised or hierarchical control of society. This combination would eventually pave the way for planned cities as we understand them – they allowed the creation of both cities and planners.[8] Settlements and urbanisation are associated with social stratification and an economic division of labour. This means different kinds of occupation and different types of land use. In the evolution of 'unplanned' urbanism, then, we assume there to be a division of labour, a distinction between land uses, and hence evolution of different types of space, different types of building, and different kinds of street. We can also infer the distinction between public and private space.

A basic original general public space could be divided into, for example, civic space, marketplace and recreation space. The Central Business District could be in a sense descended from the patch of space in the middle of the clearing where early human (or pre-human) societies did their central business. Meanwhile, private space could be divided into different types: for example, residential, religious, industrial – any or all of which might have originally taken place in a domestic setting.

In each case here, there is a switch from a more general or multi-purpose activity or space to specialisation of roles and hence a divergence of types of trade and land use – from a single common origin. So, modern land uses can be seen as just specialised descendants of more general land uses.[9]

The spaces associated with different private land uses could become buildings related to those land uses. Put another way, just as we have the evolution, adaptation and divergence of different kinds of social organisation and land uses, the same can be said of building type – and indeed, building type could be said to spring from or evolve in turn from different land uses or social organisations.

The ancient Greek *agora*, as Peter Hall notes, was not just a 'market place', or 'civic centre', but 'it was simply the place where people came together'.[10] This accords with the idea of a central space being a generic place-type that could have a resonance deep in human evolutionary history. The *agora*, then, combined the marketplace and civic centre functions. The marketplace was, in turn, divided into many specialised subdivisions, including further subdivisions for fresh and dried fruit, and 'fish city' (*ichthyopolis*) with further subdivisions for smoked and unsmoked fish.

The *agora* also provided 'a simple theatre for sacred dances and perhaps drama, and a stadium for athletic games and equestrian events. Later, the drama got its own special places, the theatres . . .' From the *agora* as a 'place where people came to gather' there evolved the *theatron*, a 'place where people gathered to witness a *thea* or spectacle' – this representing an evolutionary branching or speciation. The theatre, of course, eventually became its own *building* type, one that survives to this day.[11]

Building type brings us to architecture, where of course designs or buildings can be reproduced, varied and selected. Banister Fletcher's history of architecture is shot through with references to transformations from one kind of building to another – where the use of the word evolution seems a natural appellation, and not an academic affectation. Different kinds of architectural design or style could also be said to evolve. The transmission of ideas down the generations is seen in the case of Vitruvian ideas for 'Vitruvian man', column orders, primitive huts, and so on. This lineage of concepts can be seen strikingly in the book *Architectural Theory*, where we see architectural treatises one after another following Vitruvius. Although Vitruvius has been described as a 'second-rate architect', it was sufficient that his works (of all Roman treatises) somehow survived, and were therefore available for copying and onward propagation during the Renaissance, to be seen in hindsight as successful.[12]

Finally, we can see how the same kinds of specialisation of land uses apply to the evolution of different types of street. From what would have been a general all-purpose street, we would see divergence of street type into shopping street, residential street and so on (tied to land use and building type).

The evolution of street type may also be related to the evolution of different transport modes. For a start, Çatalhöyük (Figure 3.19a) is an example of a settlement with no streets – circulation was via the roofs, trapdoors and ladders. This represents an urban form suitable for human pedestrian use.

The domestication (and hence artificial selection) and use of large animals such as horses would tend to encourage the invention of streets (more or less horizontal; outside) lined by buildings. Street widths might be set according to the size and manoeuvrability of animals.[13]

The introduction of wheeled vehicles, and in particular the carriage, is said to have led to the fashion for wider, straighter streets. Mews streets are also naturally associated with horse-drawn technology. The boulevard – which was adapted from the long straight avenues of hunting parks – allowed for segregation of paths or carriageways for different forms of movement.[14]

So we see how vehicle technologies, streets, spaces, social and economic systems, land uses and buildings do not evolve in isolation, but all co-evolve together (in principle, with or without the existence of cities). When buildings and spaces and routes and land uses are put together deliberately, we get designed urban units that can act as urban building-blocks – streets, blocks and zones; and ultimately, whole city plans.

Evolution of city designs and plans

It was not only Vitruvius' architectural ideas that were propagated. The idea for a regular planned 'ideal city' has also been taken up by many later urban theorists. These could be seen as 'mutations' from Vitruvius' octagon (Figure 2.2) to six-, seven-, nine- and twelve-sided or -pointed cities (Figure 8.2). These are examples of 'city design', as they are clear finite compositions, each one a 'whole'. So here it is the city as a whole unit that is being reproduced, varied and selected.

The post-Vitruvian planned cities' resonance with the set of winding towers (Figure 6.13) should by now be obvious. Like the winding towers, these ideal city plans are *both* designed objects *and* products of evolution.

We can see the reproduction and recombination of design ideas for good planning and architecture; we can see the copying of plans and blueprints (Figure 8.3). Figure 8.3 shows Elbert Peets' interpretation of how one plan may derive from a previous plan or plans. This illustrates the ideas of reproduction, variation and selection – applied to city design.

8.2 • Ideal Cities: (a) Cataneo's theoretical city, 6-pointed; (b) Cataneo's theoretical city, 7-pointed, 1554; (c) Martini's theoretical city, 8-sided, mid-fifteenth century; (d) Filarete's Sforzinda, theoretical, 8-pointed, mid-fifteenth century; (e) Specklin's ideal fortress town, 8-pointed, 1589; (f) Barbaro's theoretical city, 8-pointed, 1567; (g) Lorini's theoretical city, 9-pointed, 1592, (h) Palmanova, Italy, 9-pointed, 1593; (i) Scamozzi's ideal city, 12-pointed, 1615. These have a more or less direct line of descent from Vitruvius' ideal city (Figure 2.2).

Evolution of urban ordering

It is not just blueprints – whether of cities or buildings – that may be copied and modified, but codes of practice, recipies, procedures or rules of thumb. This could apply either to official codification of regulations, or to vernacular traditions, where the practices are passed down from generation to generation, not necessarily in written form, never mind in the form of plans. These may be interpreted as instruments for urban ordering.

In *The Timeless Way of Building*, Christopher Alexander suggests that it is 'patterns' – which may be interpreted as rules of creating things as much as

8.3 • The Descent of Plans.

the things themselves – that are replicated: like recipes rather than blueprints (Chapter 6). He gives the example of the similarity and variety of traditional barns being due not just to form following function in a site-specific sense (otherwise, each barn would be more different), nor simply copying blueprints (otherwise they would be more similar). So Alexander argues that it is not the blueprints of whole barns that are being replicated and varied, but the component elements and their relationships. In the case of barns, this amounts to ordering at the architectural scale; elsewhere, we can see urban ordering, that is, ordering at the urban scale (Chapter 2).[15]

Seen from an evolutionary point of view, the copying and variation of rules for creating urban components and their relationships – whether parts of buildings or parts of cities – give rise to the similarities and differences between urban components and forms, over space and time. Ultimately we see evolution not only in terms of the long-term transformation of components and forms, but also the evolution of the recipes that create them. In this sense, an evolutionary perspective implies not a single timeless way of building, but change through time, and the likelihood of a divergence (and recombination) of *different* ways of planning, designing and building.

(a)

(b)

(c)

8.4 • Evolution of Glasgow's physical layout: (a) Early settlement; (b) First New Town; (c) Second New Town. The later changes could not be predicted from the earlier. This is *not* development 'like an organism' (Chapter 5).

Evolution of Glasgow

Here we put together the interpretations of evolution for a single place – the city of Glasgow. Here we see *in situ* evolution of combination of buildings, streets, blocks, and so on; with 'unplanned' and planned phases that are part of a continuous open-ended evolution.

Here, we take a simplified version of what happened, for illustrative purposes. We could interpret first, a rambling array of streets, where there may be order in the form of a basic street syntax (Chapter 3), but the streets are not regular in any geometric sense (Figure 8.4 a). Then, we get the first 'new town' – known as the Merchant City. Here, there is a pre-planned layout, with straight streets, perpendicular junctions and closure of vistas. However, the street pattern is not a regular grid, but is more the 'characteristic' pattern. Then, in the third phase, we get not only straight streets but regular orthogonal blocks – the 'Hippodamean grid' of Blythswood (Figure 8.5).[16]

Here we can interpret that from (a) to (b), there is a planned intervention. This could be interpreted as a change in code, or units of urban ordering (cf. San'a, Chapter 7). Then, between (b) and (c), the code changes again. The new urban order is: streets are all straight, junctions are all right-angled, and the result is an orthogonal grid. It is not that simply over time the accumulation of streets inevitably led to more four-way junctions. Rather, in effect the 'code' or urban order itself changed, such that each new street had these qualities; this was fitting with the Blythswood grid being intended as a grid from day one. The scale of the design, and the scale of the urban units used for urban ordering had increased.

8.5 • Glasgow's central area grid, looking east from the open-ended 'Hippodamean' grid of the 'second new town' to the closed vistas of the 'first new town'.

In this simplified interpretation, then, the urban order changed twice – the degree of planning changed (increased) – the scale of the units of planning changed (increased). We could say these changes were caused by external, 'environmental' factors. If these external influences had not been there – or the change to the planning or coding not taken place – then perhaps the whole of Glasgow would have continued growing like a medieval organic settlement, but much bigger, with an irregular mix of straight and crooked streets and alleys (Figure 8.4 a). Or, perhaps a Blythswood-like grid would have marched indefinitely over the hills of the west, had there not been a further change from the Hippodamean order to a post-Hippodamean, more picturesque style of development.

The point evident here is that Glasgow transformed itself, the new growth was unpredictable from what went before. This is a case of 'more than emergence'. This is identified with open-ended evolution, rather than the progressive development of an organism towards a final mature form. To relate back to Chapter 5, the city is 'not an organism' because it does not grow or develop like an organism.[17]

Evolutionary interpretation

As we have seen, evolution can be interpreted in different ways for planned and unplanned cases. In the case of a planned or designed city, these would be based on city plans or town plans. However, for 'unplanned' cities, there will be no single plan: each iteration is not of a whole 'city design', but rather each iteration is the addition of another design – of building, street, block or housing development; or pattern or component thereof – being reproduced, varied and selected. So a 'designed' city – a product of city design – may involve large-scale, purposive 'mutation', but still part of a very long-term evolution. Over the long term, all cities are 'evolved'.

Following Chapter 6 – which allows evolution to include local increments of design – we could substitute the term 'evolved' for 'unplanned', in the sense that both allow local immediate increments of design, but not wholesale coordination or long-term targeting. Only newly designed – or comprehensively redesigned – cities would be considered to be not 'unplanned', but designed objects.

While the evolutionary perspective seems useful for interpreting urban change, we can also be aware of at least four significant differences from natural biological evolution (some of which were anticipated in Chapter 6).

First, a given plan or design may have more than two direct antecedents (as is clear from Figure 8.3). These antecedents may be quite different in type (a design could be from a machine analogy or organic analogy, for example), and contribute in a way different in degree and kind, not a random half of the genes of a complementary pair.

Secondly, each plan is the result of a deliberate selection and copying, and deliberate innovative variation, in order to try to satisfy the demands of the context of application. It was not a random mix of previous plans oblivious to intended function. While the long-term effect of evolution can be recognised even if the individual steps are intentional – as argued in Chapter 6 – the individual steps do not themselves count as evolution (for example, the derivation of Washington, DC from Versailles and Evelyn's London) any more than we say a child is 'evolved' from its parents.[18] Hence recognition of evolution is at least partly contingent on the timescale of the perspective.

Thirdly, selection can be very specific, choosing consciously between just one or two alternative designs (since all reproduction is artificial, even selecting a sole 'alternative' must be considered selection), which is rather different from natural solution involving statistical selection from large numbers of minutely differing variants.

Finally, any plan need not have been actually built and proven successful in operation for it to be copied. It is sufficient that the plan, as it were, 'looks like a good idea'. For example, Evelyn's plan for London (as with Wren's) can be admired and appreciated, and inspire application centuries later, even if it were never proven actually to have been a good idea for the seventeenth century.[19]

This last point draws our attention to the fact that this process of reproducing ideas and plans did not end with the advent of the modern era, but is a continuous ongoing process. Diagrams like Ebenezer's Garden Cities or Le Corbusier's *Ville Radieuse*, that repeatedly crop up in books, may never have been built, but they have surely had an influence on later plans that were. This invites us to consider the relationship between Modernism and evolution.

MODERNISM IN EVOLUTION

We tend to associate evolutionary urbanism with traditional 'unplanned' urbanism. Modernist city planning with its rationalist intention, technological innovation and revolutionary reinvention came along and changed all that. Or did it?

Certainly, there is a view, held by some who are sympathetic to traditional urbanism, that Modernism was like a sort of bad dream, a sort of temporary aberrational phase during which we lost our sense of how to create anything good. Indeed, Christopher Alexander has more or less suggested that the entire Modernist way of design and planning of the last century was something departing injuriously from everything that went before, as if deviating from the natural order of things.[20]

However, Modernism did not just spring forth out of thin air. When browsing through some of the classic Modernist treatises – of Hilberseimer, Korn, Jellicoe, Buchanan, Ritter, Johnson-Marshall, Gibberd, and Bacon – it is quite remarkable to find their Modernist principles and proposals juxtaposed with, and indeed inspired by, exemplars of traditional urbanism. Their books are infused with and enriched by examples of traditional villages, compact pedestrian-friendly forms, piazzas: places like Miletus and Athens, Palmanova and Siena, Mont St Michel, Bath and Chester. Above all, the city of Venice provided a model of something simultaneously beautiful and functional.[21]

Therefore, perhaps contrary to the general characterisation of Modernism as hell-bent on innovation and rejection of tradition, the Modernists – or at least some of the most creative and influential thinkers – did draw from precedent, with good intentions for their planning creations.[22] Just as Hippodamus – the ancient Greek – could be regarded as being modern, here we could say that the Modernists were, in some ways, selectively building on precedent, and following an age-old tradition in this sense.[23]

The Modernist combination of innovation and tradition – variation and retention – has a clear resonance with evolution. In this sense, Modernist planning is not something that succeeds or supersedes an original evolutionary phase of urbanism (like organised society hypothetically replacing a primeval 'state of nature'). Rather, Modernism is just the latest manifestation of evolutionary urbanism. It is not so much a case of Modernism versus Evolution, as Modernism *in* Evolution.

What form does this Modern phase of urban evolution take? Let us first look at the historical change-with-continuity as the Modernist era arrived. Then, let us look at evolutionary interpretation of what happened – including what went wrong. Finally, we look at lessons for urban planning and design.

Urban evolution in the modern era

As discussed in Chapter 2, Modernism – in terms of the physical built environment – was enabled and stimulated by technological advancement. However, Modern urbanism was not just a 'catalogue of innovations', but more an interactive coevolution, with advances on many fronts – in the design of buildings, vehicles, infrastructure, and so on – building on precedent and forming new combinations.

In the case of buildings, reinforced concrete and steel-frame technology enabled the construction of tall buildings, large spanning floors and decks, giant cantilevers, buildings on stilts. The technological possibility stimulated new forms of architectural expression. The use of tall buildings was also enabled by the invention of the elevator and the introduction of the telephone (allowing business to be done from the top floor of a skyscraper). Computers also enabled the development and analysis of engineering forms not previously practical to design or even imagine.[24]

New vehicle technologies – motorised road transport, and electric trams and trains – most directly had effect on (coevolution with) transport infra-structure. With the rise of the motor age came dedicated highways – motorways only for fast-moving motor vehicles; also, separate cycle paths, busways, and so on. Modern construction technology enabled the creation of elevated motorways, flyovers and interchanges.[25]

The accommodation of vehicles also spurred the invention and evolution of new building types such as the railway station, bus station, petrol station and multi-storey car park. But it was on *urban-scale* form that transport technology perhaps had the greatest impact. At the urban scale, roads and tramways led to ribbon development, with linear arms of urbanisation accentuating the radial form of cities. Main roads became new structuring devices for cities. Echoing the bundling of transmission of forces in steel-framed buildings, the main highways formed a superstructure that bore the main burden of traffic flows, to which local areas were 'plugged in' (Figure 8.6).[26]

At the local scale, the 'Radburn' layout, with separation of roads for vehicles and paths for pedestrians, became part of the new urban order (Figure 1.2). So while the macro-form of Cumbernauld may be regarded as a planning or design innovation, unprecedented for the 'motor age', the local urban ordering is more of an adaptation, building on and combining earlier precedents of Radburn and earlier new town models.

In addition to evolution implying a direct lineage from past to present, it also implies a divergence of function from a common origin: where a more general forebear gives rise to different, more specialised descendants. We can see this 'adaptive radiation' in the case of a proliferation of different kinds of multi-storey car park, as demonstrated by Philip Steadman. We can also see this clearly in the case of a longer-term case of speciation, the *agora*.[27]

The *agora*, as we saw earlier, specialised and evolved into the theatre. Subsequently, the theatre itself diverged into other forms. As a musical venue, the theatre could be said to evolve into a concert hall; the theatre form also could be adapted in function to become the lecture theatre. With the invention of the kinematograph, some theatres started showing films, and later became dedicated 'electric' picture-houses, and hence modern cinemas.[28]

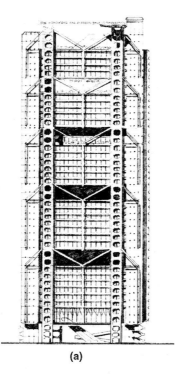
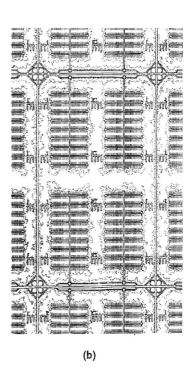

8.6 • Modern structure: (a) Steel-framed building (HSBC, Hong Kong); (b) Hilberseimer's New City, with superstructure of main roads.

(a)   **(b)**

With modern broadcasting technology allowing separation of viewer from action, the TV studio becomes the descendant of the theatre stage, and living rooms become the modern miniature auditoria (or private boxes), with the armchairs turned to huddle round the TV, rather than the communal hearth of old. While iconic of modern times and a fragmented society, the family sitting round the 'telly' is no more and no less than a combination or even fulfilment of the deep-rooted human inclinations for public spectacle and private relaxation.

Meanwhile, the agora evolved into the covered market and hence shopping mall. On the one hand, then, the modern shopping mall – especially the suburban type surrounded by a 'sea' of car parking – can be seen as a twentieth-century invention partly stimulated by the motor car. On the other hand, as a building type and public space, the mall can be seen as simply the latest in a lineage that could be traced back via shopping arcades, shopping streets, street markets and (in the case of western versions) to the Greek *agora* and beyond.[29]

Therefore, Cumbernauld's monolithic megastructure of a town centre, although on the one hand a large-scale architectural innovation, could be seen as nevertheless an evolutionary descendant of the ancient *agora*, where all those town centre functions took place in a single identifiable space, and were not spread into separate streets of shop-buildings and civic-buildings.[30]

Whereas Cumbernauld saw a deliberate innovative leap to the town-centre-as-single-building, East Kilbride – another new town near Glasgow – did it a different way. East Kilbride's town centre started out with its main shopping street as a conventional vehicular street (Princes Street).[31] This was converted to a pedestrian precinct (renamed Princes Gate, Figure 8.7a); and finally covered over to form a shopping mall (now Princes Mall, Figure 8.7b). The mall was subsequently connected up with the other shopping malls, a cinema complex, ice rink and multi-storey car parks to produce incrementally what is in effect a 'town centre in a single building' – a megastructure by stealth (Figure 8.7c).[32]

Ironically, while Cumbernauld Town Centre was built with a conceptual

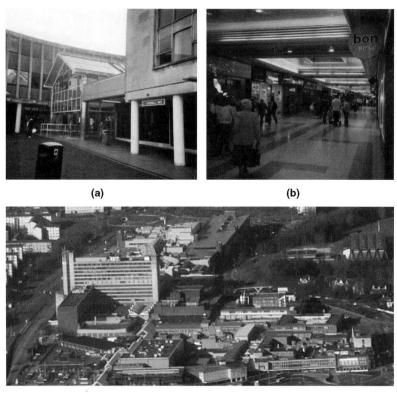

(a)   (b)

(c)

8.7 • East Kilbride Town Centre. (a) Entrance to Princess Mall – originally an exterior vehicular street; (b) Interior of Princess Mall; (c) The town centre forms a single contiguous megastructural building – a 'labyrinthine civicomplex', as Geddes might have called it.

expression of extensibility, it was East Kilbride that extended in the more 'organic' fashion over time, to create what what Geddes might have called a 'labyrinthine civicomplex'.[33]

In combining the functions of shopping, public space, and spectacle (cinema and ice rink), East Kilbride Town Centre can be seen as a descendent of the *agora*, reconciling the ancient schism between the *agora*'s market and spectacle functions. The evolution of a town-centre-in-a-building (if not quite a whole city-in-a-building) is almost a reconciliation of the original schism between private architecture and public urban space. In each case, the recombination is enabled by the way that cultural transmission allows a given urban object to have several disparate predecessors, separated in time.

One could easily colloquially describe the transformation of East Kilbride Town Centre as 'organic growth' (in contrast to Cumbernauld's 'town centre design'). But, the transformation is not like the development of an organism to a fixed programme. Rather, like the case of Glasgow (Figure 8.4), it is an example of *in situ* urban evolution: open-ended, with the outcome unknowable, even if each increment was a purposive design.[34]

A final evolutionary resonance for East Kilbride is the idea of a new town in the first place. This 'Modern' idea of a deliberately planned town descended through time – in the western tradition, at least from the ancient Greeks (Figure 8.8).

What's new with Modernism?

Even if Modernism was not a complete break from the past, there must be some change of significance, otherwise we would have an unpunctuated continuum, with no 'impact of Modernism' discernible. Here, we can identify three ways in which evolution in the modern period differed from traditional evolutionary urbanism.

First, there is the speed and suddenness of the change – this could be referred to as the 'high speed aquarium' effect. Secondly, there is the magnitude of change, in terms of the scale and scope of the units – the 'hopeful monster' effect. Thirdly, there is the diversity of the 'solution space' opened up – the 'Cambrian explosion' effect. Let us look at each of these in turn; these will help answer the question about why Modernism may some-times be dysfunctional, despite good intentions.

'High speed aquarium'

Geoffrey Jellicoe's book *Motopia* is at first sight a typical Modernist tract: as if a radical utopia 'for' motor cars. But on closer inspection, we can see that *Motopia* is actually about creating a human-friendly urban environment, that

8.8 • Set of plans for British post-war new towns. These have a 'family resemblance', because they are based on similar principles, addressing a similar context. (a) East Kilbride. (b) Stevenage. (c) Harlow. (d) Cwmbran. (e) Crawley. (f) Basildon.

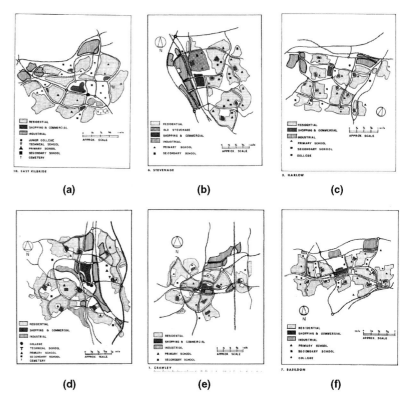

(a)   (b)   (c)

(d)   (e)   (f)

is also adapted for the motor car. Jellicoe's prose is infused with evolutionary thinking:

> The car is a metal shell which man has grown around himself. By this means he is able to propel himself at will to distances and at speeds that were certainly never the intention of nature. If all the slow-moving mollusks in the sea rocks were suddenly to acquire self-propulsion twenty times their present rate, we can imagine the collisions and disasters that would befall them. Man's condition is somewhat similar, because although he has had 60 years to adapt himself personally, he has omitted to adapt his environment as well.[35]

Jellicoe's reference to 'slow-moving mollusks' seems to be an echo of a similar point made by Le Corbusier in *La Ville Radieuse*, referring to speeded-up fish colliding in an aquarium.[36]

The high-speed aquarium effect, as we could refer to this, is the idea that we make changes to one thing (in this case, the speed of moving molluscs or cars) but the rest of the environment takes some time to adapt. In the meantime, there is a frictional, dysfunctional lack of fit. This may be to the disbenefit of the new entrant itself (technology introduced 'ahead of its time', that fails to catch on), or the environment (directly, for example by being polluted, or indirectly, getting despoiled by high-speed roads introduced to adapt to the new entrant), or directly disbenefit the other users of the environment (pedestrians forced in turn to negotiate the new barren, threatening environment of high-speed traffic roads, no longer fit for people on foot) – or all three.[37]

This then relates to the speed or suddenness of modern innovation, and the lack of time for people to adapt to them. So while rapid innovation can be exciting and deliver new solutions, the success will partly depend on how it fits with the other things around it. So this is one reason 'why Modernism failed'. Innovations on one front are not matched by adaptation on others. We are waiting for the other things to catch up: as if we are in a forever-temporary ill-fitting phase, like living in a building under constant renovation: heroic in aspiration, perhaps, but uncomfortable for living in for the time being, and with an uncomfortable doubt as to whether it will ever be fit to live in.

'Hopeful monsters'

A second effect is to do with the scale and scope of change: the nature of the innovations themselves. In the biological context, mutations in an organism – relative to an already functional, finely tuned 'design' – tend to be harmful, and the larger the mutation the more likely it is to be harmful, and the resulting organism dysfunctional.

We see this in technological evolution. An unprecedented innovative idea – like a tricycle powered by horses on a treadmill – is such a leap from either tricycle or horse-drawn carriage that it would not be surprising if it turned out to be unsuccessful (Figure 8.9 a). Something similar could be said of innovative technologies such as the Lartigue steam monorail or Bennie Railplane (Figure 8.9 b, c). These risked failure not necessarily for being dysfunctional in an internal mechanical sense, but by not fitting the social, economic and built environment into which they were to be inserted, or there being no viable paths to a future successful fit. In contrast, the motor car (or 'horseless carriage') got a foothold because it was able to exploit the environment of smooth straight streets first adapted for the horse and carriage (rather than the irregular winding alleys not adapted for vehicular traffic); while diesel and electric trains (less radical departures from their steam forerunners) exploited the conventional rail technology that the 'railplane' was unable to.

(a)

(b)

(c)

8.9 • Technological macro-mutations, or 'hopeful monsters': (a) Stockton's fictional horse-powered tricycle; (b) The Lartigue Railway, Ireland – a steam monorail with 'mutant' two-boilered, two-funnelled locomotive; (c) The Bennie Railplane, a propellor-driven monorail, near Glasgow. In each case, the innovative technology might be functional, but was poorly adapted to the contemporary environment. In the case of the Bennie Railplane, the futuristic craft is ironically shown contrasted with a contemporary conventional steam engine; the latter was nevertheless better adapted.

Something similar may be said to happen for the built environment, where there are large leaps in the 'solution space' (recall Figure 1.9). Instead of a gradual improvement in streets and blocks of flats, we suddenly leap to 'streets in the air' as a solution. Instead of piecemeal renovation of individual worn-out buildings (Jane Jacobs), we leap straight to wholesale demolition and reconstruction along Modernist lines (Anderston Cross, Glasgow). These may be regarded as 'hopeful monsters'.[38] If they are lucky they just might work; but they are nevertheless risky 'leaps in the dark'.

Here, the monstrosity is not in the monolithic size or brute ugliness of the architecture – though it helps.[39] Some Modernist architecture may indeed be 'monstrous' in terms of size or ugliness or both – as in popular expressions of some building being a 'monstrosity'. Here, what is meant is more the idea of an abnormal aberrational aspect – unnatural and (hence) dysfunctional, although it may be seen as an individualistic novelty by its own creator. Hence Unités (however aesthetically pleasing) or 'streets in the air' are more monstrous in this sense than an unsightly brick vernacular building.

A new town or new city is not necessarily a hopeful monster. It may be hopeful, but not a 'monster' unless it is a new combination of parts – reinvention or reconstitution of elements. Cumbernauld town centre was arguably a 'hopeful monster' – a leap to a town-centre-in-a-single-building. East Kilbride Town Centre, whatever its bulk and aesthetic impact, is not monstrous in this sense.[40]

In effect, we get 'monstrous Modernism' because we humans are impatiently visionary, impatiently creative: we have the ability to imagine future target solutions that would lead us to attempt to design a 'hopeful monster' rather than wait to evolve one.

While all this seems rather negative on novelty, a leap in the dark could, however, be good if it lands in a fertile new territory that could not readily be reached by more gradual means.

The 'Cambrian explosion'

The 'Cambrian explosion' is the idea of a sudden profusion of new forms, many of which become extinct, before stabilisation to a few basic forms. The original (biological) Cambrian explosion happened when a diverse mass of new species 'suddenly' appeared in the fossil record – followed by subsequent extinctions.[41]

In technological evolution, an analogy here would be the profusion of kinds of bicycles in the nineteenth century: when the bicycle 'took off', many new forms were experimented with. This meant there was much trial and

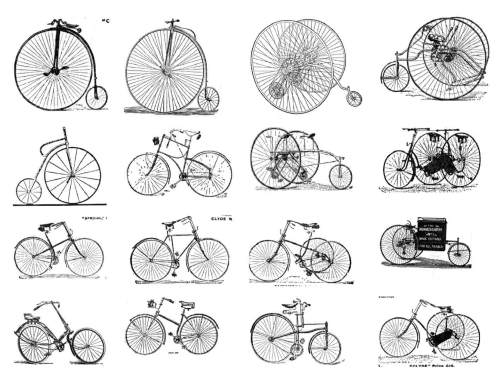

8.10 • A 'Cambrian explosion' of bicycles.

error, including types that proved to be not so useful and relatively soon became extinct (Figure 8.10).[42]

Note that in the set of bicycles here, while there is a graphic resonance with, say, the winding towers of Figure 6.12, there is a subtle difference. The winding towers represent mature technology, where there is a robust basic design that does not change much, although it may differ in detail from time to time, and place to place. However, the bicycles display a greater variety of types, because they are still (as it were) exploring the solution space, they have not yet settled down to a few basic viable types, but include all sorts of penny farthings, tandems and tricycles, and so on. This variety is – at least temporarily – viable because the newly opened-up solution space represents 'easy pickings', or finding oneself stumbling on success in all directions.[43] This is because, put crudely, almost any design that works as a bicycle is better than no bicycle. In effect, there is a diversity of successful forms – because success is *relative*. But in the long term, the less successful encounter greater competition, and became extinct.

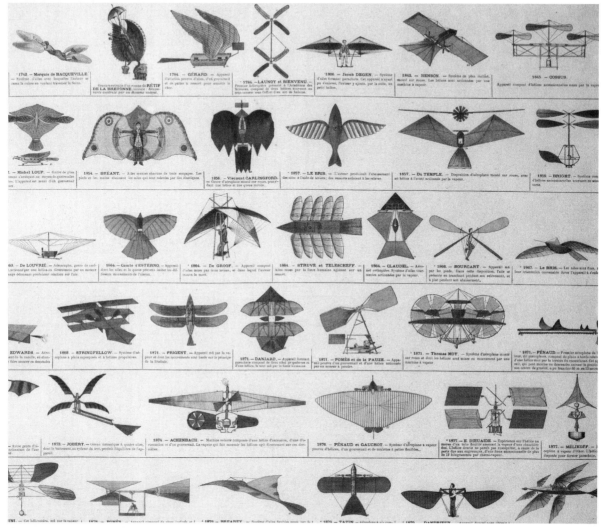

8.11 • Dieuaide's *Tableau d'Aviation*. Here, the flying-machines are more diverse, relatively speaking, than the bicycles (Figure 8.10) and not necessarily viable.

Let us now consider a third case: that of heavier-than-air flying machines (Figure 8.11). Here we see the familiar story of 'similarities and differences', of form and function, and resonance with the winding towers or bicycles. However, in this case we can note how *different* the flying-machines are from each other (unlike the winding towers, or even the bicycles; or for that matter, modern mature aircraft designs). That is, while they look similar insofar as they look as if they might fly, they are very different in detail. Compare, for example, the variation in number of wings per machine, versus number of wheels per machine for the bicycles; or the different seating positions, or number of different types of structural components, and so on.

With the bicycles, the 'similarity with diversity' is because a basic functional design is modified and applied for different purposes in different contexts. With the flying-machines, it is almost the other way around. The similarity is due to the attempt to achieve a single end – that is, heavier-than-air flight. The difference is because these are *not* gradual adaptations of an existing viable model, but are coming at the problem from different starting-points. Or, put another way, the designs are not close to each other in design space, as it were, but are more randomly distributed, reached by almost random leaps from the last untested – or tested but unsuccessful – design. The different 'leaps in the dark' were in a sense trying to bypass the gradualist evolution that might one day evolve a viable heavier-than-air aircraft. So we have three scenarios, as shown Table 8.1.[44]

Of course, once heavier-than-air flight had been achieved, there was then a great diversity of early designs partly due to the great degree of experimentation – the rapid exploration of a 'newly opened up solution space' (as with the bicycles) – then finally matured like the medley of winding towers, or a medley of modern aircraft designs. In other words, the prize for success in scenario III is to proceed to scenario II. The difference between scenarios I and II is fuzzy, partly dependent on the timescale of the perspective: how temporary is temporary?

Table 8.1 Three evolutionary scenarios

Case	Nature	Technology	Urban
(I) Mature	Extant species – all viable, with tried and tested functionality.	Winding towers (Figure 6.13).	Everyday designs of individual buildings, streets, etc.
(II) Cambrian explosion	The original Cambrian explosion, followed by extinction.	Bicycles – all viable at the time, but success is relative and temporary (Figure 8.10).	Experimental new towns (Most of those in Figure 8.2; Figure 8.8).
(III) Leap in the dark	Targeted macro-mutation not seen in nature.	Flying-machines (Figure 8.11) – not even united by being viable for the moment; could live on as design ideas, even if never proven in practice.	Unbuilt visions, e.g. Ciudad Lineal (Figure 2.9); Ville Radieuse (Figure 2.11).

The urban equivalents are suggested as follows. The urban equivalent of the flying-machines would be a set of unbuilt, untested designs – such as *Ville Radieuse*, New City, *Ciudad Lineal*. They have things in common, to be sure, but are coming at the problem from different points of view, and not directly based on a common ancestor. The urban equivalent of the bicycles is perhaps a set of new towns, with experimental variations on a theme (Figure 8.8). These are viable and built, and vary from context to context. The urban equivalent of the winding towers would be individual mature urban components such as buildings, streets, and so on. An 'unplanned' city does not have an overall design as such.

Learning from evolution

In effect, city planning is like any kind of design, attempting a creative short-cut to a successful solution. Hence it appears daring, prescient, visionary. In contrast, a step-by-step way looks no further than the next step. So it is in danger of being perceived as myopic. But, however visionary, the targeted leap (from III to II, in Table 8.1) is nevertheless a risky leap. The point here about Modernism is that modern technology allowed an explosion in possible forms of buildings and cities – *and we are still picking through the wreckage*.

Much of Modernist architecture and planning was experimental – streets in the air and pilotis and Unités – and much did not work. The problem is that while the occasional novel, aberrational building may get away with it, Modernist *planning* interventions are so large and long-lived; and moreover are part of a delicate ecosystem which could be harmed by a few crude interventions. (Unlike a bad car model which just gets sent to the scrapyard; and a new model comes along right after.) Also, while one can easily substitute one car for another, or even one building for another, one cannot easily substitute a whole district or urban quarter or city.

Nevertheless, targeted innovation can pay off. After all, the Wright Brothers got their successful solution to heavier-than-air flight without either trying to directly emulate flapping, feathered wings, or by adding fins to a balloon or car, and gradually evolving wings (although someone *could* have). Their successful aircraft design can be regarded as an invention rather than as an evolution. But, it did build from existing technologies – it did not arrive out of thin air. And, the point about evolution is the long-term perspective. However novel the design, a flying-machine is still built on precedents in engine and metal technology, and so was the long-term product of evolution. This is like the flight of a bird or bat, built on preceding muscle-and-bone technology.[45]

So it was the combination of inventive design and evolution that got us powered heavier-than-air flight. If we only had evolution without targeted invention, we would still be driving around in cars with fins, waiting for wings to sprout. But then again if we only had design-leaps on their own, we would still be jumping and flapping off cliffs with birds' wings.

So it is not a case of 'Modernism bad, evolution good', nor 'evolution natural, Modernism aberrational' (as Alexander might say).[46] Nor does it mean an evolutionary interpretation of urbanism airbrushing the designer out of design history.[47]

In effect, if we allow increments of design – as well as artificial selection – to be part of evolution, then Modernist city design is indeed part of urban evolution as described herein. In effect, cities and artefacts can be seen as products of design *and* evolution, and not just one or the other. This also means that many 'good old evolved' settlements may still owe much of their functional order to a large extent to conscious design (or selection). Conversely, the problematic 'hopeful monsters' of 'bad old Modernism' are indeed *part of evolution*. In other words, part of the problem of Modernism is part of the problem of evolution.

Arguably what both successful old urbanism and successful modern urbanism have in common is that they are *well adapted* – whether by design or accident: old urbanism often through a long process of trial and error (including prescient design; retention of the good and elimination of the bad), and modern urbanism through successful prescient innovative design or successful prescient adaptation of existing places and designs. It is mostly the unsuccessful innovative designs of Modernism (indeed, of any 'ism') that get the bad name, but these unfortunate by-products are in the end part of the evolutionary deal: products of the same kinds of process that created what we now recognise as retained good old urbanism.

In this perspective, the Pruitt-Igoe demolition (Chapter 2) does not represent the 'death of Modern architecture' (which sounds terminal, like the extinction of a species), but simply represented '*a*' death of modern architecture – part of an ongoing process of elimination of bad design (or rather, elimination of artefacts whose design turned out badly adapted for their context). In this sense, some of the dysfunctional innovations of Modernism could be seen as 'aberrations', but not Modernist architecture *per se*.[48] The elimination of 'bad design' is part and parcel of evolution. This is what is – or what appears in hindsight to be – successful about both evolved life-forms and traditional urbanism.[49]

TWENTY-FIRST CENTURY EVOLVING URBANISM

So much for Modernism. We now appear to be in a post-modern world, or some kind of mixed-up combination of modern, post-modern and neo-traditional urbanism. As we saw in the last chapter, we don't have the traditional roughly radio-concentric city; but then again we don't have the fulfilment of the Modernist reinvention of the radio-concentric model, with radial motorways and ring roads feeding megastructural town centres either. Nor do we yet have space-station-like cities-in-buildings. We do have familiar urban things, but in different combinations: out-of-town town centres, gentrified inner cities, apartments and artists' studios where warehouses and wharves and docks used to be, a new generation of back offices and small enterprises in the suburbs. We do still perpetuate a kind of quotidian Modernism, with lots of new houses, supermarkets, distributor roads, car parks and roundabouts: a twenty-first-century suburban soap-opera rather than a space-age science fiction epic.

How do we interpret this with respect to evolution? Are cities degenerating, like evolution gone into reverse, or gone off the rails? No; or at least, whatever they are doing, they are not confounding evolution. After all, the evolutionary sense of the term 'fitness' implies fitting for the present context, in a relative not absolute sense. There is not and never was an 'evolutionary track of progress' leading in any particular direction, otherwise we would have ever bigger cities with ever denser centres, ever taller buildings, ever larger blocks, ever wider roads, ever more concentric rings. We only ever seem to have more suburbs. Walking city-sized buildings may well come some day, but there is no inevitable destination of progress.

Rather, perhaps, we can see today's urbanism as simply a further continuation of urban evolution, in a new phase. In this phase, we see evolution on at least two different fronts, which can be – very broadly – interpreted as the evolution of 'unplanned' and planned urbanism. These shall be referred to, for convenience, as ad hoc Modernism and post-modern planning.

Ad hoc Modernism

On one front, then, we continue with modern architecture and infrastructure, but there is no grand plan. We retain the modern urban ordering of hierarchical Radburn-style loops and cul-de-sacs, but without the city design. It is a sort of ad hoc, laissez-faire urbanism. The result is a mix of stuff all over the place. Out in the suburbs, this is what tends to get called *sprawl*. But we also see the equivalent in the inner city, exemplified by London's Docklands, where a relaxation of planning is seen as part of the solution, while the buildings are as Modern as any. It could in some cases be described as post-planning Modernism. Planning is not actually dead, but old-style planning with the paternalistic city planner in the driving seat directing everything is superseded, while Modernism continues everywhere else with modern

8.12 • Glasgow's regenerated waterfront. Modernism is alive and well, and continues to evolve – in this case, with a variety of biomorphic architectures.

architecture, modern technology, modern cars and roads, and so on. This could apply equally to new settlements, urban extension or regenerated parts of existing cities (Figure 8.12).

The result is a familiar combination of continuity with change. The ad hoc sprawl can be seen to evolve not so much from Modernist city planning, but from Modernist components, evolving without City Design. In other words, left to own its devices, this is what a modern car-oriented, telecommunications-rich society would naturally generate – as naturally and organically as the Victorian city of trams and tenements, or the medieval city of streets and mews. Or put another way, the ad hoc Modernism and post-planning sprawl is the true evolutionary inheritor of unplanned organic urbanism, finally realising the 'natural' forms stimulated by the technological innovations of the nineteenth century – that is, forms that would arise without the straitjacket of Modernist planning.

In other words, this evolution to some extent bypasses or short-circuits the Modernist city design of the type that attempted to recreate the physical structure of the traditional city, only on a more modern, ordered, 'rectified' format; that is, the kind of design that attempted to create ring-and-radial highway systems bolstering accentuated city centres (such as in Glasgow, Chapter 2). Cities that never went through a sixties-style Modernist phase – or that never had railways and railway suburbs – go straight to the contemporary form.

This leaves Modernist *city design* (as opposed to modern roads or buildings) as a strange aberration in hindsight: even, an evolutionary cul-de-sac. Le Corbusier's unbuilt city designs may have been visionary, but being ahead of their time was not necessarily a good thing: it is tantamount to being ill-fitting to its present context, and hence risks being dysfunctional. Le Corbusier's *images* may have beguiled a generation of planners, but these were untested, hopeful monsters. The idea of having an aerodrome at the centre of a city looks strangely anachronistic and unprophetic. If it had been built, it would surely soon have gone out of date.

Post-modern planning

An alternative to ad hoc Modernism – a kind of post-planning Modernism – is post-modern planning. This is where neo-traditionalism and the New Urbanism come in. These can be seen as a reaction to 'bad old Modernism' *and* to the contemporary sprawl just described. As we saw in Chapter 2, neo-traditionalism combines an element of urban ordering – reversing the Corbusian revolution (Figure 1.2) – and an element of city design.

The neo-traditional city effectively evolves from 'city planning ideas'. It builds on pre-Modern urban order of streets and squares and courtyards; combined with Modernist city-scale and town-scale design. It is a direct descendant of Modernist city planning (Chapter 2).

Unlike Modernism, neo-traditional urbanism was not primarily stimulated by new technology. More, it was stimulated by the failure of Modernism, and by changed priorities. Hence the return to the traditional street, traditional terrace and courtyard. This return is – as suggested in Chapter 1 – due to these being functional solutions. So the neo-traditionalists are in a sense doing what the old Modernists did, but instead of optimising for limited objectives such as accommodating motorisation, they are doing it for the more pluralistic objectives such as 'balanced sustainable transport and people-friendly urban space' (Chapter 2). In this sense, rather than a counter-revolution, it could be seen as more a kind of resetting, as if to a longer-term trend or theme, after the more violent perturbations of the 1960s and 1970s Modernism. That is, a sort of gradualist Modernism, what planning might have evolved for itself had the Corbusian revolution not happened.

Planning still at the crossroads

Of course, the reality is more complex than this. The main point here is to draw attention to the sense that there is not just one 'post' Modern urbanism going on; that Modernism is still with us, and that evolution of both planned and 'unplanned' aspects of urbanism is continuing. Or, perhaps, one might say there is evolution of modern urban order without city design (ad hoc or post-planning Modernism), and evolution of modern city design, town design, neighbourhood design and street design, without the Modernist urban order (post-modern planning).

And, just to be clear that there are other combinations out there, we need only look at the burgeoning cities of today's rapidly developing countries to see on the one hand Modernism going full throttle, with grand-scale Modernist and neo-traditional city design and urban ordering in the more affluent cases, and the somewhat less than modern urban order and somewhat less than city-level design of squatter settlements in less affluent cases.

CONCLUSIONS

Evolution seems to be a useful paradigm for interpreting the complex, dynamic, collective entity that is the city and urban change, including the change arising from urban planning and design. Evolution seems a natural way of discussing things that descend from things, are adapted, succeed or fail in competition, may be steered or selected by environmental influences or conscious human intervention, and coevolve and transform themselves over time. Interpreting cities in evolutionary terms seems to be useful, and worth it, even though the processes of urban evolution do not in detail resemble processes of biological evolution.

The evolutionary paradigm is indeed a paradigm in the sense of a way of understanding and interpreting the world. The components of the evolutionary paradigm are well enough known: plans, patterns, codes, standards and guidelines are copied and selectively retained; experimental innovations are adopted or discarded. Perhaps what is new is the recognition of this amounting to evolution, in a sense that is more than figurative – in a more definite and literal sense than claiming 'a city is an organism'. Perhaps what is newly crystallised is the idea that planning and design can be considered *part* of evolution.

This means, in turn, that evolution is not just a model for a particular kind of vernacular urbanism or an historical phase of urbanism, that have been supplanted by professional planning or Modernism. Evolution need not imply a stubborn conservatism, or a denial of inventive design. It can include deliberate intervention while having emergent outcomes. It can combine innovation and tradition. As with the equivalents in nature, without some innovation and some tradition, there can be no evolution.

Evolution, indeed, turns out to amount to a paradigm within which other models or approaches can be placed. Evolution can handle both buildings and cities, embracing both physical and social dimensions, and can apply to plans and blueprints, patterns and codes. Evolution can take both planned and 'unplanned' urbanism in its stride; it can dine out on traditionalism, swallow Modernism whole and have post-modernism for afters.

Perhaps ironically it is Modernism, with its boldest and most exaggerated creativity and iconoclasm, that most clearly brings out the idea of urban evolution in a sense that means more than simply gradualism, but evolution in the sense of continuous generation of novelty, trial and error, leading ultimately to better, 'tried and tested' outcomes in the longer term. In effect, Modernism *magnified* the problems of urban evolution – in one sense literally by creating the 'big problems' of its physical macro-mutations; and in a second sense, by making large and clear in front of us, what was traditionally hidden in myriad micro-innovations and micro-extinctions of historical urbanism. Like the rise and fall of the dinosaurs, the rise and fall of Modernist planning makes a vivid and visceral case study of a phenomenon that has been happening before and since on a more quotidian scale. This is perhaps why the monstrous forms of the 1960s and 1970s still fascinate us, even if they are best seen from the safe distance of hindsight, or confined to the pages of a textbook.

The evolutionary perspective, then, can indeed provide some answers to the urban conundrum identified at the start of the book. Now we are in a position to suggest four kinds of reason why modern planned urban development and settlements are not necessarily better than traditional 'unplanned' urbanism.

First, there are reasons to do with the scope and scale of change – the 'hopeful monster' effect – where innovations proved to be poorly adapted and hence dysfunctional. Secondly, and linked to this, is the 'high-speed aquarium' effect, where even if the innovations were individually functional, their implementation was too sudden (or piecemeal) for the overall result to be functional. Both these points proved to be a particular problem for Modernist *planning* – that is, urban-scale interventions – due to their large scale and long timescale for implementation.[50]

The third kind of reason is to do with the scale of perspective in which the changes are seen. This relates to the idea of the 'Cambrian explosion' – not of itself a problem, more a perspective on the problem. Failures are part and parcel of evolution. For Modernist planning, it is just that we have been living through an ongoing period of big trial and big error. The safe, cosy traditional urbanism admired for its functionality is only that way because of being the end-product of decades or centuries of hard-won adaptation.

A fourth kind of reason (encountered originally in earlier chapters) is to do with the process by which Modernist planning tried to rectify or reconstitute conventional urban forms on modern lines – like cities with centres and radial routes. This was implicitly as if the city were a fixed kind of 'organism', requiring corrective surgery, rather than something evolving with no knowable optimal destination. In a sense, the paradigm was misleading, so the diagnosis was misguided, and the treatment misfired.

In the end, urban evolution would not be of such interest to planners and designers – as biological evolution is to agriculturalists or virologists – if it were merely an explanation of past formation; if it did not allow insights into purposeful ongoing intervention. We have seen that planning and design can be part of urban evolution; the question now shifts – to recall Geddes again – from '*whence?*' and '*how?*' to '*whither?*' And so, having suggested answers to the specific conundrum of dysfunctional Modern planned environments, we turn to the more general question of how this understanding can help us do better urban planning and design.

Notes

1   Thompson ([1917] 1948: 1020–1021).
2   Geddes (1915: 1).
3   Pinker (1999). For further discussion, see Marshall (2006b).
4   Kostof (1991: 31) refers to the 'chicken and egg' nature of trying to understand urban origins. Fletcher (1921) suggested that buildings evolved from three natural prototypes: the cave (hence stone-walled building), the arbour (hence wooden hut) and the animal skin (hence tent). See also Bellan (1971) and Morris (1994) on the origin and history of cities.
5   Unwin (1997).
6   According to Banister Fletcher, village settlements in some parts of the world were often contiguous first, and only later developed a more open-plan layout with streets. There is a logical case, then, by which cities might have formed out of large building complexes, either as a result of a societal restructuring (emergence of a more articulated society, not a tightly knit social unit) or as a result of growth in size, or both (Fletcher, 1921; Cruickshank, 1996).
7   The schism between buildings and cities could be regarded as no more or less significant to architecture and planning than the ancient schism of animal and plant kingdoms is to zoologists and botanists. It is intriguing to consider that the schism between architecture and planning could predate the emergence of *Homo sapiens*, if earlier human species developed communal and individual topologies – hearths or 'buildings' – separately.
8   See for example Clark (1958: 238), Benevolo (1980: 16), Morris (1994: 3), Diamond (1998), Kotkin (2005: xiii, 158).
9   Religious buildings might originate as dedicated 'public' buildings, or might have originally developed within private residences. See, for example, Pryor (2004). Craft industry within the home became split into residential-only and industrial-only. In expanding industries, we tend to see greater specialisation of trades – although in contracting industries, there may be amalgamations, and ultimately, extinction of trades, for example, bowyers, loriners, mercers, and so on. The

modern list of land use categories used in planning is potentially not just descriptive like a pre-Darwinian taxonomy, but could be an historical, genealogical, evolutionary one.

10 Hall (1999: 38).

11 Hall (1999: 38); Hall (1999: 39).

12 For evolution of building types, see, for example, Hanson (1998: 155), Crouch and Johnson (2001); Steadman (1979). Fletcher (Cruickshank, 1996) characterises changes in architecture in evolutionary terms; and depicts a 'family tree' of architectural traditions (1921). Vitruvius: several instances of Vitruvian ideas and depictions of 'Vitruvian man' appear in the volume *Architectural Theory*, for example, Jobst (2003a: 63), Jobst (2003b: 97), Zimmer (2003: 482); Vitruvius as 'second rate architect' (Jobst, 2003a: 60). Vitruvius explicitly acknowledges his own predecessors (1960: 198). Leonardo's 'Vitruvian Man': Nicholl (2005: 246–247); Modulor: Le Corbusier (1951).

13 For land transport, we then have the domestication of various animals, used for riding on, for bearing packs, and hauling vehicles. These include horses, oxen, also llamas, sled dogs. Also, litters and sedan chairs. Animals like horses are large and cumbersome, hence are not suitable for ladders; they are smelly and social outsiders, hence not for indoor use (Chapter 4).

14 Straight streets suitable for carriages (Barnett, 1986: 10, after Mumford); mews (Deckker, 1998); boulevards (Jacobs *et al.*, 2002). The Islamic tradition sets out requirements for streets to be wide enough to allow laden camels to pass (Morris, 1994). 'When the transport system is contemporaneous with the built environment, i.e. horse and carriages in 18th century London or York, the moving environment is compatible with the static' (Black and Williams, 1977: 225). Railways also affected the alignment of streets and urban forms (Scargill, 1979: 20).

15 Alexander (1979: 175–183). While biology now understands that organisms are genetically specified in a way that is more like a 'genetic recipe' than a 'genetic blueprint', it is not strictly necessary to know the details of genetics in order to observe the basic fact of evolutionary change in species. To the extent that this book is mostly concerned with *urban* planning and design, there is no scope here to enter the debate about the process by which buildings or architectural components should be designed – by blueprints, patterns, or otherwise.

16 Walker (1996, 1999). This grid idea may have been partly copied from Edinburgh. Finally, we later get, further west, more complex geometries – curvilinear suburbs of houses and maisonettes (Reed, 1996, 1999b).

17 This implies an evolutionary process of urban change that is different from that described as 'evolution' by Alexander in *The Nature of Order* (2002b, 2005); see also Chapter 9.

18 This is just as we do not say we 'evolved' from our parents, even if the incremental change is theoretically part of a long-term effect ultimately recognisable as evolution.

19 Indeed, the fact that Evelyn's and Wren's plans were never built suggests that, however good in theory, these did not fit the time and place, that is, London in the aftermath of the Great Fire (Kostof, 1992).

20 Alexander also sees this as a deviation from the way the natural world is structured; and from how our own built environment should be structured (2002b: xiv–xvi).

21 Hilberseimer (1944); Korn (1953); Johnson-Marshall (1966); Gibberd (1967). Buchanan (MoT, 1963) and Le Corbusier ([1933] 1964: 268) use Venice as an example of a hierarchy of circulation systems; Jellicoe (1961) actually has water-buses in his *Motopia* proposal; Ritter (1964); Johnson-Marshall (1966: 118); Bacon (1975); Hebbert describes how as far back as 1931 walkways were proposed in Manhattan, using Venice as a model; also the Barbican development in London and the City of London walkway system were also partly inspired by Venice (1993: 441, 449). Although Le Corbusier was notably reticent in his praise for the past, even he was seduced by Venice: 'Poetry flies there on multi-coloured wings' (1947a: 41). In particular, Venice provided a model of a harmonious interlocking system of separate circulation systems (in its canals and pedestrian streets) – even if the Modernist authors used that unique city as a justification for providing more quotidian cities with urban motorways for fast-flowing road traffic and elevated concrete pedestrian walkways (both features being notably absent from the Venetian original). Elsewhere, Ritter (1964: 315) shows Leonardo da Vinci's scheme as if the Modernist segregation has a noble pedigree.

22 See Birksted (2007) for discussion of Le Corbusier's hidden precedents.

23 Even Le Corbusier, the arch-Modernist, was building on a tradition of innovative iconoclasm. In *When the Cathedrals Were White* he referred to the past to justify rejection of tradition (Le Corbusier, 1947b).

24 Billington (1983), Barnett (1986: 110), Holgate (1986: 122), Graham and Marvin (1996), Slouka (1997). Vickers (1998: 153): 'Technology was a crucial factor in the development of the International Style.' Gold (1997: 24): 'In the cities, the combination of load-bearing metal frames, passenger lifts and the telephone system for communication made skyscrapers economically as well as technically viable structures.' According to Holgate (1986: 122) 'improvements in the production of steel and the development of reinforced concrete liberated building from the constraints of masonry construction. A new aesthetic was even more necessary and possible'. Structural shapes not previously attainable or calculable – or even imagined – become possible: Mainstone (1975); Fournier, (2004: 104).

25 Cervero (1998) refers to the almost Darwinian adaptation between public transport and some kinds of traditional city. The relationship between modern roads and the urban environment is explored by Tunnard and Pushkarev (1963); Appleyard *et al.* (1964: 11); Llewelyn-Davies *et al.* (1971); Banham (1971); Brodsly (1981); Dunnett (2000).

26 Marshall (1998).

27 Philip Steadman suggests that the multi-storey garage is a particularly clear-cut and instructive example of the evolution of a building type, under the pressures of a changing economic and technological environment. This was enabled by modern construction technology as well as being stimulated by the mass uptake of the private motor car (Steadman, 2006b).

28 Here the different functions of the modern mall and the ancient *agora* are not merely analogous: they are *homologous*.

29 Also, the Roman multi-storey market hall or 'shopping centre' – *Mercatus traini* (Kotkin, 2005).

30 Cumbernauld Town Centre, in straddling a main road, can also be read as a descendant of a historic megastructural form, the street-bridge (Brogden, 1996: 110).

31 Opher and Bird (1980: 5); East Kilbride Development Corporation (1987).

32 The idea of a megastructure by stealth echoes Banham's allusion to mega-structures growing wild (1976).

33 'Labyrinthine civicomplex' – Geddes ([1915] 1949: 2).

34 In fact, the transformation of the town centre is referred to as having 'evolved' on the centre's website – a colloquial use of evolution that is easily understood; not an academic affectation (www.shopek.co.uk/ 29.04.07).

35 Jellicoe (1961). *Motopia* is subtitled *A Study in the Evolution of the Urban Landscape*.

36 Le Corbusier describes the chaos that would happen if some of the fish in an aquarium suddenly speeded up – hence justifying the redesign of cities for the car ([1933] 1964: 121). Jellicoe alludes to *Motopia*'s 'pedigree' including the work of 'M. le Corbusier' (Jellicoe, 1961: 4). Note that the sudden speeding-up relates to the pawn-becomes-queen analogy in Chapter 7.

37 Banham describes the freeway environment of Los Angeles as an 'ecology' (Banham, 1971). The Sinclair C5, small electric tricycle, failed partly because of its own perceived inadequacies (required pedalling on hills) and because the street environment (big fast polluting vehicles) was unfavourable. The point here is that even were it perfectly adequate as a vehicle, a hostile environment could sink it (like one might say of bicycles).

38 The term 'hopeful monster' was originally coined by Goldschmidt in connection with large mutations in organisms (Dennett, 1996; Wolpert, 1998).

39 Monstrous forms of modern buildings (Alexander, 2002a: 14; 2002b: xiv); 'monstrous carbuncle' (Prince of Wales, 1984).

40 Howard's Garden City was a hopeful monster (recall green space at centre, circular Crystal Palace). A new town that was simply a contemporary development sited on a new location would not be.

41 Note controversy over interpretation of the original Cambrian explosion (Dawkins, 2004).

42 Solé and Goodwin (2000), Ziman (2000a). The bicycle images are assembled after Ballantyne (1979).

43 This could arise due to stumbling upon – or successfully devising – a new solution. Or, it could be finding a new environment, or the existing environment suddenly becoming more favourable (sudden heatwave).

44 See also Vincenti (2000) on technological evolution with respect to aeroplanes; Stankiewicz (2000: 243) on the nature of expanding 'design space'; and Perkins (2000: 171) on leaps over 'boundaries of non-viability'.

45 Gordon (1978) wondered if planes should have feathers. Leonardo da Vinci preferred the bat as the model for the flying-machine (Richter, 1952: 105).

46 Alexander (2002a, 2002b, 2005).

47 It is just that while human wilful creativity *may* be part of the variation part, or selection part of evolution (either wholly within a design process, or in the context of design plus external control), it is not *necessarily* involved – and we may not know if it is or is not – such as the case with some kinds of craft evolution, say, copying with accidental errors and with impersonal selective forces. Because this is a sort of alternative to the perhaps popular casual assumption that (all) man-made objects are by implication 'designed', this might seem to be pushing for a pro-evolutionary, anti-design perspective, but this is not the intention.

48 This argument here diverges from Christopher Alexander's suggestion that there is something intrinsically wrong with Modern architecture (2002a, 2002b, 2005).

49 This is like a 'reverse resonance' with Le Corbusier's argument *When the Cathedrals Were White* (1947b), where Le Corbusier looked to the past to find precedents that themselves broke with tradition.

50 The resulting environments themselves might be considered unfavourable for reasons also related to evolution and rate of change in a very long-term sense: that humans are not well adapted to such environments. That is, certain kinds of the Modernist-style environment may be intrinsically antithetical to the savannah-type environment that humans are naturally adapted to (Pinker, 1999; Marshall, 2006b).

9 PLANNING, DESIGN AND EVOLUTION

City planning is as old as cities and might count among its earliest functionaries **Cain, whose client was God; God himself, who oversaw the creation of numerous towns and the destruction of unsuccessful ones; and Romulus, planner of Rome.**
C. Abrams, *The Language of Cities*[1]

Those who see themselves in charge will legislate a built order, turning upon this wilful artifact with stern curves. But always the city has its own mind: it may refuse to go along with what has been prescribed, or find its mode of obedience that leaves it free to metamorphose without losing track of its idiosyncratic habits.
Spiro Kostof, *The City Assembled*[2]

A city's environment is shaped not only by people who have an important influence, but by everyone who lives or works there. They shape it when they vote, choose a new front door, replace their windows, complain about broken pavements, organise a community festival, give their opinion on a planning proposal, plant out their window boxes, commission building work to their business premises, or tell their children about local history.
Robert Cowan, *The Cities Design Forgot*[3]

The study of urban evolution is not simply a matter of historicism, like a romantic appreciation of bygone cities, or a fascination with antiquarian maps or artefacts, or even a kind of ancestral identity-fix, by which our roots help tell us who we are, according to where we came from. These may well apply, but no more so than in the way we might appreciate the evolutionary history of designed objects such as buildings or bridges.

That said, when it comes to a designed object like a building or

9.0 • The Glasgow skyline reflects the city's evolutionary history.

bridge, it is not necessary to know the evolutionary history of architecture or bridge design in order to actually design or adapt one. It may be sufficient to know the purpose to which the object is to be put, and to have knowledge of how an existing model works, and knowledge of how the object is to be constructed, in order to design one to fit a given purpose.

But when it comes to cities, things are different, because cities – except the most newly minted planned creations – are more significantly products of evolution as they are simple objects of design. So, it is useful to have an appreciation of the evolution of cities because in most cases knowing how a city has evolved is the *equivalent* of knowing how a building or bridge was designed and built, and why it works the way it does. This suggests that we can learn from the evolution of cities, in a direct and material way, to inform their onward planning.

To actually pursue planning as a rational intervention implies that through some kind of planning we can do better than having no planning at all: that we can somehow have an urban outcome that is better than emergence on its own, or evolution left to its own devices. The question becomes what kind of planning intervention is appropriate: which is the focus of this chapter.

First, this chapter sets out three alternative ways of thinking about planning and designing cities: Creation, Development or Evolution. This contrasts the evolutionary paradigm (Chapter 8) with two alternatives – the 'creationist' (object-design) and the 'developmental' (growing-organism) paradigms, and explores how the way we understand urbanism affects how we intervene.[4] Secondly, the chapter sets out some basic principles by which planning can be understood to operate as a combination of Space, Time and Civics, appropriate for application to cities. Finally, we consider more specifically what An 'Evolutionist' Approach to urban planning and design might be.

The focus of this chapter – as with the book as a whole – is mainly on the city design and urban ordering aspects of planning, rather than the overarching planning intentions or the details of planning instruments, both of which would be dependent on context. The discussion in this chapter is therefore set at a sufficiently general level that the ideas might be adapted and applied to a variety of contexts; there is no scope here to tie into specific planning or design guidance initiatives of particular locations. This is partly because different readers will have different planning applications and institutional contexts in mind in this regard – and some readers, none at all.

CREATION, DEVELOPMENT OR EVOLUTION

It was suggested in Chapter 5 that in science, revolutions are to do with changes in understanding about the way the universe works, whereas revolutions in planning tend to be about changes in aspiration or practice. (This is the difference between the Copernican revolution and the Corbusian revolution.) That said, when it comes to understanding urbanism – what cities are and how they came to be the way they are – scientific understanding becomes mixed up with planning aspiration and action. In other words, we need to understand what planners and designers are thinking they are doing, in order to understand the urban specimens that are subject to our scrutiny.

Earlier, in Chapter 5, it was suggested that a city is more like an eco-system than an individual organism, work of art or machine; while in Chapter 6 evolution was interpreted as an emergent effect that could include individual increments of purposive intervention. In the last chapter, it has been suggested that evolution provides a paradigm for understanding urbanism, that can accommodate both traditionalism and Modernism, both planned and unplanned urbanism. The question now becomes one of how we use this understanding to inform how we might better plan and design cities.

To do this, it will be useful to contrast the evolutionary paradigm with two other paradigms which are implicitly or explicitly used to interpret urban change. These may be described as the 'creationist' (designed-object) paradigm and the 'developmental' (growing-organism) one. Let us explore what these are and how these differ from the evolutionary paradigm.

The creationist paradigm

In the creationist paradigm, urban change is understood to result from a series of purposive acts of creation, punctuating an otherwise more or less stable condition, that passively embodies all previous creations. In the creationist paradigm, each intervention is an act of creation of sorts: as if both original and yet definitive of a final desired order. In the creationist paradigm, the creator is 'omnipotent' in the sense of having complete control of the finished work, and is 'omniscient' in the sense of knowing all the parts of the creation (including the parts remaining from previous acts of creation).

The creationist paradigm could be likened to a model railway, where everything is made or put in place by the human creator (Figure 9.1). The components added are fully formed and purpose-built from day one. The components – like water towers or grain silos or scrapyards – have fixed roles and do not interact or change between one intervention and the next. In other words, you may leave your model railway for a while, and when you come back to it, everything is still in place as before. You may then resume 'creation', introducing a new building here or laying a new bit of track there.

9.1 • The creationist paradigm, interpreted for a model railway. Every track, every tree, and every piece of junk is put in place by the creator; objects are added fully formed and purpose-built.

In the creationist paradigm, the product is functional to the extent that it has been designed to be so. Adaptations are deliberate. In the case of the model railway layout, everything fits together because it is so willed: the model hills are formed in order to be tunnelled through, and model valleys created in order to be bridged.

In the world of urban planning and design, operating in creationist mode, the designer or planner is (or aspires to be) the creator, assuming control of urban change: creating new things here, or mending existing things there. The planner may be an agent of creation acting on behalf of a ruler or controlling authority.

The creationist paradigm is clearly identifiable with the mode of design used for a building, machine or work of art; and when applied to cities equates with city design. In this case, the creator can create the city in any form that he or she wishes. This could be a grand act of symbolism (city as a work of art); it could be the creation of a complicated machine; or it could even be the creation of a city as 'organism'. In the last case, this means creation of a city with some kind of organic form – biomorphic or zoomorphic design.[5] But designing a city-as-organism in the creationist mode is no different from designing as work of art or machine; it is just the designer thinking with a different metaphor. It is exactly like the way an architect may design a building to look like an organism (as opposed to a machine, or sculptural object) even if the design is done in a completely artistic or mechanistic manner.

Christopher Alexander and colleagues evoke the creationist spirit where the architect's vision arises 'full-fledged, from "thin air" ' and where 'each act of design or construction is an isolated event which creates an isolated building – "perfect" at the time of its construction, and then abandoned by its builders and designers forever'. Panerai and colleagues make the interpretation at the collective urban level: 'Seen from a bird's-eye viewpoint, the city is a model, a collection of objects that are manipulated like so many cigarette lighters on a display shelf.' Clara Greed refers to this 'top-down process in which the "designer" looked down on "his" drawing board, taking the "God's eye view", and thus created the Grand Design'. Finally, we have Frederick Gibberd, master-planner of Harlow New Town describing his own Master Plan for Harlow: 'the three lines of communication – road, rail and river – form the base-line of the new town, from the centre of which (the site of the railway station) a semi-circle is struck to give the most compact theoretical perimeter for the town'.[6] This sounds like nothing other than the planner-God, at the drawing-board, in the act of creation.

The developmental paradigm

In the 'developmental' paradigm, the city is like an organism, but this time it is not a biomorphic creation, but is a 'living being' that is somehow following a developmental programme of growth and maturity, that it would naturally follow if left to its own devices. Here, the city-organism is a definite (if growing) whole, with subordinate parts functioning for the good of the whole.

Ebenezer Howard appears to be suggesting how a town should be seen as a growing entity, implying that this is part of the developmental paradigm:

> A town, like a flower, or a tree, or an animal, should, at each stage of its growth, possess unity, symmetry, completeness: and the effect of growth should never be to destroy that unity, but to give it greater purpose; nor to mar that symmetry, but to make it more symmetrical; while the completeness of the city structure should be merged in the yet greater completeness of the later development.[7]

The implication is that the planner's or designer's role is to somehow foster and abet this 'natural' developmental process, here training growth like a vine, there pruning back straggling growth, or effecting healing surgery (Figure 9.2).

9.2 • If the city is an organism, then planning is the equivalent of training or pruning something that would follow its own natural programme of growth if left to its own devices. If the type of organism is known, the future pattern of growth is roughly foreseeable.

As if signalling a switch from a creationist point of view to a developmental one, Patrick Abercrombie commented on the new understanding Patrick Geddes brought to urbanism by making people realise that planning was not just about manipulation of discrete objects of design, but was something more organic. In a passage which could almost apply today, Abercrombie comments:

> There was a time when it seemed only necessary to shake up into a bottle the German town-extension plan, the Parisian boulevard, the English garden village, the American civic centre and park system, in order to produce a mechanical mixture which might be applied indiscriminately and beneficially to every town and village in this country, in the hope that it would be 'town planned' according to the most up-to-date notions.[8]

However, Abercrombie suggests this was a 'pleasing dream' that was 'first shattered by Geddes'. The implication of Geddes' organic perspective is the need to take account of context, and the interrelatedness of parts, interwoven through time.

Although classically associated with the evolution of cities, Patrick Geddes' outlook seemed to mix an awareness of historical evolutionary change with an anticipation of the future that was almost developmental. For a start, he talks of the city as a 'living being'; he also refers to cities' 'embryology', and their 'true development' likened to the opening of a flower. He also anticipates the 'coming conurbations which it is time to be preparing for' as if they were already latent and part of an unfolding programme of growth. If this is evolution, it implies evolution as having a direction of progress; an idea that does not accord with Darwinian evolution.[9]

A similar impression is sometimes gained when reading the work of Christopher Alexander, who sometimes seems to imply a kind of developmental aspect to urban form, where there is an assumption of a sort of unfolding whole. For example, in *The Nature of Order* Alexander refers to the 'evolution' of Piazza San Marco in Venice, but in a way that implies the eventual whole was somehow already latent in the earlier stages, almost as if it were growing like, say, a tree, into a roughly predictable tree shape. But this is not the kind of biological evolution that is unpredictable in the long term – the kind that can turn ancestral fish into dolphins via intermediate land mammals.[10]

However 'developmental' these interpretations of urban change might be, both Geddes and Alexander see a role for proactive human intervention.

Geddes clearly sees a role for planners – he is after all writing at a time when town planning and the need for planning towns was a movement: something needing proactive promotion, rather than being part of the incumbent apparatus of state. His exhortation of the need to survey before plan hints at the idea of studying the organic specimen that is to be encouraged and steered and healed or operated upon. But at heart there still seems to be the idea that evolution is unfolding almost like something developmental, progressive; almost like ensuring healthy growth of a growing living body, towards a roughly foreseeable final form – like a mollusc shell unfolding its characteristic spiral form, or a tree growing to fruition – even if each individual case is unique and the exact form is unknowable in detail in advance.

Above all, the developmental paradigm implies that there is a pre-existing exemplar, model or archetype for what a city should be – as a mature healthy organism – which the planner should aim to help steer towards (or in Alexander's case, a natural *process* of unfolding whose workings should be mastered by the urban practitioner). The classic kinds of urban interventions that followed this developmental paradigm – as espoused by the likes of Lewis Mumford – are therefore things like the need for corrective surgery to diseased parts, or once a town or city had got to a certain size, that it should stop growing and create a new offspring.

The existence of a city as a naturally developing organism implies, if not the need for a creator, then the need for an interpreter, and perhaps manager: at any rate, the need for professional urban experts to interpret and decide on the behalf of the people how best for the organism to be extended into the future – which almost comes back round to a creationist position.

And so, while in principle we can separate the developmental perspective from the creationist, in practice there is not much to choose between the two, when it comes to urban application. Both imply there is a desired target form; in the first case, this is dreamed up by the creator, whether with reference to the past or whether a novel rational construct from first principles; in the second case, the latent target form is assumed to exist already, as if it were given by nature, a natural order to be interpreted by the planner. Both tend to imply the need for skilled practitioners: one, a bit like an artist or perhaps engineering designer (if the city is a machine); in the other case, like a skilled physician operating on the urban body.

The evolutionary paradigm

In the evolutionary paradigm, the city is not a designed object (or a series of created objects); nor is it a developing organism composed of parts that are functionally interlinked, supporting and subordinate to the whole (Figure 9.3).

9.3 • Paradigms for urban planning and design.

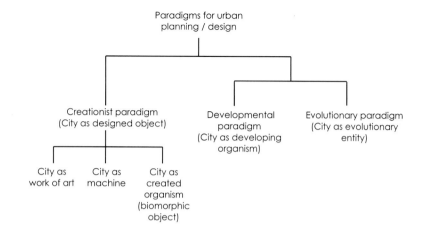

Instead, the city is a collective entity like a forest or an ecosystem, a population of coevolving things, partly in cooperation, partly in competition. It is the very interactions of the cooperating and competing parts that gives rise to the complex collective product (Chapter 5).

In the evolutionary paradigm, above all, there is no optimal target form. It may be possible to identify potential improvements as immediate targets, but there is unlikely to be a single optimal target form, and certainly no long-term knowable optimal form. The parts of the city are not fixed; there may be unexpected changes that could take cities in any direction in the future; cities may split or amalgamate; centres may become suburbs, and suburbs centres.

With urban evolution as interpreted in this book, design is recognised as a purposive activity that contributes to individual increments of change, and ultimately contributes to long-term evolution (Chapter 6). In this sense, it is not the same as the Darwinian evolution of biology, where variation is in effect random, and not premeditated. So, the urban evolution suggested here is different not only from a purely creationist perspective, or a developmental one, but also a Darwinian perspective where there is no role for design at all.[11]

In the evolutionary paradigm, designers and planners are only ever partly – only temporarily – in control. This is clearly different from the creationist case. It is also different from the developmental case, which implies that when the planner is not intervening, the city will somehow follow its own laws towards the mature adult form. However, in the evolutionary paradigm, we know that what the city does when 'left to its own devices' is unpredictable, and no more and no less than the sum of all the interactions of the individual actors with each other and the environment. This opens the door to the recognition of the role of the people in shaping their own environment.

The paradigms in practice

It is not being claimed that urban planners and designers are necessarily consciously thinking they are 'creators' when they draw up their master plans, or 'organism-physicians' when they tinker with their traffic management systems. Also, it is not claimed that planners and designers would ever assume a purely creationist or developmental position, but may mix the two up to fit circumstances. And yet, in some sense, there is a feeling that something creationist or developmental is influencing things, perhaps tacitly or intuitively, as revealed in what urban planners and designers do. And moreover, when planners and designers *do* express what they are thinking or doing, they do tend to say things that accord with these paradigms. One only needs to consult the range of literature reviewed in Chapter 5 to see this, where planners and designers refer to cities using all sorts of terms from anatomy to zoology, or actions from sketching to surgery.[12]

The talk of paradigms is more than a theoretical academic argument, as it really bites when it affects what we do. Both the creationist and developmental approaches could lead to a cavalier attitude, either by acting as if the professional is fully in control of delivering a successful outcome, or as if the city itself was somehow in control, able to heal itself after any surgery. A creationist perspective could encourage an authority to install new features such as shopping-centre decks simply assuming they would function as intended; or leave a half-finished urban motorway, and come back some years later to complete the job, as if the important thing is the good intention of the ultimate grand design, and the chaos on the ground in the meantime is just 'collateral damage'. Or, a developmental perspective could encourage planners to believe that a city should have a certain kind of form such as possessing a strong centre, distinct neighbourhoods, an optimum size, and so on. This would encourage suppression of unsolicited alternatives lest these be harmful mutations, while reinforcing existing centres, the reconfiguration of neighbourhoods as definite entities, and the creation of new towns, with their own centres and neighbourhoods, as if small 'offspring' settlements. We saw all this, of course, in the redevelopment of Glasgow, and the creation of new towns like Cumbernauld (Chapter 2).

The point at this juncture is not to criticise urban motorways, neighbourhood-based planning or new towns policies of themselves; but to suggest that the rationale for what planners were doing in these cases is entirely consistent with beliefs – whether more or less consciously held – that a town or city is either a created object (or assembly of objects) or a developing organism. And hence, the point is that if a city is not, after all, either of these things, then there is a danger of misdiagnosis of the problem, and hence mistaken treatment. Or, 'operation successful, patient dead'.

What, then, does this understanding imply for planning and design? For a start, the creationist paradigm seems quite natural and appropriate for the design of a model railway, a kitchen, a house, or a building, or a street; but the larger the scale, the longer the term and the more people involved, the less likely this kind of design is to be appropriate.

Secondly, the developmental paradigm might be useful where actually dealing with nature – with gardens or landscapes – or perhaps when intervening in large projects that are following a definite (but changeable) programme of construction. But when it comes to cities in general, there may be problems. The developmental paradigm begs the question as to where the final target comes from; if it is truly a natural form, then why should planners intervene to override this; to do so implies the planner is imposing their own will, as if they are after all a biomorphic 'creator'.

In contrast, the evolutionist paradigm allows that cities and urban change arise from increments of purposive intervention, but the outcome is still somewhat organic in being complex and emergent. So the evolutionary paradigm does not necessarily mean an absence of planning intention. In the remainder of the chapter, we look first at general principles for planning, which relate to *why* an evolutionary approach might be more appropriate than approaches based on a creationist or developmental perspective. Then we look more specifically at what an 'evolutionist' approach might entail.

SPACE, TIME AND CIVICS

If a city were physically small, could be built in a short time, and for inhabitants with a fixed social structure, then we could design a city like a building. Even if just one of the above were true, it might still be done. Perhaps a barracks town or a mining town or a resort town, where most people are of a single type in a fixed relationship to each other and the management, could be designed and built rather simply, even if housing the population the size of a village and even if construction took place over some time. That is, a reasonably simple but well-organised urban solution could be devised and constructed like a set of created objects. However, as long as cities have complex relationships between people, are large and are a long time in the making, it implies that we need more than a single fixed design like the design of a building.

In effect, we can recognise at least three dimensions implicit in planning, that typically go beyond issues faced by the designer of a building. First, is the large-scale of the object or entity to be designed and planned. Secondly, there are temporal factors relating not only to the long timescale – of the construction of a settlement relative to an individual building – but also the way that design, construction and occupation are overlapping. Thirdly, is the nature of the 'client' or user, which in the case of planning is in effect the whole population, and does not normally have the socio-political structure of the inhabitants of a building. So, for these three reasons, planning is not just 'big architecture' nor 'phased design'; and is not normally an act of creation.[13] In effect, planning is not just about 'thinking ahead', but is about the co-ordination and distribution of decision-making, among many people, over space and over time. Let us consider these three dimensions: civic, spatial and temporal.

The civic dimension

Let us assume that society exists, and that societies and cities exist in order to serve the interests of individual citizens.[14] That is, a society or city has no goals of its own, but social and urban organisation exist in order to benefit the constituent citizens. So although we sometimes talk of the collective good, of the 'good of the city as a whole' – or for that matter the good of the planet – these should not be seen abstractly as goals in themselves, but things to be pursued to the extent they actually fulfil individual citizens' needs.[15]

Let us take the purpose of planning as to anticipate and precipitate a future desired state for the collective good (Chapter 2). This includes the 'selective retention' and proactive provision that goes into mending potholes and building schools. The purpose of city planning – given that a city is a collective entity – is to generate an output that will be better for everyone, better than if there were no intervention.[16] This does not necessarily mean subsuming the interests of the individual to the city or the state. It could simply be a means of unlocking latent synergies between people and urban places and activities that would be difficult to emerge spontaneously.

There are two particular ways this can manifest itself. One is the pro-active creation of positive large-scale outcomes that would be unlikely to arise without coordination. This could be two communities on either side of a river joining forces to create a bridge, to the benefit of both. Here, one whole bridge is worth more than double the value of half a bridge. So planning purpose is to do with, as it were, 'leveraging synergies' for the collective good.

The second purpose is to avoid negative emergent effects, which no one individually wants, but that happen if people are left to their own devices. A classic case is Hobbes' social contract (Chapter 4), which aims to avoid the harmful outcomes arising from unrestrained individual freedom. Another well-known example is the 'tragedy of the commons', where if everyone is allowed to exploit a public good (such as common grazing) the result is overgrazing and worse than if there had been some control. A third example is the case of avoiding spontaneous self-segregation – the ghetto effect – an emergent outcome which no one individually seeks (Figure 7.6).[17]

There are many ways of 'planning' for a desired future state for society, or a city's inhabitants. These include legal, economic and political instruments, as well as non-physical planning instruments. Here, the focus is on physical planning whose purpose is to generate a physical urban order that accommodates the citizenry. The assumption is that the spatial order should 'in some way' reflect or support social order; and the planning process should in some way take account of the distribution of decision-making among the urban 'stakeholders'. Planning is not just a matter of having a vision, but taking care with whose vision, and for whose benefit.

Darwinian evolutionary thinking did away with the need for central intelligence or design, in the creation of functional order in nature. But urban evolution, as argued in Chapters 6 and 8, need not deny a role for individual increments of design. In the creationist mode, the planner or designer is acting ultimately for the benefit of the users and public, of course. But the user or public are not intrinsically involved in the process, except where consciously drafted in. Also, in the developmental mode, there is an implicit assumption that the city is some kind of organism that needs to be understood; and this falls most readily to mean the professional trained in understanding cities and how to operate on the 'patient'. It does not explicitly rule out the role for the citizen – indeed Geddes believes the citizen should be involved – but it still implies there is something that is knowably optimal about the city. An evolutionary perspective, however, suggests the significance of local, individual interventions: of the kind that could equate with the actions of individual citizens, and be motivated directly by the aspirations of those citizens.

The space dimension

Whatever the social organisation, the urban units – buildings, streets, neighbourhoods and so on (Chapter 3) – should in some way relate to social structure: a combination of social containers and social filters (Chapter 4).

This is about tailoring the physical structure to serve the needs of the socio-political structure and governance of the citizenry – just as one does when designing a building such as a house or office to accommodate a household or workplace.

As discussed in Chapters 4 and 5, a city is not physically a large building; nor is its citizenry a social unit like a city-sized household. A city, like a society, is rather a collective entity. In this sense, although a city may be recognisable as a distinct bounded entity, socially speaking a city is more an unpredictably straggling thing – like a society – not something for which a determinate finite 'design' is particularly appropriate.[18]

Following the evolutionary paradigm, we can't assume cities 'should' have centres and neighbourhoods with sub-centres, and so on. Therefore, city planning is about more than the creationist replication of old models, or the assumption that there is a 'natural' city form or structure to be steered towards.

From consideration of Chapter 7, we have seen that it is not – or was not – necessary to explicitly plan neighbourhoods or settlements to get them. Despite this, Modernist and neo-traditional planning are often tempted to replicate the forms of traditional neighbourhoods and villages and cities, even if society has moved on from these as formats for communities.

This is not to say that developments of different sizes – including neighbourhood-sized units – should not be planned as such; but simply that they need not and perhaps should not be *designed* (at the level of the neighbourhood) – in the way a building is designed. It implies, instead, that whatever kind of 'planning' is involved, it can allow for a certain distribution of decision-making and flexibility in terms of timescale. It may imply that the neighbourhood is not, after all, 'planned', but may be subject to design coordination of smaller-scale units, such as blocks or streets.

At the level of individual streets, the logic of 'street syntax' (Chapter 3) seems to hold. That is, it makes sense to construct a continuous network of public streets to which private plots and buildings are appended. This logic applies whatever the final ultimate shape of the city might be, and whether or not we recognise intermediate-scale features such as neighbourhoods. This makes the street a useful building-block of urban structure, as long as the 'normal' structure of a city separated into public and private areas is to hold.

So, while the street is not normally a social unit – a single cohesive decision-making entity, as defined in Chapter 4 – the street itself embodies the relationships *between* social units. The street system embodies the urban fabric of private and public, that binds together buildings and plots and routes and spaces, echoing the way that social units do not exist in isolation but link together as part of wider society. In effect, a street is like a micro-cosm of the public–private relationship that permeates urban structure generally; it is like a self-contained sample of urban fabric, like a branch of a tree that could be transplanted and a whole new settlement 'grown' from itself.

The time dimension

The future is fundamentally unpredictable; and broadly speaking, the longer the timescale for prediction, the less predictable the outcome. This makes cities – which are about as long-term as physical products get – intrinsically unpredictable. So a future city cannot simply be the built-out product of a creator's imagination, in the way a building (or model railway layout) can be. Nor is a city growing like an organism: there is no knowable optimal form (target organism) to be steered towards. Nevertheless, we can try to plan; but this should be with awareness of the limitations of planning, and, it is suggested, awareness of the evolutionary nature of urban change.

A planned settlement usually implies that someone has thought about what it would be like – or should be like – in five, ten or twenty years; not just when the current batch of things under construction is complete. Thinking ahead is clearly part of what planning is about. But it is not necessarily just a case of the further ahead the better. There are three interlinked strands of argument here.

First, there is the matter of 'long-sightedness'. As Tom Turner notes of master plans, 'They tell us what will be right in the future, instead of what is right now'. This could be interpreted as mistaking long-sightedness for far-sightedness: where long-sightedness implies not having a clear picture of crucial things in front of your nose, which (like short-sightedness) is regarded an impairment.

Secondly, is the matter of uncertainty. We don't necessarily know what a desired or optimal future state will be. So, although in general 'foresight' has virtue, it all depends on what is foreseeable. If there is a bulge in the birth rate today, then it is prudent to plan for more schools tomorrow. But if we have no idea whether people will still need typewriters in ten or twenty years' time, it is perhaps best not to demolish our existing urban fabric to accommodate typewriter factories that may not materialise. There is a danger that planning, although apparently prescient, is actually more of a leap in the dark (a 'hopeful monster', Chapter 8). The idea of the planned city as a knowable utopia is a chimera.

Thirdly, there is the matter of path choice: how to get to possible desirable future states. A master plan conventionally settles on one particular future outline form, to which subsequent details must be fitted, and future paths funnelled and steered. But from Chapter 7 we can infer that there are many ways of getting *roughly* the same answer. For example, let us suppose that a compact urban form is desired. There are many, many more ways of getting a *roughly* compact form than there are of getting *any particular* roughly compact form – this difference could be the order of thousands, or easily millions.[19] So unless the precise final form is definitely known, and known to be optimal, then the well-intentioned targeting of a precise optimal outcome may be no better than choosing an incremental approach which is still very likely to reach roughly the same kind of form, but which may more surely maximise the chance of each intermediate step being viable and adding immediate value.

Predicting the final outcome at the outset might superficially look more 'strategic', showing more 'foresight', and be more 'prudent' in 'taking care about the future', but in an uncertain context this approach may simply be more risky. The 'fallacy of forward planning' is mistaking the ambition of the timescale, and precision of the prediction, for the likelihood of the prediction coming to pass – when these may well be inversely related.

This is not an argument against planning – urban or otherwise. (Part of the problem here is the word 'planning' which seems intrinsically to connote a prudent, worthwhile activity, such that any argument against it may seem gratuitously contrarian or wilfully anarchistic.) Rather, the argument is against the presumption that *more, longer-term, centrally coordinated* planning is intrinsically better than having a more even distribution of decision-making in time. It is about being realistic about what can be reliably planned for. The point here is that if the optimal future state is not knowable, then the benefit of having a precisely specified 'target plan' may be illusory. Put another way, the longer the term (and the bigger the scale, and the more people involved) the less suitable to attempt 'creationist design'.[20]

The foregoing has set out what planning should and could be doing, in a general way. This could equally apply to Modernist city design, neo-traditional planning, or for that matter, the individual increments of intervention that form part of traditional 'unplanned urbanism'. These general purposes are summarised in Table 9.1. Now let us see how more detailed planning and design principles could be devised, consistent with the evolutionary paradigm and foregoing considerations of space, time and civics.

Table 9.1 **General planning purposes**

1. General collective mobilisation of aspiration and action towards the collective good – for individuals' benefit.
2. Steering towards beneficial macro-outcomes for the common good, over and above what would happen if individuals were left to their own devices:
   (a) Targeting positive macro-outcomes (leveraging synergies);
   (b) Averting negative macro-outcomes.
3. Fitting spatial organisation to social organisation.
4. Balancing between short-term (more certain) benefits and longer-term (less certain) benefits.

AN 'EVOLUTIONIST' APPROACH

Evolution is a robust and flexible enough concept that it can be interpreted in any kind of urbanism (Chapter 8). Therefore, almost any kind of urbanism could be described as evolutionary. That said, we could identify a distinct evolution*ist* approach, that would consciously build its philosophy around, and take advantage of, the paradigm of a city as an evolutionary entity. This would be in conscious contradistinction to approaches that were built on a 'creationist' perspective (city as designed object) or 'developmental' perspective (city as developing organism).[21]

The evolutionist approach presented here is only a sketch, not a complete or comprehensive 'theory'. But here we can, at least, explore things following what we have learned about planning, design and evolution from the preceding chapters in this book, and earlier in this chapter.

The 'Game of Evolution'

There are at least six good things about evolution, as a means of creation. First, it is very easy. Just copy what was done before, not even necessarily completely faithfully. Secondly, the process requires no foresight and no memory. Thirdly, a diversity of alternative solutions is forthcoming. Fourthly, anything seen in existence at any one time is viable, or 'mostly roughly right'. Fifthly, the solutions are robust, 'tried and tested'. Finally, the result is functional, or 'fit for purpose'.

However, there are at least six problems with evolution. First, it is extra-ordinarily slow at generating anything. Secondly, it *has* no foresight or memory: it can't aim at future targets, and can't learn from models of past successes (other than in the sense of what is already embodied in the current design). Thirdly, what it does produce is rather 'samey', at least in the short term. Fourthly, every 'design' at every increment must be viable (no 'draft versions' are allowed to coexist with final versions). Fifthly, amidst mass fecundity and redundancy, there is much waste and sacrifice, due to a relentless regime of unthinking trial and unforgiving error. While this may be statistically successful at an abstract strategic level, the waste and sacrifice is borne tangibly by particular individuals. Finally, although apparently fit for purpose, this purpose is in effect controlled by the environment, which itself has no purpose – benevolent, moral, rational or otherwise (Table 9.2).[22]

Now when we play the cultural, technological and urban versions of this 'Game of Evolution', this is when our range of human qualities come to the fore. We solve the problems of slowness and 'sameyness' by pressing forward quickly (without waiting for natural selection), and by leaping over the serried ranks of almost-the-same, almost-as-bad-as-each-other solutions, to alight on a significantly different, and hopefully improved new solution. We *have* foresight and memory, so the second problem is no problem. However, by solving or averting these first three problems, this exacerbates the fourth and fifth, by the effect of leaps of speed and scope of change, that lead to 'macro-mutations' (Frankenstein monsters) which are poorly adapted and dysfunctional in the short term. Additionally, our foresight is imperfect, and memory may seduce us into following moribund models ('dinosaurs' – or 'neanderthals').

As David Perkins has pointed out, 'human invention largely lacks two major advantages of biological evolution – massive parallelism and geological time'.[23] This is perhaps an issue if trying to 'evolve' artefacts like kettles and buildings; but relative to these, cities in some senses *do* have a kind of 'parallelism' – lots of individual actors creating their own urban objects and interventions – and *relatively* long timescales. Table 9.3 suggests the 'Game of Evolution' interpreted for traditional 'unplanned' urbanism (closest to natural evolution) and conventional planning or Modernism (furthest removed from natural evolution).

An evolutionist approach, then, should aim to keep as much of the good parts of evolution, while avoiding the problems of past urban planning (particularly, the problems of Modernist planning). Here, five principles are

Table 9.2 The 'Game of Evolution'

Good things	Bad things
1. Easy	1. Slow
2. Requires no foresight or memory	2. *Has* no foresight or memory
3. Diverse (in long term)	3. 'Samey' (in short term)
4. Viable at all times	4. No 'draft' versions may coexist
5. Tried and tested	5. Trial and error: waste and sacrifice
6. Fit for purpose	6. Purpose set by purposeless environment

Table 9.3 The 'Game of Evolution' – applied to urbanism

Traditional vernacular urbanism	Conventional planning and Modernism
1. Slow, but simple to apply.	1. Go fast and make big leaps.
2. No forecasting or 'learning from best practice' elsewhere.	2. Apply foresight and learning from best practice (some successes, some failures).
3. 'Samey', but reflects genuine similarities of taste.	3. Make big leaps; variation can be artificially applied.
4. Every step viable.	4. Problems with half-completed, ill-adapted insertions.
5. Tried and tested; involves trial and error, but on a small scale and in control of stakeholders.	5. Problems of big trial and big error, and 'unsolicited sacrifice'.
6. Purpose applied to increments of design.	6. Purpose supplied to planning interventions at all scales.

Table 9.4 Five evolutionist principles

I.   Make each step viable now
II. Proceed by small steps – avoid 'monstrosity'
III. Avoid suppressing 'unsolicited novelty'
IV. Discard moribund models
V.   Devolve decision-making

suggested that attempt to meet the kind of planning purposes set out in Table 9.1, while overcoming the problems associated with conventional city planning and city design. These do not form a one-to-one correspondence with the six items in the 'Game of Evolution', but combine to try to solve them (Table 9.4).

I. Make each step viable now

First, let us aim for a situation where everything is viable for everyone, here and now. There should be no sacrifice of the livelihoods of existing locations – especially ones that are currently viable – in the hope that some day a promised more functional future will materialise. New interventions should be introduced so they are immediately adapted to the surroundings from day one. For example, if a new transport route has to be driven through an area, the scheme should not be considered finished until all the necessary ameliorations are in place. Otherwise it will be a grievous scar on the landscape for many years. If the scheme's feasibility is dependent on the transport route being open as soon as it is connected into the network, but without completing the urban healing around it, then perhaps the feasibility calculation is faulty.[24]

To operationalise the principle of viability now, we may need to revise the way feasibility is calculated for new schemes, to better reflect the uncertain nature of future benefits and disbenefits – and, crucially, to whom these accrue.

Secondly, development briefs should ensure that physical urban design integrates new buildings and infrastructure with existing – 'joint development'. This was often aspired to, for Modernist motorway schemes, but it would require a more systematic and sensitive application – see second principle.[25]

II. Proceed by small innovations – avoid 'monstrosity'

Partly in pursuit of continuous viability, we should avoid 'macro-mutations'. That is, avoid urban interventions that are either too novel – too great departures from existing known, tried and tested formats – or that are applied at too large a scale, or too suddenly, in such a way that the urban system around it has no time to adapt. Novelty for its own sake might be rewarded in art, or to some extent in architecture, but we should think very carefully before putting novelty ahead of urban functionality. Novelty of itself is easy: just add a lobster to a telephone. Making novelty *work* – whether functioning as a work of art, or piece of technology, architecture, or intricate urbanism – requires craft and judgement.[26]

Following on from this second principle, an evolutionist approach would first of all promote novelty in relatively small-scale increments, while ensuring that any large-scale development used tried and tested formats. So, if going for a large new urban extension, perhaps traditional street-grids – or conventional residential cul-de-sacs – will have to suffice, and leave more radical, novel solutions for small-scale test schemes. This could imply that large new housing developments by a single developer or designer end up being 'samey', but at least, if they contain individually desired dwellings, this beats experimental housing schemes that no one wants to live in. If there are to be large-scale risky novelties, perhaps these should be left to the private sector, and not be paid for by the public twice over: first by having to fund them, and then having to live in them.

III. Avoid suppressing 'unsolicited' novelty

While monstrous novelty is to be avoided, we should avoid suppressing unsolicited functional novelty, or new ways of doing things that 'spontaneously' emerge – or would emerge if they had the chance. That is to say, there is a certain kind of functional novelty or invention born of necessity, not the pursuit of novelty for its own sake. And there may often be cases where people would do things differently – better – if only they were allowed to; but they are discouraged or prevented from doing so due to extant planning regulations or design standards, that may have been devised a long time ago for other purposes. Indeed, novelty could be proactively encouraged, if it is seen to be functional. In this case, it would be a case of starting small, and proceeding in small viable steps, in accordance with the first and second principles.

In support of this third principle, an evolutionist approach would be sensitive to where novelty is happening spontaneously, and try not to suppress it, as may happen currently. For example, a householder's proposal to create a rooftop garden, with a rooftop garden shed for 'home-working', powered by a wind turbine, might have planning permission refused under conventional regulations, even by an authority that ostensibly favours green design, home-working and green energy. In practice, being sensitive to novelty could mean actively monitoring planning applications, or informal proscribed behaviour – such as skateboarders or rollerbladers appropriating spaces they are not supposed to – to see if there is a pattern of use by individuals doing what they want to do, that could become part of tomorrow's collective solution (green mobility, personal health, sociality, and so on).

An evolutionist approach would also be proactive in looking out for such novel, curious, idiosyncratic things which have somehow come into being, and not been snuffed out, and by their very survival must be functional or viable in some way that might yet be exploited. Rather than considering idiosyncratic things as 'merely' curiosities that (in being not the norm) are of marginal interest, we should look to see how they might be ready-made exemplars that could be applied to new purposes. They may be marginal to today's norm, but indispensable to tomorrow's.[27]

Finally, an evolutionist approach would consider how existing, past and potential future novelties might be put together in new combinations. These might serve new purposes or be applied and adapted to new contexts. There is no guarantee that these would work – even if combinations of otherwise viable things – any more than streets in the air or megastructural town centres might. But it could be possible to learn from those cases of success and failure. After all, streets in the air do work in some contexts. And there are many cases of successful 'conjunctions' – of previously unconnected things – the steam engine and the railway vehicle to create the steam locomotive; the surfboard and roller skates fused to create the skateboard.[28]

As some concrete examples of what these 'novelties' or 'curiosities' might be, Table 9.5 lists a series of novel cases drawn from this book. The

Table 9.5 'Mutation permutator' for novel, curious, exceptional and idiosyncratic cases

	1. Bostan	2. Glazed courtyards	3. Yurt	4. Unité	5. Capsule hotel	6. Cumbernauld town centre	7. Eden	8. Animal-power vehicles	9. Human-powered vehicles	10. *Ciudal Lineal*	11. Çatalhöyök	12. Motopia	13. Venus Fort	14. Walking City	15. Floating City
1. Bostan – enclosed communal garden behind houses															
2. Glazed courtyards															
3. Yurt															
4. Unité d'Habitation															
5. Capsule hotel – stacked 'cells' instead of rooms															
6. Cumbernauld town centre															
7. Eden project – vegetative environment indoors															
8. Novel animal-powered vehicles (Stockton's tricycle)															
9. Human-powered vehicles – rollerblades, skateboards, scooters															
10. *Ciudal Lineal* – continuous city along tramway spine															
11. Çatalhöyök – pedestrian circulation on the roof															
12. Motopia – vehicular circulation on the roof															
13. Venus Fort – Interior Italianate streets, inside a shopping-centre shed															
14. Walking City – insectile megastructure															
15. Floating City – 'city' in the form of a ship															

Note: This table has 15 items. This means there are 105 permutations of pairs, and 32,727 permutations overall.

reader is then invited to imagine mutations and permutations of these, and think how they might be applied in different contexts.[29]

IV. Discard moribund models

A fourth principle – that supports the third – would be to avoid clinging to old forms and formats for the sake of it. If something doesn't work, it will be 'found out' sooner or later. If no one wants to shop in city centres, or sit outdoors chatting or playing chess, but people prefer to shop out of town and chat or play chess over the internet, then this may or may not be a matter for regret. But trying to restrict shops to the city centre, or contrive public vitality will be fighting a losing battle, unless – which is quite possible – people actually wish to do those things. Otherwise, they will surely still do them anyway, but somewhere else. If this discussion seems unduly harsh on much appreciated traditional formats, it is only to illustrate a tangible case of how an evolutionist approach does not necessarily mean clinging to the past – 'neanderthal' models.

Following from the fourth principle, the general idea here is to allow new large-scale or long-term forms to emerge or evolve, rather than trying to guess what they should be from the outset; or rather than trying to fit smaller-scale features (streets, blocks and districts) to fit a preconceived out-line target plan. An immediate way of doing this would be to discard visions of future cities, expressed through zoning, or the outline specification of a 'final target' form. Instead, a possibility here would be to have coding (or Alexander-style 'patterns') to ensure micro-scale order, and allow the macro-form to emerge. This amounts to urban ordering without city design.[30]

For example, rather than specifying that a new town should have indus-trial estates on the periphery, separate from residential areas, there would simply be an adjacency rule specifying that at no point should heavy industry be directly next to residential. This could still allow light industry near houses, or commercial areas, in many possible combinations.

The street could yet be a useful building-block for the creation of urban structure, where rules of street syntax are expanded and elaborated for accommodating relationships between different building types, land uses, street types and block types.

V. Devolve decision-making

A fifth principle is that of devolution, subsidiarity or delegation to as local a level as practicable. There are at least three good reasons for this devolution. First, devolution is about basic democratic accountability and empowerment: it should help give power back to the local level and re-enfranchise individual citizens. Devolution recognises that the whole is not superior to the parts, but only exists to serve the interests of the parts.

Secondly, devolution is about the fecundity and diversity of solutions. If we are going to encourage small novelties and small-scale incremental changes, how better to do it than allowing individuals to do their own things of their own initiative, rather than having a master designer contriving local idiosyncracy? This is the kind of process that naturally gives every village its own character, rather than the contrived differences in character between the neighbourhoods or 'villages' of planned settlements.

Thirdly, devolution of decision-making is about getting better, more fitting solutions: it is about distributed 'intelligence', or countering the unknowability of what is best for the people. The professional planner can't possibly know what is best for all the citizens, not now and certainly not in the future. It is by our own choices and habits as citizens – of choosing to work or shop from home, for example – where we express what we think is best for us. Out of the countless permutations of what the optimal city of tomorrow should be like, the least we can do is have a city that reflects individual choices. If this results in things that appear – when viewed as a whole, by cynical outsiders – to be 'sameyness', or vulgar taste, then so be it. This is surely better than relying too much on the taste, and intellectual schools of thought, of planners and designers (and urban writers), on what the abstract form of the whole city should be like.[31]

In support of the fifth principle, an evolutionist approach would empower people by allowing more individual freedom of action, with respect to their own properties, and adjacent public areas, and any otherwise unused or uncared for spaces. This would reinforce the idea of overhauling planning permission, to be more sensitive. If we were less suppressive of individual initiative, we might not have to go to such great lengths to contrive the complex and contested process of citizen participation.

An evolutionist approach could, for example, remove barriers to incremental construction and extension of buildings. Instead of having to buy or build a whole house, it could be made easier to start by creating a small building (possibly attached to an existing building, or a stand-alone outhouse) and then allowing this to be gradually developed into a whole self-contained house.

An evolutionist approach could make use of a pattern language expanded for the twenty-first century. We could take, for example, the urban and architectural patterns in Christopher Alexander and colleagues' *Pattern Language*, as a starting-point; and work out how these would fit with different kinds of design activity and planning regime (in such a way that the latter does not

Table 9.6 **Examples of possible 'new' patterns for an expanded pattern language for the twenty-first century**

Building component scale	• Smokers' porch: a place to keep the rain off people banned from smoking inside their workplace.
Building scale	• The incremental house: starts as an outhouse or contiguous extension to an existing building, extends incrementally as finances allow and space needs dictate, to a fully self-contained new house. • Communal roof garden (Bostan + Unité + Çatalhöyök).
Street scale	• Tram arcade: combination of glazed-over arcade and street reserved for trams and pedestrians and human-powered vehicles. • Rollerblade arcade: central carriageway for bicycles and fast human-powered vehicles.
Block scale	• So-ho-Co-housing: combination of 'small-office – home office' (So-ho) and Co-housing – terraced or tenement block with communal courtyard (possibly glazed) with shared facilities for residents and home-workers. • Combination of So-ho-Co-housing and communal roof garden. • Micro-neighbourhood block unit: combination of So-ho-Co-housing, with shops on the exterior of the block, and communal facilities in the interior: in effect like Perry's neighbourhood unit scaled down, to the level of actual neighbours across common courtyard.

stifle the former). The point here is to see how far these can be used as bottom-up building-blocks; and get this implemented as part of an actual system.[32]

We can also, of course, create new patterns for the twenty-first century; some possibilities are suggested in Table 9.6; some of these are combinations from Table 9.5, and some relate to *A Pattern Language*.[33]

So, let us imagine that you have a small vision of aspiration for your street or town or city – perhaps part of your own property, or an unused public space. To take one example from the existing *Pattern Language*: say you wish your street to become full of fruit trees. Or even just have one fruit tree added outside your home. Why can't you just plant one, or get the council to desist from chopping down any that might spring up naturally? Whatever the aspiration – fruit tree or home-office-shed or roof garden – we can imagine many kinds of small improvement each of which is a definitely desired, positively beneficial thing, that is clearly tangibly possible in principle, and may cost next to nothing in practice. So what is stopping us? Let us hope that 'planning' is not part of the problem.

Nurturing the evolutionary tree
An evolutionist approach, then, would specifically be one that acknowledged the lessons of evolution or change with continuity: maintain current

viability; avoid disturbing existing symbioses; experiment by using proven components and combinations in new locations or contexts, or try new components and combinations on a small scale; and devolve decision-making as far as practicable, incentivising individual initiative. Or: if it ain't broke, don't fix it; if it don't fit, adapt it; if it's new, try it small; if it's small, let the people do it; if it works, run with it.

Much of the evolutionist approach relates to removing barriers to incremental improvements that can be instigated and executed by individuals or small social units such as households or workplaces. It also responds to the intrinsic unknowability of what the best possible future outcome would be. Aiming to make each increment positive must be a start towards a city of tomorrow that is at least one definite if small step better than today.

The evolutionist approach is contrasted with interpretations of alternative approaches that are based on the creationist and developmental paradigms (Table 9.7). The evolutionist approach allows for some novel creation. It is also in some respects like dealing with something living, but not in the manner of training or pruning a tree: it is more like training or pruning an *evolutionary* tree, allowing new mutations to evolve and flourish into new lineages.

There is therefore still a role here for planners to imagine what the possible longer-term outcomes would be, but to use this knowledge to make for more sensitive interventions, with less 'suppression' (unless a town is sure it wants to stay the same as yesterday, as far as possible), and not trying to drag everyone to conform in one particular direction.

A lot of this has a resonance with Patrick Geddes (conservative surgery), Jane Jacobs ('unslumming' and 'backyard industries'), Christopher Alexander (site-responsive interventions, using patterns or recipes rather than blueprints), and Robert Cowan (quotation at start of chapter).[34] If this means the approaches suggested are not entirely novel, then at least this chapter (and book) serves to provide a new package, and a new impetus based on a fresh theoretical perspective on 'organic' urbanism from an evolutionary point of view.[35]

Evolution versus revolution

Arguably, the worst of Modernist city planning arose when going against evolutionary principles. For example, in the case of Glasgow in the 1960s and 1970s (Chapter 2), comprehensive redevelopment tore up more of the original fabric than it needed to, in pursuit of a grand vision, a 'new coherent whole' that was nevertheless based on an old model of what a city should be like (strongly structured by radial routes meeting at a centre). What might

Table 9.7 Evolutionist principles contrasted with creationist and developmental

Evolutionist	Creationist	Developmental
I. Make each step viable now.	Part-finished fragments of grand designs may be acceptable.	Focus is on the final mature target form.
II. Proceed by small steps – avoid 'monstrosity'.	Creationist inclined to promote novelty for its own sake.	Tends to avoid monstrosity.
III. Avoid suppressing 'unsolicited novelty'.	Creationist approaches tend not to 'see' unsolicited novelty; anything unsolicited may be averted, weeded out, or in some circumstances, worked in if it can be exploited.	Developmental may see unsolicited novelty as an aberration or 'tumour', to be averted, corrected or cut out.
IV. Discard moribund models.	Tends to avoid too much reliance on past for models, although may do so in the case of 'improved' or 'reconstituted' cities (Figure 2.13).	Developmental may be inclined to adhere to existing models, and enforce conformity.
V. Devolve decision-making.	Creationist approaches are intrinsically likely to act on behalf of the citizen, rather than the citizen being actively involved.	Developmental approaches are intrinsically likely to act on behalf of the citizen, rather than the citizen being actively involved.

have otherwise been viable formats of trams and tenements were discarded in favour of tower blocks and car mobility.

Put another way, too often the Modernist city planning focused on the macro-structure, and in doing so destroyed the intricate physical, functional and social micro-structure, that has taken so long to heal. An evolutionist approach would, however, do the reverse: and nurture (preserve, heal, and gradually adapt and improve) the micro-structure, and allow the macro-structure to take care of itself, albeit with checks to control against dysfunctional emergent outcomes.

So what might an evolutionist approach have done differently, in the case of Glasgow? It would not pursue a 'new coherent whole', but pursue extension of existing coherent parts. So tenement grids would be extended outwards, continuous with the existing fabric. The tenements would be modern technologically and architecturally. They could build on the ideas of Alexander Thomson, to glaze over tenement closes or courtyards (Figure 3.19d).

There would be no demolition of Townhead or Anderston. Parliamentary Road would stay. Perhaps St Enoch Station would be converted into a mall (rather than demolishing and replacing with a 1980s glazed shopping centre).

Perhaps instead of the 'Brobdingnagian and bombastic' Buchanan Galleries shopping centre,[36] Buchanan Street would be glazed over to form a mall, linking up with other arcaded streets – say, Sauchiehall Street and Argyle Street, plus the existing Argyle Arcade and Princes Square – to form a contiguous linked Galleria, just like East Kilbride Town Centre (Chapter 8).

An evolutionist approach, then, would have not comprehensively demolished the inner areas, but those would be regenerated piecemeal using the existing physical fabric. There would be no ring and radial motorway. Perhaps new motorways would have been built on the periphery – perhaps an orbital motorway placed out beyond where it would damage the urban fabric – to which those industries and businesses who benefit from good road accessibility would relocate (these would locate on the periphery anyway).

Who can say whether the result would have been better than what actually happened? We can't say, overall; but we can say that at least inner urban communities such as Anderston, Townhead and Hutchensontown would still be there.

And, lest anyone wonder if this really could have happened, all we need to do is look at Edinburgh, which had a more conservative approach: retention of a continuous fabric of tenemental quarters; no urban motorways but an orbital bypass; its share of business parks and out-of-town retail; but a city centre nevertheless popular for commerce, business, residents and tourists.

Glasgow, of course, is not Edinburgh. It will do things its own way. From where we are now, however, Glasgow could yet do many of the things mentioned above (although bringing back Parliamentary Road would be a push). The city has the potential to make the best of its retained assets – and also to take advantage of the latent assets born of its previous mutations. The scope to knit back together in a new way is more possible than in a city that never tore so much down in the first place. Evolution is ever opportunist.

CONCLUSIONS

This chapter has suggested that the evolutionary paradigm can be a useful way for understanding urban change and hence informing planning and design. This is in contrast to a 'creationist' (designed-object) paradigm, or a 'developmental' (developing-organism) paradigm. A rationale for planning has been suggested, based on collective purpose, the large scale and the long term, which it is suggested fits with the evolutionary paradigm.

The evolutionary paradigm of theory can inform the basis of an evolution-*ist* approach to practice. This chapter has suggested what an evolutionist approach might be. This has been set out as five suggested principles, and associated applications. These suggest the possibility of a more bottom-up approach to planning, which could amount to urban ordering without city design (Chapter 2). Any such programme based on bottom-up generation could yet be accompanied by a control-selection-approval mechanism, to avoid unanticipated negative macro-effects. This could be regarded either as a sort of sixth principle as part of an evolutionist approach, or, if this were regarded as an artificial selection mechanism over and above what should properly be called evolutionist, then so be it. The important thing is not the label, but what works in terms of urbanism.

From the perspective of planning at the crossroads, then, it should be clear that any approach learning from evolutionary thinking could embrace both innovation *and* tradition, and also more *or* less planning.

An evolutionary awareness does not mean to say that we cannot try to plan ahead, or we must only apply urbanism gradually and conservatively. If you know what you want when, then design can be the best way of generating it. For example, if the intention is to create a new place rapidly, it may yet be better to design as a single creation, if it is known how it is to be occupied and is used straight away. However, this is less likely to apply to settlements where construction takes place in increments; it seems natural to – and would seem foolish not to – take the opportunity to adapt with feedback, and update as one goes along.

Put another way, if the environment is relatively stable, and development is rapid, and an optimal solution for all is foreseeable, then a 'totally created product' can ensure a coordinated outcome, that is deliberately targeted to be adapted to its context. On the other hand, if the environment is volatile, then long-term advanced planning may be futile, especially if the rate of development is low. Because, either the first increments (towards a future grand plan) will be ill-fitting with respect to the reality now, or, the grand plan even once built may not fit the future (because the context will have changed), or both.

Evolution need not imply just leaving things to the 'natural selection' of market forces, since we can choose to impose the 'artificial selection' of planning control at any time. Politically, then, evolution should be thought of as something neutral like democracy, not intrinsically implying left or right: democracy implies sufficient individual freedom not to be a totalitarian state, but sufficient social organisation to have a political system in the first place.[37]

A general 'evolutionist' approach has been presented here to see what this would look like in principle, without this amounting to unqualified advocacy. Advocacy for practice would, as ever, depend on purpose and context of application. In any particular situation, it is likely that no single approach – whether Modernist or traditionalist, evolutionist or creationist – would be adopted in a completely pure form. What this chapter does advocate is the recognition of the evolutionary nature of urbanism, and for us to learn from this, even if any evolutionist approach would need further development and adaptation to context in practice. This implies further development, adaptation and application *in situ*, not least by policy-makers and practitioners.

Notes

1 Entry in *The Language of Cities. A Glossary of Terms* (Abrams, 1971).
2 Kostof (1992: 298).
3 Robert Cowan (1995).
4 The evolutionary and developmental paradigms have obvious parallels with different processes of change in nature; the creationist paradigm alludes to purposive design (where the term 'creationist' has a resonance with the 'creationist' belief in purposive design in nature).
5 For biomorphic or zoomorphic architecture, see, for example, Aldersey-Williams (2003), Cook (2004), Steadman (2008).
6 Alexander (2002b: 48); Alexander *et al.* (1975: 76); Panerai *et al.* (2004: 116); Greed (1998: 201); Gibberd (1967: 47); 'planner-God': Turner (1996); Kostof (1991: 43) refers to the 'created' city – *ville créée* – in contradistinction to the spontaneous city – *ville spontanée*.
7 Howard (1904: 45).
8 Abercrombie, quoted in editorial introduction to *Cities in Evolution* (Tyrwhitt, 1949: xii).
9 Geddes: 'living being' (1949: 84); 'embryology' (1949: 10); 'development of a flower' (1949: 53); 'coming conurbations' (1949: 24). Some of Geddes' allusions may be not intended literally. Nevertheless, the city-as-developing-organism is a definite way of thinking of cities that people continue to consciously or unconsciously follow, or act as if they do believe cities are like this. Geddes himself believed that biological evolution (somewhat like development) had an element of progressive unfolding, on which point he departed from Darwin (see, for example, Geddes and Thomson, 1889; 1911).
10 The example of the 'evolution' of Piazza San Marco seems significant, as it is clearly addressing the urban and not just architectural scale, and Alexander refers to it in Book 2 (2002b: 252–255) and then again in Book 3 (2005: 5–7). In fact, Alexander (2002a: 22–32, 33–35) seems to lump together processes as diverse as galactic formation, embryonic development, Darwinian evolution and the formation of crystals as if these are all equivalent as natural unfolding processes. Meanwhile he appears to cast doubt on contemporary neo-Darwinian accounts of biological evolution (2002: 41–42).
11 In this interpretation of urban evolution, the human designer is not removed, as would be the case in a strictly Darwinian interpretation (Steadman, 1979: 189).

12   This is not confined to professional jargon, either, and is seen in everyday language through talk of the lifeblood of the city, or urban vitality, regeneration, or the 'creation' of a new housing estate.

13   See also Lynch (1990: 254) on urban design as large-scale architecture.

14   Society must exist, at least for those who refrain from relieving themselves in the street, picking their neighbours' flowers, or causing violence to other individuals, for reasons that are social. We can't be said to have a 'world society' as long as nations unilaterally pursue internationally anti-social behaviour like polluting others' environments, appropriating other countries' resources, or bombing or invading other countries.

15   In a Hobbesian sense, this is the point of the social contract: if it benefits the individuals signed up to it. To pursue a collective goal in the abstract, that compromises or sacrifices individuals, is counter-productive, or only benefits those whose individual interests are aligned with the collective good, or those who manage to manipulate the collective good to be aligned with their own interests. This also may be related to the 'gene's eye view' of the organism (Chapter 5). We are, like genes (in a manner of speaking) both 'selfish' and cooperative (Dawkins, [1976] 2006).

16   Hall (2002: 3); the general objective of urban planning being 'to provide for a spatial structure of activities (or of land uses) which in some way is better than the pattern that would exist without planning'.

17   Hobbes (1651); Hardin (1968); Batty (2005, 2007, 2008b).

18   This assumes a modern democractic context. According to Kostof, a treasured advantage of newly founded cities was that 'the ruler could design an ideal population for his city and coerce it to live in premeditated relationships' (Kostof, 1991: 34).

19   In terms of Figure 7.19, for example, the chances of getting *some* form that is 'contiguous, tight against the existing form' (something *like* c or d or similar) is 4,845 times more likely: $(20 \times 19 \times 18 \times 17 / 1 \times 2 \times 3 \times 4)$ than getting *any particular* form (precisely c or d).

20   This relates to the 'wicked' problem of planning, where planning is in danger of being part of the problem (Batty, 2007, 2008b).

21   An evolutionist stance is a theoretical abstraction, just like a Modernist or traditionalist one; and no actual *application* would be expected to be 100 per cent 'evolutionist' any more than it could be 100 per cent Modernist or 100 per cent traditionalist. An evolutionist approach could be applied to anything – whether we call it planning or urbanism, or architecture or urban design, as with product design, or societies or nature.

22   Mitchell (1990) also discusses evolution as a strategy for creating things.

23   Perkins (2000: 171).

24   Tokyo has motorways threaded through its urban fabric unobtrusively (see, for example, Richards, 1969) – and Glasgow at its best did the same.

25   Llewelyn-Davies *et al.* (1971).

26   The avoidance of 'macro-mutations' depends on the characteristics of the 'solution space'. In some circumstances, for example in the artistic context, it is not necessarily the case that the closer to the existing solution, the more likely to be viable. An Andy Warhol painting that simply changed the brand of soup would not necessarily be more viable (as art) than one that changed the soup cans to, say, dog food. A variant of Dalí's Lobster Telephone would not function particularly well as an independent work of art if it involved only some barely perceptible change (substitution of a different individual lobster). However, a 'shrimp cellphone' or a 'prawn pager' might do the trick.

27   The issue of avoiding suppressing novelty is linked to the question of how to get from here to there: by what viable paths might we evolve desired future forms? Let us recall the example of East Kilbride, whose town centre evolved into a megastructural building complex (Chapter 8). What paths would have prevented this from happening? Well, a number of things: insisting on streets being retained for use by vehicles; banning the enclosure of pedestrian precincts; insisting on preserving some of the original buildings on the site which were demolished (an old ballroom and library); preventing in principle too large an area being con-tiguously built (perhaps for fire safety reasons); the prevention of being allowed to increase parking capacity to boost the viability a regional one-stop shopping centre, and so on. Any one of these bans might have been done for good reason, based on prevailing assumptions about what a town should be like. But any one of those bans would be enough to prevent the evolution of East Kilbride Town Centre, where the hypothetical possibilities foreclosed by such bans would not, of course, be knowable. This brings home the importance of not suppressing unsolicited novelty, that may have no particularly apparent functional benefit, but is functional enough to have a right to survive.

28   By simply listing this collection (that was assembled for other purposes elsewhere in the book), which includes extinct cases, and by not putting forward any specific combinations from the potential (very large number), it should be clear that this is not intended as an actual set of proposals, but an example of what is meant by 'novel, exceptional or idiosyncratic cases'.

29   See Borden (2001) for history of the skateboard.

30   See Sorkin's *Local Code* (1993) for a hypothetical system of coding, based on rules of adjacency, branching algorithms, and so on.

31   The accusation of vulgar sameyness may sometimes be inferred in some criticisms of new towns, although this rather ignores the prerogatives of the citizens concerned (Marshall, 2006a). Madanipour questions where the taste of the professionals comes from (1996).

32   Alexander (1979); Alexander *et al.* (1977). See also Shane (2005) for ideas for 'recombinant' urbanism.

33   See Williams (2005) for discussion of co-housing.

34   Geddes (1915); Jacobs (1962); Alexander, (1979), Alexander *et al.* (1977) – but the patterns evolve over time, rather than being 'timeless'; Alexander *et al.* (1987);

also, any site-responsive parts of *The Nature of Order* that do not presume a pre-existing 'latent whole' (Alexander, 2002a, 2002b, 2005); Cowan (1995).

35 As a particular point of departure: while sympathetic to the 'organic' sensibilities of Geddes and Alexander, this book departs from any theories or approaches that regard the city as an optimisable organic whole, that interpret urban evolution as unfolding towards such a whole, and that assert that planning and design must be applied in a specific way to attain such unfolding towards such a whole. Such theories seem incompatible with evolutionary change as understood by mainstream biology (Chapter 6), and – more to the point – the evolutionary reality of cities (Chapter 8).

36 Reed (1999d: 201).

37 This echoes the way that the beehive could be interpreted either as a despotic monarchy or a utopian workers' collective (Ramírez, 2000).

10 CONCLUSIONS

This book opened contemplating the fittingness of the built environment as a human habitat, and the question – or 'urban conundrum' – as to why it seemed that modern planned environments are not necessarily or systematically better than traditional 'unplanned' ones. This book has suggested a range of interlinked answers, that relate to the understanding of the nature of what a city is, how its parts relate to the whole, and how these change over time. These answers are enabled by three key arguments advanced by this book, regarding understanding cities, interpreting evolution and application of evolutionary understanding to city planning.

First, while a city may be 'organic', it is not an organism; realising this means we can exploit understanding of the 'organic' nature of cities, without being undermined by the inadequacies of the city-as-organism metaphor. Secondly, we can interpret evolution as a generic effect, rather than a specifically biological process; this opens the door to robust evolutionary interpretations of urbanism, that need *not* interpret cities in biological terms. Thirdly, this gives us an evolutionary perspective or paradigm that resolves the apparent paradox that a city is on the one hand a product of human will, and on the other hand something more organic, not completely under human control. This allows us to apply urban planning and design mindful of the city as an evolutionary entity, rather than as a wholly designable object (like a building or machine), or as an organism that follows some mysterious developmental logic of its own.

As we have seen, an evolutionary perspective or paradigm can accommodate both Modernism and traditionalism, planned cities and 'unplanned' ones. From this evolutionary perspective, indeed, the Modern planned environment and traditional 'unplanned' one are not, after all, so different, but are simply different manifestations of evolution, interpreted in different spatial and temporal scales. Today's modern planned environment – or, at least, the functional parts that survive – will, after all, some day be part of tomorrow's 'traditional' environment.

This concluding chapter serves first to draw out some of the key messages of the book with respect to Understanding Cities and Urbanism; secondly to suggest onward Implications for Practice and Research; and thirdly, to provide some Reflections on Evolution. Finally we shall take a look at some issues arising from the subject matter of the book, that point beyond the scope of the book itself: Beyond Cities, Design and Evolution.

UNDERSTANDING CITIES AND URBANISM

This book has articulated an understanding of cities as evolutionary entities. This does not mean that we need to consider cities as literally being living things, or metaphorically as organisms. The evolutionary perspective or paradigm is based first on the kind of thing a city is, and secondly how it changes over time.

This perspective regards a city as a complex dynamic entity, in this regard a bit like an organism, rather than a complicated object like a machine; but also as a collective entity – more like an ecosystem, or a society, than an individual organism. As a collective entity, the different components are partly in cooperation (or, at least, passively benefiting from each others' presence) but also partly in competition. Although the parts are to some extent inter-dependent – and bound up by a common social fabric – the parts are not serving the whole as such (like proverbial cogs in a machine). This understanding of the city as a complex, dynamic, collective entity sets it apart from works of art, machines and individual organisms; to design a city somehow as if it were an organism would be no better than trying to design it as a work of art or machine – or, for that matter, a building. As we have seen, it is not normally appropriate to design cities like buildings, due to their larger spatial scale, longer temporal scale, and their different social structure. Nevertheless, it seems that city designers have sometimes behaved almost as if they were designing a building, with this being part of the urban problem.

The evolutionary perspective secondly has to account for the change over time of this collective entity that is the city. A useful insight offered from contemporary science is to understand and work with the concept of emergence, by which the interactions of local components can give rise to large-scale outcomes that are unanticipated from their ingredients. The phenomenon of emergence means that the nature and behaviour of the output may be rather different from the nature and behaviour of the inputs.

This has been illustrated in cases such as the concentric pattern of cells in a honey bee's hive comb, where there is no need for any 'master planner bee' to specify what zones should exist where; from a more or less random deposition of eggs, pollen and honey, the concentric pattern naturally arises. We have seen how equivalent kinds of emergent patterns can appear in cities, by individual people simply reacting to local conditions, or at most, individuals optimising their own location with no regard for the overall collective outcome, and with no city-level control directing development into concentric zones. Emergence therefore can lead to the appearance of planning, but without planners. We can have urban order, without city design.

An evolutionary perspective is based on two further key insights. First, there is the suggestion that evolution is a kind of emergent effect – a kind of adaptive emergence. The adaptive nature means that there is feedback from the environment, so the product of evolution is likely to have a functional order to it, fitness with respect to its environment, that changes over time. Secondly, an emergent effect may be unanticipated and unintentional, but this does not mean that individual increments are necessarily random, unseeing or unintentional. This has the important effect that it has been possible to suggest a general interpretation of evolution as a long-term emergent effect that nevertheless may allow small local increments of *design*.

The idea that evolution could include increments of 'design' would, of course, be heretical in the biological context; but the interpretation of evolution in a more general sense allows design to be included as part of the local incremental processes – where there is intentionality with respect to the next iteration – while still requiring the long-term effect to be unknown and unknowable. This is useful for interpreting evolution in cultural, technological and urban contexts. It means that one can purposefully design an improved pocket-watch, without this implying any foreknowledge of, or inevitability of progress to, wristwatches or digital watches. Or, one can design individual buildings and streets, without heed to whether these might one day become enclosed as shopping malls. With non-biological evolution, we have a 'heedless' watchmaker – heedless of the long-term consequences of future iterations – but not a 'blind' one; that is, not 'blind' to the form and function of the current increment of design.

Acceptance of this interpretation of evolution as a kind of adaptive emergence, that allows design intentionality in local increments, while resulting in unintended long-term effects, is key to unlocking urban evolution. For this means that urban planning and design can be *part* of urban evolution. It means for a start that 'urban evolution' is not only not just a figure of speech – like urban 'vitality' or urban 'metabolism'. It also means that urban evolution is not only confined to some primitive historic phase of 'unplanned' urbanism, that was supplanted and superseded by modern planning. Rather, urban evolution is a continuous process, that includes both innovation and tradition, and hence Modernism and traditionalism, and a combination of local design intention and larger-scale, long-term effects that we recognise as 'unplanned'.

This in turn has the consequence for how we interpret urban change and the impact of Modernist planning. In effect, Modernism *magnified* the processes and problems of evolution. Modernism provided rapid advances in technology, and the rapid creation of novel forms of architecture and revolutionary urban formats – cities without streets, or with streets in the air, buildings on stilts with no fronts or backs, and so on. These were often applied rapidly and on a large scale, such as in new towns and comprehensive redevelopment of existing cities. This general postwar programme of large-volume, large-scale innovation and experimentation – a 'Cambrian explosion' of 'hopeful monsters' – was a case of big trial and big error.

This trial and error is, of course, business as usual for evolution. But the large urban scale and long timescale made any errors very tangible, ongoing and seemingly indefinitely enduring. We notice this downside of evolution – the waste and sacrifice – because we are living through it, like living in a house constantly under reconstruction. Traditional urbanism also made many mistakes and wrong turns, but those are buried in history; from today's perspective, we see only the successful functional survivors.

Where the Modernist innovations proved to be functional, and fitted well – were *well adapted* – we get what we recognise as all the positive qualities of modern urban living. However, where they were badly adapted, especially where ripping up the older functional order of the traditional urban fabric – then we got discord and dysfunctionality. When we compare modern planned environments unfavourably with traditional 'unplanned' ones, it is usually *badly adapted* Modernism that is being criticised, and *well-adapted* traditional urbanism that is being lauded. It is the role of the planner and designer to manage this adaptation, through sensitive generative and selective interventions.

IMPLICATIONS FOR PRACTICE AND RESEARCH

This book opened with the suggestion of city planning at the crossroads, with reference to two debates: Modernism versus traditionalism, and planned versus unplanned urbanism. What does the foregoing analysis suggest for taking these debates forward?

For a start, as already noted, both traditionalism and Modernism can be accommodated in an evolutionary approach. It is not so much a polarisation of either/or, but how to handle innovation and retention of functional tradition. We can choose to replicate traditional planning, or allow Modernism to evolve. While Modernism was, in a sense, the focus of the problem at the outset of the book, by the end it seems there is no reason to discard Modernism. It just needs a sufficiently sensitive application. Indeed, perhaps this book if anything gives a renewed boost to novelty, or the significance of different kinds of novelty, that can open up paths to future functionality.

Secondly, in the debate of planned versus 'unplanned' (or more versus less planning) it is not so much whether we should have rigid blueprints or a laissez-faire free-for-all, but what is the best scale of units to be designed, timescale, and distribution of decision-making.

This book has, indeed, suggested that urban planning can take place within an evolutionary perspective or paradigm, as opposed to a 'creationist' (object-design) or 'developmental' (growing-organism) paradigm. Evolution does not mean 'no human agency', since we can have the both the intentional generation of design proposals, and the 'artificial selection' of development control. But planning or design interventions are made in the knowledge that they are affecting a complex evolutionary system, and not aimed at any single finite optimal form.

In a nutshell, an evolutionary perspective invites us to keep what works, and innovate using small-scale changes that are definite improvements, and viable in the short term, rather than the pursuit of grand visions that would replicate the forms of the past shapes of cities, that may be disruptive in the short term and may not even be viable in the long term anyway.

This also invites us to focus on the possibilities of a more bottom-up approach to planning, where there can be urban ordering without city design. That is, rather than necessarily prescribing in advance an overall neighbourhood-scale or settlement-scale design, it is possible to create functional urban order at the level of streets and blocks.

While blocks are well enough understood as urban units, we should not overlook streets. Streets are not just unbuilt voids or utilitarian networks that, like water pipes or telephone cables, could be threaded through a city-sized building or built environment of any social construction. Rather, streets are bound up with the very social fabric – of public and private – that makes a city what it is. Streets therefore have a civic significance that other potential kinds of building-block – such as neighbourhoods – don't necessarily have.

Urban ordering by the logic of 'street syntax' can allow the construction of the urban equivalent of prose, that has a basic functional order to it, that is quite adequate for most circumstances, even if it does not have the finite compositional qualities of a piece of poetry. Instead of city planning attempting epic poetry, we have functional prose in instalments, as and when needed. It is a matter of planning intention in individual circumstances, as to whether it is worth trying to form the 'urban poetry' of finite formally planned urban compositions, where the needs of the whole are put before the needs of the parts, where individuals' interests, buildings and streets may be compromised or sacrificed for the good of the whole. In some cases, it may be worth it – providing the whole is a worthy, collectively accepted civic goal, but should be avoided if the future whole is a chimera, something that may not be achievable, and that may be of uncertain value in an unknowable future context. So what is 'right' will depend, as ever, on the context of application.

This book is not equipped to give a comprehensive set of recommendations on how to plan cities, as that would require addressing planning intentions and planning instruments, and these would need to relate to a specific context. Chapter 9 has already given some suggestions – in the form of an evolutionist approach – that include the five principles: (I) Make each step viable now; (II) Proceed by small steps – avoid 'monstrosity'; (III) Avoid suppressing 'unsolicited novelty'; (IV) Discard moribund models; (V) Devolve decision-making. These are not 'tablets of stone' – not necessarily sufficient of themselves – but could be adapted and worked in with other philosophies and principles according to individual contexts and purposes.

Over and above the suggestions in Chapter 9, here we can suggest some pointers, as to where attention could next be directed, that follow from the scope and findings of the book.

For a start, the suggestion of a greater focus on bottom-up urban ordering rather than top-down city design could imply the development of appropriate instruments of urban ordering. This could imply renewed attention to instruments such as urban coding (or Alexander-style 'patterns'). Coding could provide the 'building blocks' of generation, and their necessary and allowable relationships, and could be combined with a degree of 'selection' (development control) by an appropriate planning authority. This could give an effective combination of functional local order checked for the final outcomes; but without the kind of zoning of conventional planning, where the outline form and structure of a settlement is fixed in advance.

Attention should be given, in particular, to the possibility of the street and block as building-blocks of urban structure – rather than the neighbourhood or land use zone or whole settlement. This would mean investigating different kinds of suitable street type and block type. A possible system has already been suggested in *Streets & Patterns*. But more work needs to be done to develop these ideas further in different directions, applied to different contexts.[1]

In the pursuit of this or any other more bottom-up approach, we need to research explorations of the effects of different kinds of codes or programmes on what kinds of macro-outcomes are produced. Can we predict what emergent outcomes would arise, probabilistically, for given kinds of urban ordering, coding and design units at different scales, applied at given rates and with different kinds of context?[2] In general, it could be fruitful to pursue further kinds of application of contemporary science to urban formation and structuring. This includes things like urban complexity, environmental structure, and so on.

It would also be beneficial to have more research on learning from historical cases where planned order has been achieved by urban ordering or coding in relation to – and in the absence of – city design.[3] More generally, it could be interesting to examine urban history more widely through an evolutionary perspective, to learn from cases that are traditionally either regarded as planned innovations – as if unprecedented creations or revolutions – or on the other hand gradual conservative traditions, as if constituting periods of stasis just waiting for a revolution to happen.

It would be interesting to do further research on both novel designed forms, and also spontaneous urban forms, and how they might be generated and combined in different permutations. This could include consideration of architectural megastructures, vernacular architecture and self-organising morphologies of informal settlements.

This book has mainly been about physical urban units and urban structures. The social, economic and political implications of this book need to be worked through. What do people want – what would they like if they were given the chance? How is social organisation evolving? How does this relate to physical urban form and structure? How does the physical environment feed back to influence 'social evolution'?

Finally, we need to consider the implications of all of this for the design professions. We may need different kinds of 'planner' and 'designer'. In addition to the conventional public authority 'selector' and private sector 'designer' (master-planner), there could be a role for the urban code-writer, who could be a planner, or a private sector designer of urban building-blocks that are then adopted by the planning authority. A system of coding could imply a shift in creativity to the code-writer, whether the code-writer were a public planner or private consultant. It could also imply further delegation to allow architects to 'build' urban form using building-scale, street-scale and block-scale building-blocks, without the need for old-style master-planners.

Also, at the smaller scale, there may be opportunities for individual citizens as self-builders to contribute to the generation of urban form through smaller-scale interventions, albeit that some of these may be coded, or their combinations controlled in some way, by publicly agreed standards.

REFLECTIONS ON EVOLUTION

The theologian Williamm Paley argued that an eye, like a watch, must be a product of purposive design. Darwinian theory argued that the eye was a product of evolution, not design. This book argues that a watch is not just a product of design, but is also – like an eye – a product of evolution. Whereas Paley applied the 'argument from design' to nature, we can apply the 'argument from evolution' to human artefacts and systems.

This book has demonstrated that cities can be usefully understood as evolutionary entities, products of evolution. It is not exactly novel to suggest that cities 'evolve'. But perhaps in the past, evolution has tended to be written off as mere wordplay, like saying that a city is a 'living thing'; and perhaps evolutionary explanations of urbanism have to some extent been overlooked because cities are obviously products of human will, in contrast to the natural evolution of organisms; and perhaps because evolutionary urbanism might be thought limited to certain kinds of historic vernacular processes – as in *Architecture without Architects* – that are all very well but do not apply 'here and now'.

This book has been able to make use of evolutionary concepts by recognising evolution as an emergent effect, that where, though the long-term outcome is unanticipated and unknowable, nevertheless individual local increments that include intentionality are allowed, therefore allowing design – and planning and Modernism – to be part of evolution.

What this book has suggested is that we can interpret the meaning of evolution at a general level in such a way that the term is equally applicable to biological and non-biological contexts. That is to say that the essential meaning of evolution is sufficiently generic – like the concepts of construction, competition, cooperation, defence, and so on – that it can equally well be applied to books and ox-carts as to bookworms and oxen. On the other hand, while general enough to cover a raft of non-biological systems and artefacts, this sense of evolution is specific enough not to be confused with other kinds of change seen in nature, such as growth, development or metamorphosis.

The book has also suggested specific ways in which cities may be said to evolve: the evolution of 'unplanned cities', where the main thing is the coevolution of parts – buildings, spaces, vehicles, streets, land uses, and so on – and the evolution of 'city designs', where the evolution is more or less equivalent to the evolution of other designed artefacts such as machines or buildings (Chapter 8).

In the world of human designs, individual artefacts may (quite properly) be studied in their own right, as if these were wholly separate independent objects – just as an archaeologist may study a series of skulls of different animals as if they exist as independent objects. But we know that everything living is related to everything else by evolution (via adaptive radiation); and so it can be said for human artefacts and systems. That is, if we accept evolution as a generic effect applying to human artefacts, then these can be seen as being all linked to each other, in a single system. So we can add together all the urban things that may be said to evolve (cities, types of building, land uses, and route types; Chapter 8) plus all the other human systems and artefacts discussed in Chapter 6 (languages, steam-chariots, boomerangs, and so on) and then finally add all *these* together with humans and all the other living things and all *their* systems (beavers' dams and spiders' webs, etc.) in a single system, and say that the whole lot – as a whole and in its parts – is evolutionary.

From this perspective, we can't help seeing 'fruits' of evolution all around us. That is to say, all around us we can see animals, plants, artefacts, processes, activities, institutions, systems and other kinds of entities, each of which can be said to have had a precursor, that was slightly less well-adapted, perhaps more crude or rudimentary, perhaps less specialised . . .[4] Or, as Kubler put it, 'Everything made now is either a replica or variant of something made a little time ago and so on back without break to the first morning of human time'.[5]

So we can look around us, to see how everything ultimately links back to something simple from the natural world. The pencil sharpener descended from the metal blade which descended from the first hand axe made of stone, held by our earliest human ancestors, millions of years ago. The ball-point pen can be traced back through quill pen to bird's feather to dinosaur. The modern laptop computer – within living memory a descendant of the first personal computers – in turn can be traced right back to the first electronic computers, and before them, although the lineage is not exactly linear, to things like telegraphs, typewriters, cathode ray tubes, analytic engines, punchcard-driven looms, calculating machines, arithmometers, abacuses, and so on, right back to the first sticks and stones used to write or count with. Electric lights, that came after gas lamps and flaming torches and candles, can be traced back to the first lamp design – perhaps a cupped rock filled with animal fat – right back to the first controlled use of fire. A central-heating radiator could be traced back though various kinds of boiler or hypocaust to the first hearths and again ultimately back to the first fire. Here, the radiator and the light bulb in this sense have a joint common ancestor in the first fire.[6]

In such a way, we can take any artefact, and relate it back to an earlier product, back to the specialised use of a living thing (horsepower; animal hide; bone), or another natural object (such as a rock or sand or water). Here, we seem to end up with fundamental elements such as air, water, fire and earth, plus organic matter – fundamental in the sense that it is from these kinds of things that all products of evolution are descended. This connectedness of all evolved systems and artefacts should make us feel an intimate connection with the objects in our homes and workplaces, as with our ancestors; and hence make us feel at home among our creations.[7]

The point here is that if we allow the word evolution to apply to things other than living things – if we allow it to relate to institutions, social and economic systems, designed artefacts, and, yes, cities – then we start to notice how much of our world is in some sense a product of evolution: an improvement on a previous system or design; an adaptation; a transfer from one thing to a new context, and so on. Does this make the use of the word evolution so all-encompassing as to be redundant? No; rather it seems to enlarge and enrich its significance; and makes it an important kind of process that stands in contradistinction to other kinds of change.

Evolution implies something that is not just a series of historical accidents (meteorites impacting, or mountain-building events); nor a series of progressive, purposive stages (like the folding of a paper aeroplane); nor straightforward processes of physics and chemistry (clouds and rain, for example, whose restless processes are indistinguishable from yesterday, or last year, or thousands of years ago).

With our general interpretation of evolution, we can furthermore see that all of those generic concepts discussed in Chapter 6 – construction, competition, cooperation, defence, adaptation, and so on – may similarly be said to apply to living systems, and hence in each case the human (artificial) version is simply a local application of a more universal concept. Hence evolution, adaptation, specialisation, competition, communication and construction can be seen as terms applying to extended biological systems in general, that happen to include human systems as well. Hence economic competition, infrastructure construction, institutional cooperation are simply specialised human-system variants of those concepts that may be applied in a more general sense – and yet which we may ultimately interpret precisely *as* biological – as argued by Geerat Vermeij.[8]

What is more, we can see that these generic concepts – competition and communication and defence – *only* truly apply to living systems, or contexts involving living systems. Since when has a wind or tide been said to specialise or adapt? Since when has a crystal or waterfall been said to compete or communicate? Since when did a rock or sand dune defend itself?

A paper wasp's nest is a product of evolution – whether considered directly or indirectly as part of the living world. The papery chambered nest itself is lifeless, but the lifeless Moon has no papery chambered nests; no specialisation, no adaptation, no competition, no communication, no construction.

Hence, we may say in a general sense that most of the world as we know it only makes sense in the light of evolution. Non-evolutionary explanations could cover what made the Sun, Moon, planets or stars the way they are: explanatory processes generally covered by physics and chemistry, astronomy and geology, mathematics and meteorology. But just about everything that sets Earth apart from everywhere else in the known Universe – great walls, canal systems, dams, webs, fly-traps, flying-machines, steam engines, cities, nations, economies, industries, commodious Buildings, accounts of Time, Arts and Letters, and Society – requires biology and evolution as part of their explanation.

BEYOND CITIES, DESIGN AND EVOLUTION

The contemplation of science in general and evolutionary theory in particular has implications for how we believe the world works, and in turn how we believe it should be made to work. It is possible now to reflect on some of the implications for the interpretation of urban evolution, concerning progress, life, nature, evolution, human intentionality, and hence consequences for attitudes and action concerning environmental management and planning and the future of the built environment.

Although this book started out with a question mark hanging over Modernist planning, nothing explored in the course of this book would seem to suggest losing faith in Modernism in general, in rationality, science or technology, which on the whole make the world a better place. (Any postmodern critic of science and technology who doubts this is welcome to consider life without a fridge, hot showers and modern hospitals.) This does not mean that we should 'worship' science; nor that technology should replace human values.[9] It does not even mean that technology gives the best of possible worlds. Technology gives benefits to those who have it, relative to those who do not, when the two are in competition. Put another way, modern ways of life are not necessarily better than ancient ways of life, except when one impinges on the other, or is offered as an alternative to the other, when the latter becomes uncompetitive in practice. This gives the impression of progress. But even if we tire of this progress and competition among ourselves, and were not to 'struggle for life' so strenuously, we should expect to lose out to other species or life-forms. If it is of any comfort, it is exactly this relentless evolutionary arms race of tooth and claw that made us the crafty, dexterous and omnivorous species we are today.

This book has applied evolutionary thinking to interpreting the design and planning of cities: that is, purposive intervention in non-living entities. In claiming that things like languages, technologies and cities evolve, this does not mean that these are considered *alive*. This means that evolution is not reserved as one of those special phenomena that help define what a living thing is. Living things may still be regarded as special – and set apart from steam locomotives and wristwatches – in that they are self-reproducing, rather than being reproduced indirectly by other agencies. So living things are special, at least in that sense – but not *because* they evolve.

That said, the distinction between the living and non-living may be regarded as somewhat arbitrary in the first place. This relates to organisms and the details of their biochemical processes; the question of what is alive is also begged by the artificial life (Alife) agenda. Therefore, far from the evolutionary perspective gratuitously bestowing the 'magic' of living things on inanimate objects, the treatment here is more likely to question the existence of any such 'magic', or rather question the extent to which life should be accorded a privileged position in the world scheme of things.[10]

Philosophers have speculated for centuries that living things may simply be complex machines. Hobbes considered that human behaviour could be reduced to the effects of a mechanical apparatus, acting and reacting in response to the environment. Hooke looked down his microscope to see 'small machines of nature'. Descartes thought of animals as clockwork mechanisms, while allowing that humans had minds that set them apart from animals and machines. Le Mettrie went further, and invited us to 'conclude bravely that man is a machine'.[11]

When contemplating nature and the living world around us, one sees how well everything fits together: the insects that pollinate the flowers, or seeds floating in the wind, the microbes in the soil that help recycle dead plants into nutrients, and so on. In *Climbing Mount Improbable*, Richard Dawkins describes the almost incredible complexity of the relationships between fig wasps and figs, and how finely tuned and intricately adapted each part is that fits together, as perfectly as if they had been part of a designed mechanism. With these intricate functional mechanisms, nature is almost like a well-designed machine, that is not incidentally a homely habitat for humans. In other words, we could see *nature* as a machine for living in.

This book has assumed from the outset that humans have evolved as part of nature, and as such, a city is as much a product of evolution as a beehive or wasp's nest. At a very basic level, the evolutionary ancestry of humans – our common descent with all other living things – blurs the distinction between what we call artificial and natural.[12]

The distinction between natural and artificial may also be called into question in other ways. First, in a direct practical sense. Something that has been genetically engineered could be regarded as something unnatural, and artificial, even though it is an organism. This could apply to a genetically engineered 'anti-freeze' tomato, or a fly that has an ectopic eye growing out of its leg. The fly with the eye in its leg is surely in a significant sense a product designed by human genetic engineering, as it is a natural product. In future, it is likely that there will be an increasing blurring between the natural and the artificial, in this sense: artificial life and eye-legged flies today, cyborgs tomorrow.[13] If artificial variation makes an eye-legged fly artificial, then the distinction between the 'natural' evolution of humans and wasps and the 'artificial' evolution of cities and wasps' nests and eye-legged flies becomes a rather academic one, and we may as well call these both equally evolution, just as artificial selection and natural selection are equally selection.

The distinction between artificial and natural may be blurred in other senses. Although humans and paper wasps both make a substance we recognise as paper, we tend to regard the paper purposefully and dexterously crafted by humans differently from the paper made by a wood-munching wasp, because human will and consciousness is involved. But, as our under-standing of brains, minds, consciousness, free will and creativity increases, we may yet change our minds on the privileged position we grant to human will and consciousness, and the significance of difference between what is going on in the brain of a paper-making human and a paper-making wasp. Recall that intention was the defining difference between the set of generic concepts involving biological versus non-biological phenomena – construction, competition, and so on (Chapter 6). In other words, it is not just evolution where the non biological differs from the biological due to intention. At least, this is the case as long as human design and selection are considered as products of conscious free will, and not simply the result of mechanistic impulses in the brain.[14]

Yet, if it were to turn out that humans are just machines after all, then perhaps our free will is illusory. Apart from anything else, this would cast doubt on the special place we hold for our design and creativity, and shed more light on the difference between the brain of an architect and the brain of an ant. So the difference between a designed object and an object that emerged from a combination of mechanistic sub-routines would be blurred. If human free will and purposive design were to prove illusory, there would be no evidence for any kind of 'design' anywhere in the universe.[15]

According to David Grahame Shane, the 'shocking' part of Darwin's insight is the removal of a need for any central designer or master-planner of nature. This 'shock' is not just about how biology works, of course, but the interpretation of humanity's place in the scheme of things.[16]

Although evolutionary theory had a profound impact on religion, evolution is not intrinsically at odds with religious belief. Theodosius Dobzhansky, one of the most eminent evolutionary biologists of the twentieth century, described himself as a creationist *and* an evolutionist. That is, he believed that God created the world, but that evolution was the divine instrument of creation. Evolution may be at odds with some intepretations of some parts of some religions – but that could be said for almost any kind of science that sheds new light on old wisdom.[17]

There is no scope here to go into the full ramifications of evolutionary theory for religion, belief, human values, and so on. It must suffice here to say that acceptance of humanity's evolutionary history does invite us to question not only things like 'natural history' – including the emergence of the first humans – but things normally associated with the 'humanities', such as attitudes to nature, how society came to be, where morality came from, and so on. These will in turn affect the political choices that underpin planning.[18]

The 'shock' of the impersonal mechanistic nature of Darwinism does not just affect how we think we got to where we are, but has implications for where we are headed. While many people may be comfortable at some level with the idea that humans evolved out of a primordial biochemical soup, the 'shock' of Darwinism has perhaps not so fully worked its way into implications of what comes next, or what we should do next. For evolution implies there is no target destination; not even a direction of progress; the future is uncertain, the interpretation of success is relative to context. In a sense, Darwinism supplied all the 'uncertainty' and 'relativity' that post-modern philosophies would require, without having to resort to associations with the physics of Heisenberg or Einstein.

The kind of uncertainty and relativism that follows from Darwin is seen straightforwardly in the way that no one could tell in advance if four legs should be better than four fins, or two legs better than four. Even humans' large brains, that seem to be quintessentially identifiable with our success, are only useful relative to the prevailing context; and anyway the success is only relative to our own point of view.[19] This may be readily accepted if we come to think of it, but the point is how it affects what we do in the everyday world of work and planning and all manner of spheres of society. We so often behave as if things in the future 'should' be the way they normally are, or always were, or perhaps would be if past trends were simply projected into the future. For example, we tend to assume that because cities normally have central business districts, they *should* have them; or, because families 'always were' fundamental social units, they 'always should be'; or because we have historically seen increasing economic growth, we should continue to pursue it. While these may often be reasonable assumptions in practice, evolution removes from them a basic theoretical justification.

Learning from evolution does not mean that we should behave like our forebears – human or otherwise – because we descended from them. There is no need to accept our evolutionary ancestors' territorial behaviour or gender roles or sexual mores or dietary preferences because they are 'natural', nor reject them because they are 'bestial'. And acceptance of Darwinian evolution in biology does not mean we should have a sort of Darwinian political science, in which the default setting is unthinking conservatism, or a sort of crude economic game of 'survival of the fittest'. It is, after all, our ability to think ahead and intervene – either through generation or selection – that means we can make societal and political choices in which we try to treat everyone as members of a human community, rather than the strong exploiting the weak, or being indifferent to the weak, as if we lived in a state of nature. In short, our understanding of how nature works need not determine our moral, social or political preferences any more than our moral, social or political preferences should determine our interpretation of how nature works. But our moral, social and political preferences should at least benefit from being informed by good science in the first place.[20]

The question becomes how humanity now takes care of its own affairs; how the world's resources should be distributed among its citizens, according to our moral and political values. If the aim is to make as much of the planet habitable to as many humans as possible, then this may imply urbanity spreading over much more of the surface of the planet than is currently considered desirable, or the alternative might require stacking up our cities like beehives and termite skyscrapers at densities currently considered undesirable.

One could imagine a truly laissez-faire planetary policy that did not recognise national boundaries, but would allow anyone to live anywhere, giving rise to a more even distribution of population relative to resources. The opposite extreme could see people living in socially rigid 'beehives' – whether the beehive model here is that of workers' cooperative, despotic monarchy or 'ovarian police state'. Put another way, we could choose to make our national borders as porous as our city boundaries, or make our cities' spatial structures as rigidly allocated as our buildings.[21]

While evolution stresses the ecological connectedness of everything, and hence the importance of the environment, it does not imply sacrificing ourselves for the good of other species or the environment in general. Evolution suggests that we should look after the environment because it is our life-support system, but not for its own sake; we should not put the planet – that has no knowable goals – ahead of our own interests. If looking after ourselves is anthropocentric, it is no more selfish than the behaviour of any other species that ever survived.[22]

In the long term, as evolution teaches us, all sorts of possibilities could arise. Evolution says in effect that, given time, you can have any future you like, as long as it follows from something that works now. Perhaps one day we will have Walking Cities stalking the land (Figure 2.16c) – perhaps in response to an alien planetary environment, on Earth or elsewhere. The designers would perhaps dust down the Archigram archives for inspiration, just as L'Enfant looked back to Evelyn (Figure 8.3). Perhaps their interiors would be facsimiles of our familiar terrestrial environment: perhaps the urban interior of Venus Fort, a shopping mall in Tokyo designed like an Italianate town, with its own artificial sky (Figure 4.13 d); or something more like the vegetative landscape of Earth, such as the Eden project in Cornwall (Figure 4.4), whose geodesic-membrane exterior could one day be the bulbous 'eye' in an insectile megastructure. Perhaps a Walking City would evolve from some existing megastructure; perhaps from an already symmetrical, smooth-sided construction, like an aircraft, whose wheeled landing gear gradually evolves into legs, while losing the wings. Or perhaps they might be evolved from urban submarines whose fins evolve into legs, and later, wings . . .

In the long term, 'we' might have a post-terrestrial, post-human future. In the meantime, we should take care of the planet we have, as a human-friendly habitat. Humans have been extremely successful in adapting to the environment, and adapting the environment to suit ourselves. So far, the rate of our technological development, and our ability to migrate over long distances and to adapt to diverse environmental niches have outstripped our propensity to lose touch or fall out with each other. Despite our billions, we still hang together as a single breeding population. This suggests that – barring a planetary-scale catastrophe – speciation is likely to be held in check, at least on Earth. So, cities for *Homo sapiens* may be around for a while. Cities will still all be different, and still all the same.

And while our cities and built environments may never be as perfectly adapted as other species' constructions, this is perhaps a small price to pay for our human creativity, planetary 'reach' and individualistic choice of what to build and how to live. Unlike bees or termites, the designs of our homes are not so much tethered to our genes, nor do increments of improvement hang on the mortal fate of each generation. Instead, we can imagine and execute design innovations in our built environment, for our own direct benefit. Our cities can benefit from both design and evolution. Our built futures are in our own hands.

Notes

1 Marshall (2005).
2 Ongoing research and further testing of codes in practice; for the UK context, see Carmona *et al.* (2006), Carmona and Dann (2007).
3 Marshall, ed. (forthcoming) *Urban Coding and Planning*.
4 In his book *The Ancestor's Tale*, Richard Dawkins (2004) traces species back through time, meeting up with successive common ancestors where each ancestor further back in the chain unites us with an ever wider collection of other species. Going backwards, humans meet up first with chimpanzees and then all other apes, then all other mammals, and all other vertebrates, and all other animals, and all other eukaryotes, right back to the earliest possible entity granted the status of life.
5 Kubler (1962: 2).
6 See, for example, G. Dyson (1998), Uhlig (2001).
7 Dawkins' pilgrimage (2004) ends with convergence on a single ancestor, but our non-biological pilgrimage ends not with a single terminal point, but a series of termini – perhaps like a ring of railway termini round a city centre. One terminus is biological; others end in fire, water, rocks, metals, and so on. To link these termini up, we have to go beyond adaptive evolution, but find further unification in chemical structures and elements.
8 Vermeij (2004).
9 Modernity has been criticised for being 'the path to the horrors of the twentieth century' (after Bauman, cited in Allmendinger, 2001: 13). But while advanced technology may have abetted or magnified the horrors, the root of the horrors surely lie at the door of human free will. In effect, the human motives and prejudices that led to the horrors of the twentieth century are as old as humans.
10 On the boundary between life and non-life being blurred: G. Dyson (1998: 117); Gribbin (2005: 230); Vermeij (2004: 14). Zubay (2000: 168) refers to the 'ill-defined boundary between the nonliving and the living'. See also Levy (1993) on artificial life.

11 Macpherson (1968: 28); Bolter (1993: 11, 205). Our modern scientific understanding of the world might no longer use clockwork as the best metaphor; Bennett *et al.* (2003). That living things may be machine-like to some extent is not to say we should actually think we are machines; but just that we need not allow preconceptions about the nature of ourselves and our component particles to become a barrier to understanding the correspondences and equivalences across the living–non-living divide.

12 Paper wasps make paper to construct their nests with. If paper is considered an 'artificially processed' material, then wasps' nests are artificial and part of 'artificial evolution'. If paper is considered a natural material, then human paper products must also be considered natural – and by extension, human products made of timber, stone, and even concrete, glass and steel, since they are all ultimately made from 'natural' constituents. In this case, buildings and cities must be natural. Either way, a city is as natural or as artificial as a wasp's nest.

13 On ectopic eyes, see Halder *et al.* (1995); see also Carroll (2006). Cyborgs: 'a human that is part-machine' (Cotton and Oliver, 1994: 56). Sirius (1993: 100) provides a pop culture take on 'evolutionary mutations'.

14 See Pinker (1999: 55) on 'enigma' of free will; Pinker (1991: 147) on the inconclusive nature of our knowledge of sentience; Dennett (1996, after Chomsky) on 'mystery' of free will; Ziman (2000a: 7) reports on the view that neural events (and by implication, purposive design) 'might as well be considered random for all we can find out about them'. As Resnick (1997: xiv) says, 'How can a mind emerge from a collection of mindless parts? It seems clear that no one part is "in charge of the mind" (or else it too would be a mind).' Dennett (1996: 63) suggests Darwin's idea questions 'the illusion of our own authorship, our own divine spark of creativity and understanding'.

15 Our brains seem to find it natural to think of things as designed; Dawkins suggests (1991: xv) that it is almost as if our brains were designed to misunderstand Darwin.

16 Shane (2005: 89); see also Ayala (2007: 8573).

17 The topic of religion has been largely avoided in this book, to avoid the distraction of arguments that do not directly affect urbanism or the scientific knowledge that feeds its understanding. That said, it is probably worthwhile spelling out here three things regarding the treatment of evolution in this book, to avoid any possible confusion. First, urban evolution is suggested to be a real identifiable effect, that is not strictly speaking dependent on the veracity of biological evolution (or the relative importance of selection and adaptation to biological evolution) for its own validity. This is akin to the way that purposive design is a real and valid activity in the urban context, that is not dependent on having a belief in the 'argument from design' in biology. Secondly, although urban evolution as interpreted in this book (from Chapter 6 onwards) allows design to feature as a local incremental input, this does not imply there is any room for interpreting design or purpose anywhere in natural biological evolution. If anything, it is more likely that our own purposes

and free will are called into doubt, as discussed in this chapter. Thirdly, that the book is based on the scientific understanding of biological evolution should be considered just as natural as being based on the scientific understanding of every other aspect of the world. See also Dobzhansky (1973); Bullock *et al.* (1988). Perhaps one of the reasons that evolution is curiously subject to intrigue and speculation (Dawkins, 1991: xv; Lynch, 2007: 389) is that in a sense evolution is really not exclusively biological in character, but is tangled up with the history of the environment; Geddes considered Darwinian evolution to be an economic theory. So armchair, desktop or blogsphere philosophers can have an opinion on it – construct a belief system around it – in a way that they will not about genes, chromosomes or proteins. (Darwinian evolution has also been described as a belief system, Ruse, 2003.) Evolution has 'no need of God as a hypothesis' – as Laplace said of his own astronomical work, to Napoleon (Bolter, 1993: 41).

18 See *Darwin's Dangerous Idea* for discussion of some of these matters including morality (Dennett, 1996). In his book *Transforming Men*, Geoff Dench (1998) explores issues of society and morality from a gendered perspective. This includes the suggestion, in effect, that society and morality were invented by women, for women. This could be regarded as 'Dench's Dangerous Idea'.

19 If success is defined in anthropocentric terms, then humans win by definition. If it is measured in terms of, say, longevity as a species, or numbers in a species, then humans would not win. So as there is no clear winner in terms of what a successful species might be, then there are no particular human attributes – brains or opposable thumbs or speech – that are necessarily more valuable than others, except in a relative sense.

20 Points relating to this are discussed further by Dennett (1996), Pinker (1999) and Mindell (2006).

21 Ramírez (2000), Hrdy (1999).

22 There is a difference between being anthropocentric about how we understand the world – which can imply a limited and hence inferior perspective – and being anthropocentric about how we act in the world, which implies acting in our own interests – as adopted by any species that ever survived. See also Silver (2006) on 'the good of the planet'; Wolch (2003) on 'Zoöpolis'; and Dixon's (1998) *After Man: A Zoology of the Future*.

BIBLIOGRAPHY

Abbott, E. A. (2006 [1884]) *Flatland: A Romance of Many Dimensions*. New York: Oxford University Press.

Abe, T., Bignell, D. E. and Higashi, M. (eds) (2000) *Termites: Evolution, Sociality, Symbioses, Ecology*. Dordrecht: Kluwer Academic Press.

Abercrombie, N., Hill, S. and Turner, B.S. (1994) *The Penguin Dictionary of Sociology*. London: Penguin.

Abercrombie, P. (1933) *Town and Country Planning*. London: Thornton Butterworth.

Abrams, C. (1971) *The Language of Cities: A Glossary of Terms*. New York: The Viking Press.

Aldersey-Williams, H. (2003) *Zoomorphic: New Animal Architecture*. London: Laurence King.

Aldous, T. (1992) *Urban Villages*. London: Urban Villages Group.

Alexander, C. (1966) A city is not a tree, in *Design*, 206: 46–55.

Alexander, C. (1979) *The Timeless Way of Building*. New York: Oxford University Press.

Alexander, C. (2002a) *The Nature of Order: An Essay on the Art of Building and The Nature of the Universe. Book One: The Phenomenon of Life*. Berkeley: The Center for Environmental Structure.

Alexander, C. (2002b) *The Nature of Order: An Essay on the Art of Building and The Nature of the Universe. Book Two: The Process of Creating Life*. Berkeley: The Center for Environmental Structure.

Alexander, C. (2005) *The Nature of Order: An Essay on the Art of Building and The Nature of the Universe. Book Three: A Vision of a Living World*. Berkeley: The Center for Environmental Structure.

Alexander, C., Ishikawa, S., Silverstein, M., Jacobson, M., Fiksdahl-King, I. and Angel, S. (1977) *A Pattern Language: Towns. Buildings. Construction*. New York: Oxford University Press.

Alexander, C., Neis, H., Anninou, A., King, I. (1987) *A New Theory of Urban Design*. New York: Oxford University Press.

11.0 • Teotihuacan, Mexico, an 'extinct' city.

Alexander, C., Silverstein, M., Angel, S., Ishikawa, S. and Abrams, D. (1975) *The Oregon Experiment*. New York: Oxford University Press.

Allan, J. (2000) Lubetkin and Peterlee, in Deckker, T. (ed.), *The Modern City Revisited*. London: Spon Press.

Allmendinger, P. (2001) *Planning in Postmodern Times*. London and New York: Routledge.

Anderson, S. (ed.) (1978) *On Streets*. Cambridge, Mass.: MIT Press.

Appleyard, D. (1981) *Livable Streets*. With M. S. Gerson and M. Lintell. Berkeley: University of California Press.

Appleyard, D., Lynch, K. and Meyer, J. (1964) *The View from the Road*. Cambridge, Mass.: MIT Press.

Aristotle (1992) *The Politics*, ed. Saunders, T. J. London: Penguin.

Ayala, F. J. (2007) Darwin's greatest discovery: design without designer, in *Proceedings of the National Academy of Sciences of the United States of America*, 1 (9 May): 8567–8573.

Bacon, E. (1975) *The Design of Cities*. London: Thames and Hudson.

Baines, M. (1994) Exploring the wall: the urban facades of Alexander Thomson, in Stamp, G. and McKinstry, S. (eds) *'Greek' Thomson*. Edinburgh: Edinburgh University Press.

Bak, P. (1996) *How Nature Works: The Science of Self-organized Criticality*. New York: Copernicus.

Ballantine, R. (1979) *Richard's Bicycle Book*. London: Pan.

Banai, R. (1996) 'Neotraditional' settlements and dimensions of performance, in *Environment and Planning B: Planning and Design*, 23: 177–190.

Banham, R. (1971) *Los Angeles: The Architecture of Four Ecologies*. London: Allen Lane.

Banham, R. (1976) *Megastructure: Urban Futures of the Recent Past*. London: Thames and Hudson.

Banister, D. (2002) *Transport Planning* (2nd edn). London: Spon.

Banister, D. (ed.) (1995) *Transport and Urban Development*. London: E & FN Spon.

Barabási, A.-L. (2002) *Linked: The New Science of Networks*. Cambridge: Perseus.

Barnett, J. (1982) *Introduction to Urban Design*. New York and London: Harper and Row.

Barnett, J. (1986) *The Elusive City: Five Centuries of Design, Ambition and Miscalculation*. New York: Harper & Row.

Barton, H., Davis, G. and Guise, R. (1995) *Sustainable Settlements: A Guide for Planners, Designers and Developers*. Bristol: University of the West of England and the Local Government Management Board.

Barton, H., Grant, M. and Guise, R. (2003). *Shaping Neighbourhoods: A Guide for Health, Sustainability and Vitality*. London: Spon.

Battle, G. and McCarthy, C. (1994) Multi-source synthesis: the design of sustainable new towns, in *Architectural Design*. London: Academy Editions, no. 111: New Towns.

Batty, M. (1995a) Cities, planning, design, computation and evolution; editorial, in *Environment and Planning B: Planning and Design*, 22: 379–382.

Batty, M. (1995b) New ways of looking at cities, in *Nature* 377: 574.

Batty, M. (1995c) Cities and complexity: implications for modelling sustainability, in Brotchie, J., Batty, M., Blakely, E., Hall, P. and Newton, P. (eds.), *Cities in Competition: Productive and Sustainable Cities for the 21st Century*. Melbourne: Longman.

Batty, M. (1999) A research programme for urban morphology, in *Environment and Planning B: Planning and Design*, 26: 475–476.

Batty, M. (2000) Less is more, more is different: complexity, morphology, cities and emergence; editorial in *Environment and Planning B: Planning and Design*, 27: 167–168.

Batty, M. (2005) *Cities and Complexity: Understanding Cities with Cellular Automata, Agent-Based Models, and Fractals*. Cambridge, Mass.: MIT Press.

Batty, M. (2006) Rank clocks, in *Nature*, 444 (30 November): 592–596.

Batty, M. (2007) Complexity in City Systems: Understanding, Evolution, and Design, *CASA working paper 117*. London: Centre for Advanced Spatial Analysis.

Batty, M. (2008a) The size, scale, and shape of cities, in *Science*, 319 (5864): 769–771.

Batty, M. (2008b) Complexity in city systems: understanding, evolution, and design, in De Roo, G. and Silva, S. (eds), *A Planner's Meeting with Complexity*. Aldershot: Ashgate Publishers.

Batty, M. and Longley, P. (1994) *Fractal Cities: A Geometry of Form and Function*. London and San Diego: Academic Press.

Batty, M. and Xie, Y. (1997) Possible urban automata, in *Environment and Planning B: Planning and Design*, 24: 175–192.

Becher, B. and Becher, H. (2004) *Typologies*; ed. with introd. Armin Zweite. Cambridge, Mass. and London: MIT Press.

Bellan, R. C. (1971) *The Evolving City*. New York: Pitman.

Benevolo, L. (1980) *The Origins of Modern Town Planning*. London: Routledge and Kegan Paul.

Ben-Joseph, E. (2005) *The Code of the City: Standards and the Hidden Language of Place Making*. Cambridge, Mass.: MIT Press.

Ben-Joseph, E. and Gordon, D. (2000) Hexagonal planning in theory and practice, in *Journal of Urban Design*, 5 (3): 237–265.

Bennett, J., Cooper, M., Hunter, M. and Jardine, L. (2003) *London's Leonardo: The Life and Work of Robert Hooke*. Oxford: Oxford University Press.

Bentley, I., Alcock, A., Murrain, P., McGlynn, S. and Smith, G. (1985) *Responsive Environments*. Oxford: Architectural Press.

Berneri, M. L. (1982) *Journey through Utopia*. London: Freedom Press.

Bernick, M. and Cervero, R. (1997) *Transit Villages in the 21st Century*. New York: McGraw-Hill.

Biddulph, M. (2000) Villages don't make a city, in *Journal of Urban Design*, 5 (1): 65–82.

Biermann, V. (2003) Antonio Averlino called Filarete, in *Architectural Theory: From the Renaissance to the Present*. Cologne: Taschen.

Billington, J. (1983) *The Tower and the Bridge: The New Art of Structural Engineering*. New York: Basic Books.

Birksted, J. (2007) The politics of copying: Le Corbusier's 'Immaculate Conceptions', in *Oxford Art Journal*, 30 (2): 305–326.

Black, M. and Williams, J. (1977). The environment of transport, in Roy Cresswell (ed.), *Passenger Transport and the Environment: The Integration of Public Passenger Transport with the Urban Environment*. London: Leonard Hill.

Bloomsbury (1993) *Bloomsbury Guide to Human Thought*. London: Bloomsbury.

Bloomsbury (1996) *Bloomsbury Guide to Art*. London: Bloomsbury.

Blunt, W. (2004) *Linnaeus: The Compleat Naturalist*. London: Frances Lincoln.

Boardman, P. (1944) *Patrick Geddes: Maker of the Future*. Chapel Hill: University of North Carolina Press.

Boardman, P. (1978) *The Worlds of Patrick Geddes: Biologist. Town Planner. Re-educator. Peace-warrior*. London, Henley and Boston: Routledge and Kegan Paul.

Bolter, J. D. (1993) *Turing's Man: Western Culture in the Computer Age*. London: Penguin.

Borden, I. (2001) *Skateboarding, Space and the City: Architecture and the Body*. Oxford: Berg.

Borges, J.L. ([1962]1998) *Fictions*. London: John Calder.

Bovill, C. (1996) *Fractal Geometry in Architecture and Design*. Cambridge, Mass.: Birkhauser Boston.

Bowes, B. (1996) *A Colour Atlas of Plant Structure*. Manson Publishing, London.

Brandon, R. (2002) *Automobile: How the Car Changed Life*. London: Macmillan.

Bressi, T. W. (1994) Planning the American Dream, in Katz, P., *The New Urbanism: Toward an Architecture of Community*. New York: McGraw-Hill.

Brett, M. (1994) The view from Great Linford, in *Architectural Design*, profile no. 111, *New Towns*. London: Academy Group.

Brodsly, D. (1981) *LA Freeway: An Appreciative Essay*. Berkeley: University of California Press.

Brogden, W. A. (1996) The bridge/street in Scottish urban planning, in Brogden, W. A. (ed.), *The Neo-Classical Town, Scottish Contributions to Urban Design since 1750*. Edinburgh: The Rutland Press.

Brotchie, J. F. (1984) Technological change and urban form, in *Environment and Planning A*, 16: 583–596.

Bryson, B. (2003) *A Short History of Nearly Everything*. London: BCA.

Bullock, A., Stallybrass, O. and Trombley, S. (1988) *The Fontana Dictionary of Modern Thought*. London: Fontana Press.

Butina Watson, G. (1993) The art of building cities: urban structuring and restructuring, in Hayward, R. and McGlynn, S. (eds), *Making Better Places: Urban Design Now*. Oxford: Butterworth Architecture.

Calthorpe, P. (1993) *The Next American Metropolis: Ecology, Community and the American Dream*. New York: Princeton Architectural Press.

Calthorpe, P. (1994) The Region, in Katz, P., *The New Urbanism: Toward an Architecture of Community*. New York: McGraw-Hill.

Camazine, S. (2003) Patterns in Nature, in *Natural History* (June 2003): 34–41.

Camazine, S. (2005) *Designed by Nature*. <www.scottcamazine.com/personal/DesignNature/index.html>

Camazine, S., Deneubourg, J.-L., Franks, N. R., Sneyd, J., Theraulaz, G. and Bonabeau, E. (2001) *Self-Organization in Biological Systems*. Princeton: Princeton University Press.

Campbell, H. and Marshall, R. (2002) Instrumental rationality, intelligent action and planning: American pragmatism revisited, in Rydin, Y. and Thornley, A. (eds), *Planning in the UK: Agendas for the New Millennium*. Aldershot: Ashgate.

Campbell, K. and Cowan, R. (2002) *Re: Urbanism*. London: Urban Exchange.

Carey, J. (1995) *The Faber Book of Science*. London: Faber and Faber.

Carmona, M. (1998) Urban design and planning practice, in Greed, C. and Roberts, M. (eds), *Introducing Urban Design, Interventions and Responses*. Harlow: Longman.

Carmona, M. and Dann, J. (2007) Design codes, in *Urban Design*, 101: 16.

Carmona, M., Heath, T., Oc, T. and Tiesdell, S. (2003) *Public Places Urban Spaces: The Dimensions of Urban Design*. Oxford: Architectural Press.

Carmona, M., Marshall, S. and Stevens, Q. (2006) Design codes: their use and potential, in *Progress in Planning*, 65 (4): 209–289.

Carroll, S. B. (2006) *Endless Forms Most Beautiful: The New Science of Evo Devo and the Making of the Animal Kingdom*. London: Weidenfeld and Nicolson.

Caves, R. (ed.) (2005) *Encyclopedia of the City*. London and New York: Routledge.

Cervero, R. (1998) *The Transit Metropolis: A Global Inquiry*. Washington, DC: Island Press.

Cherry, G. E. (1988) *Cities and Plans: The Shaping of Urban Britain in the Nineteenth and Twentieth Centuries*. London: Arnold.

Chesterton, G. K. ([1904] 1996) *The Napoleon of Notting Hill*. Ware: Wordsworth Editions.

Choay, F. (1969) *The Modern City: Planning in the 19th Century*. New York: George Braziller.

Choay, F. (1997) *The Rule and the Model: On the Theory of Architecture and Urbanism*. Cambridge, Mass. and London: MIT Press.

Christaller, W. (1966) *Central Places in Southern Germany* (transl. from 1933 German edn, C. W. Baskin). Englewood Cliffs, N.J.: Prentice-Hall.

Clapson, M. (1998) *Invincible Green Suburbs, Brave New Towns*. Manchester: Manchester University Press.

Clark, C. (1958) Transport – maker and breaker of cities, in *The Town Planning Review*, 28 (4): 237–250.

Coates, P. S. (2006) A dynamic model of the growth of San'a, paper presented at SOLUTIONS seminar on Urban Structuring, London, June.

Cohen, J. and Stewart, I. (1994) *The Collapse of Chaos*. London: Penguin.

Coleman, A. (1985) *Utopia on Trial: Vision and Reality in Planned Housing*. London: H. Shipman.

Colin Buchanan and Partners (1968) The South Hampshire study, in Lewis, D. (ed.), *Urban Structure*, Architectural Yearbook 12. London: Elek Books.

Conzen, M.R.G. (1969) *Alnwick, Northumberland: A Study in Town Plan Analysis*. Publication no. 27. London: Institute of British Geographers.

Cook, P. (2004) On city objects, in Bogner, D. (ed.), *A Friendly Alien*. Ostfildern-Ruit: Hatje Kantz.

Cooke, C. (2000) Cities of socialism: technology and ideology in the Soviet Union in the 1920s, in Deckker, T. (ed.), *The Modern City Revisited*. London: Spon Press.

Corporation of the City of Glasgow (1972). *Roads in the Glasgow Area*. Glasgow: Corporation of the City of Glasgow.

Cotton, B. and Oliver, R. (1994) *The Cyberspace Lexicon*. London: Phaidon.

Coveney, P. and Highfield, R. (1995) *Frontiers of Complexity: The Search for Order in a Chaotic World*. London: Faber and Faber.

Cowan, R. (1995) *The Cities Design Forgot: A Manifesto*. London: Urban Initiatives.

Cowan, R. (1997) *The Connected City*. London: Urban Initiatives.

Cowan, R. (2002) *Urban Design Guidance: Urban Design Frameworks, Development Briefs and Master Plans*. London: Thomas Telford.

Cracraft, J. and Donaghue, M. (eds) (2004) *Assembling the Tree of Life*. New York: Oxford University Press.

Crouch, D. P. and Johnson, J. G. (2001) *Traditions in Architecture. Africa, America, Asia, and Oceania*. New York: Oxford University Press.

Cruickshank, D. (ed.) (1996) *Banister Fletcher's A History of Architecture* (20th edn). Oxford: Architectural Press.

Cullen, G. (1961) *Townscape*. London: Architectural Press.

Curl, J. S. (2005) *A Dictionary of Architecture*. Hoo: Grange Books.

Czarnowski, T. V. (1978) The street as a communications artefact, in Anderson, S. (ed.), *On Streets*. Cambridge, Mass.: MIT Press.

Dargahi, N. and Bremer, N. (1995) *Sim City 2000: Power, Politics and Planning*. Rocklin, CA: Prima Publishing.

Darwin, C. (1859) *The Origin of Species by means of Natural Selection, or The Preservation of Favoured Races in the Struggle for Life*. John Murray. London: Penguin Classics, 1995.

Davis, M. (2006) *Planet of Slums*. London and New York: Verso.

Dawkins, R. (1991) *The Blind Watchmaker*. Harmondsworth: Penguin.

Dawkins, R. (1997) *Climbing Mount Improbable*. Harmondsworth: Penguin.

Dawkins, R. ([1982] 1999) *The Extended Phenotype*. Oxford: Oxford University Press.

Dawkins, R. (2004) *The Ancestor's Tale: A Pilgimage to the Dawn of Life*. London: Phoenix.

Dawkins, R. ([1976] 2006) *The Selfish Gene*. Oxford: Oxford University Press.

de Botton, A. (2006) *The Architecture of Happiness*. London: Hamish Hamilton.

Deckker, S. (1998) *Mews Style*. London: Quiller Press.

Deckker, T. (2000) Brasilia: city versus landscape, in Deckker, T. (ed.), *The Modern City Revisited*. London: Spon Press.

Defries, A. (1928) *The Interpreter Geddes: The Man and His Gospel*. New York: Boni and Liveright.

Dench, G. (1998) *Transforming Men: Changing Patterns of Dependency and Dominance in Gender Relations*. New Brunswick and London: Transaction Publishers.

Dennett, D. (1996) *Darwin's Dangerous Idea: Evolution and the Meanings of Life*. Harmondsworth: Penguin.

Diamond, J. (1998) *Guns, Germs and Steel: A Short History of Everybody for the Last 13,000 Years*. London: Vintage.

Diamond, J. (2001) Foreword, in Mayr, E., *What Evolution Is*. New York: Basic Books.

Diappi, L. (ed.) (2004) *Evolving Cities: Geocomputation in Territorial Planning*. Aldershot: Ashgate.

Dickinson, R. E. (1961) *The West European City: A Geographical Interpretation* (2nd edn). London: Routledge and Kegan Paul.

Dixon, D. (1998) *After Man: A Zoology of the Future*. New York: St Martin's Griffin.

Dobzhansky, T. (1973) Nothing in biology makes sense except in the light of evolution, in *American Biology Teacher* (March), 35: 125–129.

Dodge, M. and Kitchin, R. (2001) *Atlas of Cyberspace*. Harlow: Addison-Wesley.

Douglas, K. (2006) Are we still evolving? in *New Scientist*, 2542 (11 March).

Duany, A. and Plater-Zyberk, E. (1994) The neighborhood, the district and the corridor, in Katz, P., *The New Urbanism: Toward an Architecture of Community*. New York: McGraw-Hill.

Duany, A. and Talen, E. (2002) Transect planning, in *Journal of the American Planning Association*, 68 (3): 245–266.

Dunnett, J. (2000) Le Corbusier and the city without streets, in Deckker, T. (ed.), *The Modern City Revisited*. London: Spon Press.

Dutton, J. A. (2000) *New American Urbanism: Re-forming the Suburban Metropolis*. Milan: Skira.

Dyson, G. (1998) *Darwin among the Machines*. London: Allen Lane.

Dyson, F. (1998) The evolution of science, in Fabian, A. C. (ed.), *Evolution: Society, Science and the Universe*. Cambridge: Cambridge University Press.

East Kilbride Development Corporation (1987) *East Kilbride: A Story of Success*. East Kilbride: East Kilbride Development Corporation.

Eaton, R. (2002) *Ideal Cities: Utopianism and the (Un)Built Environment*. London: Thames and Hudson.

Edwards, B. (1994) Alexander Thomson and the Glasgow improvement scheme, in Stamp, G. and McKinstry, S. (eds), *'Greek' Thomson*. Edinburgh: Edinburgh University Press.

Ellin, N. (1996) *Postmodern Urbanism*. Cambridge, Mass.: Blackwell.

Elliott, C. (1998) The earthly city, in Freestone, R. (ed.), *The Twentieth Century Urban Planning Experience*, Proceedings of the 8th International Planning History Society Conference and 4th Australian Planning/Urban History Conference, University of New South Wales, Sydney (July 1998), 166–171.

Engwicht, D. (1999) *Street Reclaiming: Creating Livable Streets and Vibrant Communities*. Gabriola Island, British Columbia: New Society Publishers.

Erickson, B. (2001) The 'armature' and 'fabric' as a model for understanding spatial organisation, in Roberts, M. and Greed, C. (eds), *Approaching Urban Design: The Design Process*. Harlow: Longman.

Erickson, B. and Lloyd-Jones, T. (1997) Experiments with settlement aggregation models, in *Environment and Planning B: Planning and Design*, 24: 903–928.

Evers, B. (2003) Preface, in *Architectural Theory: From the Renaissance to the Present*. Cologne: Taschen.

Farkas, I., Helbing, D. and Vicsek, T. (2002) Mexican waves in an excitable medium, in *Nature*, 419 (12 September): 131–132.

Fawcett, C. B. (1944) *A Residential Unit for Town and Country Planning*. Bickley: University of London Press.

Fernández-Armesto, F. (2000) *Civilizations*. London: Macmillan.

Fletcher, B. (1921) *A History of Architecture: On the Comparative Method* (6th edn). London: B. T. Batsford.

Forshaw, J. H. and Abercrombie, P. (1943) *County of London Plan*. London: Macmillan & Co. Ltd.

Fournier, C. (2004) On technological mutations, in Bogner, D. (ed.), *A Friendly Alien*. Ostfildern-Ruit: Hatje Kantz.

Frankhauser, P. and Tannier, C. (2005) A multi-scale morphological approach for delimiting urban areas, paper presented at 9th Computers in Urban Planning and Urban Management conference (CUPUM '05), University College London, July 2005.

Freigang, C. (2003a) François Blondel, in *Architectural Theory: From the Renaissance to the Present*. Cologne: Taschen.

Freigang, C. (2003b) Marc-Antoine Laugier in *Architectural Theory. From the Renaissance to the Present*. Cologne: Taschen.

Frey, H. (1999) *Designing the City*. London: Spon.

Friedman, A. (1998) Design for change: flexible planning strategies for the 1990s and beyond, in *Journal of Urban Design*, 2 (3): 277–296.

Friedmann, J. (2003) Toward a non-Euclidian mode of planning, in Campbell, S. and Fainstein, S. S. (eds), *Readings in Planning Theory* (2nd edn). Cambridge, Mass.: Blackwell.

Futuyma, D. J. (2005) *Evolution*. Sunderland, Mass.: Sinauer Associates.

Fyfe, N. (ed.) (1998) *Images of the Street: Planning, Identity, and Control in Public Space*. London: Routledge.

Garde, A. (2006) Designing and developing New Urbanist projects in the United States: insights and implications, in *Journal of Urban Design*, 11 (1): 33–54.

Garreau, J. (1992) *Edge City: Life on the New Frontier*. London: Anchor Books.

Geddes, P. and Thomson, J. A. (1889) *The Evolution of Sex*. London: Walter Scott.

Geddes, P. and Thomson, J. A. (1911) *Evolution*. London: Williams and Norgate.

Geddes, P. (1915) *Cities in Evolution: An Introduction to the Town Planning Movement and to the Study of Civics*. London: Williams & Norgate.

Geddes, P. ([1915] 1949) *Cities in Evolution* (new and rev edn). London: William and Norgate.

Gehl, J. (2001) *Life between Buildings: Using Public Space* (5th edn), transl. Jo Koch. Copenhagen: Danish Architectural Press.

Gibberd, F. (1962) *Town Design* (4th edn). London: The Architectural Press.

Gibberd, F. (1967) *Town Design* (5th edn). London: The Architectural Press.

Girard, G. and Lambot, I. (1999) City *of Darkness: Life in Kowloon Walled City*. Haslemere: Watermark Publications.

Golany, G. S. and Ojima, T. (1996) *Geo-Space Urban Design*. New York: John Wiley and Sons.

Gold, J. (2000) Towards the functional city? MARS, CIAM and the London plans 1933–42, in Deckker, T. (ed.), *The Modern City Revisited*. London: Spon Press.

Gold, J. R. (1997) *The Experience of Modernism: Modern Architects and the Future City, 1928–53*. London: E. & F. N. Spon.

Gold, J. R. (2006) The making of a megastructure: architectural modernism, town planning and Cumbernauld Central Area, in *Planning Perspectives*, 21(3): 109–131.

Gonzalez, M. D. (1998) Translator's note, in LeGates, R. and Stout, F. (eds), *Selected Essays*, Early Urban Planning Series. London: Routledge/Thoemmes Press.

Goodman, J., Heckerman, D. and Rounthwaite, R. (2005) Stopping spam, in *Scientific American*, 292 (4): 24–31.

Gordon, G. (1984) The shaping of urban morphology, in Reeder, D. (ed.), *Urban History Yearbook 1984*. Leicester: Leicester University Press.

Gordon, J. E. (1978) *Structures – or Why Things Don't Fall Down*. Harmondsworth: Penguin.

Gosling, D. (1996). *Gordon Cullen: Visions of Urban Design*. London: Academy Editions.

Gosling, D. and Maitland, B. (1984) *Concepts of Urban Design*. London: Academy Editions.

Gould, J. L. and Gould, C. G. (2007) *Animal Architects: Building and the Evolution of Intelligence*. New York: Basic Books.

Graham, S. and Marvin, S. (1996) *Telecommunications and the City*. London: Routledge.

Grande, L. and Rieppel, O. (eds) (1994) *Interpreting the Hierarchy of Nature: From Systematic Patterns to Evolutionary Process Theories*. San Diego: Academic Press.

Grant, J. (2006) *Planning the Good Community: New Urbanism in Theory and Practice*. London and New York: Routledge.

Greed, C. H. (1993) *Introducing Town Planning*. Harlow: Longman Scientific and Technical.

Greed, C. (1998) Design and designers revisited, in Greed, C. and Roberts, M. (eds), *Introducing Urban Design: Interventions and Responses*. London: Addison-Wesley Longman.

Greed, C. (2000) *Introducing Planning*. London and New Brunswick: Athlone Press.

Green, N. (1999) Art and complexity in London's East End, in *Complexity*, 4 (6): 14–21.

Green, N. (2005) Did Mumford misunderstand Mendel? in *Planning History*, 27 (3): 2–3.

Greenberg, K. (2000) Preservation and renewal of historic buildings, districts, and landscapes affirm the continuity and evolution of urban society, in Leccese, M. and McCormick, K. (eds), *Charter of the New Urbanism*. New York: McGraw-Hill.

Gribbin, J. (2005) *Deep Simplicity: Chaos, Complexity and the Emergence of Life*. London: Penguin.

Grönert, A. (2003) Francesco Milizia and Giovanni Battista Cipriani, in *Architectural Theory: From the Renaissance to the Present*. Cologne: Taschen.

Hacking, I. (1983) *Representing and Intervening: Introductory Topics in the Philosophy of Natural Science*. Cambridge: Cambridge University Press.

Hakim, B.S. (2001) Julian of Ascalon's Treatise of construction and design rules from sixth-century Palestine, in *Journal of the Society of Architectural Historians*, 60 (1): 4–25.

Halder, G., Callaerts, P. and Gehring, W. J. (1995) Induction of ectopic eyes by targeted expression of the eyeless gene in Drosophila, in *Science*, 267 (5205): 1788–1792.

Hall, P. (1988) *Cities of Tomorrow*. Oxford: Blackwell.

Hall, P. (1995) Bringing Abercrombie back from the shades: a look forward and back, in *Town Planning Review*, 66 (3): 227–241.

Hall, P. (1999) *Cities in Civilization: Culture, Innovation and Urban Order*. London: Phoenix Giant.

Hall, P. (2002) *Urban & Regional Planning* (4th edn). London and New York: Routledge.

Hansell, M. (2005) *Animal Architecture*. Oxford: Oxford University Press.

Hansell, M. (2007) *Built by Animals: The Natural History of Animal Architecture*. Oxford: Oxford University Press.

Hanson, B. and Younés, S. (2001) Reuniting urban form and urban process: the Prince of Wales's urban design task force, in *Journal of Urban Design*, 6 (2): 185–209.

Hanson, J. (1998) *Decoding Homes and Houses*. Cambridge: Cambridge University Press.

Hardin, G. (1968) The tragedy of the commons, in *Science*, 162: 1243–1248.

Hardy, D. (1991) *From Garden Cities to New Towns: Campaigning for Town and Country Planning, 1899–1946*. London: Chapman Hall.

Hardy, D. (2006) *Poundbury: The Town That Charles Built*. London: TCPA.

Hauman, H. W. (1984) *Neighborhoods: Their Place in Urban Life*. Beverly Hills: Sage.

Hawking, S. W. (1988) *A Brief History of Time: From the Big Bang to Black Holes*. London: Bantam.

Hayward, R. and McGlynn, S. (eds) (1993) *Making Better Places: Urban Design Now*. Oxford: Butterworth Architecture.

Hebbert, M. (1993) The City of London walkway experiment, in *Journal of the American Planning Association*, 59 (4): 433–450.

Hebbert, M. (1998a) *London. More by Fortune than Design*. Chichester: John Wiley & Son.

Hebbert, M. (1998b) *To-morrow* never came – or did it? in *Town and Country Planning*, Special supplement.

Hebbert, M. (2003) New Urbanism: the movement in context, in *Built Environment*, 29 (3): 193–209.

Hebbert, M. (2005a) Engineering, urbanism and the struggle for street design, in *Journal of Urban Design*, 10 (1): 39–59.

Hebbert, M. (2005b) The street as locus of collective memory, in *Environment and Planning D*, 23 (4): 581–596.

Higgott, A. (2000) Birmingham: building the modern city, in Deckker, T. (ed.) *The Modern City Revisited*. London: Spon Press.

Hilberseimer, L. (1944) *The New City. Principles of Planning*. Chicago: Paul Theobold.

Hill, D. (1996) *A History of Engineering in Classical and Medieval Times*. London: Routledge.

Hillier, B. (1996) *Space is the Machine*. Cambridge: Cambridge University Press.

Hillier, B. and Hanson, J. (1984) *The Social Logic of Space*. Cambridge: Cambridge University Press.

Hobbes, T. (1651) *Leviathan. Or the Matter, Forme & Power of a Common-wealth Ecclesiastical and Civill*. London, Printed for Andrew Crooke, at the Dragon in St. Pauls Church-yard. Modern edition (1968) ed. C. B. Macpherson. London: Penguin.

Hodder, I. (2005) Women and men in Çatalhöyük, in *Scientific American*, 15 (1): 34–41.

Holgate, A. (1986) *The Art in Structural Design*. Oxford: Clarendon Press.

Holland, J. (1995) *Hidden Order: How Adaptation Builds Complexity*. Reading, Mass.: Addison-Wesley.

Holzman, D. (2007) Modern times causing human evolution to accelerate, in *New Scientist*, 2634 (14 December).

Hopkins, K. (1999) *A World Full of Gods: Pagans, Jews and Christians in the Roman Empire*. London: Weidenfeld and Nicolson.

Houghton, G. and Hunter, C. (1994) *Sustainable Cities*. London: Jessica Kingsley.

Houghton-Evans, W. (1975) *Planning Cities: Legacy and Portent*. London: Lawrence and Wishart.

Houghton-Evans, W. (1978) *Architecture and Urban Design*. Lancaster: The Construction Press.

Howard, E. (1904) *Tomorrow: A Peaceful Path to Real Reform*, reprinted as Volume 2 of LeGates, R. and Stout, F. (eds) (1998) Early Urban Planning series, London: Routledge/Thoemmes Press.

Hrdy, S. B. (1999) *Mother Nature: Natural Selection and the Female of the Species*. London: Chatto & Windus.

Ingold, T. (1998) The evolution of society, in Fabian, A. C. (ed.), *Evolution: Society, Science and the Universe*. Cambridge: Cambridge University Press.

Jablonka, E. (2000) Lamarckian inheritance systems in biology: a source of metaphors and models in technological evolution, in Ziman, J. (ed.), *Technological Innovation as an Evolutionary Process*. Cambridge: Cambridge University Press.

Jablonka, E. and Ziman, J. (2000) Biological evolution: processes and phenomena, in Ziman, J. (ed.), *Technological Innovation as an Evolutionary Process*. Cambridge: Cambridge University Press.

Jacobs, A. (1993) *Great Streets*. Cambridge (Mass.): MIT Press.

Jacobs, A. and Appleyard, D. (1987) Towards an urban design manifesto, in *Journal of the American Planning Association*, 53 (1): 112–120.

Jacobs, A. B., Macdonald, E. and Rofé, Y. (2002) *The Boulevard Book: History, Evolution, Design of Multiway Boulevards*. Cambridge, Mass.: MIT Press.

Jacobs, J. (1962) *The Death and Life of Great American Cities*. London: Jonathan Cape.

Jacobs, J. (1965) *The Death and Life of Great American Cities*. London: Pelican.

Jacobs, M. (2000) *Multinodal Urban Structures: A Comparative Analysis and Strategies for Design*. Delft: Delft University Press.

Jefferson, C., Rowe, J. and Brebbia, C. (eds) (2001) *The Sustainable Street: The Environmental, Human and Economic Aspects of Street Design and Management*. Southampton and Boston: Wessex Institute of Technology Press.

Jellicoe, G. A. (1961) *Motopia: A Study in the Evolution of Urban Landscape*. London: Studio Books.

Jencks, C. (1981) *The Language of Post-modern Architecture* (3rd edn). London: Academy Editions.

Jencks, C. (1987) *Post-Modernism: The New Classicism in Art and Architecture*. London: Academy Editions.

Jencks, C. (1995) *The Architecture of the Jumping Universe: A Polemic: How Complexity Science is Changing Architecture and Culture*. London: Academy Editions.

Jencks, C. (1997a) Introduction, in Jencks, C. (ed.), *New Science = New Architecture?* London: Academy Editions.

Jencks, C. (ed.) (1997b) *New Science = New Architecture?* London: Academy Editions.

Jenkins, M. (1999) *Evolution*. London: Hodder Headline/Teach Yourself Books.

Jo, S. (1998) Spatial configuration and built form, in *Journal of Urban Design*, 3 (3): 285–302.

Jobst, C. (2003a) Fra Giovanni Giocondo da Verona, in *Architectural Theory: From the Renaissance to the Present*. Cologne: Taschen.

Jobst, C. (2003b) Pietro Cataneo, in *Architectural Theory: From the Renaissance to the Present*. Cologne: Taschen.

Johnson, D. L. and Langmead, D. (1997) *Makers of 20th Century Modern Architecture: A Bio-critical Sourcebook*. London: Fitzroy Dearborn.

Johnson, S. (2001) *Emergence: The Connected Lives of Ants, Brains, Cities and Software*. London: Penguin.

Johnson-Marshall, P. (1966) *Rebuilding Cities*. Edinburgh: Edinburgh University Press.

Jones, S. (1999) *Almost Like a Whale: The Origin of Species Updated*. London: Black Swan.

Jordison, S. and Kieran, D. (eds) (2003) *The Idler Book of Crap Towns*. London: Boxtree.

Katz, P. (1994) *The New Urbanism: Toward an Architecture of Community*. New York: McGraw-Hill.

Kauffman, S. A. (1993) *The Origins of Order: Self-Organization and Selection in Evolution*. New York and Oxford: Oxford University Press.

Keeble, L. (1969) *Principles and Practice of Town Planning* (4th edn). London: The Estates Gazette Limited.

Kenoyer, J. M. (2005) Uncovering the keys to the Lost Indus Cities, in *Scientific American*, 15 (1): 24–33.

Kitchen, P. (1975) *A Most Unsettling Person: An Introduction to the Ideas and Life of Patrick Geddes*. London: Victor Gollancz.

Kolson, K. (2001) *Big Plans: The Allure and Folly of Urban Design*. Baltimore and London: Johns Hopkins University Press.

Koolhaas, R. (2005) *Atlanta*, in El-Khoury, R. and Robbins, E. (eds), *Shaping the City*. London: Routledge.

Korn, A. (1953) *History Builds the Town*. London: Lund Humphries.

Kostof, S. (1991) *The City Shaped: Urban Patterns and Meanings through History*. London: Thames and Hudson.

Kostof, S. (1992) *The City Assembled: The Elements of Urban Form throughout History*. London: Thames and Hudson.

Kotkin, J. (2005) *The City: A Global History*. London: Weidenfeld and Nicolson.

Kreiger, A. and Lennertz, W. (1991) *Andres Duany and Elizabeth Plater-Zyberk: Towns and Town-Making Principles*. New York: Rizzoli International Publications.

Krier, L. (1993a) Poundbury Masterplan, in *New Practice in Urban Design* (Architectural Design series). London: Academy Editions.

Krier, L. (1993b) Poundbury, Dorset, in *Architecture in Arcadia* (Architectural Design series). London: Academy Editions.

Kriesis, A. (1958) Ancient Greek town building, in *Urbanism and Town Planning*. Proceedings of the 2nd International Congress of Classical Studies, Volume IV. Copenhagen: Ejnar Munksgaard.

Krugman, P. R. (1996) *The Self-Organizing Economy*. Cambridge, Mass.: Blackwell Publishers.

Kubler, G. (1962) *The Shape of Time: Remarks on the History of Things*. New Haven; London: Yale University Press.

Kuhn, T. (1970) *The Structure of Scientific Revolutions* (2nd edn). Chicago: University of Chicago Press.

Ladyman, J. (2002) *Understanding Philosophy of Science*. London: Routledge.

Lang, J. (1994) *Urban Design: The American Experience*. New York: Van Nostrand Reinhold.

Larkham, P. J. (2006) The study of urban form in Great Britain, in *Urban Morphology*, 10 (2): 117–150.

Larkham, P.J. and Jones, A. N. (1991) *A Glossary of Urban Form*. Historical Geography Research Series no.26. London: Institute of British Geographers.

Lauwerier, H. (1991) *Fractals*. London: Penguin.

Lavin, I. (1993) Picasso's bull(s): art history in reverse, in *Art in America*, 81 (3): 76–93.

Le Corbusier (1929) *The City of To-morrow and its Planning* [English edn, transl. from 8th French edn, *Urbanisme*]. London: John Rodker.

Le Corbusier ([1933] 1964) *The Radiant City*. London: Faber and Faber.

Le Corbusier (1947a) *Concerning Town Planning* (*Propos d'Urbanisme*). London: The Architectural Press.

Le Corbusier (1947b) *When the Cathedrals Were White: A Journey to the Country of Timid People*. London: Routledge.

Le Corbusier (1951) *The Modulor: A Harmonious Measure to the Human Scale Universally Applicable to Architecture and Mechanics*. London: Faber and Faber.

Le Corbusier (1960) *My Work*. London: Architectural Press.

Le Corbusier (1973 [1943]) *The Athens Charter*. New York: Grossman Publishers.

Leccese, M. and McCormick, K. (eds) (2000) *Charter of the New Urbanism*. New York: McGraw-Hill.

LeGates, R. and Stout, F. (1998) Editors' Introduction, in LeGates, R. and Stout, F. (eds), *Selected Essays*, Early Urban Planning Series. London: Routledge/Thoemmes Press.

Levitas, G. (1978) Anthropology and sociology of streets, in Anderson, S. (ed.), *On Streets*. Cambridge, Mass.: MIT Press.

Levy, S. (1993). *Artificial Life: The Quest for a New Creation*. Harmondsworth: Penguin.

Lewontin, R. (2000) *The Triple Helix: Gene, Organism, and Environment*. Cambridge, Mass. and London: Harvard University Press.

Lillebye, E. (2001) The architectural significance of the street as a functional and social arena, in Jefferson, C., Rowe, J. and Brebbia, C. (eds), *The Sustainable Street: The Environmental, Human and Economic Aspects of Street Design and Management*. Southampton and Boston: Wessex Institute of Technology Press.

Lima, A. I. (2003) *Soleri: Architecture as Human Ecology*. New York: The Monacelli Press.

Lin, Z.-J. (2007) From megastructure to megalopolis: formation and transformation of mega-projects in Tokyo Bay, in *Journal of Urban Design*, 12 (1): 73–92.

Llewelyn-Davies, R. (2000) *Urban Design Compendium*. Prepared in association with Alan Baxter and Associates for English Partnerships and the Housing Corporation. London: English Partnerships.

Llewelyn-Davies Weeks Forestier-Walker and Bor, and Ove Arup and Partners (1971) *Motorways in the Urban Environment*. London: British Road Federation.

Llewelyn-Davies, R. (1968) Town design, in Lewis, D. (ed.), *Urban Structure*, Architectural Yearbook 12, London: Elek Books.

Lloyd-Jones, T. (1998) The scope of urban design, in Greed, C. and Roberts, M. (eds.), *Introducing Urban Design: Interventions and Responses*. London: Addison-Wesley Longman.

Loasby, B. J. (2002) The evolution of technological knowledge: reflections on 'Technical Innovation as an Evolutionary Process', in Wheeler, M., Ziman, J. and Boden, M. A. (eds) (2002) *The Evolution of Cultural Entities*. Proceedings of the British Academy. Oxford: Oxford University Press.

Lock, D. (1994) The long view, in *New Towns* (Architectural Design series). London: Academy Editions.

Lynch, K. (1981) *Good City Form*. Cambridge, Mass.: MIT Press.

Lynch, K. (1990) *City Sense and City Design: Writings and Projects of Kevin Lynch*, ed. Banerjee, T. and Southworth, M. Cambridge, Mass.: MIT Press.

Lynch, M. (2007) *The Origins of Genome Architecture*. Sunderland, Mass.: Sinauer Associates, Inc.

MacCormac, R. (1996) An anatomy of London, in *Built Environment*, 22 (4): 306–311.

Macpherson, C. B. (1968) Introduction, in Hobbes, T. (1651) *Leviathan. Or the Matter, Forme & Power of a Common-wealth Ecclesiastical and Civill*. London, Printed for Andrew Crooke, at the Dragon in St. Pauls Church-yard, ed. C. B. Macpherson, London: Penguin.

McKean, C. (1996) The incivility of Edinburgh's New Town, in Brogden, W. A. (ed.), *The Neo-Classical Town, Scottish Contributions to Urban Design since 1750*. Edinburgh: The Rutland Press.

McKean, J. (1994) Thomson's city, in Stamp, G. and McKinstry, S. (eds), *'Greek' Thomson*. Edinburgh: Edinburgh University Press.

Madanipour, A. (1996) *The Design of Urban Space: An Inquiry into a Socio-spatial Process*. Chichester: John Wiley and Sons.

Madanipour, A. (2006) Roles and challenges of urban design, in *Journal of Urban Design*, 11 (2): 173–193.

Mainstone, R. (1975) *Developments in Structural Form*. Harmondsworth: Penguin/ Allen Lane.

Mairet, P. (1957) *Pioneer of Sociology: The Life and Letters of Patrick Geddes*. London: Lund Humphries.

Mandelbrot, B. (1983) *The Fractal Geometry of Nature* (updated and aug. edn). New York: W. H. Freeman and Company.

Manguel, A. and Guadalupi, G. (1999) *The Dictionary of Imaginary Places*. London: Bloomsbury.

March, L. (1998) [8 + (6) + 11] = 25 + x, in *Environment and Planning B: Planning and Design*, 25 (Anniversary Issue): 10–19.

March, L. and Steadman, J. P. (1971) *The Geometry of Environment: An Introduction to Spatial Organization in Design*. London: RIBA Publications.

Markus, T. A. (1999) Comprehensive development and housing, 1945–1975, in Reed, P. (ed.), *Glasgow: The Forming of the City*. Edinburgh: Edinburgh University Press.

Marshall, A. (2000) *How Cities Work: Suburbs, Sprawl and the Road Not Taken*. Austin: University of Texas Press.

Marshall, S. (1998) The evolution of transport networks with urban structure and possibilities for postmodern settlement design, in Freestone, R. (ed.), *The Twentieth Century Urban Planning Experience*, Proceedings of the 8th International Planning History Society Conference and 4th Australian Planning/Urban History Conference, University of New South Wales, Sydney (July 1998), 598–603.

Marshall, S. (2001) Alienated by the Planning of Science City, in *Alien Times*, 15 (9): Japan.

Marshall, S. (2003) Transport and the urban pattern, in *Town and Country Planning*, 73 (2): 106–108.

Marshall, S. (2005) *Streets and Patterns*. London and New York: Spon Press.

Marshall, S. (2006a) Living in new towns: from Utopia to Knowhere, in Buonfino, A. and Mulgan, G. (eds), *Porcupines in Winter: The Pleasures and Pains of Living Together in Modern Britain*. London: The Young Foundation.

Marshall, S. (2006b) The emerging 'Silicon Savanna': from Old Urbanism to New Suburbanism, in *Built Environment*, 32 (3): 267–280.

Marshall, S. (ed.) (2003) New Urbanism in *Built Environment*, 29 (3).

Marshall, S. (ed.) (forthcoming) *Urban Coding and Planning*. London and New York: Routledge.

Martin, D. T. (1999) Conservation and restoration, in Reed, P. (ed.), *Glasgow: The Forming of the City*. Edinburgh: Edinburgh University Press.

Martin, L., March, L. and others [*sic*] (1972) Speculations, in Martin, L. and March, L. (eds), *Urban Space and Structures*. Cambridge: Cambridge University Press.

Maynard Smith, J. and Szathmáry, E. (1997) *The Major Transitions in Evolution*. Oxford: Oxford University Press.

Mayr, E. (2001) *What Evolution Is*. New York: Basic Books.

Meller, H. (1980) Cities and evolution: Patrick Geddes as an international prophet of town planning before 1914, in Sutcliffe, A. (ed.), *The Rise of Modern Urban Planning 1800–1914*. London: Mansell.

Meller, H. (1990) *Patrick Geddes: Social Evolutionist and City Planner*. London: Routledge.

Mindell, D. P. (2006) *The Evolving World: Evolution in Everyday Life*. Cambridge, Mass. and London: Harvard University Press.

Mitchell, W. J. (1990) *The Logic of Architecture: Design, Computation, and Cognition*. Cambridge, Mass.: MIT Press.

Moholy-Nagy, S. (1968) *Matrix of Man: An Illustrated History of Urban Environment*. London: Pall Mall Press.

More, T. (2003) *Utopia*, ed. Turner, P. London: Penguin.

Morris, A. E. J. (1994) *History of Urban Form: Before the Industrial Revolutions* (3rd edn). Harlow: Longman Scientific and Technical.

Ministry of Transport (MoT) (1963) *Traffic in Towns*. London: HMSO.

Moudon, A. V. (1994) Getting to know the built landscape: typomorphology, in Franck, K. and Schneekloth, L. (eds), *Ordering Space: Types in Architecture and Design*. New York: Van Nostrand Reinhold.

Moudon, A. V. (1997) Urban morphology as an emerging interdisciplinary field, in *Urban Morphology*, 1: 3–10.

Moudon, A. V. (ed.) (1987) *Public Streets for Public Use*. New York: Van Nostrand Co.

Moughtin, J. C. (1992) *Urban Design: Street and Square*. Oxford: Butterworth Architecture.

Mumford, L. (1938) *The Culture of Cities*. New York: Harcourt, Brace & World, Inc.

Mumford, L. (1961) *The City in History: Its Origins, its Transformations, and its Prospects*. San Diego: Harcourt, Brace and Company.

Nakamura, T. (ed.) (1989) *Peter Cook, 1961–1989*. Tokyo: A & U Publishing.

Neal, P. (ed.) (2003) *Urban Villages and the Making of Communities*. London and New York: Spon Press.

Newman, P. and Kenworthy, J. (1999) *Sustainability and Cities. Overcoming Automobile Dependence*. Washington, DC: Island Press.

Nicholl, C. (2005) *Leonardo da Vinci: The Flights of the Mind*. London: Penguin.

Noirot, C. and Darlington, J. P. E. C. (2000) Termite nests: architecture, regulation and defence, in Abe, T., Bignell, D. E. and Higashi, M. (eds), *Termites: Evolution, Sociality, Symbioses, Ecology*. Dordrecht: Kluwer Academic Press.

Oc, T. and Tiesdell, S. (1997) *Safer City Centres: Reviving the Public Realm*. London: Paul Chapman.

Opher, P. and Bird, C. (1980) *Cumbernauld. Irvine. East Kilbride: An Illustrated Guide*. Oxford: Oxford Polytechnic.

Osborn, F. J. and Whittick, A. (1969) *The New Towns: The Answer to Megalopolis*. London: Leonard Hill.

Owens, E. J. (1991) *The City in the Greek and Roman World*. London and New York: London.

Oxford University Press (1995) *The Oxford Companion to Philosophy*. Oxford: Oxford University Press.

Ozeki, M., Isagi, Y., Tsubota, H., Jacklyn, P. and Bowman, R. M. J. S. (2007) Phylogeography of an Australian termite, *Amitermes laurensis* (Isoptera, Termitidae), with special reference to the variety of mound shapes, in *Molecular Phylogenetics and Evolution*, 41 (1): 236–247.

Palen, J. J. (1995) *The Suburbs*, New York: McGraw-Hill.

Panerai, P., Castex, J., Depaule, J.C. and Samuels, I. (2004) *Urban Forms: The Death and Life of the Urban Block*. English-language edn of *Formes urbaines, de l'îlot a la barre*. Oxford: Architectural Press.

Parfect, M. and Power, G. (1997) *Planning for Urban Quality: Urban Design in Towns and Cities*. London and New York: Routledge.

Parr, M. (1999) *Boring Postcards*. London and New York: Phaidon.

Paul, J. (2003) Tony Garnier, in *Architectural Theory: From the Renaissance to the Present*. Cologne: Taschen.

Pearson, B. (2006) New towns: can they be given a new life? in *The Herald*, 4 April.

Perkins, D. (2000) The evolution of adaptive form, in Ziman, J. (ed.), *Technological Innovation as an Evolutionary Process*. Cambridge: Cambridge University Press.

Peterlin, M. (2005a) Emergent Patterns in Urban Form, paper presented at 9th Computers in Urban Planning and Urban Management conference (CUPUM '05), University College London, July 2005.

Peterlin, M. (2005b) Design of Processes, paper presented at Design out of Complexity Workshop, University College London, July 2005.

Pincock, S. (2006) Biology fights computer viruses, in *The Scientist*, 20 (7): 20–21.

Pinker, S. (1999) *How the Mind Works*. London: Penguin.

Porter, R. (1994) *London: A Social History*. London: Penguin Books.

Prince of Wales (1984) A speech by HRH The Prince of Wales at the 150th anniversary of the Royal Institute of British Architects (RIBA), Royal Gala Evening at Hampton Court Palace <www.princeofwales.gov.uk/speechesandarticles/a_speech_by_hrh_the_prince_of_wales_at_the_150th_anniversary_1876801621.html> 14.05.07

Prince of Wales (1989) *A Vision of Britain: A Personal View of Architecture*. London: Doubleday.

Pryor, F. (2004) *Britain B.C.* London: Harper Perennial.

Pumain, D. (2004) An evolutionary approach to settlement systems, in Champion, T. and Hugo, G. (eds), *New Forms of Urbanization: Beyond the Urban–Rural Dichotomy*. Aldershot and Burlington: Ashgate.

Punter, J. and Carmona, M. (1997) *The Design Dimension of Planning*. London: E & FN Spon.

Ramírez, J. A. (2000) *The Beehive Metaphor: From Gaudí to Le Corbusier*. London: Reaktion Books.

Rapoport, A. (1977) *Human Aspects of Urban Form: Towards a Man-environment Approach to Urban Form and Design*. Oxford: Pergamon.

Rapoport, A. (1987) Pedestrian street use: culture and perception, in Moudon, A. V. (ed.), *Public Streets for Public Use*. New York: Van Nostrand Reinhold.

Reed, P. (1996) The breaking of the grid: Glasgow's West End, in Brogden, W. A. (ed.), *The Neo-Classical Town, Scottish Contributions to Urban Design since 1750*. Edinburgh: The Rutland Press.

Reed, P. (1999a) The forming of the city, in Reed, P. (ed.), *Glasgow: The Forming of the City*. Edinburgh: Edinburgh University Press.

Reed, P. (1999b) The Victorian suburb, in Reed, P. (ed.), *Glasgow: The Forming of the City*. Edinburgh: Edinburgh University Press.

Reed, P. (1999c) The tenement city, in Reed, P. (ed.), *Glasgow: The Forming of the City*. Edinburgh: Edinburgh University Press.

Reed, P. (1999d) The post-industrial city? in Reed, P. (ed.), *Glasgow: The Forming of the City*. Edinburgh: Edinburgh University Press.

Reps, J. W. (1965) *The Making of Urban America: A History of City Planning in the United States*. Princeton: Princeton University Press.

Resnick, M. (1997) *Turtles, Termites, and Traffic Jams: Explorations in Massively Parallel Microworlds*. Cambridge, Mass.: MIT Press.

Richards, B. (1969) *New Movement in Cities*. London: Studio Vista.

Richardson, J. (2000) *The Annals of London: A Year-by-Year Record of a Thousand Years of History*. London: Cassell.

Richter, I. A. (ed.) (1952) *The Notebooks of Leonardo da Vinci*. Oxford: Oxford University Press.

Ridley, M. (2004) *Evolution* (3rd edn). Malden, Mass.: Blackwell Science.

Ritter, P. (1964) *Planning for Man and Motor*. Oxford: Pergamon Press.

Robbins, E. (2000) The New Urbanism and the fallacy of singularity, in *Urban Design International*, 3 (1 & 2): 33–42.

Roberts, M. and Lloyd-Jones, T. (2001) Urban generators, in Roberts, M. and Greed, C. (eds), *Approaching Urban Design: The Design Process*. Harlow: Longman.

Roberts, M., Lloyd-Jones, T., Erickson, B. and Nice, S. (1999) Place and space in the networked city: conceptualising the integrated metropolis, in *Journal of Urban Design*, 4, (1): 51–66.

Rogers, R. (1998) The evolution of London, in Fabian, A. C. (ed.), (1998) *Evolution: Society, Science and the Universe*. Cambridge: Cambridge University Press.

Rossi, A. (1982) *The Architecture of the City*. Cambridge, Mass.: MIT Press.

Rossi, A. (2003) The urban artifact as a work of art, in Cuthbert, A. R. (ed.), *Designing Cities: Critical Readings in Urban Design*. Oxford: Blackwell.

Rowe, C. and Koetter, F. (1978) *Collage City*. Cambridge, Mass. and London: MIT Press.

Rudofsky, B. (1965) *Architecture without Architects*. New York: The Museum of Modern Art.

Ruhl, C. (2003) William Chambers, in *Architectural Theory. From the Renaissance to the Present*. Cologne: Taschen.

Runciman, W. G. (1989) *Confessions of a Reluctant Theorist. Selected Essays*. New York: Harvester Wheatsheaf.

Ruse, M. (2003) Is Evolution a Secular Religion? in *Science*, 299: 1523–1534.

Rykwert, J. (1976) *The Idea of a Town: The Anthropology of Urban Form in Rome, Italy and the Ancient World*. London: Faber and Faber.

Rykwert, J. (1981) *On Adam's House in Paradise: The Idea of the Primitive Hut in Architectural History* (2nd edn). Cambridge, Mass.: The MIT Press.

Rykwert, J. (2000) *The Seduction of Place: The City in the Twenty-First Century*. New York: Vintage Books.

Sagan, C. (1974) *Broca's Brain: Reflections on the Romance of Science*. New York: Balantine.

Sagan, C. (1977) *The Dragons of Eden*. New York: Ballantine.

Saiki, T. (ed.) (2001) *New Garden City International Conference 2001, Program and Abstract*. Kobe: The New Garden City International Conference 2001 Organizing Committee.

Salingaros, N. A. (1997) Life and complexity in architecture from a thermodynamic analogy, in *Physics Essays*, 10: 165–173.

Sandercock, L. (1998) *Towards Cosmopolis: Planning for Multicultural Cities*. Chichester: John Wiley.

Sandercock, L. (2003) Towards Cosmopolis: Utopia as construction site, in Campbell, S. and Fainstein, S. S. (eds), *Readings in Planning Theory* (2nd edn). Cambridge, Mass.: Blackwell.

Saunders, P. T. (1997) Nonlinearity: what it is and why it matters, in Jencks, C. (ed.), *New Science = New Architecture?* London: Academy Editions.

Scargill, D. I. (1979) *The Form of Cities*. London: Bell and Hyman.

Schurch, T. W. (1999) Reconsidering urban design: thoughts about its definition and status as a field or profession, in *Journal of Urban Design*, 4 (1): 5–28.

Scott and Wilson, Kirkpatrick and Partners (1965) *Report on a Highway Plan for Glasgow*. Glasgow: Corporation of the City of Glasgow.

Scruton, R. (1979) *The Aesthetics of Architecture*. London: Methuen and Co.

Scully, V. (1994) The architecture of community, in Katz, P., *The New Urbanism: Toward an Architecture of Community*. New York: McGraw-Hill.

Shane, D. G. (2005) *Recombinant Urbanism: Conceptual Modeling in Architecture, Urban Design, and City Theory*. Chichester: Wiley-Academy.

Sharpe, W. and Wallock, L. (1987) *Visions of the Modern City: Essays in History, Art and Literature*. Baltimore: Johns Hopkins University Press.

Shelton, B. (1999) *Learning from the Japanese City: West meets East in Urban Design*. London and New York: Spon/Routledge.

Siksna, A. (1998) City centre blocks and their evolution: a comparative study of eight American and Australian CBDs, in *Journal of Urban Design*, 3 (3): 253–283.

Silver, L. M. (2006) A nasty mother, in *The Scientist*, 20 (7): 49–53.

Simmie, J. (1993) *Planning at the Crossroads*. London: UCL Press.

Sirius, R. U. (1993) Evolutionary mutations, in Rucker, R., Sirius, R.U. and Mu, Q. (eds), *MONDO 2000: A User's Guide to the New Edge*. London: Thames and Hudson.

Sitte, C. ([1889] 1945) *The Art of Building Cities: City Building According to its Artistic Fundamentals*. New York: Reinhold.

Slouka, M. (1997) *War of the Worlds: Cyberspace and the Hi-Tech Assault on Reality*. London: Abacus.

Smith, A. (1999 [1776]) *The Wealth of Nations: Books I–III*. London: Penguin.

Smith, H. H. (1983) *The Citizen's Guide to Zoning*. Chicago: American Planning Association.

Smith, P. F. (1974) *The Dynamics of Urbanism*. London: Hutchinson Educational.

Smithson, A. and Smithson, P. (1967) *Urban Structuring*. New York: Studio Vista: Reinhold.

Smithson, A. and Smithson, P. (1968) Density, interval and measure, in Lewis, D. (ed.), *Urban Structure*, Architectural Yearbook 12. London: Elek Books.

Sohn, E. (2003) Hans Bernhard Reichow and the concept of *Stadtlandschaft* in German planning, in *Planning Perspectives*, 18 (2): 119–146.

Solé, R. and Goodwin, B. (2000) *Signs of Life: How Complexity Pervades Biology*. New York: Basic Books.

Soleri, P. (1969) Arcology: the city in the image of man, in LeGates, R. T. and Stout, F. (eds), *The City Reader*. London: Routledge.

Soria y Mata, A. (1892) The Linear City, transl. M. D. Gonzalez, in LeGates, R. and Stout, F. (eds) (1998) *Selected Essays*. London: Routledge/Thoemmes Press.

Sorkin, M. (1993) *Local Code: The Constitution of a City at 42 N Latitude*. New York: Princeton Architectural Press.

Sorkin, M. (2000) Foreword, in Deckker, T. (ed.), *The Modern City Revisited*. London: Spon Press.

Southworth, M. (2003) New Urbanism and the American Metropolis, in *Built Environment*, 29 (3): 210–226.

Southworth, M. and Ben Joseph, E. (2003) *Streets and the Shaping of Towns and Cities*. New York: McGraw-Hill.

Southworth, M. and Owens, P. (1993) The evolving metropolis: studies of communities, neighborhood, and street form at the urban edge, in *Journal of the American Planning Association*, 59 (3): 271–287.

Spreiregen, P. (1965) *Urban Design: The Architecture of Towns and Cities*. New York: McGraw-Hill.

Spreiregen, P. D. (1968) *On the Art of Designing Cities: Selected Essays of Elbert Peets*. Cambridge, Mass.: MIT Press.

Stamp, G. (1999) *Alexander Thomson: The Unknown Genius*. London: Laurence King Publishing in association with Glasgow 1999.

Stamp, G. and McKinstry, S. (eds) (1994) *'Greek' Thomson*. Edinburgh: Edinburgh University Press.

Stankiewicz, R. (2000) The concept of 'design space', in Ziman, J. (ed.), *Technological Innovation as an Evolutionary Process*. Cambridge: Cambridge University Press.

Steadman, J. P. (1979) *The Evolution of Designs: Biological Analogy in Architecture and the Applied Arts*. Cambridge: Cambridge University Press.

Steadman, J. P. (1983) *Architectural Morphology: An Introduction to the Geometry of Building Plans*. London: Pion.

Steadman, J. P. (1998) Sketch for an archetypal building, in *Environment and Planning B: Planning and Design*, 27 (Anniversary Issue): 92–105.

Steadman, J. P., Bruhns, H. R., Rickaby, P.A., Brown, F. E., Holtier, S. and Gakovic, B. (2000) A classification of built forms, in *Environment and Planning B: Planning and Design*, 27: 73–91.

Steadman, P. (2005) Experiments with an Archetypal Building. Unpublished manuscript, presentation to the Martin Centre, University of Cambridge, 1 July 2005.

Steadman, P. (2006a) Why are most buildings rectangular? in *Architectural Research Quarterly*, 10 (2): 119–130.

Steadman, P. (2006b) Evolution of a building type: the case of the multi-storey garage. Paper presented at Design and Evolution, the Annual Conference of the Design History Society, Delft, 31 August – 2 September.

Steadman, P. (2008) *The Evolution of Designs: Biological Analogy in Architecture and the Applied Arts* (2nd edn, in press). London and New York: Routledge.

Steeley, G. (1998) The path to real reform, in *Town and Country Planning*, Special Supplement (October 1998), *One Hundred Years of To-morrow*, 14–16.

Stone, E. C. and Zimansky, P. (2005) The tapestry of power in a Mesopotamian city, in *Scientific American*, 15 (1): 60–67.

Strickberger, M. W. (2000) *Evolution* (3rd edn). Sudbury, Mass.: Jones and Bartlett Publishers.

Sudjic, D. (1992) *The Hundred Mile City*. New York: Harcourt Brace.

Taylor, N. (1998) *Urban Planning Theory since 1945*. London: SAGE.

Tewdwr-Jones, M. (2002) *The Planning Polity: Planning, Government and the Policy Process*. London: Routledge.

Theraulaz, G., Gautrais, J., Camazine, S., and Deneubourg, J-L. (2003) The formation of spatial patterns in social insects: from simple behaviours to complex structures, in *Philosophical Transactions of the Royal Society of London A*, 361: 1263–1282.

Thompson, D. W. (1948 [1917]) *On Growth and Form*. Cambridge: Cambridge University Press.

Thompson, R. (2000) Redefining planning: the roles of theory and practice, in *Planning Theory and Practice*, 1 (1): 126–134.

Thomson, J. A. and Geddes, P. (1931) *Life: Outlines in General Biology*. London: Williams and Norgate.

Thurstain-Goodwin, M. and Batty, M. (2001) The sustainable town centre, in Layard, A.,

Davoudi, S. and Batty, S. (eds), *Planning for a Sustainable Future*. London: Spon Press.

Trancik, R. (1986) *Finding Lost Space: Theories of Urban Design*. New York: Van Nostrand Reinhold.

Tripp, H. A. ([1938] 1950) *Road Traffic and its Control* (2nd edn). London: Edward Arnold.

Tripp, H. A. (1942) *Town Planning and Road Traffic*. London: Edward Arnold.

Tsui, E. (1999) *Evolutionary Architecture: Nature as a Basis for Design*. New York: John Wiley and Sons.

Tunnard, C. (1970) *The City of Man: A New Approach to the Recovery of Beauty in American Cities*. New York: Charles Scribner's Sons.

Tunnard, C. and Pushkarev, B. (1963) *Man-made America: Chaos or Control?* New Haven and London: Yale University Press.

Turner, T. (1996) *City as Landscape: A Post-postmodern View of Design and Planning*. London: E. & F.N. Spon.

Tyrwhitt, J. (1949) Introduction, in Geddes, P., *Cities in Evolution*. London: Williams and Norgate.

Uhlig, R. (2001) *James Dyson's History of Great Inventions*. London: Robinson.

Unwin, R. (1920 [1909]) *Town Planning in Practice: An Introduction to the Art of Designing Cities and Suburbs* (2nd edn). London: Bern.

Unwin, S. (1997) *Analysing Architecture*. London and New York: Routledge.

Urban Design Associates (2003) *The Urban Design Handbook. Techniques and Working Methods*. New York and London: W. W. Norton & Company.

Urban Task Force (1999) *Towards an Urban Renaissance*. London: Spon.

Venturi, R. (1966) *Complexity and Contradiction in Architecture*. New York: Museum of Modern Art.

Vermeij, G. (2004) *Nature: An Economic History*. Princeton and Oxford: Princeton University Press.

Vickers, G. (1998) *Key Moments in Architecture: The Evolution of the City*. London: Hamlyn.

Vidler, A. (1968) The idea of unity and Le Corbusier's urban form, in Lewis, D. (ed.), *Urban Structure*, Architectural Yearbook, 12, London: Elek Books.

Vidler, A. (1978) The scenes of the street: transformations in ideal and reality, 1750–1871, in Anderson, S. (ed.), *On Streets*. Cambridge, Mass.: MIT Press.

Vincenti, W. G. (2000) Real-world variation-selection in the evolution of technological form: historical examples, in Ziman, J. (ed.), *Technological Innovation as an Evolutionary Process*. Cambridge: Cambridge University Press.

Vitruvius (1960) *The Ten Books on Architecture*. New York: Dover Publications.

Vitruvius Pollio (1999) *Ten Books on Architecture*; transl. Ingrid D. Rowland; commentary and illustrations, Thomas Noble Howe. Cambridge : Cambridge University Press.

von Moos, S. and Ruegg, A. (eds.) (2002) *Le Corbusier before Le Corbusier*. New Haven and London: Yale University Press.

von Thünen, J. H., (1966) *Von Thünen's 'Isolated State': An English Edition*, transl. from

German, Carla M. Wartenberg; ed. with introd., Peter Hall. London: Pergamon Press.

Walker, F. A. (1996) The emergence of the grid: later 18th-century urban form in Glasgow, in Brogden, W. A. (ed.), *The Neo-Classical Town, Scottish Contributions to Urban Design since 1750*. Edinburgh: The Rutland Press.

Walker, F. A. (1999) Glasgow's new towns, in Reed, P. (ed.), *Glasgow: The Forming of the City*. Edinburgh: Edinburgh University Press.

Ward, S. (1998) The Garden City as a global project, in *Town and Country Planning*, Special Supplement (October 1998), *One Hundred Years of To-morrow*, 28–32.

Watts, D. J. (1999) *Small Worlds: The Dynamics of Networks Between Order and Randomness*. Princeton, N.J.: Princeton University Press.

Watts, D. J. and Strogatz, S. H. (1998) Collective dynamics of 'small-world' networks, in *Nature*, 393: 440–442.

Welter, V. M. (2002) *Biopolis. Patrick Geddes and the City of Life*. Cambridge, Mass.: The MIT Press.

Wheeler, M., Ziman, J. and Boden, M. A. (eds) *The Evolution of Cultural Entities*. Proceedings of the British Academy. Oxford: Oxford University Press.

Whitehand, J.W.R. (ed.) (1981) *The Urban Landscape: Historical Development and Management: Papers by M.R.G. Conzen*. IBG Special Publication no. 13. London: Academic Press.

Williams, J. (2005) Designing neighbourhoods for social interaction: the case of cohousing, in *Journal of Urban Design*, 10 (2): 195–227.

Williams, K., Burton, E. and Jenks, M. (eds) (2000) *Achieving Sustainable Urban Form*. London: E. & F. N. Spon.

Wilson, E. (1991) *The Sphynx in the City*. London: Virago.

Wojtowicz, R. (1996) *Lewis Mumford and American Modernism: Eutopian Theories for Architecture and Urban Planning*. Cambridge: Cambridge University Press.

Wolch, J. (2003) Zoöpolis, in Cuthbert, A. R. (ed.), *Designing Cities. Critical Readings in Urban Design*. Oxford: Blackwell.

Wolpert, L. (1998) The evolution of cellular development, in Fabian, A. C. (ed.), *Evolution, Society, Science and the Universe*. Cambridge: Cambridge University Press.

Woolley, H. and Johns, R. (2001) Skateboarding: the city as a playground, in *Journal of Urban Design*, 6 (2): 211–230.

Xie, Y. (1996) A generalized model for cellular urban dynamics, in *Geographical Analysis*, 28: 350–373.

Young, M. (1988) *The Metronomic Society: Natural Rhythms and Human Timetables*. London: Thames and Hudson.

Ziman, J. *et al.* [All contributors] (2000) An end-word, in Ziman, J. (ed.), *Technological Innovation as an Evolutionary Process*. Cambridge: Cambridge University Press.

Ziman, J. (2000a) Evolutionary models for technological change, in Ziman, J. (ed.), *Technological Innovation as an Evolutionary Process*. Cambridge: Cambridge University Press.

Ziman, J. (2000b) Selectionism and complexity, in Ziman, J. (ed.), *Technological Innovation as an Evolutionary Process*. Cambridge: Cambridge University Press.

Ziman, J. (2002) Introduction: selectionist reasoning as a tool of thought, in Wheeler, M., Ziman, J. and Boden, M. A. (eds), *The Evolution of Cultural Entities*. Proceedings of the British Academy. Oxford: Oxford University Press.

Ziman, J. (ed.) (2000) *Technological Innovation as an Evolutionary Process*. Cambridge: Cambridge University Press.

Zimmer, J. (2003) Walther Rivius or Ryff, in *Architectural Theory: From the Renaissance to the Present*. Cologne: Taschen.

Zipf, G. K. (1949) *Human Behavior and the Principle of Least Effort*. Cambridge, Mass.: Addison-Wesley.

Zubay, G. (2000) *Origins of Life on Earth and in the Cosmos* (2nd edn). San Diego: Academic Press.

INDEX

12.0 • Fossil cars.